THE
LAST
EXODUS

DATE DUE

THE
LAST
EXODUS

LEONARD SCHROETER

112567

UNIVERSITY OF WASHINGTON PRESS
Seattle and London

Library of Congress Cataloging in Publication Data
Schroeter, Leonard.
  The last exodus
  Bibliography: p.
  Includes index.
  1. Jews in Russia—Politics and government—
1917-   2. Jews in Russia—Persecutions. 3. Israel
—Emigration and immigration.   4. Russia—Politics
and government—1953–   I. Title.
DS135.R92S37 1979   323.1'19'24047   79-4922
ISBN 0-295-95685-2

CONTENTS

To my wife Dorothy,
who, with her support, inspiration, and editorial assistance,
has made this book possible

PREFACE
TO THE 1979 EDITION

In introducing this new edition of my book, I originally sought to write a preface. Its purpose was to acquaint the reader with the Soviet Jewry Movement and to comment about any variations or changes that have occurred in the subject matter of the book or my attitudes toward it, in the years since I wrote it. I found this an impossible task. Whatever I sought to say required an understanding of what is in the book. Thus, these thoughts could not *precede* the reading of the book, but must *follow* it. Consequently, the preface I began is now the epilogue which you are invited to read, *after* you have read the contents.

Upon reflection I concluded that there is an idea I would like to share that legitimately belongs as a preface to the 1974 preface. Time has reinforced for me, rather than diminished, my conviction (or perhaps faith) that individuals, peoples, and nations ultimately benefit from facing facts as honestly as they possibly can. We can only be damaged and ultimately destroyed by clinging to ideologies not consonant with realities—by believing what we want to believe. The Soviet Jewry Movement continues to involve the strong passions of its participants and supporters. That is part of why it has been so attractive to me. The very strength of those passions has at times obscured clarity of vision as to its character, direction, and significance. My book as originally written was reportorial and as honest as my mind and pen could make it.

In preparing for this new edition I have reread the book several times. I still believe it to be factual and honest. But I have changed to some extent, and distance permits me to examine my passions at the time of writing it.

The epilogue gives me a renewed opportunity to place those passions in the perspective of both time and whatever wisdom we can gain from increments of experience and maturity.

June 1979

PREFACE
TO THE FIRST EDITION

The Leningrad hijacking trial of December 1970 focused world attention on a phenomenon that, until then, had been relegated to the back pages of newspapers or discussed primarily within the limited confines of "the Jewish world." Beneath the drama of the trial and the two Christmas Eve death sentences—aborted by an aroused world public opinion—perceptive observers could detect, rather murkily, the existence of a Jewish underground movement in the Soviet Union. That movement is the subject matter of this book. Its main outlines and significance are readily perceivable now. Time will add perspective, details, and dimension. Retrospect will provide insight. But a current understanding will be useful to everyone, everywhere, who is concerned with freedom movements, their dynamics and obstacles.

Writing about the Jewish movement in the USSR is especially difficult, since neither the Soviet Union nor Israel, to which most Jews who leave the USSR go, has been willing to grant freedom of information to observers and reporters. Both countries, for their own reasons, have tightly censored factual information—including matters so rudimentary as how many people have been involved and who they are—not to speak of what their motivations have been. Both countries have released only information they choose to reveal, and much of it is highly propagandistic in nature. Except for a small group of well-informed journalists, mass media in the West have tended uncritically to mirror the press releases of governments and institutions rather than to examine the evidence critically. But evidence is available. The 90,000 or more Jews

8

THE LAST EXODUS

who have left the USSR since the Six-Day War constitute a remarkable source of information. The facts and feelings that can be secured from them give us insight into Soviet society, Jewish life in the USSR, and the unquenchable striving of humankind for freedom.

But neither the contemporary character of the subject matter nor the obstacles in securing information have been primarily responsible for my reluctance to begin what I feel impelled to write. The most basic reason relates to my own political and philosophical perspective. Because I am, among other things, an American lawyer, I believe in full disclosure. My own point of view, my biases and preferences should be disclosed, so they can be weighed in reading this book.

I was born in Middle America—in a small city in Indiana, of Jewish parents, who knew little and imparted less of their Jewish background. I grew up a dissenter, a radical, a critic. Being Jewish was relevant largely because of its disabilities, real or presumed. I was of a generation that was heavily influenced by FDR, the New Deal, the Spanish Civil War, and the rise and fall of Nazism. My war was World War II, not Viet-Nam, and my searing trauma was the Holocaust, not the inhumanities that have followed it. I actively participated in those post-World War II movements that believed in peaceful coexistence, One World, the United Nations, racial equality, and civil liberties. I tended to be pro-Russian and idealistically socialist. Thus I did my graduate work in international relations with a course concentration and sympathetic focus on the Soviet Union. But increasingly I became more absorbed in questions of freedom than in international affairs. I participated in civil rights demonstrations decades before such activities became socially fashionable. My first job out of Harvard Law School was with Mr. Justice Thurgood Marshall, then chief counsel of the NAACP Legal Defense and Education Fund, and my major assignment was to assist in the preparation of what became known as the school segregation cases. I went South in the early 1950s and again in the early 1960s, when there was a measure of hazard in such journeys. As an attorney, I represented people involved in unpopular causes and took cases against police departments, governments, universities, large economic units, the military, insurance companies, medical doctors and their organizations. For two decades I served as counsel, officer, and board member of the American Civil Liberties Union and its state organizations. From all this came a strong commitment to human freedom, open inquiry, and the rule of law, which I believe to be necessary for societies where freedom can flourish.

Simultaneously, I increasingly began to identify as a Jew—as a part of a people with a long tradition and religious civilization, whose contemporary political expression is in the State of Israel. As my sense of peoplehood grew, my identification with Israel grew, and finally, at the beginning of 1970, my family and I went to Israel to live. I accepted a previously tendered appointment as a principal legal assistant to the attorney general of Israel. Shortly after the arrests of Jews in Leningrad and Riga, I was asked to assist in efforts being made to attract world public opinion to the human rights implications of the trials to come. For two and a half years I did little else except work with problems associated with Soviet Jews and the human rights movement in the USSR. As Jews began to come to Israel, I interviewed them, came to know them, and some became my close friends. As their ombudsman and public relations man, I worked intimately with them on problems associated with their struggles in Israel and with the condition of those they had left behind. I am, frankly, their partisan advocate and admirer.

Before I was an attorney, I had been a newspaperman and a teacher. Thus, given my three disciplines, I tend to be objective and am disposed to be oriented toward facts rather than ideology. The two and a half years I lived in Israel had a profound effect on me. I am a Zionist and feel strongly attached to Israel and its people. But I am also an American, a Jew, and a truth-seeker.

Thus, a major difficulty in commencing this book stems from my unwillingness to say anything that might be perceived by anyone as being hurtful to Israel. But I have even stronger reluctance to say anything that is untrue or unfactual or to omit anything that is true, factual, and relevant to the subject.

Because I have consistently wanted to do whatever I could to assist Soviet Jews and freedom movements, I traveled to the USSR in August 1972, met Jewish leaders and important figures in the Soviet human rights movement, as well as distinguished Soviet writers, few of whose works can be printed within that country.

When late on the morning of September 1, 1972, my Aeroflot plane left Leningrad for London, another chapter ended in a story that had begun, for me, twenty-six months earlier—a story that had its beginnings decades before I had become aware of it but will continue for years to come.

This book deals with relatively recent aspects of the heroic saga of Soviet Jews that are largely unknown even to those who have been both interested and involved in the struggle of Jews to leave the USSR for

Israel. It explains how a Jewish movement came into existence in the
USSR, what its motive forces were, how and by whom it has been led,
what techniques it has used in the course of its struggle, how it has not
only survived Soviet repression, show trials, imprisonment and terror,
but has grown and spread, so that today it constitutes a mass movement
that is successfully defying authority in a country where only a few
years ago such defiance would have been viewed as impossible. It explains how and why tens of thousands of Jews have forced the Soviet
state to let them go, although, for decades, that regime had effectively
prevented its citizens from leaving.

Although, in the past, there was a Zionist movement in the USSR,
the present struggle did not commence in politically meaningful ways
until after the Six-Day War of 1967, and it did not reach the apex of
its militant fight until after the Leningrad trial of December 1970. Since
then, like a raging fire, it races from place to place. Doused and smoth-
ered here, it breaks out elsewhere. None of the Soviet Union's 3 million
or more Jews are immune from the conflagration. And not only Jews
are involved. Soviet leadership correctly fears that the Jewish example
has spread to other national groups and may spread further.

The book traces connections between the Soviet Jewish movement
and the democratic movement in the USSR and differences between the
Jewish movement and other dissident, civil rights groups. It explains
how *samizdat* materials are prepared and distributed and analyzes their
signifiance. It shows how Soviet Jews create and maintain contact with
Jews in other cities of the Soviet Union and with the West. It describes
the abortive Leningrad hijacking plan, what happened, and what its
effects have been: KGB searches and interrogations leading to trials
and imprisonment of Jewish activists in Riga, Kishinev, and elsewhere.
It tells about the development of new tactics of open struggle—demonstrations, sit-downs, protests, petitions, citizenship renunciations, hunger
strikes—and even the continuation of the struggle within Soviet prison
camps. It examines the complex process of securing an exit visa, various
forms of government harassment, and individual exit experiences. All
of this is based on direct interviews with participants—on what they
say and what they in fact did—and on trial transcripts and other original documents not prevously reported or generally known.

One of my working premises is that the freedom movement in the
USSR is one of the most remarkable and least understood phenomena
of contemporary history, that aspects of it have been consciously dis-

torted, and that it is of the utmost importance that it be both understood and supported in the West. The Jewish movement—at this point in history the most prominent part of the broader Soviet civil rights movement—although unique in some aspects, is part of the whole. It not only defines the remarkable resurgence of Jewish nationalism as expressed explicitly in Zionism, but it illuminates the unquenchable desire for freedom.

I am convinced that man's progress and freedom ultimately come from his understanding and that his understanding results from free discussion of controversial, significant issues of our time.

THE UNKNOWN JEWISH NATION

CHAPTER 1

No one knows how many Jews there are in the USSR—neither the
Jews themselves nor the Soviet census officials. The Soviet Union conducts a periodic census, and it publishes the figures. But because little
is published, taught, or publicly available that is not consistent with
what the regime wants its citizens to know, and what is published reflects official policy, even the Soviet census is suspect as an expression
of that policy.

All Soviet citizens must have internal passports, which they secure
at the age of 16. Among other identifying factors, there is one—question
5—that asks for nationality. Jews are numbered among the Soviet
nationalities, and for them, the answer is *"Yevrei"* (Hebrew). These
basic political facts—that one is a Jew, that Jews are a Soviet nationality, that one's nationality appears on one's passport, and that the
passport identifies, classifies, remains with one until death—are the
starting point for this book.

According to the official census of 1970, there were 2,151,000 Jews
in the USSR, a decrease of 5.2% from the last previous official figure,
2,268,000 in 1959. Both before and since the 1970 census, however,
many observers—newspapermen, Sovietologists, Jewish organizations,
Soviet officials in official public statements, and Soviet Jews themselves
—have stated that there were 3 million or more Soviet Jews. (Some
serious, intelligent Soviet Jews estimate their numbers as nearly 5 million.) The most recent census figure for Jews in Moscow is about
240,000, but unofficial estimates range from 350,000 to 600,000. Both

figures, as well as those in between, are justified projections from established statistics. Recent census figures state that there are 55,000 Jews in Soviet Georgia, but *Jews in Eastern Europe,* a London publication which is a semiofficial expression of Israeli and Jewish-organization attitudes, states that there were between 100,000 and 150,000 Georgian Jews in 1970, including 50,000 in Tbilisi and 35,000 in Kutaisi, two large Georgian cities. Since not even the Soviet Jews themselves can declare with certainty who, indeed, is a Jew, it is not surprising that they do not know their own numbers.

The question "Who is a Jew?" has no ready answer in the West, either. In the United States, for example, despite substantial sums of money spent on Jewish demography and the ability of Jews to communicate freely with one another and with the government, Jewish population figures are debatable. In the Soviet Union, where no Jewish organizational life is permitted (except for a small number of synagogues organized on a local basis) and there is no all-Union Jewish organization, Jews have no systematic way to know or communicate with their brethren. A synagogue is the only permissible meeting place. There are no newsletters, mailing lists, fund-raising meetings, or other methods of group identification—or group life—only a passport identification with a compulsory nationality determination. In the United States, being a Jew is voluntary. One becomes a Jew or ceases to be a Jew, by desire. Jewish population figures include persons who identify as Jews by belonging to a synagogue or to any one of hundreds of Jewish organizations or by participating in Jewish communal fund-raising. How many silent Jews there are in addition is anyone's guess. What of the person who thinks of himself as a Jew but takes no affirmative step to identify publicly? What of the person who is married to a non-Jew or who has a non-Jewish parent? And what of the person who is merely indifferent? Certainly the person who affirmatively becomes a Christian ceases to be a Jew. To an anti-Semite, however, as recent history persistently reconfirms, a Jew is anyone with a Jewish ancestor, regardless of present identification or belief. To the orthodox Jew, a Jew is anyone who is a Jew by *halakhah* (Jewish law)—anyone with a Jewish mother who has not been converted to another faith, or anyone who has been religiously converted to Judaism.

But in the Soviet Union, one is a Jew by nationality—not by religious belief or desire or voluntary participation. Like Russians, Ukrainians, Georgians, Latvians, Uzbeks, and many other national groups, Jews are a Soviet nationality. Unless one wishes to go through the sometimes perilous and often impossible task of changing one's name, leaving all past associations and familiar places, and starting all over again under strange and different circumstances, one cannot cease being a Jew by an act of will. Yet, due to wars, dislocations, population transfers, territorial incorporations, bureaucratic laxity, bribery, and a host of other factors involving social turbulence, ideological change, geographic variables, human fallibility and ingenuity, during the more than half a century of Soviet rule, hundreds of thousands of Jews have done precisely that.

There were substantial periods, particularly during the early years of the Communist regime, when there was a belief in sexual liberation and a concomitant relaxation of bourgeois formalities such as marriage. Divorces were, and to some extent still are, easy to obtain in the USSR. Even today, despite several decades of almost puritanical official attitudes about sex and family, there is considerable informality and even laxity about formalizing marital arrangements. Thus, no one knows how many Jews have had offspring (in or out of marriage) with non-Jews. Certainly the frequency of intermarriage between Jews and non-Jews and the degree of formality of family relationships have varied from one geographic region to another and from one period of Soviet history to another. In the large urban centers such as Moscow, Leningrad, Odessa, and Kiev, where most Jews reside, between a fourth and a third of all "Jewish" families have one non-Jewish partner. Intermarriage takes place far less frequently in areas of traditional Jewish faith such as Soviet Georgia or of stronger group identity such as the Baltic states. Since Soviet law requires that all persons must obtain an internal passport after they reach the age of 16, that birthday becomes a time of critical importance. If one of his parents is Jewish by passport and the other is of a different nationality, a Soviet citizen can choose which of the two nationalities he wishes to adopt. For most of the past half-century, to be a part of the dominant nationality group was highly advantageous in terms of educational opportunity, job placement, Communist Party advancement, and social pressure—particularly if one parent was designated as of Russian nationality. Considerable numbers of Jews who have gone to Israel in recent years were of non-Jewish nationality according to their internal Soviet passports.

It seems evident, then, that the official census figure for Jews in the Soviet Union (assuming no official distortion, suppression, or dis-

16

THE LAST EXODUSTHE LAST EXODUS

honesty) reflects no more than the number of Soviet citizens who have *"Yevrei"* on their passports. In the procedure they followed, the 1970 census takers, unlike those of 1959, did not compare a person's passport designation with his response to the question about his nationality. Nevertheless, it seems unlikely that many people would declare their nationality to be other than what appeared on their passport. Thus, the official figure for the number of Jews, if credible, would indicate that in the eleven years between 1959 and 1970, only Soviet Jews, of all Soviet citizens, had a higher death rate than birth rate. However, there are no death rate statistics by nationality to support such a premise. One might hypothesize that more children of mixed marriages sought to escape their nationality classification by selecting the non-Jewish option. But in the years just prior to the 1970 census, exactly the opposite trend was occurring. Jewish identification and Jewish national feeling reached unprecedented heights after the Six-Day War in 1967, despite (or perhaps, partly because of) official anti-Zionism, anti-Judaism, and anti-Semitism.

Thus, if one accepts the prevailing Western point of view that a Jew is someone who identifies himself as a Jew, nationally, religiously, or even defensively (because his society views him as a Jew), it seems likely that there are substantially more Soviet Jews than are reflected in the official census figures. What is important, however, is not the precise number of Jews, but the quality, character, and social significance of the group.

Individual identification is a central issue of our time. In a period of greatly proliferating national feelings, with whom and with what does an individual identify? Does he see himself as a citizen of the world, with primary commitment to certain universal, ethical values—equality of peoples, freedom, economic egalitarianism, peace, rule of law? Is his primary loyalty to his state or regime? To his economic class? To his religion? To a race? Or is he, perhaps, alienated, fragmented, loyal only to his nuclear family or to his personal needs and desires? Jews, of all people, have been tormented by these questions for almost two centuries since the breaking down of ghetto walls in Western Europe and the beginning of Jewish emancipation. But for East European Jews, the period of enlightenment and secularization was delayed almost a century, and the questions were consequently deferred.

From the time of the destruction of the Jewish state two millennia ago, Jews have lived in other people's lands, often apart or barely tolerated. To the gentile world, separated from them by religious differences, buttressed by law, custom, and prejudice, the Jews were different. They have been the eternal strangers—prototypes of the outsider. Out of this constant experience, they have built their own special world —insular, tribal, particularist. Bound together by a unique, demanding, religious tradition, with its compound of faith and law, its premium on ethical chosenness, its belief in ultimate redemption both spiritually and territorially, Jews have survived intolerance, disdain, aggression, persecution, pogroms, holocausts, torture, and death. Out of their experiences and survival have come strong family structure, respect for learning and law, intellectual and economic acuity, and, above all, historic memory. Living in ghettos, *mellahs,* or *shtetls,* they have learned to rely only on themselves and to distrust kings, tsars, princes, generals, commissars, fuehrers, and presidents.

In the West, however, with the Enlightenment and the growth in importance of the New World, these centuries-old habits and memories were shaken. The walls of the ghetto crumbled. Capitalist opportunity, universal suffrage, an ideology of egalitarianism, a civic ethic of freedom and rule of law have strongly tempted Jews to abandon their ancient ways. For many, religious faith was shaken by scientific inquiry, intellectual and philosophical exploration, and the prospect of a world compelled by the geometric growth of technological progress to adopt universalist ethics. Why maintain the ancient ways and the ancient loyalties in a world where assimilation was not only possible but highly desirable? The age-old problem of anti-Semitism could be solved by ceasing to be a Jew—or by being a Jew as a matter of free choice, which meant that one's being Jewish was different in neither quality nor character from being a Methodist, Anglican, or Unitarian.

For Russian Jews, the *shtetl* and Pale of Settlement continued long after ghettos had been abolished in the West. Under the tsars, Jews remained separated, persecuted, and despised—victimized by pogroms, a vast accretion of discriminatory laws, and the endemic hatred of the peasantry and the church. Millions left East European oppression for the freedom and economic opportunity of Western lands. But millions remained. It has been estimated that more than 80% of all Jews in the world today have ancestors who lived, two centuries ago, in lands that are now part of the Soviet Union and that as recently as the beginning of World War I, at least half of the Jews in the world lived in those territories. But despite Russia's insulation, the technological and ideological winds of the West swept through that vast tyranny during the late 19th and early 20th century. The Jews were among the first to respond to Western ideas and challenges—some by emigrating, others by becoming radicalized politically or economically.

The Bolshevik Revolution of 1917 was a mixed blessing for Russian Jews. None wept for the fallen Romanovs. But many adhered to positions different from those of their new masters. Some were capitalists and supporters of bourgeois constitutional democracy. Some were social democrats—Bundists, Mensheviks, or Social Revolutionaries. Many were Labor Zionists or religious Zionists. Indeed, in immediate post-Revolutionary elections organized by the provisional government or by the Ukrainian Central Rada, the Zionists were clearly the largest grouping in the Jewish urban communities, defeating the social democratic Bundists and other major contenders. Jews—Trotsky, Zinoviev, Kamenev, Radek, Sverdlov, to name only a few—were among the important figures in the October Revolution and the new regime that it created. Kerensky's provisional government and its Bolshevik successors abolished all special laws against the Jews. Great Russian oppression of other nationalities was condemned, and the new government soon adopted a nationalities policy that recognized the rights to identity and self-determination for all national groups—including the Jews. The official Bolshevik hostility toward capitalism, bourgeois (Western) ways, religion, and nationalisms, such as Zionism, troubled or even endangered many Jews, but it could be seen as the nondiscriminatory ideological expression of the Revolution. Certainly it was not aimed at the Jews as such, since anti-Semitism was condemned, and many Jews accepted the new regime as ushering in a new era of freedom, socialism, and egalitarianism. At least it seemed much better than life under the tsars.

For the next decade and a half, despite ruthless oppression of the remnants of the bourgeoisie, despite repressive arrests and imprisonment of political foes and the destruction of the briefly tolerated non-Bolshevik parties and ideologies, despite persecution of the religious and deprivation of freedom of worship, and even despite the gradual hermetic sealing of the Soviet Union so that the discontented could not leave—and despite the subtle anti-Semitism that accompanied the elimination of Trotsky and other old Bolsheviks—many Jews continued to be confident that a new world of opportunity was on the way. They believed that anti-Semitism, a bourgeois pathology, would cease in a socialist society, that Jews, like other proletarians, would be essentially indistinguishable from their comrades. If some felt that the price to be paid for the end of anti-Semitism—assimilation into a classless society —was too high, many others, freed from pogroms and the poverty-stricken insecurity of the *shtetl,* thought that the new opportunities for education, for economic betterment, and even for power, made up for the absence of a Jewishness that, in retrospect, seemed based at least as much on anti-Semitism as it was on positive values.

The first census under the Bolsheviks showed that among the Ashkenazi Jews, Yiddish was the first tongue of 75% of the people. For the Yiddish-speaking *shtetl* Jews, the petty traders, the subsistence farmers, it was difficult to share in the opportunities for power and advancement available in the new regime. Nonetheless, large numbers left their small rural communities in White Russia and the Ukraine, and went to the cities, where they quickly learned technical skills and adjusted to the new life. Their children were educated in Russian-language schools, spoke little or no Yiddish, ceased to observe Jewish religious and cultural traditions, joined the Young Pioneers, Komsomol, and the Communist Party. They attended universities and became technicians and scientists, the technocrats of the new society. To those who had technical or academic education and linguistic skills other than Yiddish, the Communist regime offered limitless opportunities for the skillful, the intelligent, and the loyal. The number of Jews in government, in the Communist Party, in managerial posts in industry, in the universities, was out of proportion to their percentage of the population. For people who for centuries had never known power, power was seductive and gratifying. Just as their American and British cousins were seduced by material success and prosperity, many Russian Jews in the 1920s and 1930s found gratification in the exercise of skill and authority.

Some, wedded to the need to maintain Jewish identification through Yiddish culture, found solace in the fact that the regime, in its earlier years, consistent with its ideology of encouraging national self-expression, supported Yiddish literature, Yiddish theater, and an official renaissance of Yiddish culture. True, they had to be Yiddish in form and socialist in content, but that, too, was a small price to pay for the untrammeled opportunity to have Yiddish expression with official encouragement and approval.

Hitler's rise to power (and the horrors of World War II and the Holocaust that followed) changed the world irreparably for all Jews. Appalled by the pathological anti-Semitism of Nazism, its undisguised goal of Jewish genocide, and its unremitting hostility to the USSR, Soviet Jews were not only strongly anti-Fascist, they were also foremost among Soviet patriots. Their historic memory of the repeated oppression of their people was revived. But simultaneously, at home, the Stalin regime, safely secure in its power, and with the same kind of arrogant madness displayed by its Nazi adversaries, commenced the great purge of the 1930s. Soviet prison camps, already overflowing with class enemies, political deviationists, foreign agents, and nonconformists of every description (among whom were thousands of Zionists and other Jews) were now filled with millions of new victims. The great terror struck most ruthlessly at its own. An estimated 80% of Communist Party members were purged. Few of the old Bolsheviks and revolutionaries who had survived the 1920s managed to live through the next decade. Many were Jews. Few of the Jewish leaders of the Revolution, of the ranking Jewish military and diplomatic figures, died a natural death. With or without trials, vast numbers of people were sent to labor camps or were exiled to Siberia. Although of Georgian descent, Stalin, the father of the nationalities policy, became more Russian than any Russophile. In the name of national unity and preparedness, Jews were prominent among the victims. Yiddish culture was curbed. Opportunities for higher education, for party or government preferment, for military and diplomatic careers, for advancement based on merit, were curtailed. Jews not only became the victims of discrimination; their very concern for fellow-Jews abroad became a cause of suspicion—a reason for them to be reviled as cosmopolitans or ideological deviationists. There could be no nationalism other than Russian nationalism, and no loyalty other than to the Great Leader, Stalin.

Then came the Hitler-Stalin Pact. Soviet Jews were stunned. To a people historically habituated to betrayal by their rulers, this was the ultimate disillusionment. Jews have suffered from tyrants throughout their long history—the pharaohs of Egypt; Haman, the wicked prime minister of the Book of Esther, whose defeat is commemorated by the celebration of the Jewish holiday Purim; and countless others, including Hitler. Now Haman was embraced, and being a Jew was again perilous. But not only for Soviet Jews. Now the Soviet Union invaded the Baltic states and participated in the division of Poland. Hundreds of thousands of Jews, ancient residents of those Western territories, miraculously saved from the imminent onslaught of Hitler, now faced the paranoid suspicions of Stalin. Instead of being greeted as vigorous opponents of Nazism, they were viewed as dangerous and suspect—infected with the virus of Zionism, bourgeois nationalism, antiquated religiosity, and non-Russian origin. En masse, these unreliables were transported from their border communities to labor camps and to the distant, strange, endless expanses of Siberia and Soviet Asia.

When the Hitler-Stalin alliance of convenience ended and Nazi armies drove into the USSR, hundreds of thousands of Jews from occupied Eastern Europe fled from the Germans only to be transported farther East by the Russians. Despite the heroic military performance of Soviet Jews, and the partisan resistance of Jews in the path or behind the lines of Nazi armies, the Jews were never quite trusted. Of the more than 5 million Jews in the expanded territories of the Soviet Union, not more than half survived World War II. They died fighting or resisting the German armies, from mass murders by Nazi occupiers or at the hands of their "socialist comrades" in the Ukraine, Carpathia, Byelorussia, the Baltic states, and elsewhere. Babi Yar, Rumbuli, the Ninth Fort, and many other unrecorded places bear witness to indiscriminate and unprecedented genocide.

Although Stalin found it expedient to resurrect Jewish national feeling during World War II, in order to improve relations with his Western allies, and to raise sorely needed funds in the West for Russian War Relief, and although Soviet Jews participated unstintingly and with devotion in the Great Patriotic War, neither their sacrifice nor their loss has been separately identified or recognized in post-World War II Russia. The Jewish Anti-Fascist Committee, created in 1942 by Soviet leadership, was the first all-Union Jewish organization—and, since its demise in 1948, the last. Co-opting to its ranks the best-known Jewish figures in drama, the arts, and public life, it presented, both within the USSR and to the West, the stirring story of Jewish patriotism and maximum participation in the common struggle. With the Stalin-ordered murder in 1948 of its chairman, the dramatist Solomon Mikhoels, the arrest of its vice-chairman, the Yiddish poet Itzik Feffer, and the arrests in 1948–49 of virtually every leading Yiddish writer and every distinguished figure who was an identifying Jew (one whose prominence was based on the Jewish character of his work), the period known as the Black Years of Soviet Jewry was ushered in. Those were years of Stalin terror, unmitigated by hope or surcease from oppression. They culminated in the murder of Feffer and twenty-five other Yiddish writers and Jewish figures on August 12, 1952 and in the notorious "Doctors' Plot" in 1953. This effort by the aging Stalin to link Jewish doctors to a plot to murder Soviet leaders appears to have been designed to usher in a massive orgy of arrests, deaths, and deportation of Jews. It resulted in criminal charges against a group of "terrorist murderers in white gowns" composed of prominent Jewish physicians who taught at major medical schools and served as personal physicians to leading political figures, and headed medical services at the Kremlin. Only Stalin's death on March 5, 1953 averted show trials featuring the wild claims that the "saboteur physicians enrolled in foreign Zionist intelligence services" and committed treason by medically murdering the country's leaders; but the shock of the potential remained seared in the consciousness of Soviet Jews despite the rehabilitation of the intended victims. Even in a state that suppresses news and there is a time lag before the information can percolate through rumor or underground publication, events such as the August 12, 1952 murders (never officially acknowledged) or the Doctors' Plot (belatedly admitted by Stalin's successors) eventually become known and reinforce the fear and anxiety of people toward the regime.

The creation of the State of Israel was another event of incalculable importance to the Soviet Jews. The Zionist movement had received its major early propulsion and direction from Russian Jews, who were subsequently numbered among the most important ideologists and political leaders of the *Yishuv,* the Jewish settlement, in Palestine. (The importance of the original Russian Jewish emigration can be measured by the fact that all Israeli premiers and presidents to date have been Russian-born, and current Israeli leadership is still dominated by these pioneers.) Despite official condemnation of Zionist ideology and official repression of the Zionist movement, Soviet Jews remained deeply involved in efforts to create the new state. To their delight, the Soviet government supported the United Nations partition resolution that gave rise to the creation of the State of Israel. Their pleasure was not diminished by the fact that the policy was induced for reasons of Realpolitik in an effort to undermine the British presence in the Middle East. Similarly, the USSR supported Israel's successful effort in 1948 to survive the attacks of its Arab neighbors. Soviet support, of inestimable value to the establishment of the new state, created goodwill between the Soviet regime and Israel, and between the Soviet government and Soviet Jews, that unfortunately was quickly dissipated.

Golda Meir (then Meyerson), a Russian-born Jew, became the first

Israeli ambassador to the USSR. Her arrival in Moscow in the summer of 1948 elated the Jewish population. Crowds filed past the temporary embassy in Moscow's Metropole Hotel to see the blue and white flag of the new state. Later, when Mrs. Meir attended the Great Choral Synagogue of Moscow on Rosh Hashanah and Yom Kippur, the massive crowds were uncontrollable in their expressions of joy, pride, and love. Anyone who witnessed those scenes still thinks of them as among the most memorable in his lifetime. Here, in the capital of the great Soviet empire, was the ambassador of the Jewish state, a Jewish woman of humble Russian birth, attending a synagogue on the High Holy Days. "Praise God, that we could live so long, to see such a glorious day." But less than half a mile away, Stalin also heard of the attention and praise paid to a representative of a foreign power. Aged, paranoid, insistent that adulation be bestowed only upon him, and persuaded that this was the ultimate proof that no Jew could ever be loyal to him and to Russia, Stalin embarked upon those acts that caused the last half-decade of his rule to be designated as the Black Years.

Stalin's death, like the death of any other tyrant, was the cause of much rejoicing, relief, and some hope for many Soviet Jews. It had been more than a quarter of a century since any Jew could reasonably hope to leave the USSR for another land. Since the middle 1920s, few Jews had been granted exit visas to go to the West. A fortunate handful, usually old people with close family in other countries, had been allowed to leave. Some had gone to the United States or to West European countries, and some had gone to Palestine. During World War II, the number had increased as a result of war, defection, and population movement. In the postwar period, after the foundation of the State of Israel, about half a million of the pitiful remnants of East European Jewry had been permitted to leave for Israel by their Soviet-dominated governments, but not by the Soviet Union. About 150,000 of those Jews, originally of Polish nationality, had been permitted to return to Communist Poland, from which they emigrated to Israel. But Jewish residents of the USSR had long been resigned to living out their lives as citizens of the Soviet Union. Now, Stalin's death meant that the situation might improve. Nikita Khrushchev's 1956 speech, in which he publicly revealed for the first time the abuses of the Stalin era, seemed to open new possibilities, even though he was noticeably silent about the discrimination and persecution that were the consequences of Stalin's anti-Semitism.

In "the thaw," a period of liberalization that followed the commencement of de-Stalinization, Jews sought to play a more prominent role. The new period—characterized by the release of hundreds of thousands from prison camps, the rehabilitation of the jailed and dead, the curtailment of the power of the secret police, the creation of possibilities of criticism and discussion (albeit limited), the reinstatement of some respect (even though more formal than real) for rule of law, the curbing of bureaucratic abuse—afforded opportunity for recognition of merit. The heavy emphasis on technological progress and the need for educated people again opened opportunities in state industry, research laboratories, and the professions. Jews had always occupied a place in the Soviet intelligentsia out of proportion to their numbers in the population, and now they found some renewed hope. But as year followed year, they noted that discrimination in higher education (the numerus clausus), limitations on political, military, and Communist Party participation and advancement, exclusion from diplomatic posts, and a system of discriminatory treatment had been institutionally solidified. Preferential treatment was given to other nationalities. Jews were neither recognized on individual merit nor permitted to have schools in their national language—Yiddish—or to revive Yiddish theater, literature, newspapers, or other forms of national expression. Although by virtue of their special ability, many Jews received individual recognition, particularly in the sciences and the arts, Jews as a group were denied national expression, had limited opportunities for religious expression, and were the victims of conscious state discrimination.

Although there was no widespread official persecution of Jews as a people, there were, from time to time, trials of individual Jews. In 1959, reports reached the West of ten youths in Moscow who had been sentenced in 1958 for studying Hebrew and involvement in Zionist activities. Eight Minsk students were tried that same year for "organizing a Zionist cell" and circulating Zionist literature. Sporadic reports of other prosecutions for "Zionism" occurred during that period.

A decade after the trials of Jewish youth for their "Zionist activities" —trials that were unpublicized and rarely noted in the West—some of those who had been imprisoned became activist leaders in the Jewish repatriation movement. Their years in camps had steeled the class of 1958 for a broader and far more effective struggle. The continuity of personnel reflected a deeper truth—that the historic Zionist movement in the USSR had never completely disappeared. Kept alive by small, isolated groups of the faithful, it bided its time until more propitious cir-

THE UNKNOWN JEWISH NATION 25

cumstances arose. Its suppression, although unknown abroad, was an efficient deterrent, within the Soviet Union, for the small minority of Jews who might otherwise have been predisposed to express similar points of view.

Widespread international attention was attracted by a series of trials for economic crimes beginning in 1962 and continuing for almost two years. The Soviet Union, which had abolished capital punishment, gradually reinstated it and, in 1961, extended the death penalty to "economic crimes." Its first major application, shortly after its passage, was to defendants convicted of speculation, exploitation, theft of state property, and various other economic offenses. During 1962–63, more than 250 persons were reported as having been executed (the total may have been much higher); over 60% were Jews. Accompanying the widespread publicity and exploiting popular, residual anti-Semitic feeling were lurid newspaper accounts that featured Jewish names and employed anti-Semitic caricatures. Western critics saw these trials as anti-Semitic; Soviet Jews did, as well. They feared that the excesses of the Stalin period would be revived in what they had hoped would be the greater liberality of the Khrushchev era.

A study of the economic crimes trials, conducted by the International Commission of Jurists, concluded:

> . . . there has been an insidious and sometimes subtle propaganda campaign directed against the Jewish people of the Soviet Union, specifically against those charged with economic crimes and also against the supposed general characteristics of Jews that have been reiterated for centuries . . . the number of Jews receiving death sentences and severe terms of imprisonment is greatly disproportionate to their number as a minority group.
> The charge has been raised of Jewish persecution, linking their difficulties over synagogues or Passover bread with the unwelcome attention which Jewish defendants have received in the press in connection with economic crimes.

There were other reasons for Jewish anxiety. After its brief support for Israel in 1948, the Soviet Union began to court the Arab states and hailed them as progressive forces of national liberation. It soon regarded Israel as a Western imperialist pawn and equated Zionism, always the object of Soviet wrath, with fascism. Increasingly, the Soviet press attacked Israel and Zionism and lauded Israel's Arab foes. By the early 1960s, these vitriolic attacks were extended to include Judaism as a religion. Israel was likened to Nazi Germany, and attacks on Zionism and Judaism could not longer be distinguished from overt anti-Semitism.

In October 1963, the Ukrainian Academy of Sciences in Kiev published *Judaism Without Embellishment,* by Trofim Kichko. This highly prestigious body heralded the book as a "scientific work of distinction," and it was widely distributed throughout the USSR among party cadres and educators. Judaism was depicted not only as reactionary and subversive, but as a religious belief inculcating money-worship, greed, dishonesty, thievery, exploitation (of non-Jews), lust for power, hypocrisy, bribery, and virtually every other unattractive moral quality. Kichko, a lecturer at the Technological Institute of Kiev, was the Ukrainian specialist on Jewish matters, having previously published a pamphlet on the Jewish religion and completed a graduate school dissertation on the subject. *Judaism Without Embellishment* not only linked Judaism and money but adapted the late-19th-century anti-Semitic theme of the world-wide Jewish conspiracy of Jewish bankers, Zionism, Israel, and Western capitalism. Indeed, the book is a recrudescence of *The Protocols of the Elders of Zion,* a notorious Tsarist fabrication. To complete the picture, Kichko incorporated caricatured cartoons of Jews with beady, avaricious eyes, hooked noses, and kinky hair, reminiscent of those utilized by Julius Streicher in *Der Stürmer.*

This manifestation of primitive, gross anti-Semitism aroused intense criticism in the West. Foreign Communist parties joined in the vigorous condemnation. After an initial silence, some Soviet organs lamely defended Kichko as having been involved in nothing more harmful than constitutionally protected antireligious propaganda. But when the storm of protest abroad showed no sign of abating, the Ideological Commission of the Party Central Committee, clearly concerned about the image of the Soviet Union as officially anti-Semitic, criticized Kichko's work for containing "erroneous statements and illustrations likely to offend believers." Kichko temporarily sank into obscurity. But he was rehabilitated after the Six-Day War in 1967, to spearhead an attack on *Zionism— the Tool of Imperialism,* which he followed in 1968 by a book entitled *Judaism and Zionism.* He had lost none of his touch. Sixty thousand copies of the book, which likened Zionism to Nazism and incorporated all of the former canards, were published, and Kichko was awarded a diploma of honor "for his work for atheistic propaganda." Critically acclaimed, Kichko has been kept busy since then, elaborating on his favorite theme with the patronage of the state and to the consternation of the Jewish population.

By the mid-1960s, the social permissiveness of the Khrushchev period that had allowed the official publication in 1962 of Aleksandr Solzhenitsyn's classic account of prison camps, *One Day in the Life of Ivan Denisovich,* and had resulted in the publication of Yevgeny Yevtushenko's dramatic poetic criticism of anti-Semitism, "Babi Yar," had hardened. "The thaw" was over. But it had spawned the democratic movement, a phenomenon that is discussed in greater depth below. Western Sovietologists formally identify the beginning of the democratic movement and its public protest and dissent from the arrest in 1965 of Yuli Daniel and Andrei Sinyavsky and their highly publicized trial in 1966.

Daniel and Sinyavsky, both born in 1925, were in the forefront of the young Soviet writers who responded to the increased liberality of the post-Stalin period by their creative, daring writings. Daniel, the son of a renowned Jewish scholar, was a poet and translator. His friend Sinyavsky was a candidate in philological science and a one-time senior member of the Gorky Institute of World Literature and the Academy of Sciences.* Both men had written pseudonymously and published in the West stories that criticized Soviet society. They were prosecuted for anti-Soviet propaganda and were sentenced to five and seven years, respectively, in prison camps. Objections over their arrest, trials, and imprisonment led to a series of further protests, demonstrations, and subsequent trials. Jewish writers and other intellectuals were prominent in the protest movement and made up a high percentage of those active in the democratic movement. It became clear that, among the intelligentsia at least, there was substantial disaffection from the regime and that Jews, and persons closely linked by ties of sympathy and friendship to them, were prominent in the protest movement.

By the time the Six-Day War occurred in June 1967, it was evident that Jews still remained a disaffected, small minority of the Soviet population. Although many had adjusted to Soviet society and some occupied roles of privilege and status, Jews generally were in varying degrees alienated from Soviet norms. They may have been silent, like most of the population, but their discontent ran deeper than that of most minorities.

* A candidate is the next-to-the-highest advanced degree—closer to a doctorate than a master's degree.

When the Egyptians closed the Straits of Tiran, thousands of miles from the Soviet Union, they precipitated a series of events that within half a dozen years brought tens of thousands of Soviet Jews to the Middle East as their new neighbors.

THE OPEN STRUGGLE

CHAPTER 2

No one who has ever visited the Soviet Union and attempted, without benefit of official sanction, to talk with Soviet citizens can minimize the profound significance of the growth of a Soviet dissent movement. If, like many tourists, you fly to the USSR, you do not even know where you will stay until, after clearing customs, your Intourist representative escorts you to a designated hotel. In each city you visit, this ritual is followed. If, by chance, you have managed to retain a Western magazine or newspaper in your luggage, you soon learn that it is a valuable commodity. No Western journals except those published by Communist parties are publicly on sale anywhere in the USSR. Reading matter must be ideologically pure. You soon learn to treasure the relative objectivity of Western newspapers and journals. So do Soviet citizens. There are few finer gifts for Soviet friends than yesterday's *International Herald Tribune* or last week's *Economist* or *Time*. Blackmarket prices for such treasures are startlingly high.

If you attempt to watch television or listen to the radio, you quickly learn that all news and commentary are identical in content to what appears in the press. The same events are featured in all media with equal prominence or with the same government-ordained selectivity— or are omitted altogether. Foreign radio coverage is difficult to receive in most of the USSR, either because it is jammed or distant (and in a foreign tongue) or because some receiving sets are not designed for such reception. Nonetheless, many of your Soviet friends have learned exactly when and how to hear BBC, the Voice of America, Radio

29

Liberty, Kol Israel, and various European short-wave or high-powered stations. Indeed, some of them limit their news listening to such broadcasts, which are the only ones they regard as reliable.

Bookstores, which are fairly plentiful, have large selections—of inexpensive works published, and thus approved, in the USSR. The foreign books available are both artistically and intellectually noncontroversial by Soviet standards. Since travel outside the country is restricted to politically reliable people and mainly to the "People's Democracies," the danger of ideas being imported is very small.

There are some things you do not do. You do not use your hotel room telephone. You do not discuss anything significant in your hotel room. You do not leave in your room—even in a locked suitcase— anything you don't want the KGB to see or read. You carry such items with you at all times. You do not use public telephones to call anyone who is in any way a nonconformist. If you do, you assume the telephone is tapped. In apartments, in restaurants, taxicabs, or public places where you can be overheard, you do not carry on discussions about anything but trivia. You assume you will be overheard, electronically or otherwise. You meet friends on street corners, in parks, in front of public monuments—and you walk. Talking is done best while walking or sitting on a park bench. If you must communicate in a place that is bugged or where you can be overheard, you write what you have to say and later burn your notes and flush them down the toilet.

A tourist can tolerate such a situation for two weeks. But a Soviet citizen must stand it for a lifetime. Failure to adhere to these simple rules may endanger you or your friends. The Soviet government considers it impolite to call the USSR a police state. Soviet society is too well controlled to have rude intrusions such as strikes, protest meetings, demonstrations, or even published letters to the editor—unless, of course, such contentious behavior is sponsored by the regime. It is permissible, however, to take part in official demonstrations against the trial of Angela Davis or U.S. intervention in Viet-Nam or to write letters to the editor complaining about Israel's treatment of the Fatah or other Arab freedom fighters.

Demonstrations expressing the policy of the regime are stimulated, and even when they involve criminal behavior, Soviet police officials look the other way. In January 1971, the automobile windows of American newsmen in Moscow were smashed, in retaliation against acts that the Jewish Defense League had directed at Soviet representatives in the United States. Moscow militiamen watched the activities with broad smiles. These events were reported in the West. But simultaneous tire-slashing, breaking of car windows, and other vandalism, accompanied by anti-Semitic vituperation directed at Jews who formed part of the U.S. Embassy staff in Moscow, have never become publicly known. Since *only Jewish* embassy personnel were victimized, and since their identity was known only to top Soviet officials, the direct participation of the regime in these demonstrations was unmistakable. The World University Games in Moscow in August 1973 provided strong evidence of the use of demonstrations as an instrument of state policy. A small Israeli sports delegation participated in the games. It was the only team jeered at the opening ceremonies. On three successive occasions, the Israeli basketball team's games were assigned to the small Central Army Club gymnasium. Soviet Jews found it virtually impossible to purchase tickets. Not more than twenty succeeded. But the wooden bleachers were jammed on each occasion. Israel played before uniformed soldiers and security officers. The Israeli team was heckled, hooted, and derided throughout its contests with Brazil, Puerto Rico, and other nations. When Soviet Jews tried to cheer the Israelis, the soldiers shouted, *"Zhid! Zhid!"* (Kike). When they unfurled a small, hand-made Israeli paper flag, they were physically attacked and the flag was torn to bits. After the game, as the Jews sought to leave, they were kicked and beaten. The only arrests made were of some Jewish spectators—including a 14-year-old girl. *The New York Times* editorially described these events as "organized anti-Semitism" and a "deliberate and officially sanctioned vendetta."

But what defies comprehension, unless experienced—the understanding that is visceral as well as intellectual—is the fact that society is virtually hermetically sealed. Media-saturated Westerners find it almost impossible to understand that Soviet people are told only what the authorities want them to hear—even about the most vital or obvious developments. Characteristically, disasters such as plane and train crashes are minimally noted or unreported. For weeks, during the summer of 1972, there were huge, raging forest fires so extensive that ashes kept falling on a smoke-palled Moscow, but radio, television, and newspapers hardly mentioned the fires. The worst disaster up to that time in the history of commercial aviation occurred on Friday, October 13, 1972, when the crash and explosion of a Soviet passenger jet at Moscow's Sheremetyevo International Airport killed 176 persons.

The crash affected buildings in a small town near the airport, caused cancellation of flights, and obviously became known to thousands of people, yet it was unreported in the Soviet media for several days, and when finally noted briefly, there was no mention that a Soviet airliner was involved or that foreigners were among the dead.

How are Soviet citizens to know of an event as limited in visual or auditory fallout as an arrest or trial, or the violation of rights of an individual or group? Soviet society has been habituated by a quarter of a century of Stalinism to absolute silence about hundreds of thousands of arrests, executions, and prison-camp disappearances. Massive horror is not reportable. What is not reported, and thus perceived, does not exist. If discrimination against, or persecution of, a minority remains unrecorded, it can be denied as nonexistent. According to Communist Party chief Leonid Brezhnev and other Soviet officials, "There is no Jewish problem in the USSR." It is not reported in the USSR; ergo, it does not exist.

A top-secret instruction manual for Soviet censors bearing the title "Index of Information Not to be Published in the Open Press" stipulated that none of the following are to be mentioned without special authorization: natural disasters within the territory of the USSR, fires, explosions, train or plane crashes, maritime disasters, comparisons of retail prices of goods to earning standards, reports on increased living standards outside socialist countries, data on earnings of Communist Party or government members, Soviet food shortages, the names of KGB (State Security Committee) members, crime statistics, the number of uncared-for children or people engaged in vagrancy or begging, illness or epidemic in the population, military personnel problems, the existence of correctional labor camps, the physical condition, illness, and death rates of prisoners, and of course any reference to the fact that censorship exists or that foreign radio broadcasts are jammed.

The Soviet Union maintains a system for comprehensively controlling and impeding information and ideas, not only between its people and the outside world but among its own citizens. A complete state monopoly of all physical means of communication is buttressed by a vast bureaucracy responsible solely for ensuring total control of information, not only in a preventive sense but for affirmatively maintaining ideological correctness. Newspapers, journals, books, radio, television, cinema, drama, art, and music are censored before publication or performance. Classrooms are controlled. Although not provided for legally, postal censorship and telephone surveillance have been widespread and well known. But on August 31, 1972, the USSR Council of Ministers partially legitimized the long-term practice by promulgating a decree prohibiting the "use of telephone communications for purposes in conflict with the national interest and public order." Even carrier pigeons must be registered and their use accounted for in order to ensure tight control of communication.

The Soviet Union has jammed foreign radio broadcasts, although such practice violates both Article 19 of the UN Universal Declaration of Human Rights and the 1965 Montreux International Telecommunications Convention, of which the USSR is a signatory. In the face of foreign protests, the USSR has sporadically discontinued some jamming, no doubt spurred to adherence of its international obligations by the extremely high cost of radio interference. But with the invasion of Czechoslovakia in 1968, the visit of President Nixon in 1972, and other events that required an ensured monopoly of information, jamming was renewed. In September 1973, as a part of détente concessions, most interference in Voice of America, BBC, Kol Israel, and West German Radio (Deutsche Welle) broadcasts was halted. But jamming continued for the U.S.-government-sponsored Radio Free Europe and Radio Liberty.

It is not illegal for Soviet citizens to meet or socialize with foreigners, but for most of the years of the Soviet regime, such activity has been hazardous if not officially sanctioned. On December 25, 1972, the risks increased because of a new unpublished decree designed to discourage contacts with foreigners. That decree makes it illegal to meet foreign citizens for the purpose of disseminating false or slanderous information about the Soviet Union. That is an extension of existing subversion laws, but its specific character is clearly designed to permit punishment of dissidents who maintain contacts with foreign correspondents, tourists, or others who seek to assist them in publicizing their views abroad. Foreign newsmen have been a primary target for recent repressive limitations. Not only is their travel limited, but they are subjected to surveillance, phone taps, harassment, and even arrest, sometimes followed by expulsion.

In a country where the first public availability of a telephone directory in Moscow in August 1973 caused a major sensation, it is hardly surprising that the most valued of all commodities is the ability to communicate. Yet, elementary rights that people in Western countries take for granted are more officially inhibited today than a decade ago.

In such circumstances, it is not easy for a freedom movement to

come into existence. During the Stalin period, such a movement would
have been crushed. But widespread frustration of such magnitude that
it overcomes fear, combined with (a) a regime restrained by some
deference to rule of law or fear of the ultimate consequences of un-
bridled repression or (b) police and bureaucratic inefficiency, creates
the preconditions for a freedom movement. Movements can be tightly
organized, revolutionary undergrounds, like the Bolshevik movement
in Tsarist Russia, or popular, open struggles designed to convince and
persuade, including the use of militant methods, like the U.S. civil
rights movement or the peace or feminist movements. In the United
States, for example, despite the popular use of the term, protest movements have not been truly "revolutionary." They have not needed to
be. The media popularize them almost instantly. Militancy has news-
worthiness as its central purpose. The goal of all such political acts is
persuasion, not the seizure of political power, on the premise that by
acts of confrontation—confrontation politics—the consciousness of influential segments of the public will be changed and ultimately government will be forced to make major changes or concessions. In the
USSR, the freedom movements are not revolutionary underground
movements as in Tsarist times, nor do they engage in confrontation
politics. No matter how newsworthy, they cannot reach and be reported in the mass, public media. No matter how persuasive, they cannot precipitate political change since elections are not contested and
the regime does not depend on domestic public opinion—which it
perceives as something to manipulate, not heed.

Yet, the Soviet freedom movements have goals similar to those in
the West. They seek to inform and persuade, not to overthrow. In the
Jewish movement, a clear understanding developed that the people who
needed to be informed and persuaded were, first, fellow-Jews and
friendly non-Jewish allies, and, second, friends in the West, who could
exert pressure on the Soviet power structure. Change could be accomplished through acts of confrontation that would be newsworthy in the
West. Since, in the last few years, Soviet leadership has been unusually
sensitive to Western public opinion—to the extent that such public
opinion influences Western governmental action and economic activity
—the tactics employed were designed to elicit Western response. But,
in addition, the more widespread the internal protest, the more other
disaffected groups might learn by example, and thus make maintenance
of the status quo, or increased repression, more costly than it was

worth. Naturally, this was dangerous because Soviet power could easily crush any movement and its leaders, but the price of such a response in terms of international Soviet goals and increased domestic restiveness would, it was hoped, be seen as too high to pay. Lastly, Jewish leadership had a limited objective—not a transfer or change in domestic power relationships, not even significant domestic reform, but the right to leave the country. Such a goal, although unprecedented, was not truly revolutionary. It did not directly affect Soviet power. It was an insistence on a fundamental human right and thus a major concession, but it could be granted without fundamentally changing power relationships.

Thus, although the goals of the Jewish movement were, given the Soviet condition, similar to those of freedom movements in the West, and although the broad tactics involved were the use of the "word," and later confrontation politics, rather than a revolutionary seizure of power, the specific tactics were markedly different, again because they were the product of Soviet conditions. Since organizational activity was not permitted by Soviet law, the movement had to exist secretly. Even the preparation of literature had to be carried on under the most difficult circumstances. Meetings had to be surreptitious. Contacts between Jews in various cities had to be carefully disguised and undertaken with the greatest precision and secrecy. Choice of meeting places was always a problem. Telephones could be utilized only with extreme caution, and important messages necessarily were coded. So that a minimum of people would know who was doing what, the groups consisted of extremely small units. These efforts were substantially successful. Although after their arrests, a few people revealed considerable details, the KGB apparently was unable to infiltrate an agent into any movement activity—unlike the successful police and intelligence units in most other countries.

The function of most activity was secretly to initiate an open struggle: the creation and circulation of *samizdat* (self-published) material, which was usually signed; the organization of petitions, protests, and public demonstrations; and other activities that will be described subsequently. Above all, it was to create methods to get word of all this activity to the Western world, both to stimulate Western response and to receive assistance by radio and other media in recircularizing information within the USSR itself.

No comparable movement in recent Soviet history has achieved a similar degree of success in reaching its objectives. Considering the overwhelming obstacles, the defiance of the monolithic police power of the Soviet regime by a small, disdained minority must be recorded as one of the most stirring freedom stories of our time.

But world attention did not focus on the existence of a Soviet Jewish movement until the widespread arrests of Jews in Leningrad, Riga, and other cities during the summer of 1970 following an abortive attempt by a small group of Jews to hijack a plane in Leningrad. Indeed, it was not until after the first Leningrad trial of December 1970 that both Western Jews and the mass of Soviet Jews realized the depth and extensiveness of the national feelings of Soviet Jewry. But earlier signs had been commented upon by foreign visitors, by journalists, and particularly by Soviet Jews themselves.

KIEV:
The Heritage of Babi Yar

CHAPTER 3

During the first half-century of Soviet rule, tens of thousands of Jews—
perhaps more than a hundred thousand—were tried, convicted, and
imprisoned for years in labor camps, and died, because they stubbornly
persisted in asserting their Jewishness. Sometimes the charge was political (Zionist activity), sometimes economic (baking or selling *matzot*),
administrative (teaching Hebrew), or a violation of health laws (per-
forming a circumcision). One can scarcely meet a Russian Jew today
without a parent, relative, or close friend who knew the bitterness and
misery of lost years in prison camp or who died obscurely during the
Stalin years.

In the Soviet Union, where significant social events develop, take
shape, and smoulder, like a banked fire, unknown to residents or
foreigners because of the omnipresent censorship, news selection, and
insulation of public opinion, it was small wonder that a phenomenon
such as Jewish alienation from the Soviet motherland would pass
largely unnoticed. But there were signs, like small bursts of flame,
generally unrecognized but premonitory of consequential events.

A few victims—representative of incalculably more—were known
only to their persecutors and to their friends and relatives. Typical of
these was Iosip Gershovich Chornobilsky, a young locksmith-tinsmith
of Kiev. Like many Soviet Jews, Chornobilsky found the synagogue the
only place where he could legally meet other Jews, including an
occasional foreign Jewish tourist. (Jews from the West often visit synagogues in the USSR in an effort to locate, contact, and understand

37

38 THE LAST EXODUS

fellow-Jews.) In late September 1964, a prominent Detroit professional woman, who felt impelled to remain anonymous, visited the Kiev synagogue to attend Yom Kippur services. She later noted that, among those she met, "there was general agreement that anti-Semitism is felt in Russia as an inheritance from Tsarist times." One of the people to whom she spoke was Chornobilsky, who told her that he would have taught his children Yiddish and Hebrew but that, since there were no schools or other facilities in which to learn these languages, he himself did not know Jewish language or culture. After the services, he followed her and asked if she would take to the West a statement he had written. A few weeks later, a photocopy and translation of the document appeared in the English-language Detroit *Jewish News*.

Chornobilsky expressed feelings we now know to be characteristic of the younger Jewish generation. In 1964, most observers would have regarded such feelings as untypical of Soviet Jewish youth, who were believed to be largely assimilated. "Through all the existence of people on earth," wrote Chornobilsky, "Jews, owing to known compelling conditions, were obliged to live scattered, suffering indignities, medieval tortures, pogroms and insults." However, Israel's existence restored "the pride and life of the Jewish nation," and the governments of almost all countries, motivated by humanity, permitted Jews to emigrate to Israel. But not the Soviet Union. "Where is your humanity?" asked Chornobilsky. Jews have a right to live in Israel, he proclaimed, and no government practicing genuine freedom has a right "to forbid people of the Jewish nation to emigrate to their republic."

After citing the case of Armenians who were allowed to emigrate to their native land, Chornobilsky went on:

Why do you deny the right of a small Jewish nation which not long ago achieved its constitutional independence as a government? Did this not contradict the principles of democracy and socialism? The answer was that "sixty million Arabs under the slogan of socialism are greater than two million Jews," but even if the Arabs did not exist you would still be against the Jews, no matter how right they might be, because you hate us with a wild anti-Semitic hatred. If this were not so you would not torture and shoot, on the pretext of stealing valuables, hundreds of thousands of our brothers. If this were not so you would decide to erect one modest memorial . . . to the memory of the innocent Jews destroyed at Babi Yar and other places. If this were

not true you would not prohibit a poet to publish a poem of the Kiev
Jewish tragedy. If this were not true, you would not crush the rights
of Jews in their education and work. . . . Regardless of the terror
you may use in your relations with us for our thoughts . . . we will
remain loyal to the last minute to our nation and to our long-suffering
people. Long live the nation of Israel!

For decades, no Jewish theater of any kind had existed in the
Soviet Union. On February 13, 1966, at the Kiev synagogue, Chornobilsky tried to collect signatures on a petition asking for the establishment of a Jewish national theater in Kiev. When the Central Committee
of the Ukrainian Communist Party rejected the petition on the grounds
that no premises or experienced Jewish actors were available and that
such a theater would lose money, Chornobilsky and a group of other
Kiev Jews refuted these assertions. Shortly afterward, Chornobilsky
was arrested. He had been under long-time surveillance. Although the
precise charge is unknown, it appears that he had "slandered" the
Soviet Union and he had had contact with foreigners. The petitions
had been typed on the same typewriter as had been used for the
article given to the Detroit tourist. The photocopy in the Detroit
Jewish News was compared to the documents in KGB hands. Letters
to a sister in Israel were introduced. Testimony was given that Chornobilsky had met other tourists and accepted books about Israel and
postcards depicting Israeli scenes. He had listened to the overseas
radio, Kol Israel. He had received parcels from his relatives in Israel.

"In the Fumes of Zionism," an article in *Radianska Ukraina*, noted
that Chornobilsky had "fallen into the web of Zionist propaganda" and
had been "pushed into the ravine of treason." His efforts to seek a
token recognition of Jewish culture, to maintain contact with close
relatives and fellow-Jews, and his desire to emigrate to Israel had
resulted instead in an unstated number of years in a Soviet prison
camp. His fate was unnoticed—except by some fellow-Jews in Kiev.
Among them was Boris Kochubiyevsky.

Kochubiyevsky was a prototype of Soviet Jewish activism: young,
largely assimilated, a radio engineer, and an urban intellectual. It is
significant that his activities and trial took place in Kiev, the capital of
the Ukraine, a city of 1.6 million people, with a Jewish population
estimated at more than 200,000. Kiev, the beautiful political and
cultural center of the historically anti-Semitic Ukraine, was also the

site of the most famous of all Jewish trials—that of Mendel Beilis in 1912-13 for the alleged ritual murder of a Christian child.* Kochubiyevsky was born in Kiev in 1936. One of his relatives had served in the Jewish Ministry of the Ukrainian Central Rada, a provisional legislative body formed in Kiev in 1917, while the Ukraine was occupied by German troops, and dissolved in 1918. (It had consisted of representatives of various political parties and the main national minorities—Jews, Poles, Byelorussians.) The relative had been shot as a claimed follower of Semyon Petlyura (the commander of the Ukrainian nationalist forces fighting the Red Army) during a period when, under Petlyura's control, pogroms killed or wounded a million Jewish victims. Another relative, a commissar and admiral in the Red Fleet, also had been shot at the end of the 1930s after one of Stalin's military trials. Ukrainian nationalists murdered Kochubiyevsky's grandparents at the beginning of World War II, after the Soviet troops withdrew and before the Germans arrived. His father, a Red Army major, was killed in 1941 at Babi Yar, the ravine outside Kiev where, during their occupation of the city, the Nazis exterminated nearly 100,000 Jews.

Ukrainian nationalists, Bolsheviks, Germans, and Russians—all murdered Jews. But having no Jewish education or culture, young Boris Kochubiyevsky did not know why. Only later, as an adult, could he say what millions of other Soviet Jews have felt: "In this country, I belong to no one. I want to go somewhere where I shall belong."

During the Black Years of Soviet Jewry, Kochubiyevsky attended trade school and later received a radio engineer's degree from Kiev Polytechnic Institute. Like many other Soviet Jews during that period, in his documents he stated that he was a Russian and hoped that by concealing his Jewish nationality he would be able to avoid discrimination and enroll at the institute. In Kiev, even Jewish tragedies had been excluded from history. He was 25 years old when Yevgeny Yevtushenko, the popular young Soviet poet, electrified the country with his poem "Babi Yar," published in *Literaturnaya Gazeta* (Literary Gazette),

---

* Beilis, a worker in a brick kiln, was arrested amid a government-sponsored anti-Jewish campaign and charged with killing the child to use his blood in the baking of *matzot*. The authorities cynically fabricated the charges knowing that the murderers were non-Jewish criminals. Some of Russia's best and bravest attorneys defended Beilis, and world public opinion assisted in condemning the Tsarist frameup. After two years of agitation, Beilis was found innocent at his trial.

the weekly journal of the Soviet Writers' Union. This eloquent poem of solidarity with Jews rejects anti-Semitism, past and present, and says the unspeakable: Soviet anti-Semitism exists.

But the hope engendered by the remarkable relaxation of censorship that had permitted the poem to be published (shortly afterward, Aleksandr Solzhenitsyn's *One Day in the Life of Ivan Denisovich* also was permitted to appear) soon paled. The regime insisted that Yevtushenko dilute "Babi Yar" by changing the poem to read that the horror was not just a Jewish one, that there was no Russian anti-Semitism, and so that one could not infer that popular anti-Semitism persisted. The poet capitulated, and his more recent collection of poetry omits "Babi Yar." There is still no memorial at Babi Yar itself, or at Rumbuli near Riga, or at the Ninth Fort near Kaunas—all scenes of Jewish holocaust. Whereas the horrors of Dachau, Buchenwald, and other massive Jewish tragedies are memorialized, lest the world forget, in the USSR the unique Jewish loss is greeted by silence, as if to commemorate Jewish pain would be to recognize Jewish identity, history, and peoplehood. Jews continue to be a nationality on their passports, but for all other purposes they remain nonpersons. All of this Kochubiyevsky came to understand, as did the Jews of Kiev who undertook to memorialize Babi Yar themselves—by making it a symbolic meeting ground, a place of national identity, a hallowed spot where they could reaffirm for themselves and their children who they were and from whence they had come.

By the time Chornobilsky was sentenced, Boris Kochubiyevsky was 30 years old and a Jewish movement was beginning in Kiev. Intelligent young Jews of Kochubiyevsky's generation had become disillusioned about their future, indeed about their safety in Soviet society. World War II, the Holocaust, the Black Years were a part of their personal memory, to be added to the fragile but cherished historic memory they had inherited with their passport identification. The death of Stalin with the rising expectations of the thaw had culminated, in the Khrushchev period, with the launching of the savage economic trials, with the publication in Kiev of Trofim Kichko's virulent *Judaism Without Embellishment* (1963), with the surrender of Yevtushenko, the silencing of Pasternak and Solzhenitsyn, and the trial of Daniel and Sinyavsky. But there was a valuable legacy of those years. Out of the exposure of the Stalin terror had come, for some of the more intrepid and intellectually daring young Jews, an opening of minds—a spirit of inquiry—which once experienced could never be wholly destroyed.

Within them developed the intellectual exhilaration of freedom, the need to read and indeed to create underground literature, and the habit of listening to foreign broadcasts, which having planted the seed of doubt, would always throw into question official news, official rhetoric, and official truth. So, too, there developed an experience of freedom— the lesson having been learned from fellow-dissenters that, if only one was not too fearful, one could (within limitations that were difficult to learn) petition, protest, utilize the forms of legality, even if the law had little substance.

Kochubiyevsky and some of his more daring friends would meet at the synagogue, talk to foreign visitors, read literature from abroad, and petition for their rights. But above all, the very existence of the State of Israel was becoming important to their sense of self. Kiev would not erect a monument at Babi Yar, but Israel was a living affirmation that Jews could not only die but live. The Soviet Union would not acknowledge Jewish heroism in World War II, but Israel had demonstrated in the War of Independence and the 1956 Sinai campaign that Jews were as brave today as they had been in the time of the Maccabees. The Soviet government persisted in limiting economic and civic opportunity, but Israel had demonstrated that Jewish energy and creativity could make deserts bloom and an arid land grow and prosper. Hebrew could not be taught or learned in the USSR, but it was the official tongue in Israel. Thus, more and more young Soviet Jews, stripped of pride and identity in the land in which they were born, increasingly turned curious, then proud eyes to the land from which their people had come and to which, in recent years, many had returned.

But for Kochubiyevsky and many others, this sense of identity with Israel was to prove the ultimate irreconcilable conflict. Many educated Soviet citizens had been attracted to Western ideas and culture—an attraction that had weathered years of indoctrination and press assault upon the bourgeois, decadent, capitalist societies. The United States remained popular despite savage attacks upon its alleged imperialism, racism, Wall Street exploitation of the poor, repression of progressives, and degenerative culture. Such propaganda was expected and, after siphoning off the venom and diluting the rhetoric, America was placed in some kind of perspective. But that involved no conflict of loyalty to the Soviet motherland, because much as Soviet Jews might admire or even envy Western democracy, technological progress, and culture, they did not identify with the United States or other

Western countries. But for Israel, there were increased feelings of kinship, a shared peoplehood, and identity of fate. For the Soviet Union, however, in the decade before the Six-Day War, Israel represented the prototype of national evil. Attacks on Israel had long been a staple feature of the Soviet press. Israel was perceived as exploitative and imperialistic; as teeming with squalor and discrimination; as both degradingly poor and sinisterly powerful; as a lackey of Western imperialism and a partner of German revanchism; as sympathetic to Nazi war criminals and a conspirator in Nazi war crimes—in short, as a small but clever and powerful Zionist state, bent on aggressive destruction of the USSR's progressive Arab protégés.

From 1955 until the outbreak of the June 1967 War, the USSR supplied its Arab allies with modern weapons. It extended and accelerated its diplomatic interventions into the Middle East, and it supported the assertions of its Arab clients—notably Syria and Egypt—for a "popular liberation war." Indeed, in the late spring of 1967, the Soviet Union warned Israel that the persistence of its aggressive policy against its neighbors was fraught with danger and might involve direct intervention by the USSR itself. By late May, students in Moscow were "spontaneously" demonstrating against Israel's aggressive policies and being addressed by the Syrian and Egyptian ambassadors. In the United Nations, the Soviet Union was obstructing all attempts to solve the crisis provoked by Egypt's mining blockade of the Straits of Tiran. Soviet readers were reassured that if Israeli provocations eventuated in an imperialist war, the progressive Arab freedom forces would prevail.

Soviet citizens learned of the outbreak and progress of the war solely from Arab sources. Thus, they were informed, long after Arab air forces had been virtually destroyed, that Egyptian, Jordanian, and Syrian airplanes were operating over Israel, that Tel Aviv had suffered air raids, that Syrian troops had penetrated to the Sea of Galilee. It took several days before some of the military realities were revealed. Meanwhile, the USSR condemned the Israeli aggression and mobilized maximum opposition to Israel. In the USSR itself, factory protest meetings were organized to stress the fraternal solidarity of the Soviet people with their progressive Arab brethren and to condemn the criminal aggression of the Israeli fascist bandits. In one week, the Soviet press reported 264 such meetings, all of which unanimously passed resolutions denouncing Israel. In the weeks and months that followed, the litany of abuse was extended and reiterated. The Jewish state was constantly compared with Nazi Germany. Cartoons depicted Moshe Dayan as another Hitler and accused Israel, swathed in swastikas, of committing Nazi-type atrocities. On June 10, 1967, the Soviet Union severed diplomatic relations with Israel. They have not been restored.

The tension-filled days preceding the June war demonstrated the depth of concern and involvement felt by Jews everywhere, almost irrespective of the extent of their religious commitment or assimilationist experience. Their emotional commitment to the survival of the Jewish state far exceeded their conscious awareness. The relief, exultation, and pride that accompanied Israel's speedy victory laid bare the intensity of their inner feelings. Their sense of solidarity and identity with Israel was so profound that it required overt demonstration. In the USSR, such behavior conflicted with the stridently expressed policy of the regime.

Among the factory meetings organized shortly after the Six-Day War was one at the Kiev plant where Boris Kochubiyevsky worked. All employees were ordered to gather in the workers' club to condemn Israeli aggression. After Communist Party propagandists had expounded the official position, a resolution was proposed for unanimous acceptance—but Kochubiyevsky arose to deny it was unanimous. Such conduct is unprecedented at Soviet factory meetings. There was stunned silence as he declared: "I want the record to show that I disagree. I do not consider Israel an aggressor. This was a necessary measure of protection of the Jewish people from total physical annihilation." His assertion of Israel's right of defense and of his right to say so caused the party secretary to demand that he immediately stop his "anti-Soviet speech." Kochubiyevsky refused. In the ensuing turmoil, the trade union committee demanded his resignation. Again he refused, and he endured months of "persuasion" before he resigned in May 1968. In that month he wrote an essay, "Why I Am a Zionist," which was circulated in *samizdat* form and later smuggled out to the West. In it, Kochubiyevsky asserted that the regime and its policy reek of "the stench of narrow-minded anti-Semitism—in the highest bureaucratic elite of our government"—a phrase he borrowed from a *samizdat* essay, then circulating in the USSR, by Academician Andrei D. Sakharov, one of the USSR's most brilliant and honored nuclear physicists. A vigorous critic of repressive state policy and anti-Semitism, Dr. Sakharov was a founder and chairman of the Soviet Human Rights Committee, the principal public platform of the democratic movement.

Kochubiyevsky's essay cogently stated the feelings of a large number of Soviet Jews:

> Why is it that the most active sector of Jewish youth, raised and educated in the USSR, still retains a feeling of Jewish national unity and national identity? How is it possible that Jewish boys and girls who know nothing about Jewish culture and language, who are mostly atheists, continue to feel so acutely and to be so proud of their national affiliation?
>
> The answer is simple: Thanks for that, in large measure, can be given to anti-Semitism—the new brand which was implanted from above and, as a means of camouflage, is called anti-Zionism, and the old anti-Semitism which is still alive among the more backward sectors of Soviet society. It is precisely this anti-Zionism and anti-Semitism which prevents us from relaxing and welds us closer together. . . . One cannot yet speak of an end to discrimination against Jews in the USSR.
>
> Such discrimination is felt by the Jews in many ways: in the absence of Jewish schools, in religious persecution, when looking for jobs or applying to institutes of higher learning. In short, on almost all levels of public life. These evil and unjust policies are felt in the more advanced ranks of the Jewish intelligentsia where the memory of the nefarious "Beilis Affair" still lingers. . . .
>
> I am probably not saying anything new. This is how it always was and how it is now. But it's not how it's going to be! This decision and this faith is what makes the new generation of the seventies different. We are convinced that there can no longer be room for Jewish patience. Silence is equivalent to death. It was that kind of patience that created Hitler and the likes of him. If we remain silent today, tomorrow will be too late. . . . More and more Jews are coming to understand that endless silence and patience lead straight down the road to Auschwitz.
>
> That is why the leaders of the Soviet Union have anathematized Zionism.
>
> That is why I am a Zionist.

In June 1968, Kochubiyevsky married Larisa Aleksandrovna, a Ukrainian fourth-year student at the Kiev Pedagogical Institute, whose father was employed by the KGB and whose mother was a teacher. Shortly after their marriage, the young couple applied for exit permits to go to Israel, but they were refused. Later in the fall, they tried again and were told they would be able to leave. But for a man to whom "silence is equivalent to death," prudence is a stranger.

For some years, Kiev's Jews had informally congregated in small groups at Babi Yar, in September, on the anniversary of the murders.

The authorities, always apprehensive about any spontaneous, informal gathering, organized an "official commemoration" in 1968. The official speaker, without specifically mentioning Jews, referred to the anonymous "Soviet citizens, Russians, Ukrainians, and others" who were slaughtered by the Nazi barbarians. He also took the occasion, before a Jewish audience, to denounce Israeli "aggression" and occupation policies. After the official meeting was concluded, the Jewish mourners remained to express themselves in their own way, free of official cant. Witnesses related that Kochubiyevsky spoke passionately and grimly: "Here lies a part of the Jewish people." For him, Babi Yar was not an anonymous tragedy.

In November, the Kochubiyevskys were informed that they had been granted an exit permit for Israel and were told to appear at the visa registration office of OVIR to pick up their documents.* On the morning of November 28, while they were at that office, their apartment was searched and papers were confiscated. Later that day, Kochubiyevsky wrote and dispatched an open letter to Soviet Communist Party Secretary Leonid Brezhnev and Ukrainian Party Secretary Piotr Shelest and characteristically sent a copy to U. V. Doroshenko, the investigator of the Prosecutor's Office, who had led the raid on his apartment. The letter, circulated in *samizdat* form, became a clarion call for the Jewish movement. It found its way to the West, where its militancy belied the impression that Soviet Jews could still be described as the Jews of Silence. Although preceded by a few other appeals, it expressed the main themes of the Jewish movement that was to develop:

> I am a Jew. I want to live in the Jewish state. That is my right, just as it is the right of a Ukrainian to live in the Ukraine, the right of a Russian to live in Russia, the right of a Georgian to live in Georgia.
>
> I want to live in Israel. That is my dream, that is the goal not only of my life but also of the lives of hundreds of generations that preceded me, of my ancestors who were expelled from their land.
>
> I want my children to study in the Hebrew language. I want to read Jewish papers, I want to attend a Jewish theater. What's wrong with that? What is my crime? . . .
>
> I have repeatedly turned with this request to various authorities and have achieved only this: dismissal from my job, my wife's expulsion from her institute, and, to crown it all, a criminal charge of slandering Soviet reality. What is this slander? Is it slander that in the multinational Soviet state only the Jewish people cannot educate its children

---

* OVIR is the acronym for the Department of Visas and Registration (Otdel Viz i Registratsii) of the Ministry of the Interior.

in Jewish schools? Is it slander that there is no Jewish theater in the USSR? Is it slander that in the USSR there are no Jewish papers? By the way, no one even denies this. . . . But even this isn't the heart of the matter. I don't want to be involved in the national affairs of a state in which I consider myself an alien. I want to go away from here. I want to live in Israel. My wish does not contradict Soviet law.

I have an affidavit of invitation from my relatives; all the formalities have been observed. Is that why you are instituting a criminal case against me? Is that why my home was searched? I am not asking for mercy. Listen to the voice of reason.

Let me go! As long as I live, as long as I am capable of feeling, I shall devote all my strength to obtain an exit permit for Israel. And even if you should find it possible to sentence me for this—I shall anyway, if I live long enough to be freed, be prepared even then to make my way even on foot to the homeland of my ancestors.

Little more than a week later, Kochubiyevsky was arrested and charged under Article 187-1 of the Ukrainian Criminal Code. The charge sheet states that Kochubiyevsky, "during 1968, systematically disseminated by word of mouth slanderous fabrications, defaming the state and the social system of the USSR, the slander being expressed in his disseminating fabrications alleging that the Soviet state oppresses and keeps down Jews . . . this was also expressed in written form." On May 13, 1969, the trial began in the same court where Mendel Beilis had been tried more than half a century before. We know what occurred from *Khronika Tekushchikh Sobytii* (the *Chronicle of Current Events*) and from informal transcripts prepared by other observers which also circulated in *samizdat*.

The trial, which can only be described as Kafkaesque, was typical of those that were to follow. It was announced as an open court session, but admission was restricted mainly to KGB personnel, and an audience was selected for its hostility to the defendant. A group of twelve of Kuchubiyevsky's friends and relatives formally complained to the prosecutor that their exclusion violated the criminal procedure code. The defendant denied his guilt, contending that his statements were true but that if any were inaccurate, there was no deliberate falsification. The prosecutor objected: "You have received higher education; you have passed philosophy tests at least on the candidate level; you know the Constitution of the USSR. Therefore, you could not fail to know that everything you say cannot happen in our country." The subsequent verdict literally employed this formulation as proof of Kochubiyevsky's deliberate falsity.

Some prosecution witnesses were provocateurs. Others repudiated statements given at preliminary hearings. One admitted to pressure from KGB interrogators. Of eight witnesses who testified on one main element of the charge, only three supported the prosecution's position. The court rejected the testimony of the five defense witnesses on the ground that they were friends of the accused and supported his "Zionist views." The prosecutor taunted Kochubiyevsky by asking, "And have you thought what you did to your wife? You have contaminated this young Russian girl with your Zionist views." The judge advised her "to find herself another husband." Throughout the three-day trial, the judge questioned the defendant more aggressively than the prosecutor, interrupting and mocking the accused and permitting anti-Semitic outbursts in the courtroom. Kochubiyevsky's brother, who was finally admitted, reported that a KGB official standing next to him persistently taunted him, quietly repeating, "And you're a Yid. And you're a Yid."

In his summation, the prosecutor, Surkov, denied Soviet anti-Semitism and asserted that Kochubiyevsky's Zionist views were "formed under the influence of the West." The defense attorney's address not only accepted the basic validity of the charge and testimony against his client, but indicated his disbelief of Kochubiyevsky's testimony, pronouncing it harmful and slanderous. His sole defense was lack of premeditation and the "sincerity of his error." Kochubiyevsky's own final statement factually denied some charges and explained others. When he sought to refer to Yevtushenko's poem, the judge interrupted him and accused him of making anti-Soviet propaganda. Kochubiyevsky was found guilty and sentenced to three years.*

By the time Kochubiyevsky was prosecuted, Soviet Jews had learned the value of the written word. His fate was documented by *samizdat* materials prepared by his friends in Kiev and circulated in the Soviet Union, then smuggled abroad, where Kochubiyevsky was publicized as the first hero of the Jewish movement—"A Hero for Our Time," as a pamphlet published in the United States in 1970 characterized him.

A Western observer, Rabbi Abraham J. Heschel, understood well the meaning of the Kochubiyevsky case:

> It has been said that the history of the world is nothing more than the progress of the consciousness of freedom. At a time when such

---

* Upon his release from prison camp in December 1971, Kochubiyevsky received permission to emigrate to Israel, where he now lives.

consciousness is being suppressed and more than three million Jews are spiritually being buried alive, we witness the marvel of human beings who defy despair, who challenge adversity and declare their right to be what they are, their right to be free. . . .

Kochubiyevsky's adversity is that of his fellow Jews of Russia. While he languishes in a prison camp, his people are shut up in a stifling spiritual jail. Exposed to the scorn and hatred of enemies, the pricks and taunts of anti-Semites, the wholesale attempt by the oppressor to make him and them less than full men.

Suddenly, the Jews of silence have discovered their voice.

Suddenly, for them, "the time of fear has passed, the hour for action has come." . . .

They make their point with the simple eloquence of basic humanity.

They are Jews. They find it impossible to be Jews in the USSR. They want to live as Jews in the Jewish land.

LENINGRAD:
The Courage and the Heart

CHAPTER 4

Leningrad, the graceful city on the Neva, founded by Peter the Great in 1703 and adorned with the spacious, stately parks and squares he and his successors planned, and with its 18th-century Italianate architecture, has greater charm and grandeur than any other Russian city and is regarded as one of the most beautiful cities in the world. As St. Petersburg, the capital of the Romanovs, it was not only the seat of government, but it developed traditions of education and culture that outstripped the rest of their vast empire and compared favorably with the great centers of Central and Western Europe. Proud of their home, its residents survived the Bolshevik Revolution, the change of name to Petrograd and then to Leningrad, the movement of the capital to Moscow, and the 900-day Nazi siege in 1941–43. The heroism of the city and its inhabitants, their love and pride of place which did not permit them to cut down the stately trees in their beloved parks even through famine and bitter cold winters when anything that would burn might save lives, are remarkable manifestations. Even the Soviet state, with its contempt for the bourgeois past, has been remarkably sensitive to the people's need for continuity. The magnificent imperial palaces and public buildings remain, and have been restored.

If ever attachment to city and identification of place might be dominant feelings, they could be expected to exist among the Jewish residents of Leningrad. Yet, although many Jewish families have lived there for generations, they are strangers in a hostile land. KGB surveillance is constant. They live in fear. For them, Leningrad today is a temporary residence—a place to leave. But most of them cannot and dare not.

The records reveal that many Soviet citizens who are in prison camps or have served their time had tried to leave but failed or managed to get to a neighboring People's Democracy or to Finland, only to be sent back. But some have been successful, if for those blessed with families, eternal separation can be called success. The regime forbids emigration for the spouses, parents, or children of "defectors." No matter how long ago the sin was committed, how innocent the family member was of prior knowledge of the heinous crime, how young or how old, how destitute or how ill—there is a blood taint. The family must be a constant example of Soviet power. He who defies it by leaving without authority is forever damned—and so is his family. Since Soviet citizens generally know of this government policy, their leaving is the measure of their desperation. Many Leningrad Jews have been that desperate.

Because one such Jew who is now an obstetrician in Tel Aviv left Leningrad in the spring of 1969 without permission, his aged parents, still in Leningrad, are held hostage by the Soviet government. Born in Leningrad about 45 years ago, he grew up in a family of atheists, who had no religious training or Jewish cultural background. His father knew some Yiddish, as well as other languages, but the family went to the magnificent Leningrad synagogue on important holidays because, somehow, they wished to survive as Jews. As a child on summer vacation with his grandparents, he heard other children make scornful remarks about Jews and mock his grandfather's name, Avram.* Since he had not experienced anti-Semitism in school in Leningrad, he was shocked. But by the time he was twelve, even in cultured Leningrad, he had become used to being called "Yid" and being taunted and beaten. Evacuated with other children during World War II, he suffered from the scurrilous remarks of his peers that the Jews caused the war, that Jews were all cowards and enriched themselves in areas out of the war zone. Primitive anti-Semitism of this type was unavoidable, but more shocking was what he called the "anti-Semitic tradition of Russian literature." In spite of his love for that literature, "I felt as if I had been robbed—many great writers who seemed to be radiant symbols of justice turned out to be primitive anti-Semites as well."

* Most Jews adopt Russian names, and characteristically Jewish names are increasingly rare.

By the time he was a teenager, he had come to think of Stalin as "a bloody executioner, a psychotic maniac rather than a philosopher and politician." His political differences caused him to perceive his city and society differently, and as he found friends among older intellectuals, many of them Jews who had found an "individual solution" by intermarriage, change of name, adoption of Russian on their passports, he felt, even in Leningrad, that this was no "solution" for him. Then, in an antiquarian bookshop he found a volume of essays by Vladimir Jabotinsky, the Revisionist Zionist leader. He read it avidly, thirstily. To a teenage boy in post-World War II Leningrad, Jabotinsky provided some answers.

> Reading Jabotinsky completed my Zionist education. From that moment I knew where my place was in the world and could only wait patiently for the chance to go to Israel. My initial conversion to Zionism was above all emotional—and only afterward did I discover an intellectual basis for my feelings by studying the historical experience of our people, particularly in the 20th century.

Next, he sought to learn Hebrew, which in 1947–48 could still be done "legally." But it was extraordinarily difficult. He found an alphabet and a Hebrew grammar (which was published in 1880, before modern Hebrew was introduced), and struggled. Not until after the Six-Day War did he secure a *samizdat* copy of *Elef Milim* (One Thousand Words), a modern Hebrew grammar used in the *ulpanim* (intensive Hebrew courses for immigrants in Israel), and learned modern Hebrew on his own. Although he knew that three Leningrad libraries had good Hebrew textbooks in English, records were kept of those who borrowed them, and prudence dictated that they not be used.

He was admitted to the Institute of Medicine in 1947, at a time when some schools, such as the Institute of International Relations, were closed to Jews and small quotas were applicable to others. In late 1948, the start of the Black Years, universities began dismissing Jewish students solely because they were Jews. In 1950, over one hundred such students were dismissed from the Institute of Technology in three days. In that year also, he had his first experience with the KGB. He was interrogated for thirteen hours about a friend (a half-Jewish son of an old Communist Soviet diplomat) who was critical of Stalinism. He gave no information, but a few days later the friend was arrested and sentenced to ten years in a prison camp. Then another student friend, who in the summer of 1948 had organized and sent to Moscow a petition asking to be allowed to go and fight in Israel, was arrested. He owned an old Hebrew grammar, which in itself was proof of crime, and he, too, received ten years. A wave of arrests followed. During the next several years, the teaching staffs of the medical institutes and of other institutes were decimated by mass dismissals of Jews. Then came the Doctors' Plot, and fear turned into terror. Many doctors were arrested. Every day there was a new anti-Semitic article about "bourgeois Jewish nationalists," "Zionists," or "rootless cosmopolitans." Meetings of students and faculty were organized to denounce the shameless plotters. His institute was purged. So were the Soviet scientific press and the medical journals.

Rumors swept the city: Jewish pharmacists were dispensing poison rather than medicine; the meat shortage was caused by the poisoning of cattle by Jews; Jewish doctors attacked Russian women. He notes:

> Nobody was in any doubt about the imminent exile of the Jews, and people were excitedly waiting for the moment to come so that they could move into Jewish living quarters. There were cases of house committees receiving requests from tenants asking to be allocated the quarters of their Jewish neighbours after the expulsion. . . . The situation was still worse in communal apartments shared by several families. There were many cases of non-Jewish residents holding meetings and demanding that the Jews be forbidden to use the common kitchen so that they couldn't put poison in the food. . . . Jews were insulted and attacked on trams. Many Jews were simply afraid to travel on them. . . . All restraint was cast aside. On public transport you could hear Jews being cursed and expressions of regret that Hitler didn't kill them all.

After Stalin's death, the situation improved. He finished his studies and began a professional career that brought some satisfaction. But in the light of the trials of dissident intellectuals, he remained pessimistic about any real liberalization in Russia and wanted urgently to go to Israel while still young and professionally useful. The Six-Day War and the 1968 invasion of Czechoslovakia reinforced his need to leave. A confirmed Zionist, he felt that

> nothing has happened in the Soviet Union to eliminate that aspect of anti-Semitism which depends upon the leadership: official anti-Semitism, official discrimination. . . . According to one joke, Russians divide up Jews in the Soviet Union into four categories: the Jewish

salesman, known as "Jew-bastard"; the Jewish doctor or engineer—
he is the "little Yid"; the Jewish professor is "comrade Jew"; and the
Jewish academician is a "great Russian scientist."

His experiences, and the emotional imperatives they created, were
typical of his generation. His Zionism, arising from frustrated assimilation and nurtured by personal and national anti-Semitic traumas,
took adolescent and then adult form from his own internal needs and
striving. It was lonely being a self-taught Zionist. But like many others,
he eventually found friends who shared his feelings. Each story is individual, but most have the same core of human experience.

By the early 1960s, small groups of students and other young people
in Leningrad, Kiev, and Moscow were getting together—at least informally—in small groups, meeting on a fairly regular basis, attempting
to learn Hebrew, listening to foreign broadcasts, securing information
about Israel, thirstily imbibing Jewish culture, and sometimes, even
publicly, celebrating Jewish holidays. Friends in Riga, Minsk, or Kharkov had similar feelings and similar small groups. Books—Jewish histories, Hebrew grammars, stories of Israel—could be shared. And if
sharing a prized book or article meant it had to be reproduced without
benefit of official sanction, there was some anxiety but it seemed worth
the risk.

Without significant exception, these groups were composed of young,
educated, middle-class Jews—alienated from Soviet society, possessed
by nationalist passions, and dominated by an overpowering wish to
live among their own people in their own country. If they had a
prophet, it was likely to be Jabotinsky. They despised Stalin and were
sympathetic to the nonconformist Soviet intellectuals who simultaneously were developing into what has become known as the democratic
movement or the Soviet human rights movement. Their link was not
to the Soviet present but to the Jewish past and future. The disparity
between them and the older generation of Soviet Zionists was bridged
by historic memory, some of which was of the very recent past. They
sought out and found Zionist veterans—men who had spent half their
adult lives in labor camps, men whose lives bore witness to their commitment, whose suffering and memory of a recent history (expunged
from all written material) gave them authority, wisdom, and credibility.
These men taught the young Jews history, language, culture, and gave
them continuity, a link to their own, almost erased past.

The younger groups could look to men like Gedalia Pechersky, a dentist and medical technician and a life-long Zionist, born in 1901. In 1953–56, as chairman of Leningrad's Great Central Synagogue, Pechersky constantly struggled to obtain permission for kosher meat slaughter, for baking Passover *matzot,* for maintaining the Jewish cemetery, and unceasingly tried to teach Hebrew classes in the synagogue. Because of his energetic insistence on Jewish religious rights, he lost his synagogue post in 1956, and after struggling with the authorities over Hebrew classes, he was arrested in the summer of 1961, and tried for allegedly "maintaining close relations" with members of the Israeli Embassy staff. Evidence was introduced that Pechersky had led a campaign to raise 600,000 rubles for the renovation of the once magnificent but sadly dilapidated Central Synagogue, had organized a system for the baking of *matzot,* and had passed on information about Leningrad Jews to members of the Israeli Embassy staff who visited the synagogue. He was sentenced to twelve years in prison. After the "spying" charges were found to be false, Pechersky was released in August 1968, and, at the age of 67, he immediately requested exit visas to Israel for himself and his family. He was permitted to leave in October 1970.

Or the young groups could look to persons like Natan Tsirulnikov, an engineer born in 1910, who was arrested, tried, and convicted for receiving Hebrew textbooks from abroad—a charge he vigorously admitted, insisting that he had the right to teach his children the Hebrew language. Tsirulnikov was released from prison in April 1969. Twenty-one months later, when he arrived in Israel with his wife and married daughter, he was hailed at airport festivities as Israel's three millionth citizen.

Among the young Leningrad Jews who felt impelled to give their Zionist feelings more concrete form than could be realized through small, informal study groups was Gilya (Hillel) Butman, born in 1932 in Leningrad, a graduate of the Leningrad Law Institute in 1954. As early as 1960, Butman began studying Hebrew on his own. In time, he was able to read, translate, and correspond in Hebrew, and within a few years he began teaching the language to others. In these small Hebrew classes—called *ulpanim*—the groups also discussed Jewish history and culture. By 1965, they were well enough organized to collect money to make tapes of Jewish music and to secure and reproduce Hebrew grammars and literature relating to Jewish history and

the State of Israel. By now, Butman was married to an engineer and had
a daughter. He maintained an extensive correspondence with people in
Israel. Deciding to leave the law, he worked for and received a degree
in electrical engineering from the Leningrad Polytechnic Institute. Butman became persuaded of the need for a Zionist organization to struggle against assimilation and for permission to emigrate to Israel. He was
joined in this goal by a long-time friend and law school classmate of
the same age, Grigory Vertlib, whose emotional and intellectual odys-
sey had been similar but who, unlike Butman, continued to practice
as an attorney. The two men constituted the beginning nucleus for
the first organized, underground expression of the Soviet Jewish repatriation movement—what became known as the Leningrad center
or organization.

Butman and Vertlib were later joined by Solomon Dreizner, another friend of the same age, who had become a chief engineer at
the Leningrad Housing Design Center. Also among the initial group
were Bentsion Tovbin, an engineer three years older than Butman,
Vertlib, and Dreizner, and three younger men (all born in 1939)—
Vladimir (Zev) Mogilever, David Chernoglaz, and Arkady (Aron)
Shpilberg. Mogilever, whom all his friends regarded as brilliant, was
an outstanding student of electrical engineering who, after postgraduate
mathematical work at Leningrad University, became senior engineer-
mathematician at the Leningrad Geological Research Institute. An accomplished linguist, Mogilever is said to have a perfect command of
both English and Hebrew. Shpilberg, also an engineer, left Leningrad
for employment in Riga in 1967. Chernoglaz, committed as a teenager
to living on a kibbutz in Israel, had prepared himself by entering the
Leningrad Institute of Agriculture to become an agronomist. Expelled
from the institute in 1960 for his active interest in Jewish culture but
readmitted after army service, he was employed, after graduation, in
research at the Leningrad Agricultural Laboratory. Meanwhile, he continued his Jewish studies and wrote a history of the Jewish people,
which, given Soviet conditions, remained unpublished.

In the period before the Six-Day War, the activities of the Leningrad group were focused on raising the level of Jewish consciousness in
their city, and they resisted attempts to mobilize their efforts on behalf
of broader human rights issues. Testifying in 1971 at the trial of the
Riga Four (one of whom was Shpilberg), Mogilever noted that in 1965
(the period of the Daniel-Sinyavsky arrests) he and some of their

friends had been concerned about internal problems of the Soviet Union.*

> We thought that this country was not democratic enough and discussed those questions. Shpilberg immediately began arguing with me, proving that we must not get into the so-called "democratic activities." He was against anti-Semitism. He kept saying that we, Soviet Jews, who know neither our native tongue nor the history of our people, should concentrate our attention on studying our national culture, language, history. He strove to create a Zionist organization with the aims of studying and propagating Jewish history as well as helping Jews to leave for Israel. All Shpilberg's activities were of a cultural, educational character. I can't remember a single case when we distributed literature of an anti-Soviet character.

Mogilever's testimony was, of course, intended to be helpful to Shpilberg, but no evidence exists that it is not wholly accurate. Yet, given the memory and experience of Leningrad's Jews, activities which in most of the world would be viewed as socially benign required an underground structure. Secrecy, caution, imagination were necessary for young intellectuals who simply desired to assert their Jewishness.

In the period between the formation of the Leningrad group and their arrest and trial in 1970 (all of the original leadership except Vertlib and Tovbin, who had been permitted to go to Israel, were tried), the group continued to maintain secrecy and a tightly organized character but broadened in both size and activity. According to Mogilever, the group's early function—teaching Hebrew, preparing textbooks, and conducting cultural and educational work by the use of slides and musical tapes, and by the preparation and distribution of literature—broadened to include the preparation of collective letters and their dissemination abroad.

Other active members included Lev Korenblit, a physicist, and the engineers Lev Yagman and Lassal Kaminsky. Korenblit, born in 1922 into a traditional Jewish family in Bessarabia (then a part of Romania), had lost his parents, a brother and sister in the Holocaust. After graduating from the University of Chernovtsy (then Chernovitz), he completed graduate work in mathematical physics and then became a research chief at the Institute of Semi-Conductors in Leningrad. After visiting France in 1968 to see a surviving brother, a French lawyer, Korenblit became persuaded that he should leave the USSR. He began

* The trial of the Riga Four is the subject of Chapter 14.

working with the Leningrad organization, teaching Jewish language, history, and culture, which he had learned as a child. Yagman, who had joined in 1966, when he was a 26-year-old marine engineer, subsequently became particularly active in organizing collective letters and appeals. Kaminsky, born in 1930, was an engineer in a design institute. A long-time Zionist, in 1967 he actively began to seek the right to emigrate to Israel. In all (according to a September 1969 letter to Nikolai Podgorny, chairman of the Supreme Soviet, which was later released abroad), Kaminsky prepared thirty-two applications, petitions, complaints, appeals, and inquiries between April 2, 1967 and September 22, 1969, seeking to effectuate his right to leave the USSR. All were ignored or denied. In 1968, he became a part of the Leningrad organization, helping in the production of textbooks and distributing literature. Kaminsky soon became "treasurer" of the group, collecting contributions and selling gifts and parcels sent from abroad (including two fur coats sent to Mogilever and Vertlib) to secure funds for the group.

Most Jews of Leningrad believe that there are at least 250,000 to 300,000 Jews in the city (although, according to the last census, there were 168,641 Jews out of a total population of 3,321,000). In such a populous area, where fear is a concomitant of everyday life, it is not easy to locate one's soul brothers. Thus, it is not surprising that the precise size and leadership or even the existence of an underground Leningrad organization was not known to most Leningrad Jews, even among those, who, after the Six-Day War, considered themselves activists. On some of the Jewish holidays—on Purim, Pesach, Chanukah, and particularly Simchat Torah (the Rejoicing in the Law)—Jews did get together and express their Jewish solidarity. The Simchat Torah celebrations at times attracted thousands to the street in front of the Great Synagogue. Many Jews also read and discussed literature produced by the Leningrad organization without being aware of its origins, and some passed it on to others. Hundreds learned some Hebrew, and increasing numbers, from 1969 on, began to apply to emigrate to Israel. Small, independent groups also developed quite spontaneously, sharing ideas and discussing their feelings. But even those who were emotionally extremely militant Zionists spent years in intellectual isolation, not knowing how or with whom to share their intense national feelings. Typical of them was Mikhail (Misha) Korenblit, a young, successful oral surgeon.

LENINGRAD: The Courage and the Heart 59

Born in 1937 in a small town in the Ukraine, Korenblit moved to Leningrad after dental school in 1961, when he was 24. He received an honors degree from the First Leningrad Medical Institute and worked in a prestigious midcity clinic. He knew Yiddish and English, wrote poetry, was involved in the democratic movement, with which he strongly sympathized, and had become an ardent Zionist. Not until December 1968, during Chanukah, did he make his first contact with the Leningrad organization, and at once he began to study Hebrew in Butman's *ulpan*. Within less than a year, he had located an Israeli "relative" and secured an invitation (*vizov*) to go to Israel, but his application was refused. He plunged into the activities of the Leningrad group. When Joel Sprayregen, a Chicago attorney who visited the Soviet Union in May 1970, was at the Leningrad synagogue, Korenblit approached him and suggested a meeting. Sprayregen described Korenblit as a wiry, handsome, clean-shaven man, militant "in his outlook and manner of expression." Korenblit surprised him by the overtness of his comments, the intensity with which he expressed his Jewish feelings, and his complete alienation from Soviet society. A few months later, Korenblit was arrested and became one of the defendants in the second Leningrad trial.

Born in Siberia in 1944, Korenblit's wife, Polina Yudborovskaya, whom he married after his conviction, is a full-faced girl with a high bun of dark hair. Her voice is soft, contained, but intense, and her feelings surface as she gestures sharply with her fingers or grasps her hands tightly together. Her father was an engineer from Byelorussia and her mother a chemistry teacher from the Ukraine. After World War II, they returned to Leningrad where they had lived after migrating from their small *shtetl* communities. A graduate of the Chemical and Pharmaceutical Institute, Polina became a laboratory technician in the department of forensic chemistry of the institute and then a teacher of forensic chemistry. She learned English as a teenager.

Although her father knew Yiddish and her mother remembered the language slightly (the grandparents' first tongue was Yiddish), there was no Jewish culture in the Yudborovsky home. Most of Polina's friends in Leningrad were not Jewish, and most of her Jewish friends married non-Jews. Her parents discouraged any Jewish interest. As she recounts it, "They didn't want to assimilate, but they were afraid. If they ever spoke Yiddish, even at home, it was a small act of heroism. Yom Kippur and Purim were noted at home, but hardly celebrated.

Somewhere, deep inside, they wanted to be real Jews, but they had no choice."

In high school, Polina first heard discussions of Zionists and the State of Israel. Wanting to learn more, in 1960 she went to the public library and read a few books she was able to find—Jabotinsky, a book on modern Israel, a Jewish history. (Most such books have not been available in recent years.) At the university, she met a few other students with whom she could discuss her emerging feelings and ideas. She saw a few *samizdat* articles and books before 1967 but had never heard of an organized Jewish movement in Leningrad. It was difficult to meet other Jews except at the synagogue. The Six-Day War mobilized her feelings. She noted that some Leningrad Jews became very afraid for their future during the government's propaganda assault on Israel and Zionism—"It was shameful to see frightened Russian Jews"—but many responded with pride and strong identification. During that period, she decided independently to emigrate to Israel. "This decision to live as a Jew was a decision against fear—an affirmation of my right to be a Jew and control my own life."

But she and her other young friends knew very little about Israel. At the Simchat Torah celebration in the fall of 1967, she met new friends who decided to form a group to study Hebrew and Jewish history. A few weeks later they met Butman and joined his *ulpan* of fifteen people. (Most members today are in prison or in Israel.) Gradually, she learned of the existence of the Leningrad organization, and by early 1968, she was associated with the mainstream movement. She met Mikhail Korenblit in 1969, at a Purim celebration at a mutual friend's apartment. Polina has been in Israel since the spring of 1972. Korenblit is serving a seven-year strict-regime sentence at the Potma labor camp.

RIGA:
The Historic Memory
and the Head

CHAPTER 5

Of all the cities in the USSR, none has provided as high a percentage of activist leadership in the Jewish movement as has Riga, the capital of Soviet Latvia. Old Riga remains a small medieval reminder of the city's affluence and commercial dominance during the Middle Ages. Riga's physical charms include beautiful parklike forests and a magnificent Baltic beach with miles of amber sand. Jews have lived in Riga through Latvian, Polish, German, and Russian rule. According to the latest Soviet census, there were 30,267 Jews in a population of 605,000. Perhaps because they are fiercely anti-assimilationist, the Jews of Riga, unlike those of other large Soviet cities, claim little more population than the official census count. Long before the recent upsurge in national feeling, they wore their Jewishness as a proud badge. A visitor cannot locate the old ghetto where 25,000 Jews were slaughtered during the Nazi occupation, but he can note that many Jews are included among the Communist heroes memorialized in the Latvian Red Rifleman Memorial Museum or in the Revolution Museum of the Latvian Soviet Republic. They are not identified as Jews, of course, and their names appear with Latvian endings (for example, Kaplan becomes Kaplanis). But the Jews of Riga are, nevertheless, different and their collective memory is different. Only the young Jews do not remember earlier regimes. A Riga Jew in his forties or older may have graduated from a high school in which Hebrew or Yiddish was the language of instruction, and he certainly spoke Yiddish at home. He probably belonged to a Zionist youth movement before World War II. Unless he

61

was an active Communist (and a significant minority were), he was
not apt to have become Russianized, and since the Latvians had never
accepted him, he remained identified as a Jew and affirmed his
Jewishness.

The Zionist movement flourished in Riga as if on native soil. Zionism
ran the whole spectrum of its ideological variety among Riga Jews. Until World War II (during the "bourgeois" Latvian Republic), and later,
during the Nazi occupation in the resistance movement, the Labor
Zionists and the left-wing youth, Hashomer Hatzair, played an important role, and many of them found their way to Palestine. But in the
postwar Soviet period, it was Jabotinsky-inspired Revisionist Zionists
who dominated the Jewish scene. Trained in Betar (the Revisionist
youth movement), Revisionist groups during the Soviet regime continued to teach and inculcate in the young their militant national position. As Riga's Jews experienced the "delights" of socialist society,
Labor Zionism, with its socialist ideology and its romantic attraction of
redemption through agricultural labor, had increasingly less magnetism.
In comparison to Soviet power, even the nationalistic Latvian government, which had not been generally beloved, appeared attractive.

Thus, after more than a quarter of a century of Soviet rule, it was
not surprising that a large number of Riga Jews retained their Zionist
aspirations. Girls like Leah Pliner, who was already an adolescent
when the Nazi blitzkrieg raced across the Baltic States, experienced
early years of positive Jewish affirmation. The Pliner family lived in
a small Latvian town, where the father taught in the Yiddish *gymnasium* and the mother practiced dentistry. Leah and her older sister Rivka
studied in a Yiddish school. In June 1940, the Latvian government fell
and the Russians came. A year later, when the Germans arrived, the
Pliners, abandoning everything, headed on foot toward the old border
between Latvia and the USSR. After walking 25 kilometers, they and
other Latvian Jews were halted by Soviet soldiers. Many, discouraged,
turned back and were murdered by the Nazis. The Pliners, however,
stayed on the border, and the next day the Soviet soldiers fled east in
disarray. Running after them, the Pliners were in a no-man's land between the Wehrmacht and the Red Army. Eventually, Soviet authorities
accepted them and put them on a train bound for the Russian interior,
where Leah spent the war years. There she experienced the widespread
anti-Semitic myths that "the Jews are making money in Tashkent while
Russian boys are dying at the front" and learned that Jewish youths

of her age who had fled from Byelorussia, or the Ukraine, or Leningrad, unlike the Latvian Jews, had no Jewish background at all. The Latvian youngsters taught other Jewish youths. They also acquired friends from other parts of the USSR and sometimes maintained contact with them after the war. Leah became friendly with a dynamic 16-year-old from Kharkov, Chaim Spivakovsky (see page 256).

Boris Slovin, whom Leah subsequently married, grew up in Riga, the son of a prosperous businessman who was also a left-wing intellectual. In June 1940, the Slovins greeted the Red Army with bouquets of flowers, but within half a year, the Slovin family's hospitality was repaid by their being sent to Siberia as "socially dangerous" (capitalist) people. In the trains, the men were separated from the wives and children. The men, after hasty administrative decisions, without trial were sent to work camps, and the women and children were left to provide for themselves. Many never saw their families again. Most of the men who survived were released in 1946–47 and returned to cities like Riga and Vilna. Some managed to go to Palestine. But the wives, not having been punished, could not be rehabilitated and therefore could not get travel permission to leave Siberia. Boris Slovin's father returned to Riga without his family. Several years later, Boris managed to reach Riga and found a father he hardly knew. Shortly thereafter, in 1951, a new administrative decision humanely determined that the children should be reunited with their mothers, and Boris returned to Siberia. Not until 1956–57 were large numbers of Baltic Jews permitted to go home. But the passage of more than fifteen years had taken its toll. Death, disability, disease, new family arrangements, and the emotional distance that time, growth, and change sometimes bring were more than most families could withstand. Boris had been admitted to Tomsk University, where, shortly after the death of Stalin, he formed a Zionist student group, which is believed to have been the first such underground circle in Siberia. The young people met regularly, spoke of Israel, accumulated information, and, although they had no other activity, were astonished at their own audacity. After the 1956 Sinai War, which had a strong influence on his generation, Boris Slovin found his way back to Riga.

Leah **Pliner** and her family returned to Riga in 1945, having found that their home and the Yiddish *gymnasium* in the small town where they had lived had been destroyed. Leah graduated as an attorney in 1952. In 1956, the Sinai campaign stimulated her and her friends to think concretely about what they could do. Small but stable circles of young Zionists came into existence in those years. They functioned in underground fashion, and there was some contact between them. Among those who were very active in the Riga group were David Garber (also an attorney), Dov Shperling, Iosif Yankelevich, and Iosif Shneider. Leah describes these Zionist circles as "more than people dreaming of going to Israel. We were activists who wanted to educate through Zionist propaganda. Most of our youth were not Zionists, and who would tell them the truth if we did not?" In 1957, Leah's group issued its first *samizdat* publication about Zionism. It told of the Warsaw Ghetto revolt. Other surreptitious productions included Ben-Gurion's speeches on the Sinai campaign, material from Dubnov's *History of the Jews,* and, somewhat later, Israeli Attorney General Gideon Hausner's summation of the Eichmann Trial. The choice of material reflected the events that strongly influenced the movement. But for the Khrushchev revelations about Stalin in 1956, the preconditions of nonconformist courage for an underground movement might not have existed. The Sinai campaign of the same year ignited the latent sense of Jewish dignity and self-identification. Simon Dubnov's works were a natural object for *samizdat* publication. A world-renowned Jewish historian, Dubnov lived and wrote in Riga until the Nazis killed him at Rumbuli during the massacre of Riga Jews. His last words to his fellow-Jews were "Record everything, record!" The Eichmann trial in 1960 not only bolstered developing pride but revived the still-fresh memories of the Holocaust. The *samizdat* literature expressed the viewpoint of what was really a neo-Zionist movement—not the classical Zionism that spoke of *aliyah* (emigration) to Palestine, but rather of repatriation to Israel. That was why, of all the *samizdat* works prepared, "our Tanach [Bible] was *Exodus* by Leon Uris." Leah tells the story:

> We received our first copy of *Exodus* in a strange way. It explains many things about Soviet Jewry. Since we were Zionists, we did everything possible to have contacts with the Israel Embassy. But contact with the embassy was very difficult because they didn't want contact with the underground. They thought it dangerous for Israel-USSR relations. We told them it was far more dangerous to make contact with an occasional person rather than to make information available to us. But we could not persuade them of this and, as a result, none of the Zionist groups were able to work with them. The embassy people would visit different cities to give the Jews an opportunity to

see them—to feel their presence. In 1962, the Israeli ambassador came to Riga. He first sent his car on the train. When he came to the station to get his car, he saw a young man who appeared to him to be Jewish and gave him a book in English. Boris [Slovin] worked as an electrician at the station. The next day, this young Latvian said to Boris: "Your ambassador gave me a book in English I don't understand. Are you interested?" He gave Boris the book, which he brought home. It was *Exodus*. I could read some English and I was enthralled. It had to be translated by somebody with excellent English who was not afraid. But I couldn't think of such a person, so I did it myself. Each word I didn't know I took from the English-Russian dictionary. Most of the book came from the dictionary. It was translated literally. Then I gave it to Boris and Dov Shperling to make the Russian text. They shortened it considerably, partly for technical reasons. It was too long to reproduce easily. But they also wanted to make it better than Uris. They threw out Ari Ben-Canaan's romance with Kitty. They did not think a romance with a "goy" was good for Soviet Jewish youth. First they produced it in photo, but that was heavy and expensive. Then it was made on an Era mimeograph machine in 300 copies. Ephraim Tsal made it on the Era, but the technical side never knew who the literature side was. Uris should never see it because we'll be sued, but for tens of thousands of Soviet Jews, the *samizdat* version of *Exodus* was their greatest Jewish inspiration.

The enormous significance of *Exodus* to the growth and stimulation of the Jewish movement can hardly be overstated. It has been corroborated again and again by Soviet Jews in the USSR and Israel, and by visitors to the Soviet Union. If ever a book helped make a revolution, the Uris novel about the creation of the Jewish state can be said to have done so. The stories of how *Exodus* went into *samizdat* are varied, but they may all be true, since ideas and tactics in a great movement often develop spontaneously and independently in different places at approximately the same time.

Exodus was first published in September 1958. In its first paperback edition, Uris notes why the book received such an enthusiastic reception:

> *Exodus* is the story of the greatest miracle of our times, an event unparalleled in the history of mankind: the rebirth of a nation which had been dispersed 2,000 years before. It tells the story of the Jews coming back after centuries of abuse, indignities, torture, and murder to carve an oasis in the sand with guts and with blood. . . . *Exodus* is about fighting people, people who do not apologize either for being born Jews or the right to live in human dignity.

Such a book inspired veteran Soviet Zionists. Latvian-born Ezra Rusinek first saw a copy while living in exile in the small town of Taganrog, on the Sea of Azov. In 1963, when he was able to move back to Riga, he brought a precious copy with him. It took time to secure an old, privately owned typewriter. (The KGB registers all typewriters in shops as well as in offices and repair stores.) Type face was altered. A translator was found—Boris Taubin—and slowly, night after night, two or three pages of the 600-page book were prepared. It took more than a year to translate and type five copies. Two were kept in Riga and three were sent to friends in other cities. It was circulated from the giver to another person who read it, returned it, and then it was read by another, and another, and another. But no one in Riga knew who had made the book. In late 1964, Rusinek saw, for the first time, an abridged *Exodus* of 150 pages—doubtless the Slovin-Shperling version. Both groups had kept their secrets well.

Viktor Fedoseyev, the Moscow novelist and journalist who in 1970 became the chief editor of the important Jewish *samizdat* journal which he named *Iskhod* (Exodus), tells a different story about the origin of the *samizdat* version of Uris's *Exodus*. About 1960, an unknown Soviet citizen read *Exodus* in English and was struck by the story. Thereafter he was sent to prison camp. In prison camps, one way the inmates occupy their non-working hours is by telling stories. A man with a good memory and a wide reading background may provide the major cultural activity for his fellow-inmates. *Exodus,* as a story, was related in this fashion. Another inmate, impressed with the story, which he had heard a number of times, wrote it from memory when he got out, and in course of time this appeared in 70 to 80 pages in *samizdat* form. The *samizdat* story created a stir, particularly among Zionist groups. Not long after the first version appeared, a second (Zionist) one was issued, deliberately omitting any references to Kitty or romance, and omitting anything not supportive of Zionist ideology. Still later, a third version appeared. This was a translation from the complete English text. Because of the length of the book, it became necessary to find as many people as possible to translate it. Finally, fourteen people divided up the book and translated. They were from different disciplines and had different levels of competence. Thus, the engineers and scientists wrote with hard, precise, mathematical language; the poets with flowery imagery; and one fine Christian lady, who had learned her English in a missionary school, volunteered her services and translated Uris with Biblical phraseology.

Still another version tells how *Exodus* was translated from English to Russian inside the Dubrovlag concentration camp in Soviet Mordovia in 1963. Anatoly Rubin, a Zionist activist in Minsk, obtained a paperback copy of the book in late 1962 and passed it to other Jews inside Camp Number 7. Among them was Avram Shifrin, a Moscow lawyer, born in 1923, who, after service as a Red Army major in World War II, worked as a legal adviser to the Ministry of Defense until he was arrested in 1954 and accused of being a spy for Israel and the United States. His death sentence was commuted, but he served ten years in the camps and lost a leg. Another was Aleksandr Guzman, a former Red Army officer who attempted to escape to Israel while serving on Polish territory and also received ten years. Shifrin and Guzman are now in Israel. A third man who was involved but still has close relatives in the USSR and wishes to remain unidentified tells the story:

> Only some of the Jewish prisoners knew English, so group readings, accompanied by translations, were arranged. We soon realized that this was a very difficult solution. It was dangerous to meet to read a forbidden book—you could have your sentence extended—and, furthermore, many of us worked different shifts and this kept interrupting the readings. Then another upsetting thing happened—Rubin was accused of an attempt to help a prisoner escape and sent to solitary.
>
> However, a new idea occurred—to translate *Exodus* into Russian in writing, rather than orally. Paper had to be secured. All of the Jewish prisoners and many non-Jews brought sheets secretly to us, one at a time. Avram Shifrin knew English and started dictating the translation to Aleksandr Guzman. The lookout during this dangerous enterprise was Zolia Katz, an old Zionist and a wounded veteran of World War II who now works in a metal factory in Tel Aviv. After finishing our day's work in a woodworking plant, we started working again in the evening. Shifrin would sit on a top bunk in a corner of the barracks with the book in his hand, and Guzman would place a notebook on a piece of plywood, sit down next to him, and take Shifrin's dictation. Katz walked back and forth inside the barracks or stood in the doorway in order to warn us should any guards come. Shifrin was about to end his ten-year sentence and we worked very strenuously. We had to translate over 600 pages in two months. Late at night, the notebook would be passed on to Zolia Katz, who was serving his third term. He would be the first one to read it, and then he would pass it on to other Jews.
>
> Notebooks with the *Exodus* translation were passed from hand to hand. All of us were thrilled by it. Many became Zionists because of it. There were some tense moments. Once, a notebook with part of the book was found during a search. It took a lot of scheming and

deception to get it away from the guards. Another time, the whole transcript almost ended up in the hands of the authorities—the head guard came back to search Shifrin again, after we all thought that the search was over and had taken out all we had hidden.

The translation was originally prepared for the people in the camp, but then we decided to circulate it outside. Once again we had to rewrite 600 pages. We did it in one day. We gathered all the Jews whom we had trusted to read the book and invited a few non-Jewish friends, most of whom were Ukrainian nationalists, and gave each of them twenty pages on a Sunday morning. That evening we had two identical manuscripts.

When Shifrin was released, he managed to take one of the manuscripts with him. He recopied it on a typewriter in Karaganda, and so the first copies of *Exodus* in Russian came into being.

This was in the summer of 1963. Shifrin sent the books to Moscow, Riga, Leningrad, and Kiev. There they were duplicated. . . .

The various versions of *Exodus* may well constitute the all-time *samizdat* best-seller.

Other volumes were produced in the early and mid-1960s by the Riga groups. They included books by Jabotinsky and Chaim Nachman Bialik, the famous Hebrew poet, who had emigrated from Russia to Palestine years earlier. The Riga Zionists had good contacts with friends in other cities. As early as 1963, they gave some publications to friends in Leningrad, to Anatoly Rubin in Minsk, after he returned from his prison term for Zionist activity, and to David Khavkin, David Drabkin, and Vitaly Svechinsky in Moscow. Khavkin and Svechinsky had both spent years in the camps for Zionist activity, and were known to their fellow-prisoners. These men in turn had contacts in other cities, so the *samizdat* literature received relatively widespread circulation.

When, in January 1969, Leah, Shperling, Yankelevich, Shneider, and Garber received permission to go to Israel, they had many copies of *samizdat* literature on hand, which they placed in a suitcase and buried in the ground, not far from the home of Leah's parents at the Riga seashore. Only Ephraim Tsal knew where it was hidden. Shortly thereafter, he too got permission to leave and in turn told Isak Pulkhan and Aron Shpilberg where it was hidden. The suitcase containing *Exodus* and works of Jabotinsky and Bialik became an important part of the prosecution's case in the Riga trial of 1971.

Of the approximately 100,000 Latvian Jews in June 1941, more than 40,000 lived in Riga. When the Wehrmacht overran the small Baltic county, Latvian fascists immediately arrested about 7,000 Jews. Within a week of Nazi occupation, synagogues were burned, cemeteries were vandalized, and several thousand Jews were murdered. By the fall of 1941, the 30,000 remaining Jews were segregated into a narrow, teeming quarter of the Old City which had been the Riga Ghetto. They were kept there until November 30, 1941, while their Nazi occupiers, aided by some of their Latvian fellow-citizens, planned a final solution for Riga Jewry. About 5,000 able-bodied young people were transferred to work camps and factories, and many of them died in German and Polish concentration camp incinerators. On December 7–9, 1941, the remaining 25,000 were herded to a forest called Rumbuli, outside Riga, where men, women, and children were executed by German and Latvian Hitlerites.

The slaughter, similar to that at Babi Yar near Kiev, left no witnesses. Grass grew over this place of horror, and the world forgot. But the young Jews of Riga did not forget. In 1961, spurred by the Eichmann trial, they instigated an intensive search for the location. In time, they found burned bones, a child's shoe, an encrusted Star of David. They carefully demarcated the borders of the area and decided that they would make it a memorial park. But a dispute arose between the militant Jews and the more cautious majority, who urged the group to obtain permission from the Soviet authorities. Leah and Boris belonged to the extreme wing and opposed going to the authorities, but after lengthy discussion, a delegation led by David Garber was authorized to contact the Riga Executive Committee of the Soviet of Workers' Representatives to secure permission to clear and plant the area as a memorial to the Riga holocaust victims. After authorization was granted, Riga's Jews, particularly the youth, went to Rumbuli to work every Sunday. During the summer of 1963, as many as 500 young Jews worked on the memorial. Leah admits that "truth was on the side" of the moderates. But she, Boris, Shperling, and others erected a barbed-wire Mogen David that was large enough to be seen from the Moscow-Riga train. Many Jews feared it would be a provocation to the KGB and they sought to remove it. That resulted in altercations and hard feelings between the factions.

The continued Sunday activity, first with shovels, pails, wheelbarrows, and plants, while paths were made and graves marked, were followed by services, the lighting of candles, and then meetings of the young people. The authorities began warning the parents against their children's going to Rumbuli. Despite parental admonition and anxiety, the young people went on meeting there. Then the authorities began holding official memorial meetings, much as at Babi Yar. Afterward, the young neo-Zionists would begin their own assemblies, and on the bus back to Riga they would join together in Israeli songs. They commenced wearing the Mogen David, the six-pointed Star of David.

Every occasion that could be found was utilized. Mass dancing took place at the synagogue on Simchat Torah and other Jewish holidays. At weddings in Riga, at which telegrams were traditionally received from relatives and friends, the activists would invent messages from Israel containing slogans such as *"L'shanah habah b'Yerushalaim"* (Next year in Jerusalem) and read them to the assembled guests. In 1965, a visiting all-star basketball team of Israeli women toured the Soviet Union. When it came to Riga, the activists stood in line all night to secure tickets. The authorities had already predistributed large numbers to the local party sports clubs. Two children, Ina Slovin, then 11, and Viktor Aleksandrovich (Leah's nephew, the son of her sister Rivka and Isak Aleksandrovich), then 12, brought large bouquets—one for the Soviet captain and one for the Israeli team. But the militia (police) seized and removed the flowers, took the children to headquarters, and photographed and questioned them. When the game began with the playing of *"Hatikvah"* (the Israeli anthem) and the Soviet national anthem, the Jews proudly stood and sang. Although the Israeli team lost, hundreds of young Jews mobbed the bus on which the Israelis traveled and sang *"Hevenu Shalom Aleichem"* (We bring you peace). The Israeli girls, their eyes flowing with tears, joined the singing. Only with difficulty was the bus permitted to leave.

When Yosef Tekoah, then Israel's ambassador to the USSR, came to the Riga beach for a vacation in 1965, hundreds of Riga Jews who learned of it located him by a Hebrew newspaper he was reading. All of the Jewish youngsters wore Mogen Davids. (After the Six-Day War, this became a major technique of Jewish affirmation in cities other than Riga as well, and large numbers of Soviet Jewish youths today can be seen wearing this traditional symbol.) Ina Slovin was the same age as Tekoah's daughter. They met in the water, and Ina said, *"Shalom."* The Tekoah child did not answer but ran to her father. In a moment she returned and shook Ina's hand, and when Ina took her hand away there was a silver Star of David in it. She wore it until she left for Israel in February 1969, even though her schoolteacher insisted she remove it, and despite official protests at Komsomol meetings. When Ina left Riga, she gave it to a friend, who in turn left it with another friend when she was subsequently permitted to go to Israel. The Star of David is still being worn by a Jewish child in Riga. "It will be worn, until no Jews are left in Riga who wish to leave," Leah claims.

But despite the generally high level of activity, the Riga activists were plagued by a lack of funds and materials, and most of all by what they regarded as the indifference of world Jewry—most particularly Israel. They felt that they were the last Zionists in the world. They persisted in their efforts to contact Israeli Embassy officials. At every opportunity, they requested financial assistance and sought to advise the officials of their activity, which they believed should be known to them. They created opportunities to see Israeli representatives wherever they would travel. But no money was given to them. They begged for Jewish books, for Hebrew grammars, for a Russian translation of *Exodus*, but they were given none. An occasional copy of *Ariel*, an Israeli cultural magazine, could be secured, or a Bible would be given someone in a synagogue visit. But no sustained or meaningful effort was made to provide literature, so they could create *samizdat*, for which they were risking freedom. They implored Israeli officials to speak out insistently for the right of Soviet Jews to obtain exit visas. Only a handful of elderly Jews were being permitted to leave the USSR for Israel, and only when spouses or children were in Israel. They asked what to do and were told, "You must keep quiet. *Savlanut* [patience]."

By the summer of 1964, the Riga group were so frustrated and tense they felt they must do something to awaken understanding of their plight among Israeli and Western Jews. They decided to prepare a collective petition addressed to American Jewry. Families were willing to sign the petition and risk prison, so that the Jews in the free world might perhaps understand. The petition, initially signed by five people in Riga (Boris and Leah Slovin, Dov Shperling, Ephraim Tsal, and Mendel Gordin) and four in Leningrad (all now in prison), began: "We appeal to you, fully conscious that we will be sent to Soviet prisons, but appealing so you will wake up and understand our cries." Many other Jews were prepared to sign the petition if the Israeli Embassy would approve and see that it reached America.

Leah Slovin, who was expelled from the Latvian Bar Association in 1963 for her Zionist activities, had accepted a position as assistant to a

Moscow film producer—an opportunity that permitted her to travel in various parts of the USSR and make contact with Jewish activists. In December 1964, she located the Israeli cultural attaché, Ben-Chaim, who was having dinner in the Minsk Hotel restaurant with his wife, and quickly arranged to meet him the next morning at 8 o'clock when the dining room would be empty. She told him about the petition and asked him to arrange that it be taken out by diplomatic pouch and released to American Jewry. (At that time, the Riga movement had no contact with foreign correspondents at all. Such contacts were developed somewhat later by the democratic movement, through whom the Jewish movement worked to establish their press contacts.) Ben-Chaim refused to have anything to do with the petition. When pressed for a reason, he responded, "You will be sent to prison. Israel does not want the best people in prison." Leah suggested that they had the right to take their own risks. He then said, "This will be a provocation and give the Soviet authorities the opportunity to make wholesale arrests and thus jeopardize all Soviet Jews." Leah replied that such an answer reflected a lack of understanding of Soviet realities and the Soviet legal system. The diplomat then quietly confided: "Leah, I can't tell you all I want to tell, but we are taking an important initiative through diplomatic channels. It is quiet diplomacy, but very important for future *aliyah* [emigration to Israel] from Russia. If you do this, you will spoil our relations with the USSR and ruin our good contacts which will enable us soon to reach a secret agreement on that subject." However strong her disbelief (a skepticism confirmed by later events), she was unable to argue with this assertion. She told the others of her conversation, and they agreed that they could not quarrel with the representatives of Israel, particularly since they could not know what diplomatic negotiations might be occurring. The petition was never sent. No petitions from Riga reached the West, and no open, collective action occurred until diplomatic relations between Israel and the USSR ceased following the Six-Day War. In the absence of an Israeli diplomatic presence, Soviet Jews relied upon themselves and developed their own channels to Israel and the West.

Some benefits accrued from Israeli-Soviet relations. Occasional (although rare) cultural events were permitted between the two countries. In 1966, Geulah Gil, a popular Israeli singer, made a triumphal tour of Soviet cities. Her concert in Riga stimulated such tremendous anticipation that a volatile atmosphere was created. Riga Jews besieged the box office, days in advance. Before the concert began, the large square in front of the concert hall was cordoned off by motorcycles and militia. The Jews came decked with flowers, but the KGB came down the aisles and took away all bouquets. Anger, frustration, expectation charged the hall. Each song was greeted with stormy applause. When Miss Gil concluded, no one left his seat. Three thousand people, mostly young, applauded and stamped their feet until she returned. They wanted to sing Israeli songs. They cried out their desire to go to Israel. Finally the militia occupied the stage and insisted that the crowd leave. Arguments broke out. Then troops entered the building. The Jews shouted, "Shame! Shame! The world will know about this. Where are your tanks?" The soldiers responded by threatening prison for the audience. Some Jews shouted back: "We are in prison all of our lives in the USSR." They began singing Israeli songs. When told this was forbidden, they sang louder and shouted slogans. Leah relates: "It was spontaneous—like an epidemic. We were like crazy. The activists were in the front. Our behavior was abnormal—out of control." Suddenly people from the rear pushed forward. The soldiers and police advanced. Naomi, the 15-year-old daughter of David Garber, was pushed by the militia major in charge of the operation. Stunned, she slapped him. She was immediately seized and put in a police car. Young Jews rushed the car to free her. They struggled with the police. Clothing was torn. People were beaten. But the police feared to make mass arrests because the crowd was out of control. Then Geulah Gil entered her car with her entourage, including Israeli Embassy officials. The car could not move because young men lay under the wheels. Finally, the police and soldiers dispersed the crowd and arrested a number of the protesters. A group of Jews went to militia headquarters and demanded the freeing of Naomi Garber. They were told to select delegation leaders. Those selected were immediately imprisoned summarily on charges of hooliganism.

Leah, as an attorney, made an investigation of the riot, the beatings, the arrests, and the trials with their anti-Semitic statements and charges. She documented it carefully and prepared a protocol of events. It was detailed and dramatic. The group decided to smuggle the protocol to the West, in the hope of freeing the arrested Jews and attracting attention to conditions in Riga. A visiting American rabbi, contacted in the Riga synagogue, told of another tourist, an American social psychologist, who was in Riga for a convention. Arrangements were made to meet him, and he was taken by car to the seaside home of Leah and Rivka Aleksandrovich's parents. Rivka, who was an English teacher, translated. The visitor took the documents and gave them absolute assurance that the story would be told in America and in Israel. But the documents were not published, and there was only silence—a silence that the Jews of Riga did not and still cannot understand, although they speculate that the documents were taken to Israeli officials who were at that time following a policy of silence about Soviet Jewry.

Still the struggle continued, intensified by the Six-Day War and the Soviet Union's anti-Zionist, anti-Semitic response to it. In the summer of 1968, a rash of searches in Zionist cases was conducted by the KGB. In Minsk, Boris Slovin's uncle, a 60-year-old electrical engineer named Leopold Grinblat, was investigated for preparing a typewritten biography of Chaim Weizmann, Israel's first president. The KGB, believing erroneously that the material came from Riga, searched the Slovin home and detained Boris at work. Shperling and Mendel Gordin were searched and interrogated. KGB investigative case files were opened. Then, inexplicably, things quieted, and in January 1969, some of the Riga activists, Anatoly Rubin in Minsk, and others, received their exit visas. They immediately advised their friends in other cities, who were aware of the fact that applications had been made. Shortly before departing, they went to Moscow where they met with friends from there and from other cities. They agreed that contacts would be maintained from Israel, by code when necessary; that literature would be sent in; that *vizovs* would be secured and sent to all who desired them; that if permission was not given to leave, Jews would renounce their Soviet citizenship; and that a campaign would be intensified in the West, using Israel as a base from which contacts with American and British Jews and others could be made.

By early 1969 in Riga, what had begun more than a decade earlier as small groups of militant Jews committed to an educational program—at times dramatic and public—now had developed into a large, although not tightly disciplined, well-organized Jewish underground.

Mendel Gordin, a physician and bacteriologist born in 1937, is a soft-spoken, scholarly man, whose slim stature and thick glasses give no hint of the strength and courage he provided the Jews of Riga for a decade before he was permitted to leave for Israel in December 1970. After graduating from the Riga Medical Institute and serving as a staff physician at a Latvian regional hospital, Gordin was appointed to a key position at the Central Bacteriological Research Center in 1966. He kept his identification with the Jewish movement to himself until after the Six-Day War. By 1968, although not religious, he was openly celebrating Jewish holidays and following Jewish religious practices. In February 1969, he applied for an exit permit to go to Israel, but OVIR denied his request in March. On June 1, 1969, he sent an open letter to Nikolai Podgorny, chairman of the Presidium of the Supreme Soviet, protesting that denial, and stating: "I categorically declare that it is my will to live only in my own motherland, and I regard Israel as such. Taking this into account, I hereby give up my Soviet citizenship and enclose herewith my passport." Harassment, fines, demotions followed. On September 22, 1969, he took a second unprecedented step —he stayed away from work on Yom Kippur. The next day, he was discharged from his employment. He was fined for being without his passport (identity papers). Refused employment, he was threatened with prosecution as a "parasite." His involvement in the movement increased sharply. Gordin states with respect to these developments in which he played such a major role:

> It is difficult to say when and for how long there has been a Zionist underground in Riga. In my opinion, there was always a very lively Jewish life in Riga, but for a long time it was *deeply* underground. Given Soviet society and its characteristics, that is the only place it could be. By the late 1950s, there was a small group of people who were already publishing Jewish *samizdat* in Riga. But you can't find out the facts by asking only one person, or even a number. The nature of the way it was organized was such that no one knows more than his small piece of the truth. I don't know exactly. I knew of five to ten people in those days. Someone else knew five or so. I don't know what they were doing exactly. We learned not to ask. We didn't want to know too much. People were close to their own activity in a very narrow circle. By 1969 and 1970, when we began collective demonstrations—then the movement is easier to understand.

Viktor Fedoseyev, the editor of *Iskhod*, and his Jewish wife Rakhel, a professional translator and linguist, who lived in Riga from the early 1960s until the fall of 1968, when they moved to Moscow, never became aware of the underground and how it functioned. Fedoseyev notes:

> In Riga, there was a real feeling that there were Jews who constantly affirmed their Jewishness. This was in startling contrast to most Soviet

cities. But I never became aware of a movement, that is a real movement in a well-organized sense, during the years we lived there. Of
course, now that the Jewish movement is open and dramatic in the
Soviet Union, everyone really believes that it began in his kitchen,
and that he was "the" or at least "a" leader of it. This is not
bragadoccio. This is because the movement was so diffused—so spontaneous. It arose out of deep needs and deeper frustration. Of course,
it differed from place to place. But everywhere in the Soviet Union,
the ground was plowed and the seeds were planted.

No single person knows more about the growth of the Riga underground than Ezra Rusinek, now a watchmaker in a tiny shop in Kiryat
Menachem, a working-class neighborhood of Jerusalem. Rusinek, born
in 1914, is a cultured man with a sense of presence and quiet dignity
that commands respect. The son of a prosperous Latvian watch manufacturer, Ezra joined his father in the business after learning his trade
in France. A Zionist in his youth, he was active in Betar before World
War II and had secured permission from the British authorities in
Palestine to go there to live with his young wife Roza and their
daughter, when the war broke out. Instead, he was deported to a labor
camp in Siberia. He and his family found their way in 1950 to Taganrog, a small city in southern Russia, on the Sea of Azov, where he
eked out a living as a watchmaker, until he was able to return to Riga
in 1963. In the meantime, his older sister had settled in Israel and his
80-year-old mother had emigrated in 1961. Upon his return to Riga,
he noted that its Jewish population seemed divided between the
remnants of the old Riga residents, greatly supplemented by Jews from
other parts of Latvia, who would not return to their small towns after
World War II and congregated in the capital, and newcomers from
Russia. National feelings were much stronger in the first group, but
even among them, parents were unable or frightened to pass on their
heritage to their children. The second group was largely assimilated.
Contact with Jews from the first group reawakened Jewish knowledge
and interest among those who had largely lost their group identity.

Movement activities centered on (1) Rumbuli, (2) samizdat, (3)
"open-door" homes, (4) the synagogue, (5) slides, postcards, and
records, (6) Hebrew lessons, (7) OVIR contacts, and, finally, (8)
collective and open letters, that is, "open struggle." Rusinek points out
that "although the formal aim of Rumbuli was to put the holy place
in order, the hidden, real aim was to make Rumbuli a place for meetings for Riga Jewish youth. The KGB did not really understand this

until it was too late." Although "official" Rumbuli gatherings were attempted, forbidden Jewish meetings followed. On November 30, 1970, the KGB and militia dispersed such a meeting and detained many participants, but in 1971, on the three traditional occasions, meetings occurred—the commemoration of the Warsaw Ghetto, the Sunday between Rosh Hashanah and Yom Kippur, and the November anniversary of the Rumbuli tragedy—and despite official discouragement and harassment, there was a great increase of those who attended memorial meetings. In May 1972, the officials again prevented people from going to Rumbuli and arrested many, but at the traditional late November gathering, the crowds had again increased, and the police did not interfere.

Samizdat was the most fundamental activity of the movement and the cornerstone upon which the other activities were based. "*Samizdat* was essential," Rusinek said, "to give Jewish youth that information which was unavailable to them because of Soviet policy toward Israel and Soviet Jews." Interested young people could get information in no other way, and the growing "desire for knowledge had to be satisfied." Until 1969, there were several *samizdat* groups in Riga which had very limited contact with each other. The younger group, composed of Leah and Boris Slovin, Shperling, Yankelevich, and others, had been decimated by departures to Israel by the spring of 1969. The older group in age, of which Rusinek was one, was composed largely of former Betar members, many of whom had been in German concentration camps, in Siberian exile, or evacuees during the war. "They belonged to that generation which remembered the times of Stalin and were very cautious."

Despite their caution, they had produced a version of *Exodus*, two works by Jabotinsky, and *Aggressors*, a book about Israel by Ladislav Mnacko, a Slovak Communist writer who condemned the conventional wisdom of the Czech and Soviet governments about the Israeli-Arab conflict. The original copy of *Aggressors* had been purloined by a Jewish patient from a Latvian doctor who had innocently brought it back to Riga from a trip abroad. In 1966, the group had produced a press bulletin extracted and distilled from *Kol Ha'am,* the newspaper of the Israeli Communist Party and the only Israeli paper allowed to come by mail to the USSR. Just before the Six-Day War, they had also managed to secure copies of *L'Express* left behind by a French tourist and had prepared a *samizdat* analysis of the Middle East situation based on that journal's reportage. A friendly Jew in the information service of the Central Committee of the Communist Party had slipped to a member of the group a secret report of the Committee on the June 1967 war which was surreptitiously reproduced and distributed in small numbers. But despite such activity, *samizdat* work was limited largely to the reproduction of material prepared abroad and secured in haphazard ways. By the spring of 1969, feeling had grown that this was insufficient. At the initiative of some younger activists, notably Ilya Volk, Aron Shpilberg, and Boris Maftser, meetings were arranged to unify the existing *samizdat* groups into a Riga *samizdat* committee, which Rusinek agreed to head. Not only was there an increased demand and felt need to inform Riga youth, but it was agreed that the publications would be sent to other parts of the USSR, "where the Jews were sleeping and had to be awakened." Rusinek harbored some unexpressed concern about what he viewed as growing, dangerous militancy among some of the young, and felt that the educational work constituted a restraining type of control. He felt unable to apply for an exit visa, for fear his son Iosif would be immediately expelled from the university and drafted. *Samizdat* activity "compensated morally for my inability to apply for an exit visa."

By the fall of 1969, *samizdat* literature, growing in quantity, began to include material prepared in Riga itself. It had an added goal by then—to establish, through educational work, "a large reserve of Jews desiring to leave for Israel." In retrospect, Rusinek feels that this goal was achieved, since, with the exception of Soviet Georgia, applications for exit visas were highest in cities where *samizdat* materials were circulated, and in deep Russia, where they were not available, few Jews sought to leave.

The tactic of having open-door homes available had developed well before 1969. Originally a consequence of the host family's hospitality and desire to educate, the system became so institutionalized that Jews could visit some apartments without invitation and bring friends with them to discuss Jewish and Israeli themes. They could argue. They could learn. They could sing Israeli songs and dance the hora. In short, in a country where youth were limited to officially approved groups like the Komsomol, and where Jewish community centers could not exist, Riga Jews created their own unofficial means of socializing the young and bringing people together in pleasant circumstances.

Beginning in 1958, groups of several hundred Jews had begun

congregating in front of the Moscow synagogue to celebrate Simchat Torah by the singing and dancing traditionally associated with the "giving of the law." Within a few years, thousands had come to participate. Elie Wiesel has dramatically described the excitement of the event as he witnessed it in 1965. But years before, the same tradition had been followed in Leningrad and Kiev, and Riga Jews adopted the practice in 1960. In Riga, for those who were not religious, the synagogue became a place for meetings. Long before foreign tourists discovered that an "open house" to meet Soviet Jews took place at the synagogue (or in the street in front of it) on late Saturday mornings, the Jews themselves used the Sabbath, as well as the Jewish holidays, as nonproscribed opportunities to meet and exchange information about Jewish events, otherwise unreported and thus unknowable. The fact that KGB personnel also learned to cultivate habits of religiosity and that synagogue officials were heavily infiltrated with informers failed to dampen the enthusiasm of the activists. The Jews simply developed habits of creativity in making their contacts and carrying on their conversations.

The creative imagination of the activists was particularly exemplified by their development of visual aids. Boris Taubin, one of Rusinek's closest associates over many years and a linguist with expert knowledge of Israeli history, had translated *Exodus*. He was also the man who first secured and translated the issues of *Kol Ha'am*, and he had been a central figure in the *samizdat* project. Through the years, he had collected many Israeli picture postcards and had arranged them geographically. In 1968, after the postcards were photographed on slides, Taubin began a series of illustrated lectures, based on his knowledge of Israeli geography and history. To Jews unable to learn about Israel, let alone visualize it, such lectures were a revelation. Taubin soon received assistance from Lev Mints and Lev Elyashevich. In 1969-70, each man was conducting several home lectures a week on various Israeli subjects. They gave guest lectures in Moscow, Leningrad, Minsk, and other cities, until the activists in those cities could reproduce slides and other local lecturers could be trained. Hebrew phonograph records were secured from visiting tourists, and tape recordings were made so that there could be musical accompaniment to the lectures, as well as music for singing in the open houses.

Sporadically, Hebrew study circles had existed in Riga for many years, but word of the successful Leningrad *ulpanim* had spread and,

by 1969, Riga had organized similar classes. By 1970, regularized
ulpanim existed despite a severe shortage of books, which prevented
intensive study. The few copies of *Elef Milim* were supplemented by
old newspapers, calendars, and the Bible. But from Moscow, in late
1969, came two heavy suitcases full of well-photographed copies of the
grammar, and large numbers of Riga Jews were enabled to learn
Hebrew. A far higher percentage in Riga still knew Yiddish, so Riga's
Jews knew the two languages better than the Jews in any other city.

Riga also outstripped other Soviet cities in the number of Jews who
had applied to leave the Soviet Union. In many cities, especially those
deep in the interior, the idea of being permitted to go to Israel was a
wild fantasy—a cruel illusion—and few dared to hope, let alone apply,
for an exit visa. But in Riga, despite the social ostracism and the economic and political peril involved in such an application, there was an
awareness, based on historic experience, that difficult as it was, permission to leave might be granted. So long as it was possible, there was
hope. After World War II, some families had been given permission
to leave the country. Again in 1956-57, a few Riga Jews, primarily
older people without higher education, had been granted visas. Again in
1962-63, a number of daring families, including those with university
degrees whose financial circumstances were comfortable in Soviet
terms, began to apply. A few families were permitted to go, again
creating hope. When, in December 1966, Soviet leaders publicly indicated that applications would be accepted, there was a rush to apply.
Although few were granted prior to the complete shutdown of approvals
following the Six-Day War, some families reapplied. Riga Jews were
further heartened when some of the most active Zionists left for Israel
in early 1969. Suddenly and inexplicably, in September 1969, OVIR
recommenced acceptance of applications, and many families applied
for the first time. The OVIR office became a focal point for meeting
other Jews who desired to leave and the object of anger and resentment
when, from the late summer of 1969 until the winter of 1970-71,
refusal followed refusal. This frustration—one that Soviet authorities
might have averted by permitting the continuation of a small trickle of
emigrants—resulted in an open struggle—an explosion triggered by
the aborting of rising expectations, the brimming over of years of
frustration and anger, and the severing of any last traces of emotional
identification with the social system of a country where the Jews felt
they were strangers.

No single event can be said to have instigated the public surfacing of the movement. Certainly the fact that the years of surreptitious education and indoctrination had produced a hardened activist corps and a ready reserve of committed young people was an important element. Other factors were the Kochubiyevsky trial and the public attention in the West to the *samizdat* it created; the public renunciation of his Soviet citizenship in Moscow by young Yakov (Yasha) Kazakov in late spring 1968; the sudden spurt of open activity in Moscow and Leningrad; and the almost miraculous beginning of open struggle in Soviet Georgia, publicly proclaimed by a letter from eighteen Georgian families to Prime Minister Golda Meir in August 1969. Even the State of Israel, silent so long, seemed to some Riga Jews like Rusinek to signal its approval of activity, when Mrs. Meir made a dramatic statement in the Knesset in November 1969 recognizing and fully supporting the Jewish struggle in the USSR. But, more than anything else, the fact that the voice of Soviet Jewry was finally acknowledged in the West—that the first open letters were being published, that the early petitions were evoking comment, that Western Jews seemingly ceased to be the Jews of Silence—stimulated a small all-Union meeting of activist leaders, who prepared a program of action.

At first, according to Rusinek, "we thought that the people were not yet ready. Still, we gave way to the first two Riga letters." The first of these petitions, on April 24, 1969, was a startling cry from Dora Zak, a middle-aged former teacher and mother of two children, addressed to Brezhnev, Kosygin, and Podgorny. Mrs. Zak renounced Soviet citizenship for herself and her 19-year-old son Boris, since she had again been refused exit permission after having persistently applied since 1963.

> I am firmly convinced that only in Israel will we be able to feel that we are full and equal members of society. . . . For nearly twenty years, I have been subject to incessant moral and material deprivation, the only reason for which is the fact that I am a Jew. . . . My cup of sorrow has overflown; nineteen years without work in my profession; nineteen years without an assured piece of bread; nineteen years of jeering and insults and the joyless childhood of my children. . . . Don't drive me to madness by another refusal.

The second letter was Mendel Gordin's of June 1 to Podgorny renouncing his Soviet citizenship.

To Rusinek, "it was clear that open struggle could not be prepared without organization and coordination." He and Shpilberg compiled a file of Jewish families who had applied for exit visas. Intercity relations, particularly with Moscow, were intensified. Contacts with Leningrad and Minsk, in existence for years, were strengthened. The two main groups of Riga activists were known as Aleph (Hebrew letter A) and Bet (Hebrew letter B). Although some individuals had difficulty maintaining the distinction, for almost two years, the Aleph people were those engaged in open struggle—those who signed individual or collective letters; those involved in petitioning; those who were to contact public officials; those who would contact tourists and, later, newsmen. The Bet people operated far more deeply underground. Their primary task was the preparation, duplication, and distribution of *samizdat* literature. Gordin, for example was Aleph and Rusinek was Bet.

By the fall of 1969, the first open collective letter, signed by twenty-two people who had applied to leave and had been refused, was addressed to UN Secretary General U Thant. It concerned the right of free departure from the USSR and was based on Article 13/2 of the Universal Declaration of Human Rights: "Everyone has the right to leave any country, including his own." It stated:

> We are being kept forcibly. We are not allowed to go. Such treatment is an act of lawlessness. It is an open violation of the rights of man. We consider that to hold us forcibly is against the most elementary concepts of humanity and morality. We Demand Free Exit From the USSR!

The letter was written by Leib Khnokh, who signed it first. (In Riga, and generally in the USSR, the first signer is the author.) It was also signed, among others, by Silva Zalmanson, Ruta Aleksandrovich, and Mendel Bodnya, all of whom were imprisoned later that year. A second letter, signed by twenty-seven Riga Jews and written by Ruta Aleksandrovich, was addressed to Premier Aleksei Kosygin with noted copies to United Press International, the UN Human Rights Commission, and the Inter-Parliamentary Union. Since the group feared "that our letter may not reach you," they requested that those receiving a copy transmit it to Kosygin and publish it. They had thrown down the gauntlet. Would the authorities respond to their challenge?

Some young activists like Ruta and Silva had also been involved in *samizdat*. Now that they were open (Aleph), some of the organization members urged them to resist the temptation to continue *samizdat* (Bet) work. It was easier to urge guidelines than to maintain discipline.

In an open letter of March 8, 1970, thirty-nine Moscow Jews publicly commented on a government-inspired press conference of "loyal" Jews.* To Rusinek and others, this was "the decisive moment to unite for the beginning of the open, *mass* struggle." A steering committee of ten people was selected. The pace of activity heightened and, by June 1970, collective letters were being signed by greatly increasing numbers of persons. In Leningrad and in Riga, the Jewish underground had been tempered by years of quiet work. A hard-core cadre had been self-trained. They had done it themselves, under Soviet conditions— without assistance and despite severely repressive action by the regime. But they had not been steeled and tested in the fire of state terror. That would soon come.

* The press conference of March 4, 1970 and its aftermath are discussed in Chapter 6.

MOSCOW:
The Central Nervous System

CHAPTER 6

Moscow, the capital of the huge Soviet empire, is a city of infinite complexity and variety. Government officials, poets, scientists, film actors, bureaucrats, and intellectuals seek its varied opportunity and sophisticated life. On its streets, one sees the faces and costumes of the many Soviet peoples. Among the millions who call Moscow home, there are Jews who not long ago lived in the *shtetls* of the Ukraine or Byelorussia and Jews from the provincial capitals, Jews from the Soviet institutes and universities and Jews from Stalin's prison camps—Jews whose heritage has been lost or forgotten and whose future always seems uncertain.

Although according to the latest census there were 240,000 Jews in the city of over 7 million, Moscow's Jews estimate their number at between 350,000 and 500,000. Whatever the count, few cities in the world contain more Jews than Moscow. Yet, except in intellectual and scientific circles, a Jewish presence is hard to discern. A foreign tourist would listen in vain for a Jewish witticism, would look in vain for a Jewish neighborhood, restaurant, or cultural experience, for the Jewish imprint so evident in major cities of the Western world. The guide books declare that in this vast capital there are three synagogues, but one has been closed since 1972; a second, a small, ramshackle building in a distant neighborhood, is attended mainly by a small, dying group of Orthodox elders. The only sizable Jewish house of worship is the large, dignified, but somewhat seedy Choral Synagogue, in midtown Moscow, a short walk from the Kremlin and the well-known Intourist hotels.

Yet for all its diversity, despite all its atomization and fragmentation and lack of a sense of community, Moscow is the vibrant center of the Jewish movement. If Leningrad provided the courage and the heart, and Riga the historic memory and the head, it is Moscow that supplied the nervous system and the connective tissue. Without the Jews of Moscow—Jews from everywhere—there might still have been a Leningrad center, Riga groups that became an organization, activists in Kiev, Minsk, Kharkov, Vilna, Kishinev, Odessa, and other cities, even a messianic, Zionist surge in Soviet Georgia—but no Soviet Jewish movement. For it was in Moscow, where so many Jews have higher education and where so many, trained and sensitized in the arts and sciences, had long since been effectively alienated from Soviet society, that the movement found expression and made its contacts with the West. It was in Moscow, with its foreign newsmen, its embassies, its influx of foreign tourists, its increasingly sensitive concerns about world public opinion, that Soviet Jewry spoke in ways that could not be ignored in the West. Without the response in the West—particularly the delayed activism of world Jewry—the movement might have been ignored, neglected, and thus to a considerable degree rendered ineffectual.

It was in Moscow in February 1966 that the writers Andrei Sinyavsky and Yuli Daniel were tried. It was there, in succeeding months, that the democratic movement took coherent shape, as a result of other trials and in response to other repressive efforts to destroy this new and unexpected phenomenon. Jews, although often with little or no feeling of Jewish identity, were numbered among the victims and among the democratic activists out of all proportion to their representation in the population; and to the extent that the democratic movement was one of intellectuals, Jews were prominent in it. The Soviet democrats were convinced that they must set a personal example of overcoming fear, by legitimizing protest; thus, they relied heavily on their legality. They invoked the Soviet Constitution, Soviet law and procedure, and the international law of human rights. They spoke out, seeking publicity rather than fearfully avoiding it. They created a wide range of *samizdat* documents—letters and petitions, protocols of KGB searches and interrogations, unofficial transcripts of trials and administrative hearings, and newsletters, the most famous of which was *Khronika* (the Chronicle of Current Events), which documented, factually and pointedly, the enormous variety of infringements of rights in the USSR. But above all, they developed methods of reaching the West. They contacted Western correspondents, foreign diplomats, tourists and visiting dignitaries, some of whom carried their reports back to the West. And from the West, radio broadcasts, beaming the news back to the Soviet Union, reached millions of Soviet citizens who otherwise could not know what was happening in their own country. Thus, the democrats were able to affect and infect their own government and its citizens, and thereby break the hermetic seal of Soviet society.

All of this, and more, the Jews of Moscow had learned, and although their goal was to be the right to leave the USSR rather than to reform it, their tactics were borrowed with the full participation and blessing of the democrats, many of whom were long-time colleagues, friends, associates, or relatives.

Having come from elsewhere, most Moscow Jews were like Jews in the rest of the USSR, and their experiences were markedly similar. Their attitude patterns were affected by policies and phenomena that existed throughout the Soviet Union. Like other Jews, they had reacted to anti-Semitism and discrimination, to World War II and the Holocaust, to the Stalin period and the creation of the State of Israel. For many years, there had been some Zionists in Moscow and there had often been arrests and trials. It was in Moscow's infamous Lubyanka prison that Yiddish poets and writers had been murdered on August 12, 1952. It had been within the Kremlin walls, in the paranoid mind of the aging dictator, that the Doctors' Plot had been conceived, and most of the doctors accused were Moscow physicians. From Moscow the prison camps had received new populations of Jews. In the early 1950s, a number of Jewish students had been sentenced, some of whom, toughened and resolute, would provide important leadership to a more mature movement two decades later. In 1958, again, brief reports heard in the West told of ten Moscow youths who were sentenced on charges of studying Hebrew and conducting Zionist activities—part of a general crackdown by the regime against young Zionists. In 1961, heavy sentences were imposed on Moscow synagogue leaders who had been arrested at the same time as Dr. Gedalia Pechersky in Leningrad and linked to a plot of associating with Israeli Embassy officials in anti-Soviet Zionist propaganda. In March 1962, eight Jews were arrested and charged with illegally baking *matzot*. On July 16, 1963, four elderly Jews were tried for "illegal profiteering" in the sale of home-made unleavened bread. A number of Moscow Jews rallied to their defense. To the astonishment of the prosecution, the defendants pleaded not guilty and vigorously defended themselves. Although the authorities had explicitly warned against such unacceptable forms of Jewish expression, the sentences were relatively light.

Far more serious from the viewpoint of the Moscow authorities were the activities of Solomon Dolnik and a small group of Zionists who worked with him. Dolnik, a geodesic engineer, from 1961 until his arrest in May 1966, had maintained informal contacts with other Jewish activists in Minsk, Riga, Leningrad, and elsewhere. In his sixties at the time, he displayed remarkable energy in distributing *samizdat* literature, largely concerned with information about Israel, Jewish life and culture, but also including such forbidden works as Maksim Gorky's *Untimely Thoughts.*

Among Dolnik's young protégés was Valentin Prussakov, a student at the Institute of Transport Engineers, who was also a writer and poet. In January 1964, in the course of searching Prussakov's apartment, the KGB confiscated his diary—notes which indicated that Prussakov was interested in Jewish history and culture and that "his attitude to the State of Israel was not one of indifference." In the same year, he was expelled from the institute where he was studying. In May 1966, the KGB search his apartment again, in connection with Dolnik's case. During the search, wrote Prussakov, "criminal" articles were confiscated: the Torah, a badge from the Israeli exhibition of agricultural machinery in Moscow, and a few Israeli postcards and stamps.

Throughout 1966, Prussakov was repeatedly summoned to the KGB as a witness in the Dolnik case. And on February 16, 1967, he was arrested on charges of anti-Soviet agitation and propaganda, based on two stories he had written and Dolnik had circulated.

> In these stories [wrote Prussakov] I had written of manifestations of anti-Semitism in the USSR and upheld the right of Soviet Jews to existence as a nation. I was also accused of participating in so-called "nationalistic assemblies," which had consisted of listening to Jewish music and poetry and sometimes programs broadcast by Kol Israel. The criminal caught in the act, as you see!
>
> I paid for my "criminal deeds" with a thirteen-month sojourn in Lefortovo Prison, from which I was released in March 1968, "in connection with a change of circumstances," as it appeared in the investigatory organs' decree of my discharge.

Dolnik's group included about twenty people. On February 24, 1967, in a lengthy article on Dolnik's trial, *Izvestia* claimed that he had fully admitted his guilt; had, at the instruction of the Israeli Embassy, collected spying information; had prepared, duplicated, and disseminated anti-Soviet material, transmitted geodesic maps "used in military topography," and used the Moscow synagogue as a meeting place for his espionage contacts with Israel.

> During semiconspiratorial meetings he was given assignments to disseminate among Soviet citizens the anti-Soviet and Zionist booklets transmitted by the Israeli diplomats. He duplicated the anti-Soviet slanders and stuck them in the pockets of the believers in the synagogue cloakroom . . . there appears the image of a sinister, malicious traitor, a person who has lost all human traits. Before those present in the hall there stands a man whose moral devastation is monstrous. Just a short time ago he had been walking along the same street as we, had breathed the same air, had sat next to us in the bus, perhaps, at the concert in the conservatorium, or in the cinema hall.

Moscow's Jews understood this press report and the accompanying circumstances to be a sharp warning to avoid contact with foreigners —certainly with Israelis; to stay away from the synagogue; and, above all, to have no favorable attitude toward Israel.

But in Moscow, as elsewhere, such efforts proved futile. Many Moscow Jews had been searching for their Jewishness. They had been among the huge crowds that had thrilled at the appearance of Golda Meir at the synagogue in 1948. They had made contact in large numbers with the Israeli delegation to the International Youth Festival in 1957. They had instituted the ever-growing Simchat Torah celebrations in front of the synagogue in 1958. They had passed from hand to hand translations of *Exodus* and other Jewish *samizdat* materials in the mid-60s. They had turned out by the thousands to cheer the Israeli singer Geulah Gil in 1966. Now, in 1967, one of their number was to ignite a new spark by his daring example.

On June 13, 1967, his twentieth birthday, Yakov (Yasha) Kazakov, a student at the University of Moscow, renounced his citizenship in response to the Soviet government's vitriolic campaign against the State of Israel. His act was unpublicized, but word of it circulated among some of his friends, and through them to other young people in Moscow and other cities. But receiving no meaningful official response, on May 20, 1968, he wrote to the Supreme Soviet:

I am again applying to you, and I shall continue to apply until my request is granted. I demand what is mine by right, and any negative reply, no matter in what form it is given, is unlawful and contrary both to the Constitution of the USSR and to the Declaration of the Rights of Man, which the Soviet Union has undertaken to observe and to respect.

I, Yakov Iosifovich Kazakov, a Jew, born in 1947, residing at No. 6 Third Institutskaya St., apt. 42, Moscow 2R-389, renounce Soviet citizenship, and, from the moment that I first announced my renunciation of USSR citizenship, that is, from June 13, 1967, I do not consider myself a citizen of the USSR.

Whether to be, or not to be, a citizen of this or of another country, is the private affair of every person.

By not agreeing to accept my renunciation of Soviet citizenship, you cannot force me to become a loyal citizen of the USSR. Independently of your decision, I am not a citizen of the USSR, and I act, and shall act, as one who does not have USSR citizenship.

I am a Jew, I was born a Jew, and I want to live out my life as a Jew. With all my respect for the Russian people, I do not consider my people in any way inferior to the Russian, or to any other people, and I do not want to be assimilated by any people. . . .

I am a Jew, and, as a Jew, I consider the State of Israel my fatherland, the fatherland of my people, the only place on earth where there exists an independent Jewish state, and I, like any other Jew, have the indubitable right to live in that state.

I do not wish to be a citizen of the USSR, of a country that refuses to the Jews (and to other nations, too) the right of self-determination.

I do not wish to be a citizen of a country where Jews are subjected to forced assimilation, where my people is deprived of its national image and its cultural treasures, of a country where, under the pretext of a struggle against Zionism, all the cultural life of the Jewish people has been eradicated, where the dissemination of any literature on the history of the Jewish people or on the cultural life of Jews abroad in our times is persecuted.

I do not wish to be a citizen of a country that conducts a policy of genocide toward the Jewish people. If the fascists exterminated us physically, you are exterminating Jews as a nation. I do not wish to collaborate in this additional crime of yours against the Jewish people. . . .

I do not want to live in a country whose government has spilled so much Jewish blood. I do not want to participate with you in the extermination of the Jewish nation in the Soviet Union. I do not wish to live in a country in which have been re-established (even though in secret) limitations concerning Jews (concerning admittance to a number of educational institutions, establishments, enterprises, etc.). I shall not enumerate it all: you know this better than I do.

I do not wish to be a citizen of a country that arms and supports the remaining fascists and the Arab chauvinists who desire to wipe Israel off the face of the earth and to add another two and a half million killed to the six million who have perished. I do not want to be a collaborator of yours in the destruction of the State of Israel because, even though this has not been done officially, I consider myself to be a citizen of the State of Israel (the more so as I possess an invitation for permanent residence in the State of Israel).

On the basis of the above, I renounce Soviet citizenship, and I demand to be freed from the humiliation of being considered a citizen of the Union of Soviet Socialist Republics.

I demand to be given a possibility of leaving the Soviet Union.

This audacious letter quickly circulated in *samizdat* form in the USSR; on December 19, 1968, the *Washington Post* extensively reported it; and shortly thereafter, Kazakov was given an exit visa to Israel.

The first act of renunciation of citizenship is popularly ascribed to Kazakov, and certainly his act was the first well-publicized example of this form of protest, but it had, in fact, previously been resorted to by a few other dissenters. Its first apparent usage among those seeking to leave the USSR for Israel had occurred a few weeks earlier, shortly before the Six-Day War, by another Moscow Jew, the writer Vitold Kapshitser, whose father, a Communist functionary, had been arrested during the Great Purge of 1938 and "disappeared" forever. In 1966, Kapshitser began a book dealing with the history of the Jewish people, and his interest in the subject and his concerns about anti-Semitism led him, in early 1967, to apply to emigrate to Israel. The Soviet authorities agreed to consider his application only on condition he give up his Soviet citizenship, and he did so in a letter to the Presidium of the Supreme Soviet of the USSR on May 31, 1967. Meanwhile, he was expelled from his union, and was thus deprived of work. His elderly, pensioned mother felt compelled to support him and intercede in his behalf with the Soviet government and, ultimately, with UN officials. Her pathetic letter of September 1969, which details the story, reached the West late that year. Kapshitser was finally permitted to depart for Israel, and he now lives in Rome where he is writing about his Soviet experiences.

Kazakov dramatized resistance in Moscow, much as Kochubiyevsky did, contemporaneously, in Kiev. But the early heart of the Jewish repatriation movement in Moscow was another man—David Khavkin.

Khavkin, an engineer, had been imprisoned in the Mordovian camps because of his Zionism. Upon his return to Moscow, he renewed his activities and maintained his contacts with his former camp comrades. Concerned about the increasing assimilative tendencies among Jewish young people, he organized Hebrew classes and the creation and distribution of *samizdat* materials. By 1967, he had followers with whom he shared tapes of Jewish songs, information about Israel, and the latest *samizdat* publication. A short, stocky man of enormous strength and energy, Khavkin gave unstintingly of his time to young people, awakening in them pride in their Jewishness and strong personal affection toward him. It was to Khavkin that Ruta Aleksandrovich brought the young Riga activists for advice and guidance. It was to Khavkin that Mogilever, Dreizner, and Butman would come for consultation and the sharing of ideas. Schooled with other dissidents in the labor camps, he stressed legalism and the right to emigrate under the Soviet Constitution and international law. Knowing that he was under continual surveillance by the KGB, Khavkin perfected surreptitious techniques and was always careful not to overstep the limits which would lead to his entrapment and the destruction of the movement.

By the summer of 1969, Khavkin was among those who realized that the movement had matured to the point where it could begin an open struggle. He took the initiative in forming what became known in movement circles as the VKK (the Russian initials for the All-Union Coordinating Committee).* At the first meetings of that group in Moscow on August 16-17, 1969, Khavkin and Vitaly Svechinsky represented Moscow, and there were delegates from Leningrad, Riga, Kiev, Minsk, Kharkov, and Tbilisi. In discussing and hammering out the details of movement activities, they focused on intensified efforts to secure exit visas, disseminating open, collective petitions and letters, and intensifying and organizing *samizdat* preparation and distribution.

Much earlier, Khavkin had applied for an exit visa, and a few weeks after the meeting, he received word that it had been granted—doubtless because the KGB knew or suspected his key organizing role—and that he was scheduled to leave for Israel late in September. For three days before the Khavkins left, hundreds of people from various parts of the Soviet Union came to say goodbye. Khavkin was exalted at achieving his goal of emigration to Israel (with all the symbolic importance his release had to the movement), but he was saddened to

* Vsesoyuzny Komitet Koordinatsii.

leave the struggle just as it had become organized for success. Georgian wine, brought by friends in quantity for the occasion, lightened the conflict without resolving it, but careful plans were laid for continuing contact with Israel. The movement had learned from the Riga group which had left early in the year, and from Kazakov's presence in Israel, that much could be done with experienced contacts abroad.

On September 29, 1969, David Khavkin, his wife Ester, and their 9-year-old son appeared at Moscow's Sheremetyevo International Airport. Customs examination turned out to be a nightmare. Ester Khavkin was stripped and subjected to a humiliating gynecological examination. The search lasted more than three hours and they missed their plane. In response to protests, customs officials said, "If you hadn't brought this mob here, we'd have let you go straight away." (One hundred eighty-six people had come to see the Khavkins depart. Mass airport farewells are used by the movement as an expression of friendship and solidarity and as a morale-building demonstration.) On October 1, after a five-minute inspection, the Khavkins flew to Vienna and freedom.

With the departure of Khavkin, a heavy burden fell on Vitaly (Vila) Svechinsky, a 39-year-old architect who had grown up in Moscow. Tall, rugged, square-jawed, quiet, and determined, Svechinsky combined the features of a sensitive philosopher and a professional boxer. Few Jewish leaders in the USSR commanded the uniform respect Svechinsky received. His father, about whom Svechinsky is naturally reticent, was a KGB officer who operated as a counterintelligence agent behind German lines during World War II. In 1948, Svechinsky and two schoolmates planned to escape to Israel by illegally crossing the Soviet-Turkish frontier. They were betrayed by a secret police informer and in 1950 were sentenced to forced labor camps. In 1955, Svechinsky was released from the Kolyma camp and returned to Moscow to study architecture. By now a confirmed opponent of the Soviet system, he sought outlet in democratic and Jewish activity but chafed at the apathy around him. In 1960, he voluntarily returned to Kolyma to practice architecture there. Like other political prisoners, Svechinsky had developed friendships among his prison comrades, many of whom (with their lives disrupted by years away from family and familiar surroundings) had chosen to settle in the Kolyma area. By the mid-60s, a new wind was blowing, even in Siberia, and Svechinsky, encouraged by the increasingly open dissent, the lack of fear in young people, the renewed spirit of former prisoners, decided to return to Moscow. The Six-Day

War confirmed his resolution and reawakened his commitment to leave for Israel. By early 1968 he was deeply involved in the burgeoning Jewish movement in Moscow, and his apartment became a center of activity. His experience and quiet judgment were instrumental in forging the movement, which soon grew to number several hundred activists. In September 1968, Moscow's OVIR office again began to accept applications to leave.

Moscow's Jews, like those of other cities, did not have a single leader or a single unified movement. Much of what came to be recognized as "the movement" developed as a pragmatic adjustment to the exigencies of the times. At most it was an appellation for the mainstream, and there were other people and other small groups who spontaneously and independently did their own thing. But Moscow, more than any other city, reflected a wide range of individual opinion and philosophy. Unlike Riga, which had a strong Zionist tradition and virtually no democratic movement, and where differences were largely between people of different ages and temperaments (cautious v. militant), or Leningrad, where strong, emotional, early leadership tended to pre-empt the field, Moscow, to this date, has groups and opinions which coalesce for important unified actions. That is no doubt inevitable in a large city with such strong, divergent currents of intellectual enthusiasm. The same observations may be made about the democratic movement, which in reality consists of a number of movements or trends and directions. The repressive nature of the Soviet state, which views any nonpermitted movement as a criminal, anti-Soviet organization, inevitably produces a climate of fragmentation, lessens the possibility of open debate about differences, and reduces the opportunity for democratic experience and majority decision-making.

Perhaps the most fundamental split of viewpoint was in the attitudes within the Jewish movement toward the democrats. Although there will be subsequent analysis of this question, it is fair to say here that the Jewish movement is basically distinguishable from the democratic movement by the fact that it does not seek to reform or change Soviet society but only wishes to leave it. Thus, many Jews urged that their movement should be known as the Jewish repatriation movement, that is, a movement of Jews wishing not to emigrate but rather to be repatriated to their ancient national homeland, Israel. Yet few would deny that the tactics of the movement were those first employed by

the democrats, and none would question that the right to leave is a
fundamental human, not a specifically Zionist, right. Thus, although
they were often saddened by the loss of people of strength and talent
who might otherwise contribute to the liberalization and democratization of Soviet society, the democrats strongly supported the right of
Jews to leave because that right is fundamental for any Soviet citizen.
So, too, the Jewish movement, in its insistence on legalities, the right
to dissent by communication, and procedural correctness in criminal
trials and administrative procedures, was upholding premises cherished
by the democrats which, if achieved in the Jewish struggle, would represent breakthroughs of psychological and historical importance.

Nonetheless, among the Jewish leadership, the intense nationalism of
the movement often led to an exclusivity which could be criticized as
extremely chauvinistic. The most extreme Jewish activists decried any
contact or connection with democrats or non-Jews. They distrusted
anyone who did not share a complete Zionist commitment. Like some
of their ghetto or *shtetl* ancestors, they were provincial and feared the
contamination of liberal assimilationism, the carriers of which were
thought to be the democrats. Most Jews, nevertheless, admired the
democrats for their courage and moral example. However much some
Jewish leaders sought to avoid any appearance of collective action, or
even open cooperation with democrats, this was largely a tactical judgment. Soviet conditions were held to enhance the degree of danger in
direct relation to the extended ambit of cooperative activity. To a KGB
obsessed with nightmares of conspiracy, any unofficial meeting of two
or more persons was suspect. Intercity or intergroup contact—particularly if regularized—was considered to be dangerous. Other Zionist
Jews disagreed, and cooperated with varying degrees of openness with
the democrats.

Among the Moscow Jews whose influence had become more pro-
nounced by 1969 was David Drabkin, an industrial engineer in charge
of a spectroscopy department in Moscow for research into the chemical
reactions of metals. Born in Kharkov in 1924, Drabkin had early
Zionist feelings, but concentrated on his career until after the Six-Day
War. In October 1968, he telephoned a Tel Aviv relative to request
a *vizov*. His application for an exit visa resulted in his discharge from
his research post, and thereafter he became an electrician to support
his family. On April 18, 1969, he wrote President Podgorny com-

plaining of OVIR practices and notably about the comment of a Moscow OVIR official: "There are too many of you Jews. We shall not let you out. We shall finish you off here." Drabkin declared that, under these circumstances, "I can no longer consider myself a citizen of the USSR. I hereby declare that I consider myself a citizen of the Jewish State of Israel." The renunciation of Soviet citizenship was not new, but the assertion of Israeli citizenship was. It set in motion a series of events that were to culminate in legislative change in Israel's citizenship law and a major confrontation between Soviet Jewish activists and the government of Israel.

Several months later, on September 28, 1969, Drabkin wrote to Premier Kosygin. He likened the actions of OVIR in refusing to grant him the right to leave and refusing explanation to a return of serfdom, which had been abolished in Russia in 1861. Asserting that OVIR's actions were lawless, he demanded Kosygin's personal intervention. A month later, he wrote again to Kosygin. After complaining about the lack of reply and about administrative lawlessness, he noted: "My wife and I, after completing our education, worked for over twenty years, and we consider that by our work we have repaid the expense of our education." * Drabkin's appeals were publicized and followed by a group of collective letters he composed or signed. Not until February 1971 was Drabkin permitted to leave. In the meantime, he was involved in conflict within the movement by the character of some of his views, which rejected both conventional Zionist ideology and the desirability of any contact with the democrats. He was a strong, avowed Jewish nationalist, who applied his energies and organizational skills when they were crucially needed.

During the summer and fall of 1969 and the early winter of 1970, some remarkable individual letters and petitions were sent by Moscow Jews, and circulated in *samizdat* form throughout the USSR and in the West. The VKK's determination in August that collective letters should be commenced—that the movement should become an open struggle—found vigorous expression that fall. It came in September

---

* Three years later, after the imposition in August 1972 of an education tax, such an argument had particular pertinency. To discourage or prevent the exodus of Soviet Jews, old as well as new applicants for exit visas were made subject to the payment of a fee (known as a "diploma tax"), ranging from 4,000 to 35,000 rubles, as compensation for educational expenditures in universities, special schools, and other institutions of higher education.

1969 in a letter of ten Moscow Jews to world Jewry, in effect announcing that the movement had become open and appealing to the Jewish
community in the hope of receiving active help in exercising their legal
rights to repatriation.

It was followed by the Letter of the Moscow 25 to U Thant, which
was virtually identical in form and language to the Letter of the Riga
22, which followed shortly (see page 82). The letters, read together,
announced that (1) they had a common author; (2) there was syn-
chronization of planning, or at least cooperation, between Moscow and
Riga; (3) the Jewish movement was taking its struggle into international forums, not with cries or appeals, but with shouts.

The letter to U Thant is stylistically a model of clarity, directness,
and rhetorical effectiveness. Its invocation of international human
rights law is legally unimpeachable. The Moscow letter contained one
paragraph that does not appear in the Riga version: "We, the signatories to the present appeal, are persons of various ages, occupations,
education, and tastes and are not connected with one another in anything except the wish to leave the USSR for Israel, in order to be
reunited there, in our own land, with our relatives." The first signature
was Drabkin's, and those that followed included Svechinsky and some
who had sent, or would shortly thereafter send, open, individual letters
of their own. The actual author of the letter was Viktor Fedoseyev, a
non-Jew.

Fedoseyev and his wife Rakhel, who is Jewish, played a significant
role in the development of Jewish *samizdat* materials. Born in Moscow
in 1930, Fedoseyev is a blond, blue-eyed man with high cheekbones
which give him an appearance consistent with his Russian origins.
When Viktor was five months old, his father, a railroad engineer, was
sent by the Soviet government to China to assist the Kuomintang's
railroad-building program. Because the family was unable to leave
China due to the outbreak of war in 1937, Viktor grew up in Shanghai,
where he attended school for foreign children and was taught, and
knew, both French and English. Russian was the language of his home
and Chinese the language of the street. It was not until the end of 1945
that Viktor's parents could return to their native land, and by then
Viktor, already turning 16, had decided to become a merchant seaman.
Two older sisters had met and married Westerners and both had
settled in the United States in small towns in Wisconsin and California.
Viktor became a seaman. He also became a radical. His frequent,

extended visits to the United States coincided with the rise of Mc-Carthyism, and his responses to that phenomenon resulted in his becoming unwelcome to American officials. He returned to the USSR, which he had never known except through language, citizenship, and propaganda slogans, and he was horrified at what he saw. Stalin was still alive. The prison camps were full of the best and bravest Soviet citizens. Silence and fear were everywhere. Once he had returned, there was no escape. "Half a million dogs were guarding the frontiers and they had more meat than the citizens." His family had moved to Sverdlovsk in the Urals. There, in 1952, he met Rakhel Koliaditskaya.

Rakhel, small and intense, with flashing dark eyes, was born in Tientsin in 1933 of parents who fled to China after the Revolution. She, too, had grown up in China, where the English she learned in school was her primary tongue and where life for her, as a child, consisted of the horrors of war and the miseries it brought in its wake. At the end of the war, her father, Samuel Rubin, left for Palestine, settling in Haifa. Her mother, Dora Koliaditskaya, in an optimistic surge of idealism and patriotism, took 14-year-old Rakhel back to the USSR, a country neither knew. For the next two years they lived a displaced life, drifting from transit camp to transit camp until, in late 1948, they arrived in Sverdlovsk. When Viktor and Rakhel met, they understood that their reaction to Soviet life was the same, and shortly after their marriage in 1953, they moved to Riga, "as far West in the Soviet Union as we could get." Viktor worked in an auto plant and began writing—four of his books subsequently were published with a considerable measure of success. Rakhel's linguistic skills permitted her to work at translating, editing, and teaching. Both became sympathetic to, and connected with, the democratic movement. Meanwhile, Dora Koliaditskaya, realizing her error, had moved to Moscow and was seeking to emigrate to Israel to join her husband. In the process, she became involved in the Jewish movement and, when her daughter and son-in-law joined her in the capital in 1968, they became involved as well. Viktor's writing skills found instant use. His personal knowledge of the West and its ways was also a valuable asset to a movement which desperately desired such contact and support. The Letter of the 25 clearly expresses a point of view easily understandable in the West. Fedoseyev did not sign it (although Dora Koliaditskaya did), because he did not think it desirable that it became publicly known then that a non-Jew had written the letter of the Jewish move-

ment. Drabkin originally refused to sign the letter at all but ultimately
was prevailed upon to become the first signer, and he never ceased
criticizing Fedoseyev's inclusion in the movement.

By the end of 1969, inspired by the example of *Khronika*, some
Moscow Jews decided to publish their own chronicle of current events.
Prepared and edited by Fedoseyev, with others, the first issue of
Iskhod (Exodus) appeared in April 1970.

> It was important to publish *Iskhod* [Fedoseyev explained], because
> the main achievement of the Soviet regime upon Jews was that they
> were deprived of the *word*. You can't buy a Bible which speaks of the
> history, morals, and religion of the Jewish people nor can you read
> and learn about Jewish culture and life. A people deprived of the *word*
> face assimilation; to stop assimilation, to recreate a nation, a people
> must know and read the *word*. In the Bible, the exodus of Jews from
> Egypt is reported as a migration. What if it had never been reported?
> What if the Jews had been denied knowledge of their heritage? Jewry
> is great and strong because it recorded everything that happened.
> We needed to record every word—the *word*. That was the most im-
> portant task for us; we had to report the events of Soviet Jewry for
> those who wished to avoid assimilation; for those who wanted to know
> their rights and to know how to struggle; and for those who would
> support and encourage the Jewish repatriation movement. This is the
> second exodus of the Jews. This was the reason for the journal and
> the reason for its name.

The second issue appeared in July 1970, the third in November, and
the fourth issue at the beginning of February 1971. (Shortly thereafter, the Fedoseyevs left the USSR for Israel.) The cover page of
Iskhod featured two quotations: Psalm 137, v. 5, 6 ("If I forget you,
O Jerusalem"), and Article 13 of the Universal Declaration of Human
Rights ("Everyone has the right to leave any country, including his
own"). Its purpose was to report and mirror the Jewish movement—
to be its underground voice, not only to Soviet Jews but to "all honest
people everywhere in the world." That was no easy task.

Samizdat production involves a constant struggle with the ever-
watchful authorities. First, the information must be gathered—by
word of mouth, by surreptitious meetings, by clandestine reportorial
techniques. To produce it, there must be a typewriter, paper, and
carbon paper. In the Soviet Union, one cannot buy a new typewriter
without showing one's internal passport, and usable second-hand typewriters are difficult to locate. Type face (traceable by the KGB) must

be periodically destroyed, disposed of, and replaced. A 200-page document is prepared in twelve to fifteen copies (the risks are high and to type fewer copies would decrease effectiveness). This means 3,000 sheets of paper are needed. But the KGB is aware of "samizdatchiks," and thus stores usually are limited to thick paper from which only three to four copies can be made. When thin onionskin paper is available, the KGB watches shops that sell it. A plainclothesman checks to see who buys more than a few packs. The same is true of carbon paper. Since a person who buys large quantities of paper is suspect, a number of people must discreetly make small purchases. Documents and supplies must then be kept where they cannot be found if a search occurs. Finding a place to work is difficult. The next-door neighbor may contact the KGB if one types late at night. Since a knock at the door is always expected, the writer must be able to clean up and hide his material speedily. (Fedoseyev relates that it originally took him seven minutes to get his documents and supplies hidden. He trained himself to the point where he was able to secrete his materials in two minutes and ten seconds, at which point he would flush the toilet and calmly open the door.) Once the typewritten copies are completed, they are given to long-time, close friends. They, in turn, pass on such copies, saying they received them from *samizdat*, not knowing who produced them. Such copies, or microfilms of them, are taken out of the USSR by a friendly visitor, and journalists would sometimes report *samizdat* contents as information received from "unofficial Jewish sources."

How widespread was the circulation? No one knows for sure, but Fedoseyev often had copies typed by someone else given to him in Moscow by persons from Odessa, Minsk, Riga, or other cities, with an exultant whisper concerning how widespread the movement had become.

All four issues of *Iskhod* were collections of documents divided into three parts and containing thirty-six to forty-five pages. The first part usually included collective appeals and petitions, the second printed individual letters and declarations, and the third section included documents or unpublished Soviet laws, ordinances, or instructions. Read together, the four issues present a chronological kaleidoscope of the changes and developments in the Jewish movement.

The initial April 1970 issue was a report of the first outcry—a testament to the fact that Soviet Jews had ceased being silent—and the first document was the August 1969 Letter of the 18 from heads of Jewish families in Georgia to the UN Committee on Human Rights. It then included other significant and dramatic collective and individual documents through March 1970. Each was an essential part of the growing history of resistance; each documented a facet of the movement—demonstrating its ideological breadth, its geographic and class representations—people of different backgrounds sharing the single goal of repatriation to Israel. Each is a testament of courage. The third part of each issue, by citing Soviet law, documented that Soviet Jews had rights and established the legality of movement. It proved that their struggle for these rights was legal and that unpublished official instructions constituted government illegality.

Appearing after the arrests of June 1970, *Iskhod* No. 2 shows how the movement developed and how Soviet officials reacted. Some of the signatories included those arrested, subsequently tried, and now "prisoners of Zion." The cry is no longer "Let us out" but includes strident protest of illegal arrest, renunciation of Soviet citizenship and request for Israeli citizenship, and a search for new forms of struggle. It is eloquent and increasingly militant. It does not plead; it demands. The cries come from new people and new cities. They disdain anonymity. They list the addresses, ages, and professions of more than six hundred signers of over fifty appeal letters.

Iskhod No. 3, in November 1970, makes clear that the movement has consolidated and matured, that it is an open struggle for legality and rights. Among the official Soviet documents published are the academic reference issued to Lev Elyashevich by Riga Polytechnic Institute which expelled him for applying for the right to leave, and the records of KGB house searches of David Chernoglaz and Vladimir Slepak.

Iskhod No. 4 is wholly dedicated to the Leningrad trial of December 1970. The first part—an annotated, day-by-day transcript of the trial from December 15 to 24—is based on four reports from the court plus the observations of other spectators which appear in footnotes describing events within and outside the courtroom. The four reports include those from people who secretly taped part of the proceedings, or surreptitiously took shorthand notes, or memorized portions of the colloquy, or from those who made extensive notes after the sessions.*

---

* The combination and comparison of this material made an accurate unofficial transcript (official transcripts are not available in the USSR). An earlier sixteenpage version was released to the West shortly after the trial to feed the need for information not made officially available.

The second part includes immediate post-trial responses in the Soviet Union to the severity of the trial and sentences. The third part, a transcript of the Court of Appeals proceedings and decision, includes commentary on the post-trial arrests of some of the Jews who protested in front of the Court of Appeals.

Although all four issues of *Iskhod* were received shortly after they first appeared in Moscow, only the second and fourth were ever translated into English and issued in the West. The London-based Institute of Jewish Affairs published them many months after their *samizdat* appearance. Fedoseyev first learned that the IJA had received and published the journal through a radio comment heard in Moscow in November 1970. He believes it performed a great service. But he, and many Soviet Jews, found it inexplicable that two of the issues did not appear and that other *samizdat* material remained unpublished.

As Fedoseyev pointed out:

> Russian Jews put their freedom in jeopardy to speak out. They regard the distribution of factual information and documents of their struggle as essential to its continuance. Documents were published not just for Soviet Jews who needed to know of their rights and how to secure them, but for all people who believe in freedom. For people in the free world—who may freely publish material—not to do so is a crime. The greatest crime is the crime of silence.

Documents were sent, at great risk, to Israel and the West. Yet the authorities who received them long ago have never made many available for publication.

Fedoseyev revealed that before he left Moscow, material was ready for a new issue of *Iskhod,* which was to be known as *Vestnik Iskhoda* (Herald of the Exodus). Subsequently, the editors of *Vestnik* were given permission to leave the USSR, and they told of three issues of *Vestnik* (in effect *Iskhod* Nos. 5, 6, and 7) that were published in Moscow between the spring of 1971 and the late winter of 1971-72. *Khronika* reports their *samizdat* appearance in the Soviet Union. At great risk, they were smuggled to Israel, in the expectation of prompt publication. They include highly detailed documentation of the Jewish movement, but like *Iskhod* Nos. 1 and 3, they have never been published in the West.

The movement activists, including Fedoseyev, lament this.

The movement continues to exist as it is reflected—when it is reported. It withers and dies in silence. How little we know in the West about the Crimean Tatar movement or the Baptist movement in the Soviet Union. Though they are numerically more significant, they are paralyzed because no one speaks of them. The reflection of the movement is the main thing. Not to report our movement because of fear that the Soviet Union will be angered and will close the door is wrong—historically and practically. No one angered Hitler when he put millions of Jews in gas chambers, and no one angered Stalin when he murdered innocent people. The KGB began to let people out, not because no one angered them, but because Jews shouted about their rights. To be silent—to fail to report everything—is to play the KGB's game. Not to reflect all of the facts is to permit the movement to decline—to betray Jewish history.

Few Jewish *samizdat* publications appeared before 1969, when the trial of Boris Kochubiyevsky mobilized attention on the existence of a Jewish repatriation movement, but *samizdat* output increased exponentially after 1969—as Jews found their voices and their courage. *Iskhod* and *Vestnik,* however, were the only underground journals reporting only the news of the Jewish movement.

At the August 1969 meeting of the VKK, and again at the November 1969 meeting of that group in Riga, there was intensive discussion of the necessity for increased *samizdat* activity. The August meeting determined that there would be a focus on collective petitions. The November meeting decided that a new Jewish journal to be called *Iton* (the Hebrew word for newspaper) would be prepared—not a news report of the movement, like *Iskhod,* but rather a *samizdat* journal that published (or reprinted) articles of specific interest and educational value to Soviet Jews. An editorial committee was selected, composed of Riga, Leningrad, and Moscow activists, and assignments were made for the editorial and physical preparation of the journal. Two issues appeared—*Iton Aleph* (in January 1970) and *Iton Bet* (in April). (Although available since 1970, they have never been published in the West.) A third issue was prepared but never circulated because the arrests of Jews in June 1970 interfered.

Iton Aleph and *Bet* contributed important prosecution evidence of "anti-Soviet" publications and "anti-Soviet" organization at the trials in Leningrad, Riga, and Kishinev, but an objective Western reader would be hard pressed to understand how Soviet authorities could justify long-term prison sentences for publishing or possessing them. They are typewritten magazines of Jewish interest, of the kind that one might reasonably expect in Jewish communities anywhere.

The lead unsigned article in *Iton Aleph* is entitled "About Assimilation." It discusses physical assimilation (intermarriage) and linguistic, cultural, and religious assimilation. It is anti-Soviet only to the extent that discussion of such an issue (that is, free discussion) can be viewed as anti-regime. An article entitled "Purim and Pesach" is a tribute to the role of freedom in Jewish tradition, and would appear no more or less subversive than is the idea of freedom. Similarly, "May the Jewish People Live"—an account of the Warsaw Ghetto uprising—would appear criminal only if one views the concept of Jewish resistance against Nazi oppression as criminal. Among the reprints are an interview from *The Times* (London) with Golda Meir; an extract from the book *The Shining Sword,* which discusses the "Israeli People's Army"; a 1968 article, "An Open Letter to all People of Goodwill: to Fidel Castro, Sartre, Russell and many others," by Amos Kenan, an Israeli journalist; a 1957 feuilleton, "How Israel Lost the Chance to Acquire the Sympathy of the Entire World," by the Israeli satirist Ephraim Kishon; and Jabotinsky's half-century-old essay, "About Trumpeldor" (an early hero of the settlement of Palestine). Such articles were treated as criminal, apparently because sympathy toward Israel was perceived as "anti-Soviet." (Article 70, the Criminal Code section involved, prohibits "agitation or propaganda carried out with the purpose of weakening or subverting the Soviet regime or of committing particularly dangerous crimes against the state.") There would appear to be nothing in *Iton Aleph* which meets that legal test.

Iton Bet could also not be viewed as seditious in Western eyes, although it does include texts of some of the better-known collective letters prefixed by an article entitled "Let My People Go," which is sharply critical of the Soviet Union's "anti-Jewish and anti-humane policy." *Bet* includes a solemn and touching story entitled "September 29, 1969—Babi Yar." It prints Israel's Declaration of Independence. It reprints a detailed newspaper account, "The Fifth of June"; newspaper articles about the Israeli raid on the western bank of the Gulf of Suez on September 10, 1969; a *U.S. News and World Report* interview of Golda Meir; and a *Jerusalem Post* article of September 1969, "The Soviet Authorities Will Not Be Able to Break the Jewish Spirit." More self-assured in tone than *Aleph, Iton Bet* is more intense in its criticism of Soviet policy and more assertive in its insistence on Jewish rights.

Apart from *Iskhod* and *Iton,* the two journals of the Jewish movement, the numerous letters and petitions, and separate reprints of books and articles, a number of other individual political essays (or, perhaps more accurately, polemics) appeared—some of which were involved in the trials and will be subsequently discussed. These *samizdat* documents expressed the working philosophy of people or groups constituting the Jewish movement. There were differences in viewpoint, just as there were differences between *Iskhod* and *Iton. Iskhod* was heavily influenced in style by the democratic movement, and its chief editor, Fedoseyev, was advised and assisted editorially by Svechinsky, Dr. Meir Gelfand and Aleksandr Balabanov, all Zionist activists from Moscow who had long sympathy and association with the democratic movement. The only non-Muscovite who worked directly with Fedoseyev was Isai (Sanya) Averbukh, a young, militant Odessa poet and philosopher, who spent much of his time in Moscow and later in Riga, where he subsequently was engaged to Ruta Aleksandrovich. Yakov Roninson, who provided technical assistance, and Leonid Rigerman, who passed *Iskhod* to Western newsmen, were Moscow Jews. *Iton,* however, was all-Union in its preparation, with a multicity editorial board and with material submitted from various cities. Unlike *Iskhod,* which reflected the movement by straight reporting, *Iton* not only reprinted materials from abroad, but carried polemical articles created within the USSR. It was overtly a Zionist magazine of political selection and commentary. Even when the two journals included the same material, as they occasionally did when they both published certain collective appeals, there were small, subtle differences. As it appeared in *Iskhod,* the Letter of the Moscow 25 to U Thant had Drakbin's signature first and Svechinsky's third. In *Iton Bet,* the order of signing was reversed. *Iskhod* sought to stay within the narrow, permissible line of dissidence that had been worked out through the experience of half a decade of democratic activity. *Iton* plunged forward, sharply confronting and attacking authoritative figures and policies of the regime. Thus, the Open Letter of the Jews of the City of Moscow specially prepared for *Iton Bet* reads:

> Lately in the newspapers published by the supreme organs of the USSR, there has appeared material that attracts special attention by

its efforts to make a deliberately false presentation of the attitude of Jews residing in the USSR toward the State of Israel and of the situation of Jews in the Soviet Union. . . .

The authors of the present document categorically reject such assertions. We and our acquaintances (and the majority of us are far from being old people) have wished and wish to go to Israel not because of religious motives, but because of national ones. We are refused this without an explanation of the reason for the refusals, and this is done in violation of the Soviet law and of international laws, and also in violation of the publicly given promise by the chairman of the Soviet of Ministers of the USSR. . . .

In order to intensify fear and indecision, letters about the terrors of life in Israel from invented persons are published. Such is the material reprinted by *Pravda* from *Vecherny Tbilisi*. Even had one not taken the trouble to check this false document, its contents alone would have disclosed it. . . .

We are told about another way out—assimilation. Let us remind only the honest adherents (the dishonest ones remember this themselves) that assimilation had never delivered the Jews from being the first victims of any persecution that took place in Russia and in the USSR. Not a single campaign of murders, pogroms, or "purges" against the rightists, the leftists, the moderates, the revolutionaries, the counterrevolutionaries, the nationalists, the cosmopolites, the revisionists, the sectants, etc. ever took place without having an anti-Semitic taste accompanying it. And assimilation itself had been conducted not in a natural way, but by way of cultural genocide. It is generally known that the Jews were saved from physical genocide not only by the victory of the Soviet Army (in whose ranks one-third of the adult Jewish population had fought), but also by a historical accident—the death of Stalin.

Are there any guarantees that such a thing will not happen in the future? Oh, yes, we almost forgot, "equality!"

Is Jewish life in the USSR really determined by equality—by the beautiful statutes of the Constitution, the utterances against anti-Semitism by Lenin (and by Stalin), by the fact that there exist dozens or even hundreds of Jews who are academicians, heroes, or carpenters? No, it is determined by the paragraph about nationality inscribed in the passport and in the questionnaire that has to be filled in when applying for work or for enrollment in the institution of learning. . . .

It is determined by the lost talents, by the swallowing of insults, by unjust reproaches against hundreds of thousands of people, by the dozens of thousands of "cosmopolites" who have been physically and morally tortured to death. Your comrades in journalism and in ideological work touchingly unite with Black Hundred hooligans in suburban trains and in government offices . . . from a member of the Party Bureau of the Moscow department of the Union of Writers,

Arkady Vasilyev, up to the Minister of Foreign Affairs of the USSR . . . , and to the secretaries of the regional committees, who tell at party instruction meetings about the threat of Zionism to the USSR on the part of those who observe Jewish feasts and who study Hebrew.

Like the majority of thinking people in the USSR (and not only Jews), we cannot consider the State of Israel as an aggressor, just as we would not have been able to consider the Soviet Union an aggressor had it, on June 21, 1941, delivered a preventive blow against the Hitlerite troops on its borders, in spite of the pact of nonaggression. Such a pact has not been concluded between Israel and the fascist-acting "progressives" and "socialists" from the Arab countries. But let us be frank. We do not expect truth from you. And we do not expect equality here, either. The centuries-old traditions of Russia and the half-a-century-old traditions in the Soviet Union have deprived us of illusions. . . .

It is useless to thank the provisional Kerensky Government, which abolished the pale of settlement and the numerus clausus, or the Soviet government which has quietly re-established this clausus. In civilized countries man has already stopped thanking the government and his neighbors for not eating him alive.

Experience might have suggested that the Soviet authorities—up to and including Premier Kosygin and Foreign Minister Gromyko—would resent being called liars, lawbreakers, genocidists, and allies of the Tsarist Black Hundred (an extremely reactionary, rascist group). The passing praise of the Kerensky government must have been the last straw. This change in the sharpness of expression, overt hostility to the regime, and blanket condemnation of Soviet society as anti-Semitic had taken place within half a year from the fall of 1969 to the spring of 1970. Although they spoke of the Soviet policy of forcible assimilation of Jews, earlier letters, such as that of Tina Brodetskaya in October 1969, were appeals to be released.

Tina Brodetskaya, born in 1935, was typical of the core of the Moscow activist group. Her father was killed in World War II, and her mother, who served as an army doctor, remarried. Her stepfather, an engineer, brought the family to Moscow, where Tina, by now a university student, became interested in Zionism. In 1957, she was one of the students who enthusiastically greeted the Israeli delegation to the International Youth Festival in Moscow. Her enthusiasm led to conviction for Zionist activities and three years in a labor camp. As she later declared, "My stay in prison did not change my convictions. I still consider Israel as my native homeland." Upon her release, she finished her studies, became a speech therapist, and resumed her Zionist activities.

Neither prison nor age seemed to be a deterrent to action. Luba Bershadskaya, who was 53 years old when she made public the twentieth letter she had sent to Premier Kosygin—an entreaty to "please allow me to go to Israel. Nobody needs me here; my departure will be entirely unnoticeable. Be kind and humane to me, I beg you." Bershadskaya had grown up in Kiev, the daughter of a wool merchant and a cultured, well-traveled mother. Dispossessed by the Revolution, she became a ballet dancer and teacher, married an Orthodox baker's son at the age of 17, and the family expanded by three children. They moved to Moscow. During World War II, the English she had learned as a youngster stood her in good stead. She found employment at the U.S. Embassy and, at the end of the war, at the U.S. Military Mission. But suddenly in 1946, she was arrested. Her post-Stalin release and rehabilitation resulted in years of restlessness. Her family had become estranged and emotionally distant. Housing in Moscow was impossible to secure. Finally she met an artist, Nikolai Roitburd, also from Kiev and one of the few survivors of Babi Yar. They married and spent the next half dozen years working where they could—in the frozen north at Murmansk, on the Black Sea at Sochi—until in December 1966, back in Moscow, they learned of huge crowds of Jews at the Israeli Embassy spurred by Kosygin's promise that Jews could leave the USSR. Having long since determined that life in the USSR was no blessing for them as Jews, Luba and Nikolai were anxious to find out how they could depart. Like all who came to the embassy, they were directed to OVIR, where the crowds were even larger. Now began an almost four-year ordeal of forms, applications, and rejection. But it put them, after years of wandering, in touch with other kindred souls. They had found a family— fellow-Jews wishing to leave the USSR forever. There was even a kind of club room for applicants—an apartment in the middle of Moscow— the walls of which were plastered with large pictures of Moshe Dayan and Golda Meir and a map of Israel. They had found a cause—the Jewish repatriation movement. By May 1969, the movement was brave enough to celebrate Israel's Independence Day with a picnic in a wooded park outside Moscow. The two hundred people unfurled a home-made Israeli flag, sang "Hatikvah," and cooked shashlik. (It was not until the annual celebration of 1973 that the police broke up the picnic and dispersed the celebrants.) Luba signed individual letters as well as collective ones. She became a fighter.*

Other energetic older women were also involved in the movement: Dora Koliaditskaya (Rakhel Fedoseyev's mother), already 65; Lutsia Muchnik, a 50-year-old physician, whose husband, the distinguished scholar Avram Muchnik, died while they were struggling to leave; Rosalia Plotkina, also a physician, who, after she applied to leave for Israel, was subjected to collective judgment of her fellow-workers and discharged, with a recommendation that she not be re-employed—all of these women signed the important collective appeals, including the first letter (in the fall of 1969) to the women of the world—an eloquent plea for the right to leave, addressed to "Women, no matter who you are—a student or a minister, a salesgirl or a cinema star, a housewife or a queen, we ask you, Women: Help us, won't you, to appeal to the Soviet government with the words, 'Let them go in peace! Don't keep them by force!" It was signed first by Tina Brodetskaya. The tenth and last signer was Ruta Aleksandrovich, a young nurse from Riga.

These collective letters, particularly those suggesting that there was coordination between Jews in different cities, provoked a strong officially stimulated response. Letters from other Jews suddenly began to appear in the Soviet press. On December 14, 1969, the official government newspaper, *Izvestia,* prominently carried a letter entitled "To Whose Tune Do the Zionists Dance?" signed by I. Berenshtein, a doctor of history, and M. Fridel, a journalist. The letter, repeated in similar language in scores of other newspapers throughout the USSR, condemned as a "crude fabrication" the charge of "gentlemen Zionists" that there is anti-Semitism or discrimination within the USSR. The reason for this "shameful and hypocritical anti-Soviet campaign is to divert attention from Israel's acute problems insoluble under its bourgeois system; to stifle protests against Israeli annexations and crimes against the Arabs; to convince the credulous that Israel is a promised land." The letter rejected the notion that Soviet Jews wished to live elsewhere than "under the sun of Socialism" but warned the few misguided or degenerate Jews against "betrayal of their true fatherland." It asserted that "in principle, the question of the departure abroad of those who wish it is

---

* But her years of loneliness and estrangement had taken their toll. When she was finally permitted to go to Israel, the temporary camaraderie of the struggle was replaced by the hard realities of adjustment to a new society, and she again became bitter and disillusioned. After two years, she left Israel and applied to return to the USSR.

solved by Soviet jurisprudence with maximum democracy," but "if in connection with Israel this has become more complicated in the past two and a half years, it is Israel that is to be blamed because the USSR had to break off relations with Israel because of its aggression against the Arab countries." Israel is not interested in reuniting families, the article asserted; it only wants a cheap labor force for its deserts and swamps, and "cannon fodder" for its army. The article repeated the frequent charges found in the Soviet press that those who have gone to Israel have led lives of pitiful misery, poverty, and exploitation. It closed by warning that the Zionist "enemy" seeks "to persuade his 'brethren' to commit treason and betray his true homeland," and linked the fight against Zionism as an integral part of the class struggle requiring constant vigilance to combat "the black forces of imperialism."

Among the replies (never printed by *Izvestia*, but circulated widely in *samizdat* publications) was a lengthy collective letter written principally by Fedoseyev and signed by Svechinsky and five other Moscow Jews, attacking the assertions of Berenshtein and Fridel and concluding: "And to the Great Power which gave shelter to many generations of Jews, we repeat the words of our distant ancestors who demanded the right of Exodus from Egypt: *'Let My People Go.'*" Following the letter, this Biblical phrase became a major slogan of the Jewish movement, inside and outside the Soviet Union.

Another response to the Berenshtein-Fridel article came from Iosif Kerler, a well-known Yiddish poet. Born in the Ukraine in 1918, Kerler, a man with intense, deep-set eyes, grew up in a *kolkhoz* in the Crimea, published his first poems when only seventeen, fought and was severely wounded in World War II, and later published a second book, *Poems from the Battlefront.* He was arrested in 1950 and worked as a miner in a labor camp until released at the end of 1955. "I don't know why I was arrested," he has said. "There was no real reason except for the fact that Stalin decided to liquidate Jewish culture. So they made up reasons. I was accused of disseminating propaganda harmful to the Soviet Union and of being a bourgeois nationalist. What this meant I don't know. My struggle to get an exit visa lasted the same length of time as my stay in the labor camp—six years." He first applied in 1965, but despite initial indications that he would be permitted to leave, he was refused. "I had been witness to the death, the murder really, of Jewish culture in the Soviet Union. I knew personally the Yiddish writers who had been killed by Stalin, and if let out, I could tell the world. If there is one thing the Soviet Union is afraid of, it's the truth."

Kerler's letter to *Izvestia* sought to speak this truth. He noted that the total destruction of Jewish culture had left him, a Jewish writer, without a public, without contact with a living Jewish language, cut off from any Jewish cultural life. "Who needs me in the Soviet Union?" he bitterly asked. He condemned the accusation of treason made by the *Izvestia* writers, describing it as an "incitement to a pogrom. We remember that because of a similar criminal interpretation of 'treason to the homeland' in 1952, the most prominent representatives of Jewish culture were shot—shot although they were innocent. . . . In the long and glorious Jewish history," he concluded, "there have been various kinds of 'brother Jews.' There have been malicious converts; there have also been assimilators and defeatists who pretended to be liberal; and there have been *Judenrat-Polizei,* the henchmen of the German fascists. But learned Jews calling for a pogrom, and in the total absence of anti-Semitism at that—there have never been people like that."

With Kerler, and with most of the Jewish activists who had suffered prison camp experience, there was an understandable and deep-seated abhorrence for the brutalities of Soviet society. Political prisoners— which they all had been—were rarely "rehabilitated" by imprisonment. Their punishment was merely additional corroboration of their original political appraisal of the Soviet regime. Prison camp reinforced and made more sophisticated the capacity for dissent. Among the camp alumni was Dr. Semen (Meir) Gelfand, born in 1930 in the small Ukrainian Jewish town of Zhmerinka to parents with traditional Jewish education, which, out of fear, they did not teach him. By the time he was a teenager, life—in the form of the Holocaust—had taught him, quite naturally, to be a Zionist. In 1949, he was sentenced to ten years in a camp at Vorkuta. The camp completed his political education and enabled him to acquire a Jewish education from other Jewish political prisoners who taught Hebrew, Hebrew literature, and Jewish history. After he was released in 1955, he became a physician and later a cardiologist in Moscow, but he maintained ties with his camp comrades and their ideals. He and Svechinsky were close friends, and a group of Zionists—men who also had concerned sympathy for the other dissent movements—developed around their leadership. Gelfand was involved in the *Ishkod* group, but he also recognized the need for other *samizdat* publications. With a close associate, Vadim Meniker, a Moscow economist, Gelfand asked a third member of their group, Mikhail Zand, to prepare a draft of a theoretical article on the Jewish question in the USSR. The document, completed in early January 1970 and entitled "The Jewish Question in the USSR (Theses)," was originally written under the pseudonym "N. Palmoni," but after discussion and editing in Gelfand's apartment, the pseudonym was removed, Gelfand typed it, and it was circulated in *samzidat*. (Portions, entitled "On Assimilation," were included in *Iton Aleph*. The entire document appeared in the West, published in Russian by Possev and in English by the IJA.)

"Theses" describes the many forms of discrimination against Jews in the USSR and analyzes the widespread nature and dissemination of anti-Semitism.

> The national dignity of Jewish inhabitants is offended by the Jew-hating campaign in which all the means of mass propaganda are engaged. This campaign is conducted officially under the guise of a struggle against Zionism and Judaism. The fact that some Jews take part in it does not change its essence. Throughout the centuries, Jewish renegades have been tools used by anti-Semites in the persecution of Jews. The basic motive for this campaign is the sympathy of most Soviet Jews for Israel, which is in sharp contradiction to the rabid anti-Israel foreign policy of the government. Since nothing happens without the consent of party organs, there is no doubt of the organized character of this campaign, directed from above.

Noting that discrimination is "the tool" used by Soviet authorities in their assimilationy policy, "Theses" describes the various types of assimilation—physical, linguistic, cultural, and religious. The only possible solution to the Jewish question is that (*1*) "Jews who have already completely lost their national consciousness and who strive for complete assimilation with the native population . . . should have a real opportunity of dissolving themselves in the majority"; (*2*) "Jews who have recognized the total impossibility of a national existence of the Jewish people in the USSR and who strive for repatriation to Israel . . . should obtain an unconditional right to repatriation"; and (*3*) "those who have not yet realized the inevitability of a choice between assimilation and repatriation . . . will have to make their own choice."

Mikhail Zand, the author of this document, was one of the most distinguished intellectuals of the Jewish movement. Zand was born in

1927 in the small town of Kamenets Podolsk, near the former Polish-Russian border, where his father, a Communist political emigré from Poland, had been sent as chief of the Jewish section of the Communist Party. There he met his wife, the daughter of a Hasidic family. When Mikhail was quite young, the Zands were transferred to another Ukrainian town and then to Kharkov, at that time the capital of the Ukraine. In 1930, they moved to Moscow, where the elder Zand lectured in philosophy at the University of Moscow, but his primary post was at the special Comintern Institute which trained Communist leaders from African and Asian countries. The Zands lived in the institute as well, always with the foreign cadre, and Mikhail from his earliest years was exposed to Asian languages, including the Hebrew of Communists from Palestine. In 1937, his father was arrested and put to death as a part of the Great Purge. Many associated with the Institute were similarly destroyed. But 10-year-old Mikhail had already absorbed the linguistic and cultural variety of his childhood experiences and of the other children in the special classes he attended. Although his mother had been a Yiddish teacher in the Ukraine, she never taught him the language and Russian was spoken at home. The family had been so consciously assimilationist that Mikhail's maternal grandfather had suffered criminal difficulties for allegedly kidnapping 8-year-old Mikhail in order to circumcise him. Now Mrs. Zand found employment as a teacher outside of Moscow, and Mikhail and his sister were cared for in Moscow by his traditionally Jewish grandparents.

In World War II, the family was evacuated to the Urals. By then, Mikhail's Jewish interests had been awakened. Already polylingual, he taught himself Yiddish at the age of 14 and began a lifelong interest in Hebrew. He managed to learn some Jewish history and studied about Palestine. Even more, he began thinking a great deal about his father's death, the sudden purging of the unique little society of his youth, the tragedy of the Jewish people, the Hitler-Stalin pacts, the collapse and defeat of the Red Army in 1941. By 1944 he was a confirmed but not outspoken anti-Stalinist. After the family returned to Moscow, shortly before the end of the war, he began to listen to foreign broadcasts. Although jamming of foreign Russian-language broadcasts became severe, he was able to listen to broadcasts in foreign languages that he knew, such as German and English, and for over twenty years the BBC was his primary source of information. By the early 1950s, he began to listen to Kol Israel, which then, inexplicably, was broadcast in English. Later,

MOSCOW: The Central Nervous System 113

when Kol Israel switched to Russian, it became, and remained, poor in information and quality—but at least it brought some news of Israel.

In 1945, because of his excellent academic record, Zand had been admitted to the University of Moscow's Institute of Oriental Studies. (His decision to become an Orientalist stemmed from his early interests and his growing fascination with Hebrew and Palestine.) There, he learned Persian, Arabic, and other Asian languages and, on his own, he learned Hebrew. In 1948, he and a close friend, Lunia Rotshtein (now a pathologist in Petach Tikva, Israel) wrote Stalin asking permission for young Soviet Jews to go to Israel to help in the "anti-imperialist war." Zand signed with a pseudonym, and Rotshtein signed with his own name. As a consequence, Rotshtein spent eight years in prison camp and Zand learned to be cautious. At graduation in 1950, he married Nili, also an Orientalist born in Moscow of assimilated Jewish parents. Although Zand had graduated with highest honors, his father's record prevented Moscow employment or continued study, so the Zands went to Dushanbe in Central Asia, where he taught at the Tadzhik University and did research at the Tadzhik Academy of Science. The seven years in Tadzhikistan had their compensation, including the company of Jewish intellectuals from Russia proper, who were unable to find employment elsewhere because they were Jewish or otherwise nonconformist. Also, he had ample time to develop proficiency in various Oriental tongues and learn the languages and cultures of the Soviet Union's Oriental Jewish communities. In 1957, his father was posthumously rehabilitated and Zand returned to Moscow for further study, teaching, and research, and remained until he left for Israel in June 1971. By that time, he was an internationally known Orientalist, a specialist in Persian and Tadzhik literature, the editor of a journal, author of many books and articles, and a research fellow at the Oriental Institute.

By the early 1960s, Zand also became involved with nonconformist friends in *samizdat* work, discussion groups, and the nascent democratic movement. After the Six-Day War, he and some of his circle made contacts with the Jewish movement. His old friend Lunia Rotshtein, out of prison and now a doctor, introduced him to Meir Gelfand and his associates, who had constant contact with other people in the Jewish movement. They viewed some of their colleagues, such as the Drabkin group, as "a little too chauvinistic," but they cooperated with them in teaching Hebrew and preparing *samizdat* materials. *Ulpanim* had begun in 1968, and at Vadim Meniker's apartment, Zand taught a group of Jews who had come out of the democratic movement. As more and more people applied for exit visas, activity intensified. In the fall of 1969, a number of activists, including Khavkin, received permission to leave, and sharper, more political collective appeals began appearing. Even at the time Zand wrote "Theses," he was not involved in the open struggle.

Perhaps the most significant rallying point in that struggle—both for Moscow Jews and for those in the rest of the USSR—in the period before the June 1970 mass arrests was the Letter of the 39 of March 8, 1970. Its drama stemmed from the directness of its confrontation with Soviet power. Frustrated by their inability to stem the tide of exit applications by media propaganda or press campaigns—against Israel and life there; or Zionism as an enemy ideology; or the USSR as the loving motherland of all nationalities, including Jews, or the stern fatherland which would deal harshly with traitors—Soviet authorities decided to stage a spectacular political event. Up to March 1970, the existence of a Jewish movement had been publicly almost ignored in the USSR; now it was recognized and confronted. On March 4, Leonid M. Zamyatin, head of the Press Department of the Foreign Ministry, produced forty Soviet Jews for a press conference to which all foreign journalists and the Russian press corps were invited. The conference was broadcast on television and radio and repeated on television three times during the week. Soviet newspapers carried the full text of the conference—coverage reserved for major events.

Among the star performers were the Soviet Union's highest-ranking Jewish office-holder, Vice Premier V. E. Dymshits; Lt. Gen. D. A. Dragunsky; Aron Vergelis, the editor of *Sovietish Heimland,* the USSR's only Yiddish-language journal, and a long-time principal Soviet spokesman on Jewish affairs; Generals Milshtein and Rubinchik; Aleksandr Chakovsky, editor of *Literaturnaya Gazeta* (organ of the Writers' Union); academicians Hersh Budker, Isak Mints, and Mark Mitin; ballerina Maya Plisetskaya; violinist Leonid Kogan; Professor L. M. Volodarsky, an economist; and comedian Arkady Raikin. Among the others were actors, writers, doctors, scientists, and some identified as "workers." The group generally had status, and some had name familiarity. Apart from Dymshits, Dragunsky, Vergelis, and Mitin, who served frequently as Soviet spokesmen on Jewish questions, most were appearing publicly as Jews for the first time.

Professor Volodarsky began the conference by reading a statement signed by more than fifty Jews. It condemned Israeli policy, linked it to international Zionism and imperialism, claimed it had launched a subversive campaign against socialist countries, national liberation movements, and progressive regimes, denied Soviet anti-Semitism, pointed with pride and statistics to political, educational, and economic accomplishments of Soviet Jews, lauded the USSR for saving Jews from racist annihilation and mankind from fascist slavery in World War II, praised the Communist Party and the Soviet government, warned "gullible victims of Zionist propaganda throughout the world" and reaffirmed Jewish love for the fraternal blessings of Soviet society. The question period evoked additional answers in the same vein.

Four days later, Zamyatin received a letter with an accompanying declaration signed by forty Moscow Jews.* Drabkin signed first. Many had already written individually or signed collective letters discussed above. Other signers included Gelfand and some of the Jewish activists who had previously been identified with the democratic movement, notably Yulius Telesin, a well-known mathematician whose energy matched his intelligence. Telesin became a thorn in the corpulent side of the Moscow bureaucracy by his insistence on legality and his persistence in asserting rights for writers, scientists, Crimean Tatars, Jews, or any other oppressed persons. His application for an exit visa to Israel and his public identification with the repatriation cause must have impelled officials to respond with alacrity and relief, since they granted him his visa within a month after he had signed the document. Most of the other signers were given permission to leave within less than a year. The major exceptions were Vladimir Slepak, a 43-year-old engineer, his wife Maria, a physician, and Vladimir Prestin, a 35-year-old engineer.

The letter was not only delivered to Zamyatin; it was simultaneously circulated in *samizdat* form and given to the foreign press. (*The New York Times* carried it prominently on March 11.) It began:

> We are those Jews who insist on their desire to leave for Israel and who are being constantly refused by the Soviet authorities.

* Forty actually signed. Yulius Telesin added his signature just before delivery of the document. Nevertheless, it is known as the Letter of the 39.

> We are those Jews who have more than once addressed open statements to the Soviet press, but whose letters were never published.

and continued:

> We are those Jews who had not been invited to the press conference on March 4 of this year and who had not been asked to express their views.
> We suppose that you must feel uncomfortable for the one-sidedness of the conference, especially as you of course know, if only from the press, that since the renewal in 1968 of the acceptance by the Soviet administrative organs of applications from Jews desiring to go to Israel, over 80,000 applications have been submitted up to November of 1969 alone (see the weekly *Newsweek* of November 24, 1969, which is well known to the Soviet press). And all this occurs under conditions when the desire of a Soviet Jew to live in the land of his ancestors is, to put it mildly, not encouraged.
> If it is admitted that behind each of the applications submitted by the Jews within this short period of time there is even a very small family, let us say of only three persons, even then it transpires that over 240,000 Jews of the Soviet Union are unsuccessfully trying to get permission to go to Israel.
> Proceeding from the elementary concept of justice, expressed in ancient Rome in the well-known formula "The other side should be heard, too"—you, of course, will want to correct the unpleasant misunderstanding that has arisen out of the one-sidedness of the representatives at the press conference you conducted on March 4 of this year.
> Therefore we, the Jews—in distinction from "citizens of Jewish nationality"—who are prepared to leave at any minute, just as we are, and to go even on foot to the State of Israel, we appeal to you with the request to give us also an opportunity to speak at a press conference before Soviet and foreign journalists and to make a statement.

The attached statement asserted that the opinion it expressed was "characteristic of many of our fellow-Jews, although we admit that indecision is preventing many of them from openly expressing their views." It answered point by point the major themes of the conference, among other things stating:

> The essential task of the press conference was to show that its participants had reached prominent positions in society, in spite of their Jewish origin. But this was all they could show, for their Jewish origins do not mean that they have preserved their spiritual link with the national Jewish culture. Every Jew has a right to any degree of

assimilation. We, however, do not want to forfeit our national identity and our spiritual link with our people. . . .

And it is the very preservation of the national identity of Jews that is the problem in the Soviet Union. No references to completely equal and joyful labor with Russians and no examples of a brilliant military or social career can divert our attention from the problem, for in this, Russians remain Russians, and Jews cease to be Jews. Forcible assimilation in this case does not mean, for example, that reading Jewish books is prohibited. It means that young Jews do not know how to read Jewish books because there are no schools in the Soviet Union where the Jewish language is taught. . . .

One of the basic issues of the Jewish question in the USSR is a guarantee of the right of repatriation. The Soviet Union does not recognize that right, and many thousands of Soviet Jews who want to leave for Israel are being refused.

We shall insist on our right to decide our own destiny, including the choice of citizenship and country of residence. We ourselves are capable of assessing all the possible difficulties awaiting us concerning military events, change of climate or of social order.

The present state of our citizenship includes the right of the state to demand from us no more than obeying the laws, and our claims to freedom of repatriation are based òn Soviet laws and guarantees of international law.

The Jewish people has undergone many persecutions and suffering, many malicious or well-intentioned assimilation campaigns, and has succeeded in maintaining its identity.

We believe that now also Jews will respond to the anti-Israel campaign not by abdicating, but that, on the contrary, their pride in their people will grow stronger and that they will declare "Next year in Jerusalem!"

Following the Moscow statement, there was an even stronger declaration from twenty-one Leningrad Jews who described those attending the official press conference as only "passport" Jews who "have no right to speak in the name of our people. It is also doubtful whether you can consider yourself as part of the Jewish people in general." They condemned the utter lack of interest in Jewish affairs or Jewish culture. "In distinction to you, we are Jews not only because of our passports. We feel deeply the irrevocable ties binding us to the entire Jewish people no matter where it is, whether in the Soviet Union, or Israel, America or Australia."

To the Soviet leaders, the once-small brush fires must have appeared to be getting out of control. UN Secretary General U Thant was scheduled to visit Moscow in mid-June. On June 10, shortly before his scheduled arrival, seventy-five Moscow Jews addressed an open letter to him. The signers included familiar names, but many new ones were added. The first signer was Pavel Abramovich, a young engineer who, with Slepak, Prestin, and Viktor Polsky (another engineer who had already signed a number of strikingly cogent open letters) were to provide leadership when most of the early activists had departed. Also publicly signing for the first time were Rakhel Fedoseyev and Karl Malkin, the mathematician, who had been quietly working as the Moscow representative on the editorial committee of *Iton*. The appeal, clearly stating the case and urging U Thant's intervention, concluded as follows:

> We, the children of the Jewish nation, which has experienced the most cruel persecutions, torments, and physical extermination, cannot any longer imagine our existence away from our national homeland. And to achieve this aim we are prepared to go to the limit.
>
> We sign this open appeal to you fully aware of the fact that if the Rights of Man are not implemented, humanity has no future.

The signers did not know that U Thant would cancel his visit, nor did they know that their preparation "to go to the limit" would soon be sorely tested.

GEORGIA:
Messianic Judaism

CHAPTER 7

Georgia, one of the fifteen Soviet Socialist Republics, lies along the Black Sea, in the central-western Caucasus. Nestled between the snowy peaks of the Greater and Lesser Caucasus Mountains, much of it is subtropical. For thousands of years, the Georgian people and their ancestors were part of the Babylonian, Persian, Parthian, Mongol, and Turkish empires, until they were swallowed up by the expanding Russian Empire in the late 18th and early 19th centuries. The 4.7 million Georgians remain fiercely proud of their ancient civilization, which accepted Christianity long before the Russians, whom they regard as possessors of a more primitive culture.

Castles, cathedrals, monasteries, and ancient walls and towers—some from the 11th and 12th centuries—testify to the advanced civilization of the Georgian kings and princes. But under the tsars, Georgia, exhausted by centuries of strife, was a neglected and backward hinterland. It did not join in the Bolshevik Revolution and was not annexed to the USSR until 1921–22.

Georgian Jews claim to be descended from the ten lost tribes exiled to Assyria some 2,700 years ago, and some evidence suggests that Jewish descendants of those exiles may have settled in the southern Caucasus. Ancient documents and gravestones clearly confirm a Georgian Jewish presence in the early Middle Ages. Physically and culturally, Georgian Jews resemble the people in whose midst they live. The men are swarthy and wiry and wear the fierce, drooping mustache which has come to symbolize the Georgians. From earliest

119

times, the Georgian nation absorbed its Jews with minimum difficulty, and the Jews fought alongside their country's princes in Georgia's efforts to maintain independence. Traders traveling the famous "silk route" maintained contact with other Oriental Jewish communities, and during the Middle Ages Jewish centers in neighboring Turkey, Persia, and Mesopotamia influenced Georgian Jewish liturgy, religious ritual, and literature. Contact with the Ashkenazi Jews of the Russian Empire, begun in the 19th century, was somewhat accelerated by the early, enthusiastic acceptance of Zionism, which appealed strongly to the Georgians, with their orthodox, messianic religious beliefs.

Georgian delegates attended early 20th-century World Zionist Congresses and were photographed in their exotic costumes, which included bandoliers, filled with bullets. But otherwise, the Jews of Georgia were strange and unknown to the Ashkenazi majority of Russian Jewry, and even more so to the Jews of the West. Their isolation helps explain the lack of "Europeanization" until very recent years. General education, already commonplace among Russian Jews by the time of the Bolshevik Revolution, became well-nigh universal thereafter, but Georgian Jews did not begin to send their children to general schools until the 1930s.

The strong Zionist commitment of Georgian Jews was even more remarkable because of their substantial freedom from anti-Semitism and their long acceptance by their neighbors. (The Georgian Orthodox Church had been free of the religious intolerance that characterized sections of the Russian Orthodox and Polish Catholic churches.) Their first language is Georgian. They are, in fact, the only Oriental Jews without a dialect of their own. Only the younger, better-educated Jews read or speak Russian. Few know any Western tongues, and Yiddish is, of course, altogether unknown. Because of their orthodoxy, most Georgian Jews understand some Hebrew, but their level of religious and Hebrew learning is basic and unsophisticated. Their family names, like those of the Georgians, have endings such as "-shvili" or "-adze."

Because many Georgian Jews were excellent artisans and craftsmen, Tsar Alexander I granted them the right, in 1804, to live outside the Pale of Settlement created in 1791 as a territorial reservation for Russian Jews. They have been traditionally involved in the production and sale of the famous Georgian wines, and many were small traders or artisans. For centuries, they had lived in small villages, town ghettoes, or other separate settlements. Under Communism, they formed collectives or artisan cooperatives, many of which were disguised "socialist enterprises," more entrepreneurial than state managed. Some Georgian Jews have tended to become *Luftmenschen,* and smuggling and black marketeering are quite commonplace in the easygoing, leisurely pace of Georgian communal and economic existence.

To the inhabitants of large Russian cities like Moscow, Georgians are traditionally associated with free-market flower selling and fruit and vegetable peddling. Small fortunes, in Soviet terms, are believed to be made through this entrepreneurial initiative. Planes from Tbilisi to Moscow often are laden with dealers (Jews as well as non-Jews) carrying goods to the Moscow market. They return with consumer commodities that are unavailable in Georgia and are sold "informally" there. Questionably legal, the practice is usually tolerated.

The patriarchal family has maintained and transmitted the Jewish heritage and insulated its members from assimilation. Georgian Jewish family groups of three or four generations generally live together in one house or in adjoining ones. The grandfather heads the clan. Each family tends to have from six to eight children. Ten to twenty people eat together at a meal, and Sabbath and holidays bring together the entire clan. Male children—even those with Communist fathers—are circumcised. Bar mitzvah, wedding, and funeral ceremonies are in accord with ancient religious traditions. Religious observances include young as well as old. Each family supports its synagogue—almost half of the less than fifty remaining synagogues in the USSR are in Georgia —and the communities support *kashrut* facilities and *mikvahs*—but rarely Hebrew schools or Torah study.* Although the Soviet regime effectively repressed synagogues in the USSR (they decreased from 3,000 in 1917 to 1,011 in 1941, and to the present 40 to 50), the Georgians fiercely maintained their traditions and institutions and, with the lenient or generally friendly assent of Georgian officials, continued to transmit the basic elements of their tradition.

Nevertheless, there has been persecution under the Communist regime—increasing pressures for the extinction of religious institutions and widespread anti-Zionist and anti-Israel propaganda. Six Jews were shot as a consequence of "economic crimes" trials in the early 1960s (the only reported executions in Georgia). There have even been spora-

* *Kashrut* is the body of dietary laws prescribed for Jews. A *mikvah* is a ritual bath to which Orthodox Jews are required to go to cleanse and purify themselves.

dic revivals of the blood-libel accusation. But the highly nationalistic Georgians tend to sympathize with, and understand, the Zionism of the Jews. They have no tradition of anti-Semitism—which they regard as a Russian import and reject as part of the hated Russification process.

Most Georgian Jews live in Tbilisi (formerly Tiflis), the capital, with a population of 875,000 (including 40,000 Jews); Kutaisi, Georgia's second city, with a population of 170,000 (about 20,000 Jews); Kulashi (9,000 in a town inhabited mainly by Jews); or Poti (3,000 out of 4,600); but considerable numbers still live in small mountain villages or are otherwise dispersed. Some Ashkenazi Jews also have settled in Georgia, largely in Tbilisi and Kutaisi. All these figures relate to the period before 1971; since then, significant changes have occurred.

Given their long-standing messianic Zionism, it is not surprising that some Georgian Jews had gone to Palestine in the late 19th and early 20th centuries. Even after the Revolution had severely curtailed any mobility, a trickle of Georgian Jews had been permitted to reunite with their families in Palestine and later in Israel. Unlike most Soviet Jews, the Georgians generally do not have relatives in countries of the West. They were emotionally affected by the Six-Day War, as were other Soviet Jews, but OVIR would not accept exit visas until the middle of 1968. When they discovered that OVIR would receive applications, the Georgians secured invitations from relatives in Israel and applied. In the winter of 1968-69, forty-nine families received visas and departed. (Only in Riga was there anything like a comparable experience at that time.) Word of this miraculous occurrence quickly spread, and hundreds of families hastened to apply.'But the door closed as mysteriously as it had opened, and refusal followed refusal. Frustration was high for thousands who had dreamed of Israel. Some of the more militant began writing individual letters of protest to OVIR and to Georgian government authorities. A few wrote to Moscow and even sought a Kremlin interview. There was no response.

On August 6, 1969, eighteen families, mainly from Kutaisi but also including Georgian Jews from Poti, Kulashi, and Tbilisi, addressed a letter to the UN Human Rights Commission (together with three accompanying letters). Released in *samizdat* form with the assistance of Moscow friends—a few Georgian activists were already in contact with Jews in other cities—this collective letter was to have dramatic repercussions. The first accompanying letter, addressed to "friends of Anne Frank" and asking that a letter be transmitted to Golda Meir, was sent to the Netherlands Embassy in Moscow, which exercised consular functions in the USSR for Israel since the rupture of diplomatic relations between Moscow and Jerusalem in June 1967. It assured the Dutch that the Georgian Jews were "loyal citizens and that our appeal is not caused by a desire to disparage the USSR. Therefore, the transmission of the letter cannot be regarded as intervention into the domestic affairs of the Soviet Union." The next letter, to Mrs. Meir, requested her to transmit the letter to the UN. "We also ask that the letter should be published in the press and should be broadcast in Russian over Kol Israel. We shall listen to the transmissions of 2, 9, 16, and 23 Elul and on the first day of Rosh Hashanah." The third letter, to Yosef Tekoah, Israel's representative at the UN, requested that exit visas be obtained in the shortest possible time, that the letter to the Human Rights Commission be delivered, and that it be distributed to all UN members and published in the press with the full names and addresses of the signers. "Because the time of fear is over—the time of action has come. Because if not I myself, then who? And if not today, then when?"

After some preliminary, customary obeisances in the direction of the Soviet authorities, for the just nationalities policy, the absence of pogroms, the status achieved by some Jews, and the open synagogues, the main letter read:

> Our prayers are with Israel, for it is written: "If I forget thee, O Jerusalem, may my right hand forget its cunning." For we religious Jews feel that there is no Jew without faith, just as there is no faith without traditions. What, then, is our faith and what are our traditions?
>
> For a long time the Roman legions besieged Jerusalem. But despite the well-known horrors of the siege—hunger, lack of water, disease, and much more—the Jews did not renounce their faith and did not surrender. However, man's strength has its limits, too, and in the end barbarians broke into the Holy City. Thus, a thousand years ago, the Holy Temple was destroyed, and with it the Jewish state. The nation, however, remained. Although the Jews who could bear arms did not surrender to the enemy and killed one another, there remained the old people, women, and children.
>
> And whoever could not get away was killed on the spot.
>
> But whoever could went away into the desert; and whoever survived reached other countries, to believe, and pray and wait.
>
> Henceforth they had to find a way to live in alien lands among people who hated them. Showered with insults, covered with the mud of slander, despised and persecuted, they earned their daily bread with blood and sweat, and reared their children.
>
> Their hands were calloused, their souls were drenched in blood.

But the important thing is that the nation was not destroyed—and what a nation.

The Jews gave the world religion and revolutionaries, philosophers and scholars, wealthy men and wise men, geniuses with the hearts of children, and children with the eyes of old people. There is no field of knowledge, no branch of literature and art, to which Jews have not contributed their share. There is no country which gave Jews shelter which has not been repaid by their labor. And what did the Jews get in return?

When life was bearable for all, the Jews waited fearfully for other times. And when life became bad for all, the Jews knew that their last hour had come, and then they hid or ran away from the country.

And whoever got away began from the beginning again.

And whoever could not run away was destroyed.

And whoever hid well waited until other times came.

Who didn't persecute the Jews! Everybody joined in baiting them.

When untalented generals lost a war, those to blame for the defeat were found at once—Jews. When a political adventurer did not keep the mountain of promises he had given, a reason was found at once—the Jews. Jews died in the torture chambers of the Inquisition in Spain and in fascist concentration camps in Germany. Anti-Semites raised a scare—in enlightened France it was the Dreyfus case; in illiterate Russia, the Beilis case.

And the Jews had to endure everything.

But there was a way that they could have lived tranquilly, like other peoples; all they had to do was convert to another faith. Some did this—there are cowards everywhere. But millions preferred a life of suffering and often death to apostasy.

And even if they did wander the earth without shelter—God found a place for all.

And even if their ashes are scattered through the world, the memory of them is alive.

Their blood is in our veins, and our tears are their tears.

The Prophecy has come true; Israel has risen from the ashes; we have not forgotten Jerusalem, and it needs our hands.

There are eighteen of us who signed this letter. But he errs who thinks there are only eighteen of us. There could have been many more signatures.

They say there is a total of twelve million Jews in the world. But he errs who believes there is a total of twelve million of us. For with those who pray for Israel are hundreds of millions who did not live to this day, who were tortured to death, who are no longer here. They march shoulder to shoulder with us, unconquered and immortal, those who handed down to us the traditions of struggle and faith.

That is why we want to go to Israel. . . .

We will wait months and years, we will wait all our lives, if necessary, but we will not renounce our faith or our hopes.

> We believe: our prayers have reached God.
> We know: our appeals will reach people.
> For we are asking—let us go to the land of our forefathers.

One hundred days later, having received no answer from the Netherlands Embassy, Mrs. Meir, Ambassador Tekoah, or the UN, and having heard no broadcasts on Kol Israel, the eighteen families again wrote to the same people (except that this time they addressed the UN through the secretary general rather than the Human Rights Commission) with the same requests. But this time their appeal was more pointed and urgent:

> We, the eighteen religious Jewish families of Georgia, wish to remind you that we are alive and pray for our return to Israel.
> A hundred days ago we applied to the UN with the request that we be helped to emigrate. . . .
> As before, our bread is bitter, our tears are salty and the conditions in which we live are difficult. Here is an example: one of the families is huddled together in one room—small children, their parents and old people; at night there are rats. . . .
> Who will help us?
> We have still not received the permit to emigrate; one might think that our case is the first one of its kind and that the competent organs are deliberating how they should act in this very case. However, there are known precedents.
> There is much in common between the fate of the Armenians and the Jews: both nations had for centuries been the victims of oppression. Both had been scattered all over the earth; in both cases the majority of the nation for many generations lived outside the boundaries of their historical fatherland. The USSR has done everything to realize the centuries-old dreams of the Armenians; today hundreds of thousands of them have been repatriated to Armenia.
> They can say: the Armenians left the capitalist hell for the country of victorious socialism, and that no comparison can be made here. Let it be so. But then, let us remember something else: The Spaniards who emigrated to the USSR at the end of the thirties returned at the end of the fifties, together with grown-up children who were born in the USSR, to their fatherland—to Franco Spain; at that time the Spanish Republicans were not called betrayers and traitors by anyone.
> Why is it that what has been permitted to the Armenians and the Spaniards is forbidden to the Jews?
> We know that the famous internationalist and Leninist, W. Gomulka, has widely opened the gates for all the Jews who desire to go out of Poland; in this he is fulfilling his duty as a communist.
> And so, there are precedents. What, then, is the matter? . . .

We believe that we shall return. We are convinced of this on the basis of the Leninist doctrine on the right of nations to self-determination, which lies at the foundation of the national policy of the USSR, and on the statements of official persons, in particular of A. N. Kosygin (Paris, December 3, 1966).

There are also other documents well known to you: The Universal Declaration of the Rights of Man and the International Convention on the Elimination of All Forms of Racial Discrimination, signed by the USSR as well; in these international agreements is confirmed the right of everyone "to leave any country, including his own," and this is precisely what we ask. Since the UN Human Rights Commission, to which we first wrote, was unable to help us, we turn to you with the same request. . . .

May our prayers penetrate your mind and your conscience, Mr. Secretary General. We are expecting help from you, because time is short. . . .

Who will help us?

The letters of the Georgians, as well as other individual and collective letters, generally became available to the Israeli government shortly after they were issued in the USSR. But there was a well-established policy against their publication.

For a decade and a half, Shaul Avigur, a man of great power and prestige in the Israeli government, had headed an office responsible for problems of East European Jews. His policy was government policy, and his policy was not to publish or acknowledge open letters and appeals. For a quarter of a century, Avigur has remained one of the most influential yet least-known men in Israel. An early settler from Russia and one of the few survivors of the battle of Tel Hai, Avigur helped create the Haganah, the self-defense organization that later formed the nucleus for the Israeli Army.* He became its commander and an intimate confidant of David Ben-Gurion, Israel's first prime minister. Subsequently, he founded Operation Gideon, the first illegal immigration network that brought Jews from Europe to the Palestine Mandate territory, directed it during the War of Independence, and later converted the network into one that purchased arms from Czechoslovakia and other European countries. After statehood was established, he became deputy defense minister and part of Ben-Gurion's kitchen cabinet on defense policy until he was named to head the "office without a name"—the operation concerned with Jews in

* In 1920, Tel Hai, a Jewish settlement in the northern Galilee, was the site of the first major military encounter between the Jewish settlers and the Arabs.

Eastern Europe—that smuggled out, and even purchased, Jews from countries now under Communist rule.

Avigur not only has sought personal anonymity but has insisted that any project in which he participates must be tightly controlled and free from public inquiry, with all decision-making done by a handful of people who can be trusted ideologically and by virtue of years of association. Thus, his office was totally committed to the principle that any work done to help Jews leave the USSR would be achieved under strict military censorship, with responsibility only to the head of government. Nominally a part of Israel's Foreign Office, Avigur was responsible only to the prime minister. He believed that Russian Jews would be freed from the USSR through secret negotiation, the tried method that had been utilized for the illegal immigration and later for securing emigration for Romanian, Bulgarian, and Polish Jews during the 1950s. When Avigur retired to his kibbutz at the end of 1969, having reached the age of 70, his handpicked successor, Nechemiah Levanon, attempted to continue his policies, but Prime Minister Meir continued to rely heavily on advice from Avigur as had Ben-Gurion before her.

These matters were not known, and could not be known, to the Jews in the USSR. But they knew that Israel—their promised land—did not heed their cries. And it was precisely that inactivity (perceived by them as indifference) that had prompted the Georgian Jews to plead for broadcast of their appeal over Kol Israel, to implore Mrs. Meir, Ambassador Tekoah, and the UN to publish and distribute it, and to repeat their requests after one hundred days had elapsed. In the lead article in *Iton Bet,* "The Jews Break Their Silence," Soviet Jewish leaders also recognized that fact. They commented, in connection with the Letter of the 18 and other open statements, that it was these that eventually "forced the Israeli government to turn its attention to the situation of the Jews in the Soviet Union."

Two factors helped to produce change. First, Soviet Jews, through their contacts with the more experienced democratic movement and then, through their own initiatives, had learned how to reach Western news media. They thus had created possibilities of public attention in the West without any assistance from Israel. Second, recent Soviet immigrants to Israel, although small in number, vigorously insisted that the policy of silence should be terminated. Furthermore, they received information from their friends and relatives in the USSR about activities, letters, and appeals occurring there and began to reveal them publicly, or at least to insist that the government do so.

Earlier, in August 1969, after Israeli newspapers had discussed the issue and the matter had been raised on the floor of the Knesset, twenty new Soviet immigrants had managed to get an audience with Prime Minister Meir. They declared that Israel's policy was a betrayal of Soviet Jewry. Mrs. Meir made no commitment to the group, but events forced her hand. The dramatic appeal of the Georgians, including their letter to her, was being circulated in *samizdat* form in Israel and might soon be more generally known in the rest of the world. Mrs. Meir decided to act.

One hundred and six days after their first appeal, on November 19, 1969, the Israeli prime minister read the appeal of the eighteen Georgian families to the Knesset and acknowledged, for the first time, individual letters such as the October letter from Tina Brodetskaya. She said:

> The USSR had no alternative but to realize that it had failed, after half a century and more, to silence the Jewish voice. It had failed to force the severance of millions of Jews from Jewish and Hebrew creativity and its leaders should have the courage to admit their failure and to let the Jews go.
>
> We sincerely believe the day will come when we shall witness a large wave of immigration from the USSR, of old and young alike.
>
> We have always wanted to live at peace with the Soviet Union. We never sought to interfere in its internal affairs just as we never expected the Soviet Union to interfere in ours. The nature of the Soviet regime is of no consequence when it comes to the question of internal relations, and Israel cannot be blamed in the slightest for the state of these relations at present.
>
> But we cannot abandon our legitimate interest in the fate of Soviet Jewry for the sake of some doubtful friendship with the Soviet Union, a country which, by its actions in this region, has put a question mark on our very existence.

Once Mrs. Meir had spoken, the Soviet Union was compelled to acknowledge, abroad at least, the situation in Georgia. On November 29, a Soviet overseas broadcast charged that the Letter of the 18 was a forgery perpetrated by the Israeli government. Shortly thereafter, Novosti, the Soviet overseas press service, in a statement distributed by the Soviet Mission to the UN, assured UN members that the eighteen signatories had continued on their jobs and were not being molested.

In Georgia itself, officials asked the signers to withdraw their signatures and warned worshippers at the Tbilisi synagogue that more such activity would be dangerous to the Jewish community.

The Georgian Jews answered with more petitions. One, addressed to U Thant and virtually identical to the Letter of the Moscow 25 and the Riga 22, was signed by, among others, the Georgian representative at the earlier meeting of the VKK. The Georgians were making it clear that they were a part of the total Jewish movement. In February 1970, Albert Mikhailashvili, a 34-year-old engineer from Poti who was the principal author of the Letter of the 18, wrote from Moscow:

> Nothing has changed in our lives except that they are getting worse from day to day. All the eighteen families including mine are in a critical condition. I am referring to thirty-two children and 104 adults. If I were the only one in distress, I wouldn't have cried for help. I am truly and honestly crying for help for many others who are suffering with me. I have not been working for over a year. I have sold all my belongings and ever since have been living in a cellar with nine other members of the family. Rats run about in this humid and terrible cellar, making our lives unbearable. To hell with my own life! But what about the children's lives? The tears have dried on our faces. The children are in great agony and they don't understand why they are being punished so!

The number of people who signed the collective letters increased and so did the number of addresses to which the letters were sent. In May 1970, an American visitor to Tbilisi, Joel Sprayregen, reported that, as a foreign Jew who had been to Israel, he had been greeted with extraordinary enthusiasm at the impressive, well-maintained, and vital Tbilisi synagogue and that he had been repeatedly told that 90% of the Georgian Jews would go to Israel if given the opportunity.

After the eighteen families and other Georgian Jews were permitted to leave for Israel in April 1971, the OVIR offices in Georgia were deluged with applications. Most were granted. The Georgians constituted the largest single group of immigrants to Israel in 1971, and as of the fall of 1973, 15,000 to 20,000 Georgian Jews had emigrated to Israel. Clearly, the Soviet authorities placed fewer obstacles in their way than for Jews from any other republic. Whether that was because they constituted less of a technological and educational loss to the USSR or because the regime was unusually sensitive to Jewish nationalist expression in an already highly nationalistic area, or whether both motives and others were present, is not known. What is indisputable is that the Georgian Jews have a special flair, a picturesqueness and eloquence that aided their cause and later found expression in ways that will be subsequently described.

It is a quirk of history that one of the most remote and least educated segments of Soviet Jewry should have captured the imagination of their fellow-Jews and forced the government to some action—albeit a limited one. Yet the Georgian Jews and the Letter of the 18 were symbolically important to Soviet Jews and thereafter to world Jewry— perhaps precisely because of their inaccessibility, their strangeness for most Ashkenazi Jews, who had previously caricatured them, somewhat contemptuously, as flower peddlers or thieves. Their seemingly sudden activism was reassuring confirmation that the movement, and support for it, was widespread and that no Soviet Jew, no matter how remote, could be counted out. And in the West, where most Jews had never heard of or seen a Jew from Soviet Georgia, it was as if the Maccabees had again arisen on the opposite side of the moon—a miracle of Jewish survival.

VILNA:
The Right to Be Jewish

CHAPTER 8

Few cities have a more Jewish or more tragic heritage than Vilna—Vilnius in Lithuanian—the capital of Soviet Lithuania. Vilna used to be called the Jerusalem of the North, because of its flourishing Jewish religious, cultural, and educational institutions. There are few Jewish communities anywhere in the West or in Israel where some Jews have not settled who had relatives in Lithuania or whose friends or ancestors did not live full Jewish lives in Vilna.

Of the 170,000 Jews of Lithuania at the beginning of World War II, about 100,000 lived in Vilna, where they constituted approximately 40% of the population of that city. Now, according to the latest census, there are 16,000 Jews in a population of about 250,000 (although some Vilna Jews claim they constitute 10% of the city's total population). Clearly, more than 100,000 Lithuanian Jews perished during the Holocaust.

The story of Vilna and its Jews strongly resembles that of Riga. The sister Baltic states suffered the same sequence of interwar independence, reactionary regimes, incorporation into the Soviet Union in June 1940, Nazi invasion in June 1941, and Soviet domination from 1945 to the present. But relatively little is known of the growth of the Jewish movement in Vilna, even though the first collective letter of Jewish protest was written in Vilna on February 15, 1968. Unlike the lonely defiance of the roughly contemporary individual letters of Kochubiyevsky in Kiev and Kazakov in Moscow, it was a group protest, which bespoke careful preparation, organization, and thought. Unlike other collective

letters that were written eighteen or more months later, it was not a cry
to "Let my people go" but an insistence upon the right to be Jews—
to be free of anti-Semitism. Yet its context was strikingly premonitory
of things to come, and its themes are recurrent, although it was un-
coordinated with other cities. It was careful yet daring; subtle yet
overt. The letter was addressed to Comrade A. Sniečkus, first secretary
of the Central Committee of the Lithuanian Communist Party. In it,
the Vilna Jews called attention to Ponar, a forest on the outskirts of
the city, and the Ninth Fort, a military structure in a suburb of Kovno
(Kaunas, Lithuania's second city), where mass murders of Lithuanian
Jews occurred. They noted that no monuments had been built to commemorate these sites, though edifices had been erected in recognition
of places where a hundred innocent Lithuanians died. The writers of
the letter lamented anti-Israel propaganda and cartoons in the Lithuanian press which had "revived anti-Semitic passions . . . we cannot
be silent when the press publishes material that nourishes local judeo-
phobia." Accusing leading government figures of openly promoting anti-
Semitism, they named incidents involving the deputy minister of trade,
the deputy chairman of television, the president of the Pedagogical
Institute.

> Here are the facts. During the entire period, not a single Jewish stu-
> dent living in Lithuania (except for a few children of privileged
> persons) was given a state scholarship to continue his studies at insti-
> tutions of higher learning in Moscow or Leningrad. Not a single Jew
> originating from Lithuania has taken postgraduate courses in the
> institutes of Moscow or Leningrad. Not a single Jewish Communist
> has attended the Academy of Social Sciences or the Party University.
>   And here are the facts about the distribution of cadres. Ten percent
> of the inhabitants of Vilna are Jews. Until now, not a single Jew has
> ever been elected chairman, deputy chairman, or secretary of the city
> or of the city's four regional executive committees. . . . Not a single
> Jew has been elected judge of a people's court. Not a single Jew has
> been elected to any higher position in the trade unions. During the
> entire postwar era, not a single representative of the Jewish youth has
> risen to a leading position in the state, party or trade union activity—
> while at the same time the mass of Lithuanian cadres has been edu-
> cated and promoted during the postwar years. In fact, only a handful
> of meritorious Jewish revolutionaries of the older generation are still
> merely tolerated in higher positions, and they are now being hurriedly
> pushed out to pension as soon as possible.

They decried the punishment of those who "dared to teach a group
of young Jews the alphabet of their native tongue." They protested the

neglect, abandonment, and destruction of synagogues and Jewish cemeteries, the use of Jewish tombstones in public buildings: "Pink marble from the old Jewish cemetery in Vilna was used for the pedestal of the Pushkin monument. . . . This act of vandalism insults not only the Jews but everyone who respects Pushkin's genius." They noted that "even the Hitlerites had left Jewish cemeteries untouched throughout the period of their occupation of Lithuania." Yet, they continued,

> the situation of the Jews is considerably better in Lithuania than in other parts of the USSR. . . . During the entire postwar period in Lithuania there was only one bloody pogrom, in Plunge in 1958, while, according to our information, not fewer than twenty pogroms occurred in the Ukraine.

Commenting on the observation that "emigrational tendencies are increasing among the Jewish inhabitants," they stated:

> It is known that if the borders would be opened for emigration today, some 80% of the entire Jewish populace would leave Soviet Lithuania and depart for Israel. These people would leave everything here— despite the unsettled conditions in the Near East, despite the fact that our people in this country are used to a damp climate and would find it difficult to acclimatize there, despite the fact that almost no one among the Lithuanian Jews knows Hebrew any more or observes religious traditions, despite the fact that their present qualifications (most economically active people are employed in service occupations) would not make it easy for them to become integrated into Israel's society.
>
> We are confronted with a paradox here. We are not wanted here, we are being completely oppressed, forcibly denationalized, and even publicly insulted in the press—while at the same time we are forcibly kept here. As the Lithuanian proverb goes, "He beats and he screams at the same time."
>
> We are not speaking to you about the noble Communist ideals, about the equality of men and nations, about proletarian internationalism. All those slogans have been thrown into the dustheap of demagogy long ago. . . . Do all in your power to put down the menacingly rising wave of anti-Semitism. It is not too late yet. If that is not done now, Lithuania will again "adorn itself" with new Ponars and Ninth Forts.

In conclusion, they

> decided not to make public the surnames of the twenty-six signers of this document. We know well how people who protested against

flourishing anti-Semitism in the Soviet Union at one time or another
were dealt with summarily. The Party has taught us to be watchful,
and we have to be watchful now as we write to the Central Committee
of the Lithuanian Communist Party.
What painful irony.

They had reason to be watchful. Among them were men who knew
of prison camps, of arrests, of official harassment. One of the signers,
Munik (Zalman) Holtsberg, a 47-year-old journalist, had been detained
by the KGB in 1963 and accused of making Zionist propaganda because
he had read a poem in honor of the 100,000 Jewish victims at a
memorial ceremony at Kovno.* Others—following the example of Riga
Jews at Rumbuli and Kiev Jews at Babi Yar—had sought to maintain
their tragic historic heritage by similarly commemorating Ponar and the
Ninth Fort.
The Jews of Vilna did not continue to be unwilling to sign letters.
On September 30, 1969, Jonas Damba, a 40-year-old Vilna Jew, who
had been seeking to go to Israel to join the sole surviving member of his
family—a younger brother from whom he had been separated since
1941—wrote to the International Red Cross, appealing OVIR's refusal
of permission because of his being a citizen of the Soviet Union and
"materially secure." It is a tragic, desperate letter—personal and nonpolitical. There were many like it—largely unpublished. By the beginning of 1970, the tone of letters was sharper. The long waiting and
despair had changed entreaty to demand, request to struggle. On February 1, 1970, a group of Vilna Jews sent a signed collective letter to U
Thant, the UN Human Rights Commission, and Golda Meir, reviewing
the recent history of Lithuanian Jews and Soviet Jews:

Terrible is the fate of a person without a homeland, tragic are the
ways of a people expelled from the land of its ancestors. The two-
thousand-year-old orphanhood of our people is an unquestionable
example of this. For twenty centuries our plea for shelter could be
heard, but there is no country in Europe that, while giving a roof over
the head of the "eternal Jew," has not tainted its own history with
innocent Jewish blood. Perhaps it is the subconscious awareness of
this terrible guilt that is the source of the hatred toward us. . . .
We no longer want to be called guests. We don't want to be hostages

* In 1969, the KGB directed Holtsberg to write an article depicting "imperialist" Israel as a place where Soviet Jews who emigrated would suffer discrimination and poverty. His refusal led to his loss of employment as a
journalist.

or lightning rods in the game of the black passions of the world gone mad.

We, the undersigned, have repeatedly applied to the Soviet authorities with the request to allow us to emigrate for permanent residence to the State of Israel. All our requests were refused, without explanations, without motivation. All this has driven us to appeal to you, to the world public—help us, heed our plea, use your prestige so that we should be allowed to go to Israel.

Ten days later, a trial involving a Lithuanian Jewish youth began in Ryazan, an old Russian city 200 kilometers south of Moscow. Ryazan is noted, among other things, for its university, which includes an Institute of Radio Engineering (RIRE) and facilities for training teachers and other engineers. Since Lithuanian Jews could rarely secure admission to universities in Moscow and Leningrad, numbers of them had been admitted to, and received their training in, Ryazan. Among them was Simon Grilius, born in 1945 in Klaipeda (formerly Memel), a Lithuanian seaport, where his family continued to reside. Grilius maintained contact with friends in Vilna and Kovno. In the middle and late 1960s, these young Jews, like young intellectuals elsewhere in the Soviet Union, were intensely interested in *samizdat* literature. Leon Uris's *Exodus*, Randolph Churchill's *The Six Day War*, Dubnov's *History of the Jews*, various essays by Jabotinsky, a few volumes of Jewish encyclopedias, and Hebrew textbooks circulated at the universities in Kovno, Vilna, and Ryazan. Grilius possessed these and other *samizdat* works and shared them with his friends at RIRE. At Ryazan, he had become friendly with two young Jews, Yury Vudka (born in 1947) and his brother Valery (born in 1950), from the large industrial center of Dnepropetrovsk in the central Ukraine, and with Oleg Frolov, Semyon Zaslavsky, and Yevgeny Martimonov, all born in 1948. (Frolov, although he had a Russian father, identified himself with the Jewish people.) All of them were interested in and read and circulated Jewish *samizdat* materials. But their interests were far broader.

According to *Khronika*, the six students formed an illegal group— a "Marxist party of a new type." Yury Vudka (described as "an external student and a turner at the Ryazan agricultural machinery factory") wrote—under the pseudonym L. Borin—a pamphlet called *The Decline of Capital* which was the programmatic document of the group. In July and August 1969, the KGB arrested the members of the group and confiscated a typewriter, photographic equipment, and literature that was later submitted as evidence in court: (a) *The Decline of Capital*, (b) *Dror* (Hebrew for Trumpets of Freedom)—on the individual in contemporary society, (c) *Marxism and the Magicians*—on the events in Czechoslovakia, (d) *What Lies Ahead* (in Russian and Ukrainian)— a version of *The Decline of Capital* specially written to be "intelligible to workers." The arrests were preceded by a denunciation by two members of the organization—Martimonov and Zaslavsky—and by their confession of guilt. Charges were brought under Articles 70 (anti-Soviet propaganda) and 72 (anti-Soviet organization). Apparently the group was linked with other towns; a group in Saratov, sentenced a month earlier, also had *The Decline of Capital* as its programmatic document.

The case was heard in the Ryazan Regional People's Court, February 10-19, 1970. According to *Khronika*,

> The trial was held behind locked doors—entry was by special pass. Besides KGB officials, there were present in the courtroom "representatives" of large factories, educational institutes, military academies, and the regional committees of the Communist Party and the Komsomol. Altogether there were not more than thirty people in court, including relatives and fiancées of the accused. More than twenty persons appeared as witnesses. [Some came from the Moscow area, some from Leningrad, Kiev, Saratov, and other towns.] The accused pleaded guilty, but when the sentences were delivered, the judge remarked that the repentance of Grilius and the Vudka brothers was insincere.
>
> The decision to plead guilty was taken by the accused at the suggestion of the investigator, who cited Article 38 of the Russian Criminal Code (extenuating circumstances) on the role of sincere confession; in court, however, the accused learned from their lawyers of the existence of Article 39 (aggravating circumstances), which essentially cancels out Article 38 if the deed is defined as a group action.
>
> The court accepted that contact with persons abroad, which had been established by preliminary investigation, consisted in no more than the transmission of *The Decline of Capital* to a Czechoslovak citizen and a Dutch citizen. It was also established that the group engaged in the propaganda of its views and the recruitment of new members, seminars being held on the book *The Decline of Capital*.
>
> Procurator Dubtsov demanded for the accused: Yury Vudka—seven years of strict-regime camps and three years' exile; Froliv and Grilius —five years' strict-regime; V. Vudka—three years' corrective labor. The sentence of the court differed from the procurator's demands in that Yu. Vudka's term of exile was reduced to a year, while Grilius and Frolov each received three additional years of exile.
>
> In view of the fact that Zaslavsky was said in court to have come

voluntarily to KGB headquarters and given frank testimony, the court gave him a suspended sentence of three years; Martimonov, too, received a suspended sentence of three years as being seriously ill (he had previously suffered one heart attack, and during the trial his condition suggested that another attack was impending).

Several dozen people who had read *The Decline of Capital* or who had known of the existence of the group but not reported it were expelled from the Komsomol and from their institutes.

Many Jews in Lithuania were aware of the trial since the KGB had widely interrogated Jews in Vilna and Kovno from the summer of 1969 to the winter of 1970. Grilius had been arrested at his home in Klaipeda, which was searched, and *samizdat* documents were confiscated. Other searches had occurred among the witnesses interrogated. Both before and after the trial, numerous meetings were called by various faculties at the universities of Kovno and Vilna. Students at these compulsory indoctrinations were addressed by party and Komsomol officials who warned the students that "Zionist organizations" discovered in Lithuania had been duplicating and distributing Zionist literature, which had now been confiscated. This was connected to the Ryazan defendants, notably Grilius, and the offending Lithuanian students were identified and warned. As a result of the Ryazan trial, some Jewish university students were expelled.

Additional information about the trial became known when relatives of Grilius and some of the witnesses were permitted to emigrate to Israel in the early spring of 1971, to be followed in 1973 by Valery Vudka. Romiel Orliok, a long-time friend of Grilius, noted that the KGB had interrogated him twelve times and had searched his home. At the trial, questioned about his connection with the defendants and his knowledge of their distribution of *samizdat,* Orliok had acknowledged receipt of Jewish documents from Grilius and the existence of discussion groups among Lithuanian Jewish groups but had denied their activity was anti-Soviet since its sole basis was education about Jewish culture and Israel and the desire of the participants and the defendants to emigrate to Israel. Orliok reported an additional exchange between Judge Matveyev and Yury Vudka:

Vudka: The only people in the USSR without its own schools, language, and homeland is the Jewish nation.
Judge: But the Jews are dispersed over all the territories of the Soviet Union.
Vudka: So what? In Vilna there are Polish schools; in Moldavia,

Romanian ones. Neither Poles nor Romanians have national territories in the USSR. Only Jews have none.

Judge: You are a nationalist!

Vudka: If a man who desires for his people culture, schools, and books in his own language, and study of his homeland, is a nationalist, then I am a nationalist.

Among the *samizdat* documents found was an appeal by Bertrand Russell to the Soviet government demanding the cessation of anti-Semitic activity and the right of emigration for Jews. The prosecutor, Dubtsov, angrily asked the defendants to identify "Bertrok and Russel," these "two anti-Soviet propagandists," and to indicate "what anti-Soviet library was the source of the document." (This was apparently even painful to Judge Matveyev, a more sophisticated man.)

Orliok further reported that after the judgment was read, Grilius called out: *"L'shanah habah b'Yerushalaim. Lehitraot b'Yerushalaim"* (Next year in Jerusalem. We will meet in Jerusalem).

In prison Grilius and the Vudka brothers demonstrated their commitment as Jews. Sent to Potma in Mordovia, Grilius insisted on wearing a *kipah* (skull cap) on Sabbath and on Jewish holidays, for which he was placed in solitary confinement for fifteen days. Yury Vudka demonstrated in protest against the refusal of the authorities to make kosher food available and was eventually punished by transfer to the dreaded Vladimir prison complex. All requested Hebrew textbooks, and they joined other Jewish prisoners from later trials, who were sent to the same camp complex, in hunger strikes, renunciation of Soviet citizenship, requests for Israeli citizenship, and the varied militant camp activity characteristic of some Jewish political prisoners.

Reported promptly and in detail by *Khronika,* the Ryazan trial remained largely unpublicized in the West for better than a year, and when finally reported in some detail in the London journal *Jews in Eastern Europe,* it was referred to as "the unknown trial." Reports in Jewish publications in April 1971 stated that "news only recently reached the West," although such news had been available for fourteen months. An article in the Tel Aviv newspaper *Maariv* described the case as one of "six Jewish youths tried for Zionist activities." In fact, many details of the Ryazan trial had been known in Israel by the spring of 1970. By late summer, reports from the USSR made its main outlines clear: The defendants had been involved in the dissent movement; they had been arrested for democratic activities; like many young Jews, they were both democrats and Zionists, and inevitably they were involved in the *samizdat* activities of both movements. Insistence on full national rights for Jews and the right to leave were part of the demand for human rights in the USSR. But information about Ryazan was consciously suppressed in Israel because the defendants had a "democratic" coloration and the Israeli government avoided any link with the democratic movement or any criticism of internal Soviet affairs. Only the Zionist goal of *aliyah* to Israel was supportable. The Ryazan prisoners were not included in any early listings of prisoners of conscience. They became known only as a consequence of the later sentencing of other Jews for "Zionist" activities. When the other prisoners, in solidarity, insisted that their fellow-prisoners from Ryazan also receive support, some revision in attitude was necessary. So, too, some Jews coming to Israel from Lithuania could not understand why Grilius and Vudka should be forgotten men. Jewish activists in Riga expressed outrage at the silence about Ryazan and saw no excuse for ignoring men whose bravery had resulted in their loss of freedom.

A few weeks after the Ryazan trial, despite some apprehension, fourteen more Vilna Jews addressed the UN and President Zalman Shazar of Israel. Since 1956, they had attempted to emigrate to Israel but had been rejected by OVIR with explanations that "You are working, you are a separate family unit, you are young and have received your education in the USSR." The education levy was two and a half years in the future, but OVIR comments at the time prompted them to state: "If the Soviet government considers us to be in debt for our education, we are ready to leave behind all the belongings we have earned by our work and to go home [Israel] with just a rucksack on our backs."

By now, the Jews of Vilna were contributing to *Iton,* which, in its second issue, published their long, angry tirade against Vergelis, Dragunsky, and the other Jews who had participated in the press conference of March 4, 1970 and reflecting their own militant participation in the Jewish movement:

> Do you understand what a shameful step you took on March 4? By consenting to play the dummy in this huge farce, you have . . . rejected everything, your people, your conscience, your honor. This evening of lies will long be remembered. . . . From now on, always, when the authorities need this, *there you will be*. History repeats itself: They have always tried to persecute the Jews by the hands of the Jews themselves. . . .
> Now you too have chosen their way—dishonor on a full stomach.

But do you realize that your right to call yourselves Jews out loud
has been won not by your licking of hands, but by the courage of
those who in 1948, 1956, and 1967 have defended this right in the
sands of the Sinai and on the banks of the Jordan?
And this makes your words of today sound even more vile.

The militancy of the Vilna Jews was ultimately rewarded. When the
flow of emigration commenced, Jews from Vilna and other Lithuanian
cities received exit visas far more easily than did those from any other
area except Soviet Georgia. Since Lithuania already had a strong
nationalist and religious movement, and historic resentment against the
Russian occupiers remained commonplace, the Soviet authorities apparently feared additional, virulent nationalist resentment. Jews from
the Baltic republics flowed out by the thousands, but those who were
highly trained still could not go. Continuing to protest, they joined their
fellow-Jews throughout the USSR in the growth of the Jewish movement.

THE HIJACK AFFAIR
AND THE JUNE ARRESTS

CHAPTER 9

By the late spring of 1970, Jewish discontent, ignited in 1967, had produced a fast-growing movement. The simmering anger of Soviet Jews had erupted, and the relative restraint of the Soviet authorities had worn thin. Riga, Leningrad, Moscow, Kiev, Soviet Georgia, and Lithuania showed clear signs of organized activity. Of the five largest cities of Jewish population (Moscow, Leningrad, and Kiev are largest) only Odessa and Kharkov did not demonstrate the existence of a well-organized movement, yet both had functioning groups and some militant leaders with connections to the movement elsewhere. Among other communities of major Jewish population, the ferment in Kishinev, Minsk, and Chernovtsy was undeniable, and some signs had begun to appear in Sverdlovsk and Novosibirsk. Virtually all the agitation was based on the claimed right to leave the USSR. The government was being told, "You have only two choices: Let me go to Israel or send me to Siberia." Which choice would it make?

The answer was not long in coming. On the morning of June 15, 1970, in a series of well-planned raids, the KGB arrested more than a score of people and simultaneously searched the homes of more than sixty Jewish activists and movement leaders in Riga, Leningrad, Moscow, Kiev, Odessa, and Kharkov. That evening's Leningrad paper *Vecherny Leningrad* and the next morning's *Leningradskaya Pravda* carried a brief report: "On June 15, a group of criminals trying to seize a scheduled airplane was arrested at Smolny Airport. Investigations are in process." Given the Soviet policy against carrying news of

crime, even this laconic notice was unusual. Almost six months passed
before there was any official comment on what had come to be known
as the Leningrad hijack plot.

Although airplane hijacking was not as frequent or as anxiety-pro-
ducing as it became later, in the summer of 1970 it was viewed with
both abhorrence and alarm by most of the civilized world. Most countries had expressed their intent to extirpate it. Israel, world Jewry, and
most Soviet Jews shared that opinion.

In the days and weeks following June 15, interrogations and searches
continued and additional arrests were made. After a brief initial silence,
Soviet Jews were the first to find their voices. But there were aspects
of the case about which they did not speak at first. Only *Khronika,* in
its issue of June 30, 1970, carried the news in its typically understated way:

> At 8:35 a.m. on June 15, at Smolny Airport in Leningrad, a group
> of twelve people were detained in the vicinity of an AN-2 aircraft
> (bound for Priozersk) and later arrested.
>   They were: Eduard Kuznetsov (Riga), Aleksandr Murzhenko (Lo-
> zovaya, Ukraine), Yury Fedorov (Moscow), E. Kuznetsov's wife Silva
> Zalmanson and her two brothers—one an officer of the reserve (his
> name is not known to the *Chronicle*), the other Isaiah [*sic*], aged 21—
> (all of Riga), Mr. and Mrs. Khnokh (Riga), Penson, an artist (Riga),
> Mark Dymshits, a pilot aged 45, his 15-year-old daughter (who is
> now in a children's home) and his wife (Leningrad).
>   (Kuznetsov, Murzhenko, and Fedorov have previously served terms
> under Article 70, Part 1, and Article 72 of the Russian Criminal
> Code. . . .)
>   On June 15, eight persons were arrested in Leningrad: Gilel Butman,
> Goldfeld, Solomon Dreizner, Lassal Kaminsky, L. Korenblit, Vladimir
> Mogilever, David Chernoglaz; Lev Yagman, from Leningrad, was
> arrested on the way to Odessa.
>   On June 15 searches were carried out under Article 64-a of the
> Russian Criminal Code: in Moscow at the homes of V. Svechinsky,
> D. Drabkin, and V. Slepak. There were forty-one searches in Lenin-
> grad and other searches in Riga and Kharkov.

Even *Khronika* had omitted the names of some of those who were
initially apprehended. Dymshits's older daughter, 18-year-old Elizaveta,
was in the group at Smolny. Other persons from Riga included Iosif
Mendelevich, 23; Mendel Bodnya, 30; and Anatoly Altman, 28. Four
of the group—Leib and Meri Khnokh, Silva Zalmanson, and Boris
Penson—had, in fact, been detained at 4 a.m. in the forest near

Priozersk, a town on Lake Ladoga, 40 miles from the Finnish border. As Meri Khnokh later told the story, "Twenty men suddenly emerged from the darkness, shooting in the air and squirting gas into our eyes. We were bound to each other, back to back, bundled into waiting trucks and taken to the Leningrad KGB."

Of the twenty-four people placed under arrest on June 15, there were two readily distinguishable groups: those arrested near the airport and in the forest, most of whom came from or lived in Riga, except for the Dymshits family from Leningrad and the two non-Jews, Fedorov and Murzhenko; and the Leningrad residents, who were seized at their homes, places of work, or while they were on vacation. The Leningrad arrestees constituted many of the top activists in the Leningrad organization. Their arrests decimated the leadership of the group. It was not just the arrests that caused disarray within the movement. Searches, interrogations, and additional arrests continued through much of the summer and into the fall. Viktor Boguslavsky was arrested in Leningrad on July 9. Other Leningrad arrests soon afterward included Grigory Vertlib (who was subsequently released without charges being filed), Gilya (Hillel) Shur, a 34-year-old engineer (on August 5), Mikhail Korenblit and Viktor Shtilbans, a 30-year-old physician (October 27). Aleksandr Galperin and David Rabinovich were arrested in Kishinev in late July; Arkady Voloshin and Lazar Trakhtenberg were detained in August. In Riga, Arkady Shpilberg and Boris Maftser were arrested on August 5. Additional Riga defendants were Ruta Aleksandrovich, arrested October 7, and Mikhail Shepshelovich, arrested October 16. The Kishinev defendants were completed by the arrests on November 17 of Gari Kirzhner and Semyon Levit. Ultimately, thirty-four people were to stand trial. Meri Khnokh, who was an expectant mother, and Mark Dymshits's wife and daughters were released.

Not only the prosecution actions created confusion. The movement itself was deeply split over the proper response. As early as December 1969, Jews in Leningrad, including top leaders in the Leningrad organization, had discussed the feasibility of hijacking an airplane. Some months later, that discussion had been extended to Riga, and some knowledge of it doubtless had reached other cities, notably Kishinev and Moscow. After the arrests of June 15, the leaders, at least, knew that there had in fact been a hijack attempt. There was great anxiety that it might compromise the tremendous momentum the movement had achieved in the previous half-year. Furthermore, it was known that except for the arrestees at the airport and in the forest, most of the defendants had not been involved in the hijack attempt, whatever they might have known about the plans of the others. To many in the movement, it seemed singularly important to separate the hijack-attempt defendants from those who appeared to have been arrested because of their activism in the movement and in the effort to go to Israel. But that was not easily done. For months, it was not known when the trial or trials would occur, where they would take place, who, or how many defendants, would have to respond to charges, and what the charges would be. As late as early November, it was believed that a mass trial of most of the defendants would begin on November 20 in Leningrad. Even after the trial began on December 15, Western newsmen were unable to learn how many and who were being tried. Furthermore, there was no doubt that the KGB had advance knowledge of the hijack plans. The broad geographic scope of their June 15 arrests and raids indicated careful advance planning. It was widely feared that a KGB provocateur had infiltrated the group. The most common suspect was Mark Dymshits, who was known to be the principal promoter of the hijack plans. (The suspicion has not subsequently been confirmed.)

Dymshits, an airplane pilot born in 1927, was a latecomer to the Leningrad group. After World War II, he had been trained in a state security school and then had gone to flying school. After graduation, he served in the air force and attained the rank of major, but—because of his Jewish origins, he felt—he was unable to find civilian work as a pilot in his home city of Leningrad. Consequently, he went to Bukhara in Soviet Central Asia, where he was employed as a commercial pilot. His wife, Alevtina Ivanovna, was a Russian laboratory technician. They had two daughters, born in 1951 and 1955. Dymshits was a member of the Communist Party and was not expelled until his arrest. For many years he lived in Bukhara, and even after receiving additional training in an agricultural institute and working elsewhere as an agricultural engineer, he would return periodically to Bukhara. In addition to his flair for adventure and change, he was apparently a ladies' man and several times had been separated and reunited with his wife. She worried about his enormous attraction to flying and was distressed by his frequent returns to Bukhara and a flying career. Consequently, she had secured a divorce, although they continued a relationship thereafter. Dymshits not only had suffered frustration from anti-Jewish discrimination, he had also developed some affirmative Jewish enthusiasms and wanted to go to Israel. After the Six-Day War, he decided to study Hebrew. He met Butman in 1969 and began to attend the *ulpan* taught by Lev Korenblit. Meantime, his sense of adventure and his grandiosity led him to conclude that since he could not freely emigrate to Israel, he would build a balloon which would take him there. Abandoning that idea, he determined to build a small plane. When he relinquished that fantasy, he concluded that it was necessary to hijack a plane. Since such a task could not be accomplished alone, he decided to locate people who might think along similar lines. He broached the matter to Butman, and some of the Leningrad activists discussed variations of the plan. Among those who were later involved in the discussions was Eduard Kuznetsov.

Kuznetsov was born in 1939. His father, who was Russian, died during the war in 1941, and his mother, who was Jewish and who raised him in Moscow under difficult, impoverished circumstances, registered him as Russian on his passport. A precocious student and gifted writer, Kuznetsov, while in the philosophy department of the University of Moscow, became involved in the early stages of the democratic movement. *Syntax,* the first of the important underground literary journals, appeared in 1958–60. Twenty-year-old Kuznetsov had a hand in its production, as he did in 1960 in the shortlived *samizdat* journal *Boomerang.* In 1961, *Phoenix,* the most outspoken of these publications, was first issued. Kuznetsov contributed to and helped edit this 140-page anthology, devoted primarily to poetry. In that year, also, the young democrats began public demonstrations for the first time. Kuznetsov and a friend, Ilya Bokshtein, organized a group of Moscow University students to read the poems of Vladimir Mayakovsky, the lyrical poet of freedom in the early years of Communism. A major square in downtown Moscow bears Mayakovsky's name although, by 1961, his poems were disapproved of and largely unavailable. In Mayakovsky Square each Sunday, the group read his poems aloud, to the consternation of the KGB, which could hardly arrest them for reading Mayakovsky's poems there. Little by little, the number of people attending the readings increased, and as the crowds grew larger, other works by the young poets in the group were read aloud. Finally, one Sunday, when the crowd numbered more than a thousand, Bokshtein climbed up on the statue of Mayakovsky and delivered a passionate oration against Soviet tyranny. The KGB seized him and Kuznetsov. A melee ensued and many were arrested. Kuznetsov was tried and sentenced to seven years. In the camps, he came to know political prisoners from all over the USSR with whom he made common cause in resistance to the prison authorities, and he developed intense feelings about his Jewish origins, ceased to regard himself as a Russian, and sought to have his passport changed to reflect that he was Jewish. By the time he was released in 1968, he had determined that he must leave the USSR. He had been married shortly before his imprisonment, but his wife had not waited for his release. Abandoned by her, forbidden by the terms of his release from living in Moscow, where his ailing mother resided, unable to secure a change in his passport, prevented from getting work in other cities such as Leningrad, where he had friends—he met a young Zionist activist and engineer from Riga, Silva Zalmanson, married her in January 1970, and resettled in Riga. There he found employment as an English translator in a psychiatric hospital, and he also found a cause—the Jewish repatriation movement.

Soon there was a confluence of his troubled youth, his cultural and emotional turmoil, and his desire to leave the Soviet Union. He described this in a diary, which he prepared when he was in prison again and which was smuggled out to the West in the fall of 1972. His entry for December 19, 1970, written during the course of his trial, read:

> How did all this start? It was the end of February [1970] when Silva introduced me to Butman.
> One day we went to see the modest memorial in the place where thousands of Jews were killed by the Nazis. On the way back, Butman talked of this and that. I felt quite strongly what he was leading up to.
> "What are the chances of getting out of here?" he asked finally.
> "At present, nil," I answered. "That's how it will be in the near future unless . . ."
> "Unless what?"
> "Unless an episode occurs that they can't hush up. As long as we think only of ourselves, nothing will happen. It is not a question of a few people leaving but the problem of all of us. The problem of free emigration for all who wish to leave. Only in this way will we get anything, and not through letters of entreaty to the Kremlin and the UN."
> "What do you suggest?" asked Butman.
> "At the moment I have no concrete suggestion. I don't know the situation or the people in Riga. When I speak of an episode, I don't mean a provocation. Many people have reached the end of their patience after years of waiting and arbitrary refusals. One may suppose that one of these days a group of people united by despair will commit an unprecedented act. There is no doubt that they will

suffer greatly. But for the others this will be the first break in the Wall of China."

"In spite of all this, what can we do?"

"What do I know? One can organize a group of 30 or 40 people who will hold a hunger strike against the turning of Paragraphs 13 and 15 of the Declaration of Human Rights into a dead letter. We need a serious hunger strike, not one of those strikes that whets the appetite. Another solution: everyone can burn his favorite mother-in-law in Red Square."

"No jokes, please."

"As for me, I'm collecting hate. When it overflows, I'll find something."

"Whisper," said Butman. "I asked about you in Riga and Leningrad. I know a good pilot. We must form a group."

"The chances of success are very small," I said. "But if we succeed, this will be the first time that individual interests coincide with common interest."

Kuznetsov had come to the conclusion that he must find a way to leave, in ways he described in an earlier diary entry of December 13, as he reflected about what he should say to the court:

A long time ago I abandoned any thought of struggling against the regime. The political tradition of the Russian people is one of despotism: Its origin is in Ivan the Terrible and Peter the Great. The Soviet regime is the ideal inheritor of these two rulers, and I have not the slightest hope of seeing the process of democratization in the near future.

As for myself, I understand quite well that a man with such thoughts wants to leave Holy Russia, but will the judges understand me? I am a Jew, and I want to live in Israel, the land of my forefathers. That does not mean that Russia is not my homeland; it is my homeland just as Israel is, but I must confess that the homeland does not take first place in my system of values. In the first place I put freedom. Israel attracts me because it is a homeland and freedom together.

But a man like Kuznetsov, with his history in the democratic movement and his lack of Zionist orthodoxy, posed problems for some Jewish movement leaders after the arrests—problems that were made much more complex because Kuznetsov had recruited into the hijack attempt two prison-camp friends—young men like himself who had reached the point of emotional desperation at the prospect of spending the balance of their years in the Soviet Union. But these two men were not Jews.

Yury Fedorov was a 27-year-old Muscovite who had already served two prison-camp terms as a political offender. First sentenced in 1962, at the age of 19, he was pardoned in 1965 only to be resentenced a year later. He had also been under psychiatric observation and was briefly incarcerated in a mental hospital. His mother described him as "of kind disposition and very fond of books." She noted that he regarded hitting a carp on the head with a hammer before cleaning it as "like flaying someone alive" and thereafter he refused to eat fish. As early as 1962, he had written, "I need freedom to carry on the task I have started—the struggle for freedom."

Aleksei Murzhenko was a 28-year-old Ukrainian who had been sentenced in 1962, at the age of 19, for anti-Stalinist utterances. He was not released until 1968. He had spent eight years in Suvorov College (a military school for boys with very strict discipline) and six years in prison, and experienced only two years of freedom as an adult. Still, he had managed to attain a command of five languages. After release from prison, he twice tried to enter an institution of higher education but was refused although he had done well in his competitive exams. After a second refusal at the Kiev Institute of Foreign Languages, he was told that because of his record he would never be permitted to attain his goal of being a translator. Like his friends Fedorov and Kuznetsov, he had an absolute passion for freedom. But the background of the three and the circumstances of the attempted hijacking made it more difficult to contend at the time, as did Jews in the West, that the arrests were made solely as a consequence of the desire of the defendants to go to Israel.*

The first news of the wave of arrests reached the West through telephone messages to friends and relatives in Israel and through a handful of brief, speculative newspaper reports. It was immediately noted that many of those arrested had been prominent among the signers of collective or individual appeals that had been made public—peculiar behavior for persons involved in a secret, criminal conspiracy who presumably would seek anonymity. Strong suspicion was voiced that the KGB had provoked the hijack attempt. Fuel was added to such suspicions by reports such as the following that appeared in the London *Jewish Chronicle* on July 10:

* Subsequently, in prison camp, the three men renounced their Soviet citizenship and sought to become Israeli citizens. Application for Israeli citizenship was accepted for Kuznetsov, but there was no response to Fedorov and Murzhenko despite their support by the Jewish prisoners.

The hijack affair has reminded Soviet Jews of the trap set by Stalin's secret police in 1945, just after the Second World War. A number of Vilna Jews who wanted to get to Palestine were approached by a Soviet pilot who offered to transport them to Rumania (from where it was then possible to reach Palestine). But, after taking off, the pilot returned to the airport and the Jews were handed over to the secret police. Once in custody, they were forced to write letters to relatives, saying they had got safely away. The Russian pilot was then able to repeat his trick, which he did six times before it was exposed by a young child. All the Jews held in these round-ups were sent to prisons and camps for long periods. Not all of them survived.

Some weeks after the arrests, a *samizdat* document entitled *Communiqué* was prepared in Riga to explain the events. It was smuggled out to the West although most of the details had already been communicated by telephone from Jews in Riga to friends and relatives in Israel. It began: "On June 15, 1970, starting at 1500 hours, searches were carried out in Riga in the families of those persons who had been arrested in Smolny Airport." The ten Riga names followed. The communiqué noted that Kuznetsov was a recent settler in Riga and that "Altman comes from Odessa and was living in the Shpilberg flat." It then states: "All the people named disappeared from Riga on June 14 and nothing is known of their fate." It further reports KGB interrogations and searches on June 15 of Ruta Aleksandrovich, Aron Shpilberg, and Boris Maftser, during which "all materials connected with Jewish culture, such as manuscripts, textbooks, letters, photographs, etc. were confiscated." The search warrants were reported to be connected with a charge of high treason and to be signed by the Leningrad Region Procurator Petronin. It was noted that most of the people involved "had applied repeatedly to the Soviet authorities for permission to leave and settle permanently in Israel." There followed brief biographies of the ten Riga arrestees, who ranged in age from 20 to 30. The youngest, Meri Mendelevich Khnokh, had been a biology student at the University of Latvia before her marriage to Leib Khnokh. Since 1968, the Mendelevich and Khnokh families had applied to go to Israel. The oldest, Lieutenant Vulf Zalmanson, was a mechanical engineer until called into the Red Army in 1968.* Silva Zalmanson Kuznetsov, born in 1944, like her older brother was a mechanical engineer, and she, too, had applied to go to Israel since 1968. The youngest Zalmanson

* Because he had left his unit without permission, Vulf Zalmanson was subsequently tried separately *in camera* by court martial, and on January 6, 1971, he received a ten-year strict-regime sentence for his participation in the hijacking attempt.

arrested was Israil, 21, a fifth-year student at the Riga Polytechnic Institute. Leib (Arie) Khnokh, born in 1944, had been trained at the Railway Technical Institute, and, after brief military service, had worked as an electrician. He and Meri Mendelevich were married on May 23, 1970. His brother-in-law Iosif Mendelevich, born in 1947, had withdrawn from the Riga Polytechnic Institute in his fourth year because he felt that his continued attendance there might be an obstacle to his receiving permission to go to Israel, a goal he had long sought. His struggles with OVIR, his appeals, petitions, and general militancy had caused him to lose his job some months before his arrest. At 23, he was a prominent activist. The Khnokhs, Mendeleviches, and Zalmansons were large, interrelated Riga Zionist families. Three of the arrestees were less well known to those preparing the communiqué. They were Anatoly Altman, a 28-year-old lathe operator and artistically gifted wood engraver from Chernovtsy and Odessa, recently arrived in Riga; Boris Penson, an artist, 25; and a 32-year-old machine shop operator, Mendel Bodnya. All three had been denied permission to emigrate to Israel.

The first reports from Leningrad were also sent to Israel by telephone, and an undated fact sheet, which appears to have been prepared less than a month after the arrests, was smuggled out:

> In Leningrad there is no authenticated information as to whether a plane hijacking was in fact attempted. However, if it did take place it was done by a handful of irresponsible people who have nothing to do with the nine persons arrested in Leningrad. The attempted hijacking was without any doubt a provocation thoroughly prepared by the KGB. The provocateurs led the people to the plane and [also] followed close behind.
>
> The evidence is as follows:
>
> 1. The first regular plane takes off from Smolny Airport in Leningrad not earlier than 8 a.m. However, by 9 a.m. at least forty homes and places of work were visited by KGB men. Thus the provocation concerning the plane was only a signal for thoroughly prepared searches of Jews who had some, however slight, interest in Israel.
>
> 2. Everything relating to Israel and Jewish matters was taken in the searches. Letters from relatives, poems, materials on Jewish culture, etc., were taken away. Many were compelled to give up some press cutting or similar item on Israel (with no relationship to the USSR) regarded as "criminal" by the KGB men. Thus illegal watching of Jews wanting to go to Israel was in force well before the day concerned, i.e., June 15.

3. Searches and arrests included people who were not in Leningrad on June 15—which indicates the KGB had been watching them for many days before June 15 and had been waiting only for the "hijacking."

4. Material taken from the nine arrested Jews—e.g., quantities of copies of poems by Bialik and favorable writings on Israel (including translations from Howard Fast about Israel), while in no way illegal, would not have been kept in his house by anyone in his senses who was helping in a plane hijacking—if one takes into account the realities of the Soviet situation.

The fact sheet gives detailed biographies of those arrested,* then answers the question "Who was then arrested in Leningrad and for what reason?" with remarks such as the following:

- Mogilever: "Not wishing to arrest Mogilever in direct connection with his struggle to emigrate to Israel, the Soviet authorities 'linked him up' with the 'attempted hijacking of a plane.' "
- Chernoglaz: "The Leningrad authorities, consistent proponents of forcible assimilation of Jews, were simply afraid of David Chernoglaz—a man of great erudition."
- Lev Korenblit: "He loved his people. For this he could not be forgiven. The arrest of L. L. Korenblit is an attempt to prevent by any means Jews knowing their language and the history and culture of their people."
- Butman: "Popularizer of the Hebrew language, educator of Jewish people—such a man just could not be left free, in the opinion of the Leningrad authorities."
- Kaminsky: "He wrote thirty-two complaints to various Soviet authorities; he signed two letters to the UN Human Rights Commission, and the telegram to Kibbutz Bar-Am. This was enough to get him arrested."
- Dreizner: "A highly gifted man, with a deep love for his people, he evidently became dangerous to the Leningrad authorities . . . He has been thrown into prison only to frighten, by his example, other Jews wishing to emigrate to Israel."

Among the other defendants described in detail was Lev Yagman, 30, a graduate of the Leningrad Shipbuilding Institute, who was an engineer-designer at the Russian Diesel Works. He was arrested while in Odessa on vacation. Like most of the others, he had been denied an exit visa and signed the major petitions. "That was his 'guilt.' In addition, he is an intelligent, educated person of considerable authority

* Butman, Dreizner, Mogilever, Chernoglaz, Lev Korenblit, and Kaminsky have already been mentioned.

capable of influencing others to share his 'rebellious ideas' about the right of Jews to live in Israel." Another defendant was Anatoly Goldfeld, a 24-year-old-engineer, who, "despite his youth, exercised great authority . . . He attracted people to himself, especially young people. Young Jewish people should not, in the opinion of the KGB, know anything at all about their historical motherland—Israel."

The first protest letter was sent from Leningrad on June 28 by Grigory Vertlib and Hillel Shur. It charged that the arrests were "revenge of the political authorities for being unable to break the spirit of the people. . . . Those thousands of people who are now awaiting permission to leave for Israel have been waiting 2,000 years. They do not want to wait any longer and they will not be frightened by any repression."

> In these sad and hard days we remember the trials of Dreyfus and Beilis, we remember the "doctors' plot." The trial that is now being prepared may enter history side by side with those infamous cases and it may cause untold and irretrievable harm to the Soviet state.
>
> We do not know in which way the organs of the KGB will attempt to accuse the arrested men of something criminal. (Their predecessors had rich experience of this—it is enough to remember thousands of people who were posthumously rehabilitated, the victims of the trials of the thirties; it is enough to remember the "doctors' plot.") But we know for certain that the first cause for this trial to begin is the unshakable desire of the arrested to leave for the historic land of the Jewish people—to go to Israel. . . .
>
> What comes next, Procurator-General of the USSR?
>
> Shall we have to face another trial?
>
> And then more trials—concerning other people who wish to leave for Israel?

Vertlib and Shur were arrested several weeks later, and although Vertlib was inexplicably released and eventually allowed to go to Israel, Shur stood trial the following summer in Kishinev.*

On July 8, Viktor Boguslavsky, a building engineer, 30, who headed a group in the Leningrad Transport Design Center and had previously

---

* Although he had signed many other open letters, Vertlib, almost alone of the Leningrad leadership, was not prosecuted and was permitted to go to Israel in 1971 with his family. After not finding suitable work in the legal profession there, he went to Vienna, where, for a long period, he waited with other Soviet Jews to return to the USSR. In 1973, from a strict-regime labor camp in Perm, Hillel Butman addressed a remarkable open letter to Vertlib, which appears as an appendix to this book.

signed collective letters, wrote an open letter to the procurator-general of the USSR, Roman A. Rudenko, asking him to "Liberate my friends" (the Leningrad eight then arrested). He ironically commented that the search for "removal of instruments of crime" turned up letters and postcards from Israel; texts containing the words "Jew" or "Jewish," particularly if typed; all typewriters and "an even more terrible weapon —Hebrew-language textbooks and self-teaching manuals." He noted the impossibility of his friends' having participated in the Sunday airport incident since they were all at home, at work, or out of town when the plane was scheduled to leave. (Boguslavsky wrote the letter although the KGB had served a search warrant on him early on the morning of June 15.) He declared that their only "guilt" was that "they were born Jews and longed to remain Jews."

> They never intended to steal a plane. But they would have been happy if they could have bought a ticket to go to Vienna on a plane. Even if that meant selling their last shirt. They dreamed of bringing up their children in the spirit of Jewish national culture and traditions.
>
> Chernoglaz's daughter is six months old; Dreizner's son, two months; Mogilever's son, one year; Butman's daughter, three years; Yagman's children, three and five years; Kaminsky's children, four and sixteen years; Korenblit's daughter, nineteen years.
>
> A keen interest in the fate of one's own people, love of one's people, cannot be considered a criminal offense.

The following day, Boguslavsky was arrested on a charge of anti-Soviet propaganda and agitation.

The second issue of *Iskhod*, in mid-July, carried these letters as well as noting, after other individual and collective letters, the names of their signers who were arrested or searched and questioned by the KGB.

In mid-July also, other cities began to respond. A petition of forty-five Jews, largely from Moscow, but including some from Kharkov and Novosibirsk, drew analogies to the Beilis case and the 1953 arrests in the Doctors' Plot. It expressed fear over "the escalation of reprisals by a spread of trials—both a geographic spread and a spread in time," but it reaffirmed confidence that such reprisals would never stop the desire of Jews to go to Israel because that desire "is the will of history." In August, an open letter to Procurator-General Rudenko from the wives and relatives of the Leningrad defendants charged that "the arrests were made on the basis of charges that would be the result only of a monstrous mistake." It further contended that if there had been any admissions of guilt, as the relatives had been advised by KGB investigators when they had been interrogated, such confessions had been coerced.

A comprehensive and carefully drafted petition to the Supreme Court also appeared in August. The first signer, Iosif Kerler, was joined by nine other Moscow Jews, including Leonid Rigerman, a 30-year-old Moscow-born computer scientist, who later that fall claimed U.S. citizenship through his American-born mother.* Rigerman had also been closely connected with the democratic movement and with another signer, Boris Tsukerman, a 45-year-old physicist who had become an expert in Soviet law, in which capacity he had instituted important law suits attempting to get judicial confirmation of the rights of Soviet citizens.†Tsukerman was a legal expert to the prestigious Committee on Human Rights headed by the distinguished academician Andrei D. Sakharov. The petition questioned what the Supreme Court proposed doing about the "nonexistent Jewish question" that had become "an unhealing sore on the body of the Great Power which you represent." It noted that the Jewish question not only compelled major domestic attention but now attracted worldwide concern. It had been handled by "periodically reactivated press campaigns," by "a gross disregard of almost all appeals for permission to leave," by flimsy and illegal official explanations for denials (which were enumerated), and now by a new element of policy "aimed at a final solution of the Jewish question—cruel repression of Jews who insist on their rights." It referred to "obviously fabricated rumors about the motive" for the arrest of the Leningrad Jews: "that they had known about the alleged preparations for a hijacking but didn't report them." It claimed that the real motive was their Jewish affirmation. The writers declared: "We are guilty of the same crimes." They then recited their activities and asked whether they, too, had violated code provisions relating to anti-Soviet propaganda (Article 70), anti-Soviet organization (Article 72), and furthering racial or national hostility (Article 74). But, they claimed, it is not enough to assert such "crimes" have been committed. The authorities must choose the correct moment and the correct defendants "to frighten and edify others." They concluded by asserting:

* After a protracted struggle, Rigerman and his mother were permitted to go to the United States on February 20, 1971.
† Now that he is out of the Soviet Union, Tsukerman spells his surname, Western style, Zuckerman.

History now demands that you choose, and you have only two possibilities: either let us depart in peace, or enter onto the well-trodden
path of mass reprisals. Because as long as we exist, we will continue
to demand the freedom to depart—and we will raise our voice louder
every day and our voice will become intolerable for you.

But remember that afterward you will not succeed in justifying
yourselves as you have been justifying yourselves for connivance in the
crimes committed in the recent past: "We didn't know, and if we
knew we didn't believe, and if we believed then we couldn't do
anything."

These letters, and others, began reaching the West in the fall of 1970,
and substantial concern about the prospective trial (or trials) developed
into a crescendo of anxiety and anger. Soviet Jews and their problems
became more prominent on the agendas of Jewish organizations in the
West; and in the USSR itself, after the initial shock of the arrests had
dissipated, the movement's forward motion accelerated. The major
emphasis was on the Leningrad arrestees, those with the least connection
to the airplane incident, and few Jewish groups ever bothered to mention the names Fedorov or Murzhenko. By now, those arrested, and
the handful of other Jews (such as Kochubiyevsky) who had previously
been sentenced, were being labeled "prisoners of conscience"—a term
taken from Amnesty International, an organization centered in London,
which for years had protested the incarceration in all countries of people
who could be regarded as political or religious offenders. But in the
various lists of Jewish prisoners being publicized, the name of Mark
Dymshits could not be found. This was true of the comprehensive report,
Soviet Jewish Political Prisoners, published by the American Jewish
Conference on Soviet Jewry in early December 1970 just before the first
Leningrad trial began. That report reflected the absence of reliable
information but, based on *samizdat* and other communications, it asserted that the purpose of the forthcoming trials was "to stifle the voices"
of Soviet Jews. It concluded that the arrests stemmed from a "high-level
policy decision" resulting in "a nationally coordinated, concerted KGB
action against militant Jews which used entrapment and provocation,"
and which would ultimately involve "forced confessions" in public "show
trials." Prime Minister Golda Meir declared in a radio interview shortly
before the trial commenced that "there is no doubt whatsoever" that
this would be a "farce trial" aimed at frightening Soviet Jews. Some
Western attorneys attempted to secure permission to assist the accused
in their defense, or at least to be admitted as observers at the trial, but

they were refused. Those traveling to the USSR, including Lawrence Speiser, the head of the Washington office of the American Civil Liberties Union, were barred from the courtroom, although a few succeeded in speaking to Soviet officials who expressed amazing ignorance of facts surrounding, or the very existence of, the trial. One, on his return to New York, labeled the trial "a fraud and a frameup."

As the trial opened, over a dozen former inmates of Soviet prisons, who had recently emigrated to Israel, led a hunger strike and vigil at the Western Wall in Jerusalem, protesting the trial. Other recent Soviet immigrants joined them. Gideon Hausner, the former attorney general of Israel who had prosecuted Adolf Eichmann, told a special session of the Knesset that "the facts available show, beyond any doubt, that the entire hijacking was a figment of the Soviet authorities' imagination." The Knesset called upon the people of the world to raise their voices in anger against injustice. They voted (with the exception of the three New Communist members) to appeal to parliaments, world public opinion, and international institutions to put an end to the "farcical court proceedings."

The Soviet Union's tactical decision to force a showdown with the Jewish movement by the arrests was beginning to backfire.

THE FIRST
LENINGRAD TRIAL

CHAPTER 10

On December 15, 1970, at 9 a.m., the hearing of Case #15 began in Room 48 of the Leningrad City Court. That morning, *Leningradskaya Pravda* had carried a brief report that the case of the plane hijacking was to begin that day in "open court." * Hundreds of people—mostly Jews—braved the brisk cold to come to the court building. At the entrance, typed notices were displayed indicating which cases were to be heard that day, but there was no information about Case #15 or Room 48. Nonetheless, the approximately two hundred seats in the courtroom were occupied throughout the trial. People who sought admission advised the guards that it had been announced as an open trial, but they were told, "Go away. Don't disturb. Admission only on passes." Immediate relatives of the defendants—parents, spouses, siblings, children over 16—were admitted only after their passports had been checked against special lists. The first day, most of the "public" turned out to be KGB officials. On the second day, passes were issued to senior Communist Party staff people; on the third, workers from the procurator's office, etc. The relatives occupied front-row benches on the left side of the courtroom. The defendants were escorted to and from the courtroom by uniformed guards who, with each entry and exit, would stamp their heavy, shining boots and click their heels. At recess, everyone was required to clear the room. After recess, passholders were

* Soviet proceedings are either closed, semiclosed (restricted to immediate family and officially concerned persons), or open (theoretically, anyone is admitted).

157

admitted before the relatives. On several occasions, seats the relatives had occupied were taken and they were forced to the back of the room. Once, Boris Penson's aged mother, who was partially blind and deaf, was denied her customary seat. Her protests that she couldn't see or hear from the back of the room were rejected and she was asked to be quiet. This provoked a courtroom controversy, and Dr. Pinkus Khnokh, Leib Khnokh's older brother, vigorously protested. No foreign newsmen were admitted. The only Soviet journalists identified were from Tass, the official Soviet news service, and *Leningradskaya Pravda,* the morning government paper.

The three-man court consisted of the chairman, Chief Judge Yermakov of the Leningrad City Court, and two people's assessors (carefully selected laymen who sit with the judge and rarely participate). The prosecutor was S. Y. Solovyev, the Leningrad city procurator, whom Leningrad Jews regarded as an anti-Semite.* The prosecution staff included a deputy prosecutor, Katukova, and a social prosecutor, Metanogov.† Except for Israil Zalmanson and Aleksei Murzhenko, who were jointly represented by Mrs. Ilyina, each of the eleven defendants was represented by separate counsel. Counsel were privately retained, except that Dymshits was given court-appointed counsel.

The formal charges accused all eleven defendants of violating Articles 64/15—"betrayal of the fatherland" (high treason). This is defined as an act intentionally committed by a USSR citizen to the detriment of state independence, territorial inviolability, or military strength by various means, including "flight abroad or refusal to return from abroad to the USSR." It is punishable by death or a term of 10 to 15 years. Article 64 was modified by Article 15, "Responsibility for the preparation of a crime and for an attempted crime," which provides, among other things, that "an intentional action immediately directed toward the commission of a crime shall be deemed an attempted crime, provided the crime is not brought to completion for reasons independent of the will of the guilty person." Punishment is the same as for the crime involved, but "the court shall take into account the character and

---

* In 1961, while serving as a City Criminal Court judge, Solovyev imposed a series of death sentences on Jewish defendants in an economic crimes case, and, in another case, he sentenced Leningrad synagogue leaders, including an 84-year-old man, to lengthy prison terms on charges of subversion.

† Soviet prosecutors are laymen sometimes appointed in important trials to represent a portion of the public that may have a special interest in the proceedings. Metanogov was a much decorated pilot and Hero of the Soviet Union.

degree of social danger of the actions committed, the degree to which the criminal intention is carried out, and the causes by reason of which the crime is not brought to completion." All defendants were also accused of violating Article 93–1—misappropriation of state or public property on an especially large scale, which is also punishable by death or a term of eight to fifteen years.

All defendants except Fedorov, Murzhenko, Penson, and Bodnya were also charged with having violated Articles 70 and 72. Article 70 punishes by terms of six months to seven years: "Agitation or propaganda carried on for the purpose of subverting or weakening Soviet authority, or of committing particular, especially dangerous crimes against the state, or circulating, for the same purpose, slanderous fabrications which defame the Soviet state and social system, or circulating or preparing or keeping, for the same purpose, literature of such content." Article 72, which carries the same punishment, prohibits "organizational activity directed to the preparation or commission of especially dangerous crimes against the state, or to the creation of an organization which has as its purpose the commission of such crimes, or participation in an anti-Soviet organization."

Dymshits, Silva and Israil Zalmanson, and Bodnya pleaded guilty. Fedorov pleaded not guilty. The rest conditioned their pleas by pleading partly guilty—some denying some of the charges, others admitting facts but not legal conclusions from the facts. The prosecution presented its case by calling to the stand, first, each defendant, and then additional witnesses—including Butman, Lev and Mikhail Korenblit, Aron Shpilberg, Boris Maftser, Vulf Zalmanson, and other persons who stood accused in other pending cases. At least sixteen more witnesses were called in the eight-day proceedings, but no extra witnesses were presented by the defense.

Dymshits was the first witness. After detailing his background and the reasons why he wanted to go to Israel—(1) Soviet anti-Semitism; (2) Soviet policy in the Middle East; (3) Soviet policy on the nationality question as it related to Jews—he explained the three successive versions of his hijacking plan. The original version, which was called Operation Wedding, was to take a TU-124 airplane (48 to 52 passengers) flying the Leningrad-Murmansk route. This was communicated to Butman and others and planned for May 1. But the Leningrad Center decided to inquire what Israeli opinion would be, and Dymshits was forbidden to act further until an answer arrived. Meanwhile, after re-

ceiving 50 rubles from Butman for the purpose, he flew with a friend
in the pilot's cabin of a TU-124 to make a feasibility study. This plan
was abandoned by April 20. Next, Dymshits considered seizing an
AN-2 (12-seater) at an airport at night and flying away with passengers, and in late May he called Kuznetsov, in Riga, to help him
check out this idea. Kuznetsov and his wife, Silva, came to Leningrad.
After the three made trips to Smolny Airport, they decided against this
version because the presence of dogs, armed guards, searchlights, etc.,
would make it impossible to get to the plane. The Kuznetsovs returned
to Riga, believing the plans had been abandoned. By June 5, Dymshits
had worked out a new plan. Again he called Kuznetsov, who in turn
summoned Fedorov. The three men flew to Priozersk and determined
that it would be possible to seize an AN-2 plane at the small airport
there. They decided to fly as ordinary passengers from Smolny to
Priozersk, where, after the plane stopover, they would tie up the first
and second pilots without harming them, put them outside the plane in
sleeping bags, take on board the four Priozersk passengers, and then fly
to Sweden.

The group's only revolver was found on Fedorov. Dymshits admitted
it was his and said that he had made it himself in 1961 in Bukhara. He
had test-fired it with great difficulty on two occasions, and therafter it
had never functioned. All witnesses agreed it was not to be used in the
course of the operation, but only to frighten someone, such as Finnish
officials in the event of a forced landing in Finland before the Soviet
Jews could reach Sweden.* All defendants foreswore the intention of
killing, assaulting, or injuring anyone.

The next witness, Silva Zalmanson, immediately declared that she
was a Zionist, an adherent of an ideology which she denied was hostile
to Marxist-Leninist theory. She described her protracted and frustrated
efforts to secure an exit visa, for herself and, later, her husband. (One
of her letters in early 1970 addressed to U Thant described her alienation in the USSR and stated that her "helplessness vis-à-vis the authorities drives me to despair.") She also testified that since 1968 she
had been typing Zionist materials at the request of Shpilberg. She had
brought a suitcase of *samizdat* materials to Dreizner in Leningrad. (This
was the suitcase buried at the Riga beach in 1969 by Slovin, Shperling,
and others.) When Butman and Dymshits came to Riga in early 1970
with the escape plan, she had introduced them to her husband and to

* Finland has an agreement to return any defectors to the USSR.

some others. She had talked about the plan to her brother Vulf when he came home on leave in May, and Kuznetsov had discussed it with her younger brother Israil. Both agreed to participate. Kuznetsov noted in his diary that the male defendants agreed to exculpate Silva. "We agreed to pretend she knows nothing and acted in blind obedience to the men's will." But Silva refused, saying, "No, I want to do like the others." And she did assume her factual responsibility.

The third witness, Iosif Mendelevich, strongly asserted his traditional Jewish family background, their long-time effort to go to Israel, and the repeated OVIR refusals. When first approached about the hijacking, he had conditionally rejected it since an emigration application was pending, but when it was again refused, he agreed to participate. He admitted buying lead for a "knuckle-duster" and giving it to the Zalmansons. When he noted that the weapon was wrapped only in a rag and rubber, he covered it with plaster "to soften any blow." He objected to the exclusion of this fact and others from the pre-trial interrogation transcripts. Also, during the preliminary investigation, he had been sent from Leningrad to Riga for compulsory psychiatric examination. He had been on the editorial committee of *Iton* and had written articles for the journal. He had also prepared an information file card system. He acknowledged being the author of a letter which the group decided to leave behind for publication in the event the operation failed. This letter came to be known as the Testament, and was labeled by the prosecutor "a slanderous anti-Soviet document." Although frequently referred to in testimony, it was never introduced into evidence. In discussing his philosophy Mendelevich stated, "I am a Jew." He asked nothing of the USSR, in which he was not interested, since he only wanted to go to his homeland. The prosecutor rejoined, "The Russian people has allotted you Birobidzhan. Go there." Mendelevich replied: "Permit me to decide for myself which state and not which province is my homeland." For him, the sole aim of the attempt was to reach Israel.

The questioning of Kuznetsov was unusually protracted. He indicated that he was a Jew by nationality despite his passport entry. He considered himself a citizen of the USSR only "formally." Question: "But you lived and worked in this country?" Answer: "Yes, I lived and worked and sat in prison. After camp, I lived under very difficult conditions, under open supervision." After his marriage and move to Riga, "I decided to make use of the right in our Soviet constitution to emigrate from the USSR, but I was unable to submit documents to OVIR because neither I nor my wife could get character references. It therefore transpired that the *right* existed only on paper." He denied that Article 64 applied because he had no intention of harming the USSR abroad. "This part of the charge is therefore incomprehensible to me. Evidently it is not a question of harm, but of the prestige of the state, which would have been affected if the action succeeded. It is only in the countries of the Communist bloc that people are brought to trial for escape." (The judge interrupted: "Come on, Kuznetsov, don't talk about other countries. We know ourselves. Speak about the case.")

Kuznetsov denied that Article 93-1 was applicable. "If a crime has not been committed, how can one talk of hijacking or taking property? There is an old Jewish law: no crime—no punishment." He also denied any anti-Soviet agitation or propaganda. "There were simply inquisitive people with whom I shared my opinions." He had been accused of distributing to Dymshits's wife *The Memoirs of Maksim Litvinov* and David Shub's *The Political Figures of Russia*. Asserting that the Litvinov memoirs had not been disproved, he said, "I don't consider this book anti-Soviet. It speaks of Stalin's entourage and about Litvinov. The document is no more revealing than the materials of the Twentieth Congress of the CPSU. I made a copy of Shub's book from the film of a friend, so as to read it myself. The only person I gave it to in Leningrad was Avram Shifrin who is now in Israel." (Later, Mrs. Dymshits agreed, in response to Kuznetsov's questioning, that he had not given these *samizdat* materials to her but had merely left them at their apartment and that she had looked at them.) As for the hijacking, Kuznetsov had first heard of it from Mikhail Korenblit and later, in Riga, from Butman, who had previously talked to Silva Zalmanson. He, Butman, and Korenblit had discussed the Wedding version, which was already known to Silva, Anatoly Altman, and Israil Zalmanson. He knew that the Leningrad people, having consulted Israel and been asked not to go ahead with hijacking plans, had decided to proceed with the third version without Butman and Korenblit. He had involved Fedorov in late April and suggested that Murzhenko be contacted. He told Dymshits and Butman of these additional participants. Butman thought this desirable since it would disguise the "national character" of the venture. Fedorov, "not being anti-Semitic," was unconcerned that the other participants were all Jewish. Kuznetsov admitted making the knuckle-duster and when the prosecutor asserted that Silva had admitted doing so, he said, "She takes too much upon herself." He claimed to have brought into the action "Fedorov, Mendelevich, Israil, Silva, and practically all the rest." Kuznetsov was very sharp in his responses to general political questioning and made it clear that he was a proud nonconformist and had contempt for the Neanderthal rigidity of the prosecution.

Israil Zalmanson's testimony was brief. He didn't think he had caused harm to the USSR. There would have been no material loss since the plane would have been returned intact. He put the signatures of some of the others on the Testament. He tried to shield his sister from the charge of typing *samizdat* and Kuznetsov from the charge of preparing the knuckle-duster by claiming he had done these things himself.

Murzhenko spoke of his background and his motives which were personal rather than anti-Soviet aims. There was no intent to appropriate the plane, which would have been returned. He was not involved in any preparations since he had come to Leningrad for the first time on the evening of June 14. Prior to the evening before the attempt, he knew nothing except the bare outlines he'd been told by Fedorov.

Altman's testimony largely consisted of delineating his Jewish background and his efforts to get an exit visa to Israel. He had moved to Riga, in part because he thought it would be easier to secure OVIR permission there. But not being domiciled in Riga, he was again denied. He did not hear of the hijack plans until June 9 and played no role in the preparation, but he had participated in compiling and typing *Iton*, which aimed at "national enlightenment" and was not anti-Soviet.

The third day of trial began with the examination of Leib (Arie) Khnokh. Like others, he detailed his Jewish family background, his desire to go to Israel, and the repeated frustrations he had suffered. He had heard about the flight from Mendelevich, and realizing the impossibility of leaving the USSR legally, he had immediately agreed to the escape plan. He persuaded his wife and Bodnya to take part. (Bodnya later testified that he had been first told by Kuznetsov.) Meri knew nothing of it. "She, as my wife, had to follow me. I didn't ask her opinion in the matter." He had taken Meri with him in a preliminary flight from Leningrad to Priozersk to assess the feasibility of the plan. He was not guilty under Article 64 because his sole purpose was to go to Israel, not to injure the USSR. There was no intent to appropriate state property. All precautions had been taken so that the pilots would not be hurt. He had prepared a place for them after they were tied up. No arms were required or needed. If the pilot's cabin couldn't be opened at Priozersk, the whole operation would have been abandoned. The reason no one was to be injured was that they were humane: "We are not bandits. None of us has ever killed or beaten anyone." Furthermore, if anyone had been injured they would have been extradited from Sweden as criminals. He admitted taking a piece of scrap pipe and placing it in a rucksack.

> We were sixteen. Only twelve of us could board the plane with tickets. Therefore four were left out. They made up the Priozersk group which was to board the plane at the airfield in Priozersk when it landed with the other twelve people.
> The groups were formed in this way:
> For chivalrous reasons, the Priozersk group, less exposed to danger, was to include the women—Silva Zalmanson and my wife, Meri Mendelevich.
> I didn't suggest that I be included in the group because I arrived late. I was offered the place and agreed. The twelve had to arrive at Smolny early to fill the plane on the Leningrad–Priozersk run to prevent that flight which was essential to us from being canceled for lack of passengers.
> The fourth Priozersk member was Penson. He proposed his own candidacy. Nobody opposed it.
> The four of us left Leningrad on the evening of June 14 from the Finland Railway Station. There, we had the impression of being shadowed. We tried to maneuver. We changed trains and directions. We entered the forest and returned. The first to doubt the expediency of the operation, or rather our participation in it, was Penson. He suggested we go back. An ambush at the airfield was conjectured. Later on Silva began to doubt. I opposed this. I believed, once the decision had been made, it was all the same—we would be tried. And furthermore, we weren't sure whether or not we were really being shadowed. And it was impossible to warn the main group. We checked the contents of our rucksacks and I tore to pieces a map of the route which was given me by Dymshits. Penson threw out two rubber clubs that were in his rucksack.
> There is one reason more why I opposed returning. Should it have emerged that we had only imagined we were being shadowed and the group had flown without me, I would never have forgiven myself.

Because of their evasive actions, the four did not arrive at Priozersk until 1 a.m. They entered the forest, lit a campfire and slept, with first Penson, and then Khnokh, standing guard. A few hours later they were arrested.

Khnokh also denied guilt under Article 70, claiming that an article, "Nekhama Has Come" (about the famous Russian Jewish singer, Nekhama Lifshitz, who had emigrated to Israel in 1969), found in his apartment and given to him by Yankelevich, then already in Israel, was not anti-Soviet. He admitted that he had received one hundred copies of the pamphlet *Your Mother Tongue* from Silva, but denied its anti-Soviet content. This *samizdat* pamphlet was the basis of criminal accusations in a number of other trials as well. Four separate, slightly different variations of it had circulated widely in the USSR in December 1969 and January 1970. It is a brief appeal (of approximately 400 words) to the Jewish population to enter the answer "Jewish" after the question "mother tongue" in the January 1970 census.* The pamphlet reads in part as follows:

> Three previous census registrations held in the USSR show the gradually diminishing percentage of Jews who call the Jewish language their mother tongue. Is this not the best proof of the "fruitfulness" of that solution of the Jewish question in the USSR, which from time to time is proclaimed openly and is gradually carried out in practice: The solution of the Jewish question through assimilation, that is by the method of linguistic and cultural genocide. . . . I shall not give those who would like to destroy my people the possibility of stating, on the basis of data in the census, that as the Jews of the Soviet Union have lost their language they have nothing in common with the Jewish people.

Khnokh testified that he agreed with the appeal but after the census had been completed, he had burned all the copies of the pamphlet he had received. He denied that the Testament was anti-Soviet or had been intended for agitation. It explained the motivations for their actions and was to have been used only in the event they died, so they would not perish unnoticed. His signature was added to the Testament with his approval but without his having read it.

Much was made in Khnokh's examination of his pre-trial contentions that he was not a citizen of the USSR since his homeland was Israel. On September 22, 1970, the Soviet Union formalized a pre-existing practice by compelling anyone over 16 years old who received an exit visa to Israel to pay 500 rubles for compulsory renunciation of Soviet citizenship. There was a legal theory among some of the activists, including Boris Tsukerman, that upon application to OVIR, Jews lost their status as Soviet citizens. Thus they could not be found

* In the USSR, the term "Jewish" covers both "Yiddish" and "Hebrew."

guilty of treason since one of the elements of Article 64 was the requirement that the act be "committed by a citizen of the USSR." Khnokh had made this a contention in the pre-trial interrogation. At trial, the following colloquy occurred:

> Question: "In your preliminary testimony you pledged: 'If I am a citizen of the USSR, it is just nominally.' How can this be explained?"
>
> Answer: "My homeland as you see it is nominally the USSR. I understand the word 'homeland' in its emotional sense. Furthermore, while submitting the application to OVIR, I signed a document which said that in the event of permission, I would be deprived of USSR citizenship. As I had no intention of giving up permission, I believed my citizenship to be just formal."

Khnokh also refused to answer questions about people who were not defendants or to respond to inquiries concerning any accusations that were not the subject of a formal charge. Article 254 of the Code of Criminal Procedure gave him that right. Lastly, he protested vigorously the distortion of his pre-trial interrogation, claiming that it contained statements he had never made and omitted explanations he had given and that generally he had experienced exhausting, continuous, and fruitless struggle with his investigator in a hopeless effort to make an accurate pre-trial transcript.

Penson and Bodnya both gave brief testimony, essentially dealing with their motives which were the unbearable frustration of persistent applications and refusals of request for exit visas to Israel. (Bodnya, who was a partially disabled pensioner, had a mother living in Israel.) They confirmed the other testimony. Penson, who was drawn into the hijacking only three days before it occurred, maintained his dignity, accepted his responsibility, and avoided implicating others. Bodnya, alone among the defendants, thanked the authorities for having opened his eyes, and failed to express solidarity with the others.

Fedorov was the most intransigent of all the accused. Only he refused to make any statements whatever during investigation, stating that he had "no confidence in the state security service, whose conscience was stained with too much blood." He refused to cooperate during the trial, and he alone pleaded not guilty to all charges.

Butman, the first to testify after the accused, acknowledged that he was a member of the Leningrad center. He told of his meeting

Dymshits in the fall of 1969 and of Dymshits's plan for an organized escape. The Wedding version was accepted by him but opposed by the Leningrad center. When Dymshits persisted in his plan, Butman decided to seek advice from Israel. An inquiry was prepared and transmitted through a foreign tourist. The reply was strongly negative. When Dymshits was advised of this, he initially agreed to abandon his plans but soon reopened the matter by suggesting the second variant to Kuznetsov and, on June 5, he developed a third version. Butman, in the hope of getting Dymshits to confirm renunciation of his plans, asked him to sign a collective telegram of condolence to Israeli mothers of kibbutz children who had recently been killed when the Fatah fired on a school bus near the Lebanese border. Dymshits refused to make his name public in this way but did ask that Butman secure a *vizov* for him from Israel so he could apply to OVIR to leave legally. Butman agreed to contact Israel to find a fictitious relative for Dymshits.

Lev Korenblit, who was Dymshits's *ulpan* teacher, also acknowledged that he was a member of the Leningrad center and was the principal editor of *Iton*. He had known of the first version of the escape plan and had opposed it, as well as opposing a proposal of Butman's that, after a successful escape, there should be a press conference in Sweden. He felt that both the escape plan and the press conference would attract the attention of world public opinion to the negative, illegal side of the Jewish struggle. When he last spoke to Dymshits on May 24 or 25, he had urged that the hijack plan be abandoned once and for all, but he feared he hadn't been successful in his persuasion. The following day, Butman told him Dymshits had given up the plan. He was now reassured that no hijack attempt would take place. Korenblit discussed the editing of *Iton* and the participation of Mendelevich as the Riga representative to the editorial committee. He credited Mendelevich with being the author of two articles in *Iton Aleph* and of the lead article, "About Assimilation," in *Iton Bet*.*

The Riga witnesses, Maftser, Shpilberg, and Vulf Zalmanson, were also called to corroborate the principal testimony. Maftser, looking extremely frightened, pale, and ill, did so in a garrulous, confused way,

---

* Among the factual determinations upon which Mendelevich's guilt was established by the court was a finding that he "personally wrote the following articles included in the collection *Iton*: 'On Assimilation' and 'The Jews Are No Longer Silent' . . ." In April 1972, however, Mikhail Zand, then in Israel, executed an affidavit, with supporting affidavits from Dr. Meir Gelfand and Vadim Meniker, that he, Zand, was the author of both works and that Mendelevich's conviction was therefore based on erroneous factual conclusions.

acknowledging that the two issues of *Iton* had been typed at his apartment with Altman, Mendelevich, and Israil Zalmanson participating.

Shpilberg was vigorously noncooperative, having almost total memory failure about any fact the prosecution viewed as significant. He acknowledged that he had picked up the suitcase full of *samizdat* literature left him by a friend who had gone to Israel. He had allowed Silva Zalmanson to go along only because it was pleasant to be accompanied by an attractive lady. The material in the suitcase was a collection of poems by Jewish poets, a book of Bialik's poems, *Exodus* by Leon Uris, and a Hebrew-language textbook. He had asked Silva to take the suitcase to Leningrad as a favor and give it to a mutual friend whose name he didn't recall. Silva had never received copies of *Your Native Tongue* from him. Thus, she had never had them and couldn't have distributed them to Mendelevich or anyone else. Since the defendants had testified quite differently about these matters, Shpilberg, however heroic and gallant, was not very credible.

Vulf Zalmanson added little except some minor confirmation and dignified maintenance of his point of view, except his assertion that, apart from agreeing to participate when asked by Silva, he had no other involvement until he came to Leningrad with his brother Israil and Mendelevich on June 14. He had been given the task, with Bodnya, of tying up the second pilot. Since the Smolny Airport staff had been informed in advance that the Leningrad-Priozersk flight on the morning of June 15 had been canceled, no second pilot had even been detailed to the AN-2 plane. Lieutenant Zalmanson's subsequent ten-year sentence was based on Articles 64, 93-1, and 247 (desertion from the armed forces). It was a heavy price to pay for a day away from his unit and a stillborn intention.

The most interesting nondefendant witness was Dr. Mikhail Korenblit, and then largely because of what he was not permitted to say. Korenblit had met Dymshits through Butman. The three men had became very friendly and had discussed and agreed upon the first plan, which they named Wedding because the prospective hijack group was to board the plane on the pretext that they were going to attend his wedding. He had participated in checking the feasibility of the proposed hijacking of the Leningrad-Murmansk flight but began to have serious doubts. By April 20, the plan had been abandoned, and he was not privy to any later variants of it. He advised Dymshits not to give up his job, and when his friend later resigned and told him that he had to go through the project because he'd lost his job, Korenblit told him to get another job at once.

Korenblit's testimony was constantly interrupted by the prosecutor who seemed nervous about his appearance as a witness. Korenblit kept trying to make a statement about Dymshits and his wife and at one point stated, "I considered Dymshits a decent man who had suffered for the Jewish people, but . . ."; and at that point (as at many others) Procurator Solovyev interrupted him. Later, Korenblit said Butman had told him that Dymshits had abandoned the project permanently. On June 13, when the Leningrad Jews were signing their collective letter to U Thant, who was scheduled to visit the USSR the following week, Korenblit, at Mogilever's request, had gone to Dymshits's home. He was, therefore, astonished when at first, he was not allowed inside. Finally, after the doors of all the rooms had been closed, he was led into the kitchen, "and I saw . . ."

At that point, both the judge and the prosecutor interrupted Korenblit. The court guards rushed him from the stand and were leading him out of the courtroom (and back to prison) when Korenblit shouted, "I ran to telephone Kaminsky and to the center and I said, 'You've got to ring Edik [Kuznetsov's nickname] in Riga urgently— everybody knows everything. . . .' "

Whether Korenblit "saw" someone he recognized—for example, a KGB man—or "saw" in the sense of "understood" is not known. It is clear from his wife Polina that he now believes that the entire hijack affair was a KGB provocation from the start. The facts upon which he bases this conviction have never been disclosed. Korenblit has been in prison since October 1970—he and Polina were not married until the following year—and if Polina Korenblit knows the facts, she has been unwilling to reveal them to this date.

Most of the rest of the witnesses added little. Mrs. Dymshits's testimony was interesting for its omissions. She had agreed with her husband's plan to reunite their family. She had told her daughters of the plan to go to Priozersk. But she dated this on her birthday, April 19, when the plan still was the Leningrad-Murmansk flight. With the two girls she was detained at the airport and then released (unlike Meri Khnokh, who was not released until November 12, when her pregnancy had become very obvious, and perhaps embarrassing to the prosecution's desire for a good public image). Yet she was the wife of the principal actor in the drama. Furthermore, it is not clear why the prosecutor needed her testimony, since she added nothing.

Boris Azernikov, a 27-year-old Leningrad dental surgeon, testified
that he had met Dymshits in late 1969, knew what was being prepared,
but hadn't intended to take part in the hijacking. He had purchased a
starting pistol at Dymshits's request. Question: "A firearm?" Answer:
"A starting pistol. It's a sport implement and can't be a weapon any
more than a stick can." (Some months later Azernikov was arrested on
related charges and subsequently sentenced.)

Tragicomic relief was provided by the pilot originally scheduled to
fly the AN-2 plane on June 15. He first explained the plane's technical equipment, noting it was worth 35,000 rubles and not 64,000 as
the prosecution had asserted. This was significant because it took the
charge out of Article 93–1 (theft "on an especially large scale"). The
prosecutor interrupted and asked him to speak about the case. "Oh,
about the case. Very well. I taxied to the emplaning area. The passengers were brought along and were arrested outside the plane after a
little fight. There you have the whole case." The courtroom burst into
laughter. (The fight referred to, watched with bewilderment by the
defendants and many others, broke out at Smolny between the Moscow
security service and their Leningrad colleagues. The Moscow KGB had
failed to make precise arrangements with the Leningrad office, which
had decided on its own to make the arrests at the airport. The Moscow officials knew what the members of the Jewish group looked like
but were not certain that there had been no last-minute changes, so, to
be on the safe side, they arrested every person approaching the aircraft.
Some of the Leningrad KGB agents, who resisted arrest, required
prompt medical care.) The prosecutor was livid.

Question: "Would you enjoy a gag being pushed into your mouth?"
Answer: "Would you?"

The pilot obviously felt no resentment toward the accused, but he took
a dim view of the prosecution's bullying.

Kuznetsov then asked: "Tell me, when the pilot gets out to meet or
to see off his passengers, does his cabin door stay open?" Answer: "It
depends." Question: "But according to regulations?" Answer: "It
should be closed." Since previous testimony had been that if the pilot's
door had been closed, the operation would have been called off, a point
had been scored. Another one occurred in response to a prosecution
question, when the pilot made it clear that he thought it entirely possible to be tied up without bloodshed, if taken unaware.

In his summation, Solovyev devoted much time to the "intrigues of international Zionism" and the absence of a Jewish question in the USSR. According to him, the defendants, with the exception of Bodnya, were unrepentant and had been prompted by anti-Soviet motives. Their crime was a group offense and they should not be judged individually but collectively. He asked for a reduction of charges against Bodnya and for a declaration that Kuznetsov, Fedorov, and Murzhenko were "especially dangerous recidivists." He demanded the following penalties: Dymshits and Kuznetsov—death; Mendelevich and Fedorov—fifteen years; Murzhenko—fourteen years; Khnokh—thirteen years; Altman, Israil Zalmanson, and Penson—twelve years; Silva Zalmanson—ten years; Bodnya—five years intensified regime. He asked special regime for Murzhenko and Fedorov and strict regime for the others. (The degrees of severity of prison camps range upward from "intensified" to "strict" to "special" in terms of such matters as the receipt of food parcels, letters, and visits, nature of work, and the right to buy necessities in the camp shop.)

Defense counsel had played little role until this point, neither asking probing questions, nor cross-examining witnesses, nor objecting to prosecution insults or bullying—let alone calling defense witnesses. (Any significant questions were asked by some of the defendants themselves who, in effect, acted as their own lawyers.) Counsel now had their day in court. Each gave a lengthy final summation. None asked for a dismissal of all charges against his clients. All asked for reduced charges or argued that some were inapplicable. Counsel were unanimous in criticizing the theft charge since obviously there was no intent to expropriate property but rather to seize it or use it, knowing it would be returned. Silva Zalmanson's attorney, Drozdov, was strongest in his advocacy, while Dymshits's appointed counsel, Pevzner, was the weakest. All sounded as if they knew they were going through the forms of a legal defense, without hope that it would matter. They pointed to mitigating circumstances in the personal lives of their clients; they reminded the court that nothing had really happened. As Drozdov said, "We have been speaking about what might have been." Most appeared to have done their best under the highly limited opportunities for defense in Soviet political crimes.

The forensic drama was reserved for the final statements of the defendants themselves. Dymshits concluded his summation by saying:

Our group of defendants is made up of different kinds of people. Many of us had not met until the last days. And yet, it is good to see that even here, in the dock, we have not lost our human face. And we have not started biting one another like spiders in a jar.

And there is one more thing I want to say—that in spite of everything, I believe the day will come when I and my family will live in Israel.*

Expressing her shock at the penalties sought, Silva Zalmanson declared:

The procurator has now proposed that heads should roll for *something that has not been done.* And if the court agrees, then such wonderful people as Dymshits and Kuznetsov will die. I don't think that Soviet law can consider anyone's "intention" to live in another country "treason" and I am convinced that the law ought to bring to court those who *unlawfully deny our right* to live where we want to.

Let the court at least take into consideration that *if we were allowed to leave* there would be no "criminal collusion" which has caused so much suffering to us and even greater distress to our families. . . . Some of us did not believe in the success of the escape or believed in it very slightly. Already at the Finland Station [in Leningrad] we noticed that we were being followed, but we could no longer go back . . . to the past, to the senseless waiting, to life with our luggage packed. Our dream of living in Israel was incomparably stronger than fear of the suffering we might be made to endure. . . . Even now I do not doubt for a minute that some time I shall go after all and that I *will* live in Israel. . . . This dream, illuminated by two thousand years of hope, will never leave me. Next year in Jerusalem! And now I repeat:

". . . if I forget you, O, Jerusalem, let my right hand wither away . . ." [She repeated the words in Hebrew. The procurator interrupted her . . .]

Mendelevich noted that he was guilty of "having allowed myself to be indiscriminate in choosing the means of achieving my dream. These past six months have taught me that emotions must be subordinated to reason." Kuznetsov concluded his reasoned rebuttal of the logical fallacies of the prosecution with the statement: "I ask the court to show leniency toward my wife, Silva Zalmanson. For myself I only ask justice." Murzhenko, Fedorov, Altman, Khnokh, and Penson all ap-

* Dymshits's two daughters were permitted to emigrate to Israel in the fall of 1973.

pealed to the court to spare the lives of Dymshits and Kuznetsov and to show leniency to Silva. None seemed as concerned about himself. Murzhenko noted: "Fourteen years of confinement which the prosecutor has demanded means that it has been decided to write me off." Fedorov asked: "The prosecutor has not doled out the terms of punishment sparingly, but does he know what it means to spend only three years in a camp?" Penson ironically remarked: "I am ready to bear the consequences for what I have not done." Bodnya said he had only wished to see his mother, thanked the authorities "for having opened my eyes," and promised not to break the law again. Israil Zalmanson, Altman, and Khnokh all reiterated that their sole goal was, and remained, to live in Israel.

The court's sentences conformed to the prosecution's request except for Israil Zalmanson, who received eight years instead of twelve; Penson, ten instead of twelve; and Bodnya, four instead of five. When the verdict was announced, a group of "spectators" began applauding in a disciplined manner. When someone cried, "Why applaud death?" they responded, "It serves them right." Then the relatives, their voices strained by sobs, called out reassurances: "Children, we'll wait for you"; "We'll all be in Israel"; "Everything will be all right"; "You will be free"; *"Am Yisrael chai"* (The people of Israel live). Someone began singing *"Shma Yisrael . . ."* The voices of the prisoners joined the ancient prayer. It was Christmas Eve.

Within minutes of the verdict in the Leningrad court, a carefully planned operation went into effect. The facts were quickly gathered and couriers spread to the nearest telephones and transportation. Time was of the essence, since it was necessary to get the news to the outside world if there was to be any hope for the defendants to escape the death penalties. Jewish activists and democrats cooperated in this urgent mission, as they had in many others. In Moscow, within a few hours, the 28-year-old writer Vladimir Bukovsky received the information and quickly made it available to Western newsmen.

Except for two periods totaling three years, Bukovsky, from the age of 20, has been detained by Soviet authorities, either in prison or in mental hospitals.* Nevertheless, during the short period of his freedom, he was regarded as "the conductor of the whole human rights' orches-

* Bukovsky was given a twelve-year sentence on January 5, 1972, for "anti-Soviet activities."

tra." After the Leningrad arrests, he had been among those non-Jews who most vigorously urged that since the hijacking had been provoked and even compelled by the government's policy of suppressing the human right to leave, the state was more culpable than its victims. A friend of Kuznetsov and an acquaintance of some of the other defendants, Bukovsky urged maximum publicity about the case, contending that this was the only protection that could be afforded. An organizer of the "red line," he arranged for instant translation into English of the high points of the trial, the last words of the defendants, and the expected harsh sentences. All of this—the use of untapped telephone lines and of couriers who could evade the inevitable KGB "tail," the rapid preparation of English-language material—had to be done surreptitiously and expeditiously. It was a major logistical accomplishment.

Among the participants in the red line were Vladimir Telnikov, a Russian writer and democrat and the son of a Moscow literary critic, and Galya Ladyzhenskaya, a Jewish girl from Odessa, who subsequently married after their emigration to Israel. Telnikov has provided much of the information about Bukovsky's activities. Young Jewish students at the University of Moscow also acted as red-line couriers, at substantial risk, since contact with foreign journalists has often led to arrest—and for the newsmen, possible expulsion from the USSR. But in a country where there is no freedom of the press, the presence of foreign newsmen can be a major restraint. Unpleasant hassles during demonstrations, or at airport farewell parties for Jews leaving the USSR, might well be avoided because of the presence of a foreign newsman. Bukovsky arranged such "coverage."

Although the Christmas Eve death sentences were initially unreported in the Soviet Union, any hope Soviet authorities had that the holiday timing would permit the punishment to go unnoticed in the West was quickly aborted. Indeed, much of the world reacted with shock and horror to the macabre, profane disregard of human life in a season devoted to peace on earth and good will toward men. On Christmas Eve, thousands spontaneously demonstrated and mourned in Israel. Jewish groups in all the Western nations immediately protested. In all, the leaders and governments of twenty-four countries intervened officially on behalf of the Leningrad defendants. The Socialist International cabled protests to Moscow on Christmas Day. The Communist parties of a number of countries, including the largest Western parties in France and Italy, urged clemency for the accused. Leading newspapers, the Pope and other religious leaders, Nobel Prize winners, writers, public personages in many countries deluged the Kremlin with protests. A day before the Leningrad judgments, six Basque nationalists had been sentenced to death by a Spanish court martial at Burgos, but the announcement was deferred until December 26. Many protests linked the two events, and General Franco, in response, commuted the Spanish sentences. The world-wide uproar startled the Soviet authorities by its intensity.

In the Soviet Union itself, there was immediate reaction. On December 26, a group of Moscow activists telegraphed Soviet leaders condemning the "anti-humanism of [the] Leningrad tribunal" and demanding the quashing of the sentences and free emigration. Meir Gelfand wrote publicly to all former concentration-camp prisoners and to Amnesty International, citing his own camp experience, condemning the convictions as "merciless," labeling the intent to seize a plane as a "pretext," and urging those who "have covered a road of suffering and death" to "save those who are being led along the same road. Large numbers of Jews from Moscow, Minsk, Riga, and Kiev sent collective letters and telegrams of protest. Key figures in the Soviet Human Rights Committee—Valery Chalidze, Aleksandr Yesenin-Volpin, A. N. Tverdokhlebov, and Boris Tsukerman—joined by Leonid Rigerman, wrote President Podgorny:

> Do not permit the murder of Kuznetsov and Dymshits! You must understand that their attempt to break the law was motivated by extreme necessity—no state is safe from similar attempts as long as it holds people in the country by force.
> Let all those go who want to.
> Recognize the Jews' right to *repatriation!*
> Execution and terror are no evidence of the strength of a state.

The head of that committee, Academician Andrei Sakharov, also wrote to Podgorny, requesting commutation of the death sentences and reduction of the harsh prison terms because of the alleviating circumstances. He cited the intent to avoid injury, he rejected the charge of treason as inapplicable, and he noted that the attempt had been motivated by the authorities' restriction on the lawful right of tens of thousands of Jews to leave the country. On the same day, in a letter to President Nixon, Sakharov associated himself with an appeal circulated the previous week by Soviet scientists in defense of Angela Davis. Then he jointly addressed both Nixon and Podgorny:

> I place my hope in your humaneness, in your consideration for the superior interests of mankind. Executions or brutal judicial violence are no proof of the strength of a state; they do not serve the interests of international peace, democracy, tolerance, justice, and the rule of law.
>
> I call on all freedom-loving people in the USA, in the USSR, in the whole world, to stand up against injustice, terror, oppression, wherever they are rampant.

Although an appeal could not legally be heard until January 5, at the earliest, the Supreme Court of the RSFSR convened six days after the Leningrad verdict to hear the appeal of the case. So short an interval was unprecedented in Soviet legal practice, but the authorities were obviously hurried and troubled. In the courtroom were about a dozen "public representatives," some of the relatives, and Dr. Sakharov. Outside the building, despite the subzero cold and snow, dozens of Moscow Jews and democrats gathered to seek admittance—unsuccessfully. Nor did the cold deter an unusually large contingent of militia. Even some foreign correspondents braved the inclement weather. Esfir Mostkova from Novosibirsk told them of the plight of Jews and of OVIR's persistent refusals which prevented her from joining her son in Israel. KGB agents dragged her to a car, questioned her for hours, and demanded that she return to Novosibirsk. Bukovsky notified Western reporters, who instantly queried the KGB. She was released.

The next day, the Supreme Court resumed its hearings. Mrs. Mostkova returned. So did Dr. Sakharov. There was a much larger crowd, including Lev Shenkar, a Moscow activist who taught an *ulpan* and who (after persistent exit denials) had renounced Soviet citizenship. With him was his 5-year-old daughter. He wore a cloth sign in Hebrew: "No to death!" Both he and the child wore a Star of David. Shenkar was interrogated by a police colonel, arrested for "hooliganism," and given two weeks in jail.

Inside, the Supreme Court continued its deliberation and, at 11 a.m. on December 31, announced its decision. It found error with regard to some specifications in Khnokh's case and mitigating circumstances in the cases of Khnokh, Mendelevich, and Altman. Mendelevich received twelve years instead of fifteen; Khnokh, ten from thirteen; Altman, ten from twelve. The death sentences of Dymshits and Kuznetsov were reduced to fifteen years. The court ruled that it "finds it possible not to apply the death penalty as their criminal activity was stopped at the stage of an attempt, while the death penalty is an exceptional measure of punishment."

The Jews had won. The Soviet state had capitulated. It was symbolically significant that such a triumph should occur on the last day of the year. Few would have dreamed, a year before, that the Jewish movement could have successfully resisted the full force of Soviet power —widespread propaganda attacks, searches, interrogations, arrests, a major trial, and all the accompanying fearful implications which might have been expected to flow from this exertion of the state's might. It was particularly unpredictable since the small group of Jews, driven by frustration and desperation, had intended to commit an unquestionably foolish, compromising, and universally unpopular illegality. But the humanly understandable and pathetic error of the Leningrad trial defendants was dwarfed by the monstrous stupidity of the regime's response. Instead of treating it like the criminal attempt that it was, the Soviet authorities chose to convert it into an ideological attack on the entire Jewish movement. In their desire to revive fear through terror, they insisted upon death for a group of misguided idealists who, at worst, could be said to have clumsily sought to do something potentially serious. By overplaying their hand, they had enraged rather than persuaded. They had created stiffened defiance rather than supplication. They had focused widespread world attention on the plight of the Soviet Jews—something the Jews themselves had been unable to achieve.

But the great psychological and public relations victory was minimal in terms of the movement's objectives. Eleven prisoners had been sentenced to terms of five to fifteen years. Several dozen more defendants were awaiting trial. And, above all, the right to leave remained unrecognized. OVIR, a constipated, confused, bureaucratic centipede, neither moved nor permitted others to do so. As the New Year opened, the trial of the Leningrad organization leaders, postponed from its originally announced date of December 29, 1970, to January 6, 1971, was delayed again without a stated reason. (The Western press speculated that it was because of the world-wide protest over the first trial.) A third date of late January and a fourth of mid-February were abandoned without explanation. Demanding that they be permitted to have observers at the trial, thirty-one Moscow Jews selected as their representatives Boris Tsukerman and Vitaly Svechinsky, who had strongly protested the first trial. Unexpectedly, both men received permission to go to Israel. In Ja.uary and February, dozens of prominent activists in Moscow, Riga, Kharkov, and other cities also suddenly received exit visas for which they had been waiting, in some instances, for years. The selection was not random. If Jewish activist leadership could not be silenced by prison, as in Leningrad, then it might be silenced by emigration—or so the Soviet authorities appeared to reason.

But the confrontation continued and increased in intensity. March 1971 not only brought the long-awaited Twenty-fourth Congress of the CPSU, with its deluge of foreign Communist dignitaries and world-wide press coverage. It also saw an unprecedented series of public demonstrations by Jews and a sit-down strike by twenty-four Moscow Jews at the Supreme Soviet. A government decision was made, and the dam broke. In all of 1970, 999 Soviet Jews had been permitted to leave for Israel. In March 1971, more left than in all the previous year. Newspaper reports told of OVIR officials "working overtime to process and grant visas, to implement the decision to permit large-scale emigration." What had happened at Leningrad had focused world attention on the Jewish struggle to leave the USSR and accelerated the necessity for the regime to seek a solution—through trials and persecution, through permissions to depart, or through domestic and foreign propaganda campaigns.

THE FIRST LENINGRAD TRIAL REAPPRAISED

CHAPTER 11

In evaluating the significance of the first Leningrad trial, we now have the perspective of additional testimony elicited at the second Leningrad trial which began on May 11, 1971, the Riga trial beginning on May 24, and the Kishinev trial which commenced on June 21. All three trials were linked by the prosecution to the hijacking attempt, although this effort was minimal in Riga. We also have additional information from the families of defendants and from some defendants who have been released and permitted to go to Israel.

According to Dr. Pinkus Khnokh, Leib Khnokh's older brother, who is now a physician in Afula, Israel:

All of the relatives of the Leningrad defendants are convinced that this was a 100% KGB provocation—or at least we're sure that it was 80% provocation. It was well planned in advance. Why was it so successful? Because it fell on extremely well-prepared ground. The conditions in the Soviet Union caused our people to feel that legal emigration was impossible. Leib had been told, "You'll never get out until you grow old." Yossi Mendelevich had been warned, "You'll rot here." So they jumped at the first plan to escape. But we know that Leningrad party boss Tolstikov had told a small group of party leaders, six months before the arrest, that a Zionist organization existed, but not to worry. "At a suitable time and place soon, we will strike and destroy them." After all, there was experience in such provocations. Look what happened to the Lithuanian Jews in 1945, who were trying to get to Palestine illegally. The KGB got a pilot on the USSR-Romanian run to tell them he would take them. Several groups boarded secretly in

179

Vilna and wound up in prison camps. The KGB knows that when the
Jewish situation becomes unbearable, this is a way to get our leaders.

Dr. Khnokh was emphatic in denying that Mark Dymshits was the
provocateur:

> Dymshits certainly was not, although the KGB wants us to think he
> was. We don't know the identity of the first person who instilled this
> idea. Dymshits, by his personality, his bitterness, and his persistence,
> was a good carrier. But the identity of the person, or people, is of no
> real importance. It was arranged and staged by the KGB from the
> start. I knew of the whole hijacking plan before it happened. Dym-
> shits had told us we had a 5% chance to make it and remain alive.
> Those who went said, "If we have a 1% chance, we agree to take
> the risk." All doubts and fears had disappeared and they believed in
> their 1% chance. Remember, too, there was still another plan to take
> a personal plane. When the KGB knew that was abandoned, they
> had their chance. They created this new flight route from Leningrad
> to Tallinn, with a stopover in Priozersk. The KGB knew this would
> work. They had followed everybody for three months. They knew all
> the plans and intentions.

Boris Maftser, one of the Riga defendants who served his time and
now lives in Israel, confirms some of Dr. Khnokh's comments and
adds details. From months of KGB interrogation, confrontation with
other witnesses, and testimony in all of the major trials, he concludes:

> We know that the KGB had been watching the Leningrad organization
> for a year before June 15—from the spring of 1969. Since they had
> the Leningrad organization under surveillance, they soon learned of
> the hijacking discussions. They knew of the plans and preparations
> and were just waiting to arrest people. At first the hijack plan was
> separate from the investigation of the Zionist organization; then they
> decided to make a big trial tied to it and to *samizdat,* on the basis of
> anti-Soviet activity and propaganda. But though they knew of the
> Leningrad organization, they did not know about other cities, and
> they didn't know how we conducted *samizdat* activity. They didn't
> know anything of the VKK and its earlier meetings until *after* the
> arrests. They knew very little about Riga activities.
>   Even the first search of my house on June 15 was made accidentally
> because Kuznetsov, whom they were watching, had called me by phone.
> This happened because Rusinek asked me to photograph a New York
> edition of a book by Osip Mandelshtam [a famous Jewish Soviet
> writer of an earlier period, disapproved, and thus difficult to secure]
> owned by Kuznetsov. This was photographed by a Russian friend.

The book was legal, but the calls about it from Kuznetsov to me and my Russian friend caused both our houses to be searched. In the search of my apartment, they found the literature connected with Jewish *samizdat;* addresses, telephones, names, codes, literature connected with the Leningrad organization. The searches in Leningrad on the 15th produced material about the Leningrad organization and the VKK. The KGB actually began to watch me closely in May, after some Leningrad people had visited me.

We knew of the discussions about a hijacking, but we had been told that if the hijackers were arrested, they would refuse to give any evidence. I went to Leningrad for a meeting of the VKK on June 13 and 14. I wasn't warned in time to clean out my apartment before I left, and the search was on the 15th. Later, I learned that Ruta Aleksandrovich and Sasha Druk tried to warn me to clean my apartment, but I was in Leningrad. Mendelevich was the only one of the hijackers who knew of the Leningrad meeting of the VKK on the 13th. We now know that the final plans for the escape had been made on the 8th. On June 10, the hijackers had a final meeting about what to do. On the 9th, I had met with Mendelevich and Druk to discuss the VKK meeting of the 13th. I trusted Mendelevich, so when he told me the whole plot was canceled, that they weren't going to do it, I believed him. Why, even on the night of June 14, the Leningrad people—Mogilever, Dreizner, and Lev Korenblit—told the VKK there would be no hijacking. I met Mendelevich at the airport in Leningrad on the 13th. He had a new suitcase. We talked. But the hijacking didn't occur to me. They didn't warn any of us so we weren't prepared for the raids. But the KGB even knew where, when, and in what city Mendelevich bought the bag. When the hijackers met in the cemetery to finalize their plans, the KGB was on the other side of the wall, bugging the whole thing. The KGB investigator, Pavlovsky, said to me: "We know what's happening on the other side of the moon, and these kids think we don't know what's happening on the other side of the wall." They followed Mendelevich and knew about the Testament and our collective letters. They knew about Rusinek and the organizers of the letters.

Mendelevich's testimony corroborated that, at the meeting in the cemetery at Shmerli Forest Park, the question of the Testament was fully discussed.

The story of the so-called Testament and its relationship to the hijacking is one that neither the Soviet prosecutors nor the Jewish movement was willing to tell in or out of court. Although, as previously indicated, the Testament was cited as a piece of criminally anti-Soviet propaganda, it was never released, nor did its signers intend it to be released unless the group met its death. The KGB had a copy but never introduced it at the trial—presumably because it indicated, among other things, no intent to harm the plane's pilot and a lack of motivation to do more than leave the USSR without permission. A microfilm copy is now available. It is a four-page document, hand-written by Mendelevich, signed first by him and then by the other Jewish members of the group except Silva Zalmanson (whose name appears to have been scratched out) and Bodnya. Their cities of origins are given—Riga for all but Dymshits, who identified himself as from Leningrad, and Altman as from Chernovtsy. Mendelevich affixed many of the signatures, but subsequently those persons attested by their initials after their names. This appeal, or contingent last will and testament, one of the most interesting political suicide notes ever written, is prefaced by the following quotation:

> Flee from the Northern land . . .
> Escape, daughter of Zion dwelling in Babylon
> Zechariah 2:10, 11

It then continues:

> We, nine Jews living in the Soviet Union, are attempting to leave the territory of this state without requesting the permission of the authorities. We are part of those tens of thousands of Jews who, for many years now, have proclaimed to the appropriate organs of the Soviet regime their desire for repatriation to Israel. But unfailingly, with monstrous hypocrisy, distorting human, international, and even Soviet laws, the authorities deny us the right to leave. We are impudently told that we shall rot here, that we will never set eyes on our fatherland. Jews who desire to become citizens of Israel are subjected in the USSR to all kinds of persecution, even to arrests. Being an alien element in that country, we are constantly threatened with a recurrence of the events of the 40s and 50s when the policy of spiritual genocide reached its apotheosis in the physical annihilation of Jews. The fate which awaits us here is, at best, spiritual assimilation. . . . By our action we want to draw the attention of the leaders of the Soviet government to these eternal truths, to the endless tragic situation of Jews in the USSR, and to declare to them that it is in their own interests to let our people go home.
>
> We also appeal to international organizations and, in the first place, to the UN and to Mr. U Thant personally. Mr. U Thant, the Jews of the Soviet Union have repeatedly appealed to you with a plea for help. But, apparently, you are indifferent to the fate of a whole people. You try, by all means, to elude resolving this question. You failed to respond to our letters, even though we set high hopes on you. You con-

demn Israel's actions, which are caused by the obvious necessity to defend its very existence, and thus you have no time for us. Are you simply afraid of infringing upon the interests of a great power? But if so, who needs you? What right have you to speak in the name of the peoples of the world? We demand that you take steps to put an end to the violation of elementary human liberties which has been going on for many years, to lighten the plight of the three million Jews of the Soviet Union. We have enough of the bloody lessons which have befallen our people.

Jews of the world! It is your holy duty to struggle for the freedom of your brothers in the USSR. Know that, to a great extent, the fate of the Jews of Russia—to be or not to be—depends on you. We experience a keen envy of freedom—of its blessings which have become commonplace for you. We appeal to you to use them to the hilt, including in the defense of our rights. And until we obtain freedom, it is your duty to build our Jewish home and take our place in the land where we passionately desire to be.

We are motivated by the desire to live in our homeland and share its fate.

P.S. We appeal to all of you with the request that, if our attempt fails, our relatives and close ones be taken care of and protected from paying for our action. It should be stressed that our actions represent no danger for outsiders. When the plane takes off, we will be the only ones on board.

It is not difficult to see why the prosecution did not wish the Testament to be introduced into evidence. What is much more puzzling is why the Jewish movement prevented its publication afterward and through the years, since it is an eloquent statement, not only of the motivation of the Leningrad defendants, but also of the Jewish condition in the USSR and of the imperative need for support from an indifferent, if not hostile, UN and a dormant world Jewish community. Bitter debate raged for almost three years over the document's public release, but concern for a man's safety was the single most compelling reason for its suppression. Since that person, Lev Elyashevich, finally arrived in Israel in April 1973, the story can now be told.

Elyashevich, born in 1946, was a close friend of Mendelevich, Khnokh, and other Leningrad defendants. A tall, slim, bespectacled, young Zionist, precise in speech and manner, Elyashevich was a graduate student in chemistry at the Riga Polytechnic Institute. After his family presented their documents for emigration to Israel, Lev joined the Riga movement, and when, following another application and rejection in late 1969, he was expelled from the institute in early

1970 the intensity of his involvement increased and he became an important intercity courier. On February 24, 1970, he renounced his Soviet citizenship. Subsequently, he publicly released letters to the Supreme Soviet complaining of his "illegal" expulsion from the institute, OVIR's refusal to grant him an exit visa because he might go into the Israeli army as "cannon fodder," and the failure to accept his citizenship renunciation. Complaining bitterly of official harassment and of threats that he would be arrested or drafted into the Soviet Army, he declared: "I am no serf! I, myself, can decide whose cannon fodder I will be."

On May 23, 1970, he married Natasha Slepyan, a pretty Moscow girl who, with her mother, Inna, had been active in the Jewish movement in Moscow. (Inna Slepyan had signed the Letter of the 39 and other collective appeals.) Three weeks later, on June 14, Lev Elyashevich received the Testament from Mendelevich. Following instructions, he returned to Riga, and on June 15, at 11 a.m., he brought two letters to Ezra Rusinek, at Rusinek's place of work. Rusinek had not been aware of the hijacking plans. He opened the letters and read them. The first explained what the group intended to do, how they planned to carry out the act, and who knew of their plans. It expressed concern (as it turned out, unnecessarily) that people who were aware of their plans and who had rejected participation in it might inform the KGB. (There were no informants, but at the time the letter was written, the KGB knew everything, including when and where, probably from hidden microphones and phone-tapping.) Rusinek destroyed the first letter at once. He photographed the second, the Testament, and returned it to Elyashevich. It is from the photographic slide that the foregoing quotations were taken. That day, a Thursday, Elyashevich's home was searched, and shortly thereafter, he was called to the KGB. Questioned extensively, he denied that he had been asked to take part in the hijack attempt. All the next day, he was questioned further and was asked to turn over the two letters. After each session, he met with Rusinek and others, although they knew he was being shadowed by the secret police. On the third day, Saturday, the KGB confronted him with Mendelevich, who told him the KGB knew all about the letters. "Lev, if they're not destroyed by now, please give them up." That weekend, Elyashevich, Rusinek, and Dr. Mendel Gordin (and another man still in Riga) discussed the question extensively. They determined there was no point in Elyashevich's facing arrest, too, so he relinquished the original of the Testament. But Elyashevich continued his open activity. Meanwhile, his wife Natasha and her family were given permission to go to Israel. The KGB, still questioning him regularly, threatened that if he ever mentioned anything about the Testament, he would not only be prevented from joining his wife in Israel but would also be arrested. Although he had been rejected from military service because of his nearsightedness, in October he was called to the induction office and, without physical examination, drafted into the Red Army. On November 14, he was sent to Birobidzhan in Soviet Asia and detailed to a penal battalion. He was forced to take an oath despite his protestations that he had renounced Soviet citizenship and could not swear allegiance to the Soviet Union because he considered Israel his motherland. Before he had left, the KGB had told him they did not want him available for the trial because he knew the contents of the Testament. Even though the letter was sealed when given him by Mendelevich and when they received it, they told him that a KGB expert had determined, through saliva testing, that Mendelevich had not sealed it.

The movement leaders in Riga, including Rusinek, had promised Elyashevich that the contents of the Testament would not be revealed until he managed to get to Israel. But to avoid arrest, he first had to complete his military duty. Meanwhile, his family remained in Riga until his discharge, even though they had received exit permission. In Riga also, despite these considerations, debate raged over revelation of the Testament, the existence and general tone of which were known to movement people. Some, like Ruta Aleksandrovich and, after her arrest in October, her fiancé Isai (Sanya) Averbukh, urged that it should be made public. Averbukh, a poet and philosophy student from Odessa, argued that

> the arrests became a kind of litmus paper test of the moral quality of political Zionism people possessed. The question immediately arose of whether we should vigorously defend our arrested comrades by all the methods available to us, including open letters and *samizdat* documents. Sorrowfully, from my point of view, many of the activists opposed issuing open letters in defense of those arrested that might jeopardize their own chances of getting exit visas. I wanted to publish the Testament in *Iskhod*, which I helped edit with Fedoseyev. The world needed to know the motivations for the acts of our comrades. But I was told, "It's dangerous. It's harmful. If BBC comes out with what's in *Iskhod*, only bad results can follow.". . . The old Zionists

in Riga refused to release the Testament despite our pleas that it be publicized and released in the West to help protect and defend our people in the trials. That was not politically moral. The impression should never have been created that from the moment people were arrested, those who were free failed to place their interests first.

There was another reason for the early decision not to release the Testament. Israeli statements and the declarations of Jewish organizations in the West denied that there had ever been any hijacking attempt at all. They claimed the hijacking had been a KGB fabrication. The Testament, however, not only made it clear that such a plan had been made, but spelled out why, and among the reasons was the failure of Israel and Jews in the West to express vigorous commitment to Soviet Jewry. Moreover, the hijackers themselves consciously saw the hijack attempt as a political act designed to shock and to force action. Afterward, however, some Zionist activists still felt it necessary to do nothing to embarrass Israel. Thus, for totally different reasons, the Testament was suppressed for years. As late as the summer of 1973, efforts were made to prevent its publication. It didn't fit the script of the Soviet prosecutors or of Israel and the Western Jewish establishments.

Israel's role and attitude toward the hijacking case is one of the strangest facets of the story. No other country had a stronger interest in the suppression of hijacking as a political act. Dependent on air communication, Israel has experienced hijackings and been constantly threatened by hijacking threats from Arab nationalists espousing the cause of a free Palestine. It has insisted upon vigorous prosecution of hijackers and no sanction to air terrorism. And after an initial silence following the arrests in June 1970, Israeli officials and government spokesmen vigorously asserted that the entire hijacking accusation was merely a KGB provocation. But at the trial, the Soviet prosecution asserted that the defendants had close links with Israel and that the Israeli government was aware of the hijacking plans in advance.

In fact, neither position was supportable. However much there were factors of entrapment, desperate reactions of frustration to Soviet violations of human rights, and possible incitements by KGB provocateurs, there *was* a hijack attempt. But the Israeli government did know about the hijacking plans before the attempt occurred, although it did what it could to discourage the effort, and it was less than candid for Israel to deny the facts.

The Soviet Union is a member of the Universal Postal Union and a signatory to both the International Postal Convention and the International Telecommunications Convention. Israel participates in the same international arrangements. Soviet domestic laws and regulations forbid interference with the mail or with telephone conversations. One can write to or telephone persons in the USSR with no more technical difficulty than in other countries. Yet until 1970, there was almost no communication between Jews in Israel or in the Western countries and those in the Soviet Union. This was due partly to an unwarranted assumption that it could not be accomplished and partly because Western Jewish leadership discouraged it on the grounds that it might endanger Soviet Jews. However, when Jewish activists reached Israel, they communicated (to the extent economics permitted) with their friends and families in the Soviet Union, and they encouraged Western supporters of Soviet Jewry to do the same. By 1971, an elaborate communications network had been created. It was understood, of course, that the KGB monitored telephone conversations and that incoming and outgoing postal communications were opened and read. So nothing was said or written that the KGB should not know, or that would criminally jeopardize the Soviet recipient. But the activists in the USSR soon realized that they were protected, not endangered, by extensive communication. Through telephone and letter, they openly passed on news of their activities and requested assistance, knowing that if they were punished, that, too, would become known in the West. Certain individuals or apartments were designated to receive calls at specified times. Some mail was never delivered by Soviet authorities, even if sent registered, and that led to formal complaints and legal action against Soviet postal authorities. Telephone conversations would be mysteriously cut off, and during some periods, activist phones would be disconnected without notice or stated reason. Thus, Soviet Jewish activists found it necessary to use prearranged coded messages by post or telephone and to create and maintain channels for smuggling information, messages, and *samizdat* books and papers back and forth. Since telephone calls to or from the USSR would surely be tapped and letters sent by regular post would be either opened or not delivered, if formal methods of communication were to be utilized, coded messages had to be established. Thus, names were agreed to in advance—and even within the USSR, references to Riga, for example, became Roman; Moscow, Misha; Leningrad, Lonya, etc. But often messages could be sent only through channels. Tourists were the most commonly used channels, and members of the movement with foreign-language proficiency were designated to contact tourists, generally at, or outside, a synagoguge, and appointments were made for later contact. Foreign newsmen, businessmen, merchant seamen, and even foreign diplomats sometimes acted as additional channels for communication to the West. Channels were used for transmitting letters, messages, and *samizdat* materials, and for other communications that, except in a police state, would be regarded as normal, usual, or legal.

Communicating in this fashion was not unduly difficult for people who had grown up in the USSR. They had been doing it for years in their ordinary daily contacts with each other. Surreptitious behavior, extreme caution, extraordinary precautions had become a way of life— a method of survival in a country where, for many years, any utterance of unacceptable ideas could result in prison camp or worse.

When a trusted member of the Jewish movement was about to leave the Soviet Union, plans for further contact were made. It was extremely important that, once they were in the free world, people who knew the difficulties of the local Soviet conditions, the individuals involved, and the needs of the movement could render assistance. The movement required Hebrew grammars, literature on Israel, information about Israeli and Jewish history and culture, and economic assistance. People who desired exit visas needed invitations (*vizovs*) from relatives they had been unable to locate or from people who were willing to pose as relatives. Short-wave radios, tape recorders, Hebrew- or English-faced typewriters, and other equipment that was difficult to secure in the USSR were desirable. Specific individuals needed economic help, clothing, or even medicine that could not be obtained in Russia. But the main value of a movement activist who emigrated to Israel was that he could be an outside voice for the friends he left behind—not only publicly, to the outside world, but in interpreting needs, desires, and goals to Israeli authorities and world Jewish groups. By and large, members of the movement within the USSR had learned that they could expect little help or guidance from Israel. It had been even more difficult before 1967 when Israel and the USSR had diplomatic relations and Israeli diplomatic officials had behaved with (what seemed to the Soviet Jews) maddening propriety.

In Israel, Soviet immigrants found that all matters relating to Jewish activity within the USSR were under the direction of an office technically attached to the Foreign Ministry—one that had for many years been directed by Shaul Avigur. As of January 1970, it was headed by Nechemiah Levanon, an Israeli of Baltic origin, who for years had worked under Avigur's direction. He had served in the Israeli Embassy in Moscow and subsequently in the embassy in Washington. Taciturn and secretive like Avigur, Levanon succeeded to his post at a time when the question of Soviet Jewry was taking on new dimensions. He sought, often with conflict and difficulty, to handle a task that now had world-wide public relations dimensions. Levanon was well known to the Soviet authorities. In a pamphlet, *Deceived by Zionism*, published in 1971 by Novosti, the Soviet Union's international press agency, Levanon is described as follows:

> Up until the time diplomatic relations between the Soviet Union and Israel were severed, an intelligence service codenamed Netiva oper-ated under cover of the Israeli Embassy in Moscow. It was headed by Nechemiah Levanon, a colonel in the Israeli Secret Service, who officially filled the post of second secretary of the embassy.

Whatever may be the facts as to Levanon's personal background, it was his office that was important. Since it had no official name, and its very mention in the media was subject to Israeli censorship, Soviet Jewish immigrants came to call it Nechemiah's Office, and immigrants who wished contact, material assistance, or other help from Jews in the Diaspora were referred to it. Earlier immigrants experienced a good deal of difficulty in their contact with "the office." *

Dr. Asher (Sasha) Blank, now a physician on the staff of Hadassah Hospital in Jerusalem, was an original member of the Leningrad organ-ization and served on its executive committee prior to his departure for Israel in July 1969. His wife and Hillel Butman's wife were sisters. He was among the first of the activists to receive permission to leave the USSR. The Soviet press pictured Blank as a superspy, but few people fit the image as poorly as he. Well known for his jovial, outgoing nature and his distinctive physical handicap—a limp resulting from a congenital foot defect, which forced him to wear a built-up shoe—Sasha Blank is a kindly, middle-aged man with sparkling brown eyes, a shock of unruly dark hair, a quizzical look, and a mouth that constantly threatens to break into laughter. When he arrived in Israel in July 1969, he was

* The Diaspora is the term used for countries other than Israel where Jews live.

advised that any messages or requests should be channeled to Nechemiah's Office, and he immediately began to act as representative for the Leningrad organization, and the organization maintained contact with him as regularly as possible.

Within the Leningrad group, Vladimir (Zev) Mogilever was detailed to be the principal person to make foreign tourist contacts. Attorney Joel Sprayregen of Chicago describes such a meeting on May 28, 1970. After attending services at the synagogue, about three blocks away "a short man of about 60 approached and asked me in Hebrew if I could meet someone later that day. I arranged to have the meeting at 6 p.m. in front of my hotel and asked whom I would be meeting. He said: 'A young man with glasses!' At 6, the young man with glasses appeared. On first sight, I knew he was authentic, a tall young man with a most typical Jewish intellectual appearance." His name was Vladimir (Zev) Mogilever.

> Zev is 30, a mathematician, married with a young child. He spoke English well but is presently learning Hebrew and would sometimes lapse into it. I requested that he speak in English since we had only one hour, but while agreeing, he touched me by saying it would be "*yoter naim*" (Hebrew for pleasanter) to speak in Hebrew. When I asked him how he had obtained the Hebrew book, he said there would not be time for him to explain this to me but that he had obtained the book. He had taught himself Hebrew and is now teaching others. He also spoke of his exclusive desire to emigrate to Israel. He had already applied, had not yet been downgraded in his work but pressure was being placed upon him and his boss and he expected this to happen.
>
> He asked me if I would take a letter which he wanted mailed to a friend in Israel. He said there was nothing anti-Soviet or illegal in the letter but that mail sometimes took as much as 40 days to go between Russia and Israel. I agreed to do so and he said he would come to me sometime during intermission at the Kirov Ballet that evening and hand me a Communist book with the letter in it. His friend was Asher Blank, Beit Brodetski, Tel Aviv.

After Mark Dymshits had secured the approval and support of Butman and Mikhail Korenblit for the Wedding hijacking plan, the committee intensively debated it. A majority regarded it as dangerous adventurism, but Butman and Korenblit, in particular, stubbornly insisted that it was the only available dramatic way to attract world-wide attention to their plight and, besides, it might possibly work. Finally, the committee decided that Asher Blank should be asked to secure the

opinion of Israeli authorities. This enabled the opponents of the plan
to secure authoritative disapproval, since they were confident that would
be the result. Proponents such as Butman and Korenblit, who were in
any event beginning to have second thoughts about the proposal, would
be relieved of proceeding if the plan was discouraged, but if the answer
was favorable, their position would be enormously reinforced.

Butman prepared a coded letter to Blank, detailing the hijacking
proposal and asking advice. Mogilever located two tourists, a Norwegian
psychiatrist named Rami Aronzon and a Swedish philosophy student,
Carl Litsman. The three met in a park and after talking for some
time, Aronzon agreed to take the letter and mail it outside the USSR.
Early in April, the pair left. As they went through customs at the airport, Litsman cleared first, and Aronzon nervously tried to pass the
letter to him. The customs man intervened and asked to see the document, which was turned over to him, and he disappeared from sight.
The letter, wholly undecipherable, was opened, photographed, resealed,
and returned to Aronzon and Litsman, who were permitted to leave.
They mailed it later that day. Its meaning did not become clear until
after the arrests when Butman, under intensive questioning, deciphered
it. Butman also stated that, a few days later, he had received a telephone call from Asher Blank in Tel Aviv. Blank is alleged to have
said: "Gilel, I visited your uncle, Dr. Shimon Butman, and consulted
him. He gave the following prescription—the medicine can do harm."
Butman explained that he had no uncle in Israel, that the initials of
the name given were S. B. This stands for Shin Bet (the Israeli Secret
Service). The message was that the Shin Bet had disapproved the plan.

Obviously, Dr. Blank was immediately in touch with Nechemiah's
Office, and the Leningrad organization was told promptly, and as
clearly as circumstances would permit, that the hijack project should be
abandoned. It is also clear that, after April 10, Butman and Mikhail
Korenblit joined the other executive committee members in opposing
and actively discouraging the hijacking plan. But it is equally evident
that the Israeli officials responsible for Soviet Jewry matters (including
advising the prime minister, the foreign minister, the Knesset, and
world Jewish groups) did know that a hijacking plan had been prepared
and was under continued serious discussion, only a few months before
the Leningrad arrests occurred.

Although, from the viewpoint of the Leningrad group, Blank's message effectively aborted the escape plans, it had no such effect on

Dymshits. He angrily opposed asking Israel, since "it was clear to me that the answer from Israel could only be negative," and when Butman told him the reply, the two men "separated on cool terms" and Dymshits said he'd "handle the idea himself." Butman and Lev Korenblit tried to dissuade him from continuing, but "I was evasive," Dymshits later admitted. He last saw Butman on May 26, when Butman asked him to sign a joint telegram to Kibbutz Bar Am. "I refused those suggestions in order not to attract attention to myself so that I could better proceed with my plans for action."

The Israeli disapproval also did not dissuade the Riga group. Even Mendel Gordin, who had been approached in March by his younger cousin, Iosif Mendelevich, and had held virtually no hope for its success, had originally approved the plan in principle, because he felt the act itself would attract world public opinion to their plight, and at the time the Riga movement felt that more radical and dramatic steps were required. (They were particularly disturbed by a statement of Dr. Nachum Goldmann, the president of the World Jewish Congress, that this was not the time to talk of Soviet Jewry, that until there was peace in the Middle East, the time was not propitious for the USSR to agree to release Jews.) But Gordin, a member of the Aleph group, had again applied for an exit visa and OVIR had not yet rejected him. As he weighed the slim chance of success, the high danger, and the questionable morality, he determined to reject the offer. Others considered it essential to proceed. Kuznetsov, for example, saw no reason to seek the blessings of "any government." By mid-May, the Riga group realized that their Leningrad confederates were now strongly opposed and they "tried to conceal everything" from them. The position they took, said Kuznetsov, "gave us grounds to fear two committees at the same time—the KGB and the committee of the Leningrad organization, even though in our hearts we did not believe the Leningrad people would go so far as to denounce us to the authorities. Therefore, in our trips to Leningrad, we tried to avoid being seen." Silva Zalmanson also confirmed that "after finding out that the Leningradites were categorically against the idea, we carefully concealed our preparations from them. We told them that we, too, had given up the project, because we were afraid that they might cause our plan to fail."

It failed without additional help. But, in a larger sense, if its objective was to attract world-wide attention, it succeeded beyond the wildest expectation of its planners. Many Soviet activists, both in the USSR and among those who have left, retrospectively approve of the escape effort. Indeed, virtually all Jewish groups speak of the defendants in the first Leningrad trial as prisoners of conscience and regard them as heroes. Their motivation was heroic. They had great courage. They self-sacrificingly performed a symbolic act to dramatize the plight of their people. They are the martyrs of the movement, and all movements need martyrs.

Some, like Ezra Rusinek, remained confirmed in their opposition to the plan:

> The action of June 15, 1970 was a crime against the Zionist underground in Russia. It gave the KGB an opportunity to strike at the Jewish underground, stopping the *samizdat* work and Jewish education for a long time. The participants knew perfectly well that the open struggle had begun by March 1970. But they did not understand that only such a mass struggle can bring success. They also knew that no country suffered as much from hijacking as did Israel. In their last letter, they wrote that they were going to their death, but if they were caught alive they would refuse to give evidence and would remain silent. Within the first week, they'd begun to talk, not only about the "plot," but about the VKK and the *samizdat* work. They bear some responsibility for the additional arrests. Their behavior at the trial was often admirable, but it was the cruel death sentences that aroused the indignation and protests all over the world. If they had received a few years, the West would have remained silent.

Of all the paradoxes of the case, one rarely mentioned was that the USSR had no provision in its criminal code punishing the hijacking of an airplane. For that attempt, they tortured the clear language of the law and applied Article 64, which made punishable escape abroad with intent to cause harm to the USSR. On January 3, 1973, the Supreme Soviet promulgated a decree "on criminal responsibility for hijacking an aircraft." Its provisions, if in effect earlier, would have meant much lighter sentences for the defendants. Following its announcement, 82 Soviet Jews petitioned President Podgorny asking for leniency for the prisoners based upon a Soviet procedure permitting reconsideration when there is newly applicable law. They concluded:

> One cannot ignore the moral side of the case. Not base instincts, but rather passionate aspiration for a national homeland, a clear vision of their national heritage—this is what guided our comrades and incited them to this action. Only the difficult situation of those days, occa-

sioned by the rage of reactionaries who, despite the Constitution, characterized the repatriation of Soviet Jews as treason in print and at meetings, and who created insurmountable obstacles for emigration —only this situation and their feeling of being trapped induced despairing people to consider extreme measures. They were unfortunate victims of oppression and tyranny.

THE SECOND
LENINGRAD TRIAL

CHAPTER 12

The second Leningrad trial, which began on May 11, 1971, was a political conspiracy trial of the leadership of the Leningrad organization. The delays in commencing it not only violated Soviet criminal procedural law (under which trials must start within nine months of arrest—six of the nine defendants had been arrested on June 15, 1970) but also reflected external political factors—the outcry following the first trial and the meetings of the Twenty-fourth Congress of the CPSU. But the primary reason for the delay appears to have been an effort to secure greater cooperation from the defendants. The Soviet authorities were partially successful in this respect, but the extent of their success is still difficult to measure, since reports of the trial from Soviet news comments vary markedly from the oral commentaries of those who witnessed it and from the unofficial, partial *samizdat* transcript.*

The following, at least, is known: (1) Soviet press reports that all of the defendants abjectly confessed to a whole series of crimes are false. (2) None of the nine defendants was involved in the hijacking effort, although most of them had advance knowledge of hijacking plans during the late winter and early spring of 1970. Hillel Butman and Mikhail Korenblit originally were involved in the planning, and Viktor Shtilbans had a lesser, but still meaningful involvement. Most

---

* For the first Leningrad trial and the subsequent Riga trial, the full unedited *samizdat* transcripts were independently received in Israel and the West and are generally available. But although Israeli authorities have had full transcripts of the second Leningrad trial and the Kishinev trial since 1971, they have not released them, except in heavily edited versions.

of the accused, notably Lev Korenblit (who is not Mikhail Korenblit's brother), Lassal Kaminsky, and Vladimir Mogilever, were bitterly opposed to the entire scheme. By mid-April 1970, all those who knew of the plans actively opposed them, but none reported their knowledge to the Soviet authorities. (3) All defendants except Shtilbans, and to some extent Viktor Boguslavsky, were actively involved in the executive of the Leningrad center. In such capacities, they created and distributed literature, raised funds, and did other organization work which was the subject of testimony and which they admitted. (4) The major area of dispute in the trial was whether these political activities could be viewed as anti-Soviet and thus criminally subversive. (5) As a consequence of either pressure and duress, or of a promised prosecution "deal," most of the defendants abandoned their unwillingness to testify by the time the final pleas were made on the ninth and last day of the trial.

But even this analysis obscures the cardinal fact to be discerned from the trial. The government's purpose in carrying out the prosecution was to discourage, or if possible to destroy, the Jewish movement in the USSR. In that it failed, even though the repressive effect of the two Leningrad trials greatly retarded the movement in Leningrad for over a year. Because that was the regime's goal, the focus, as in almost all political subversion trials in all societies, was on a sinister conspiracy—in this case, on international Zionism.

The trial can also be understood only in terms of the overheated political atmosphere in Leningrad—an atmosphere in which Soviet officials, angered by the resurgence of Jewish identification, exemplified by efforts to emigrate to Israel, permitted endemic anti-Semitism to be openly expressed. An example of this was the experience of Igor Borisov.

Borisov, the 28-year-old son of a Russian father, had declared his nationality to be Jewish. He and his Jewish wife had openly stated that they regarded Israel as their motherland and desired to emigrate there. On September 1 and 2, 1970, they were called to the KGB, which stated that the police had received reports that the Borisovs intended to cross the frontier illegally to go to Israel. The Borisovs denied this and declared that they were seeking an OVIR application. Returning from the KGB on the train, they were seated next to a group of Russian drunks, the most vocal of whom, a man named Kulagin, between swigs of vodka, was discussing the Jews: "*Zhids, zhids,* I hate them. I'd murder them all. I'd cut their throats. So many of them are around, stealing and sending gold to Israel." Borisov expressed his resentment, noting that he was Jewish and intended to go to Israel. Another drunk rejoined: "It's a pity we saved you during the war. Hitler would have done away with the lot of you. Whoever heard of *zhids* opening their mouths in Russia? We've always beaten you and we always shall." With this, at least three men jumped Borisov, tore his shirt and pummeled him. He resisted effectively and then moved away. Another passenger, Colonel Vodnev of the KGB, approached and asked the whole group to go with him to the police station. Some of the drunks quickly left, but the Borisovs, Kulagin, and another man accompanied him. At the police station, Kulagin again insulted Borisov in the presence of policemen and witnesses. Although his anti-Semitic epithets constituted a crime under Soviet law, the remarks were ignored. On October 14, Borisov was summoned to a formal confrontation with one of the drunks, Shishkin. To his astonishment, he was detained and charged with hooliganism—malicious assault of Kulagin. During the two-day trial, which took place in the suburb of Toksovo on the last two days of the Leningrad hijacking trial, the prosecution placed much emphasis on Borisov's desire to go to Israel, and the court sentenced Borisov to three years' imprisonment.

Shortly thereafter, Leonid Rigerman, commenting in Moscow, noted that the statute under which Borisov was jailed (Article 206/2 of the Russian Criminal Code) applied only to recidivist hooliganism and thus was inapplicable and illegally applied. "I want to emphasize the seriousness of the trial of Borisov. It is pure anti-Semitism. Tomorrow—for the same reasons, with the same accusations—they may seize any one of us, when he applies to go to Israel."

The Leningrad City Court was the site of the second Leningrad trial. Although the trial was billed as public, admission was by pass only, and most passes were reserved for KGB officials and Communist Party faithful. The courtroom seated 150 persons, but only about fifteen relatives of the nine defendants were permitted entry, and on opening day, eight relatives wired Roman A. Rudenko, procurator-general of the USSR, protesting their exclusion. All foreign newsmen were excluded and Intourist canceled the Leningrad leg of the tour of a visiting delegation of Italian journalists on the pretext that no hotel rooms were available. But Tass and Novosti reporters were present, and the trial's coverage both in the Soviet press and in foreign releases far exceeded even the most important political "show trials" of recent years. The ambivalence and selectivity of the authorities about what could be stated and what was to be hidden defied rational comprehension.

The judge, Nina Isakova, and the senior assistant prosecutor, Inessa Katukova, were not as well known as their counterparts in the first Leningrad trial, but they were at least as contentious.

Among the defendants only Butman and Mikhail Korenblit were accused of organizing, abetting, and being accomplices in the hijacking effort. All but Boguslavsky and Shtilbans were charged with concealing a crime—the theft in Kishinev of an Era duplicating machine which had been brought to Leningrad for reproducing literature. All nine defendants were charged with violating the two subversion statutes— Articles 70 and 72.

At least forty-six witnesses testified during the nine-day trial. They included Dymshits, Kuznetsov and his wife Silva Zalmanson, and Iosif Mendelevich. Many other Leningrad movement activists were among the witnesses called to confirm various details designed to buttress the forty-volume KGB investigative protocol. Some of the witnesses desired by the defense had suddenly received long-sought exit visas and de- parted for Israel. One, Rudolf Brud, soon went to Copenhagen, where he set up a monitoring command post during the trial period. Brud's service permitted the West to learn some otherwise unpublished trial details. Others, such as Yury Mekler and Vladimir Friedman, had been dispatched by their employer, on pain of discharge, on extended busi- ness trips far from Leningrad. Two of the prospective defense witnesses had been sent to Siberia. Still others, such as Yevgeny Shmilovits, had been threatened that they would be permanently denied exit visas if they testified favorably for the accused. Similar warnings had been given to Vladimir Knopov and others who had refused to become prosecution witnesses. Despite harassments, most witnesses did little but confirm basic facts that the defendants readily admitted. Indeed, there was little dispute of facts. The differences arose over motivation and the legal consequences of the acknowledged behavior.

The case the state wished to prove was summarized in the indictment:

> International Zionism is conducting disruptive activities against the
> socialist countries. Zionism is trying to carry out ideological sabotage
> against the USSR and the other socialist countries by propagating
> slanderous articles and by sending tourists [to these countries]. These

activities have induced [some persons] to set up a Zionist organization in Leningrad. The preliminary investigation established that persons who became members of the organization maintained close contacts with Zionist circles in Israel, that the said persons were conducting hostile activities, that they were slandering Soviet internal and external policies, that they have been fomenting [among Jews] sentiments supporting emigration to Israel, and that they were actually able to induce individuals of Jewish nationality to go to Israel. For these purposes they used anti-Soviet Zionist literature, and even works published in the capitalist countries. They organized a committee, which communicated with other towns [and cities]. The activities [of the said people] were directed toward a conspiratorial organization; these persons were collecting membership dues for material support [of their organization]; for the same purpose they used parcels sent to them from Israel through the firm of Dinerman [in London].

The indictment also added the following: "Existing facts irrefutably prove the direct involvement of the Zionist centers with the events in Hungary in 1956 and with the activation of the counterrevolutionary forces in Poland and Czechoslovakia in 1968."

Among the "anti-Soviet Zionist literature," the charge sheet included Leon Uris's *Exodus*, the two issues of *Iton*, issues of *Iskhod* that contained petitions and letters described as "slanderous," and several *samizdat* brochures created by the movement.

The essential testimony confirmed the involvement of Butman and Mikhail Korenblit in the original hijacking plans and their subsequent disavowal of them. Shtilbans, the most cooperative of the defendants, admitted that he had helped prepare sleeping drugs for the pilots in the original Wedding plan, but later renounced his participation. The testimony also included details of the inquiry through Asher Blank in Israel and of the Israeli rejection of the escape plan. The prosecution was thus left with testimony showing that by mid-April 1970 all the defendants had opposed any hijacking effort and thought such plans had been discontinued. Indeed, Butman had been so unworried that from May 26 until his arrest on June 15, he and his 4-year-old daughter were on vacation at his summer *dacha*, miles from Leningrad; and Mikhail Korenblit had gone to Dymshits's apartment on June 13 to secure his signature on the petition to U Thant. But the prosecution had one additional piece of controversial evidence that hinted, at least, that Butman and Mikhail Korenblit had known about the ongoing nature of the plan. Dymshits testified, and Eva Butman (Hillel's wife) and Korenblit confirmed, that at about 6 a.m. on June 15, Dymshits unsuccessfully sought to telephone Korenblit and then phoned Eva Butman asking her to transmit to Korenblit a prearranged coded message, "Marusya has tonsilitis and is going to see the doctor within three hours." (The code meaning was that the hijacking effort would begin within three hours.) On cross-examination, Dymshits stated that Korenblit had seen him at the beginning of June and "asked that if we do anything, to inform him beforehand so they could be ready for any possible searches." In response to a question asking what else Butman could have done to dissuade him by additional pressure, Dymshits replied, "Nothing."

That evidence fell far short of indicating that even Butman and Mikhail Korenblit knew ahead of time the specific hijacking plans for June 15. But clearly there was preknowledge and preparticipation in events preliminary to, and ultimately resulting in, the hijacking attempt.

The Section 189 charge—concealment of a crime, theft of an Era duplicator—was factually not denied; many of the defendants had known about the machine. But the duplicating machine never worked and apparently was never used despite the criminal risks involved in securing and transferring it to Leningrad. Yet, although a number of witnesses testified that they had no idea it was stolen, knowing the nature of their society, they could not seriously have believed its possession was legal.*

The most damning accusation in a propaganda sense was that the defendants were part of an international Zionist conspiracy. Although the prosecution asserted that the Scandinavian tourists Dr. Rami Aronzon and Carl Litsman were in the employ of Israel and/or Zionist intelligence, there was no proof, even circumstantially. The Soviet news agency Novosti on May 13 reported that Mogilever testified:

> Through intermediaries, I forwarded to the Israeli authorities a list of names of those persons we recruited for anti-Soviet activity. Through an American trainee in the USSR, Donald Melament, I informed Israeli government agencies about forms and methods of subversive work of our organization; plans to hijack a plane and escape from the USSR . . . through Aronzon I sent a long list of titles of anti-Soviet publications issued abroad, which I asked to be sent secretly to our group to use in our activities.

* Clearly, in the Soviet Union, possession of such an unpurchased machine was a breach of criminal law. (The main facts of the expropriation and transfer of the copier are presented in Chapter 13, on the Kishinev trial.)

Although Novosti made this sound sinister, it simply recounts the frequent practice of asking tourists to mail letters to overseas contacts listing names of people who wanted invitations from Israel and books on Israel, the Jewish people, or Hebrew studies, for reading and reproduction in the USSR. The reference to Donald Melament, also contained in the prosecution's opening statement, became the most sensational charge in the trial, although to this date the character of the proof is unknown.

The charge, reported by both Tass and Novosti, claimed that "Donald Melament, born 1945, a Zionist and a citizen of the United States, who received the necessary training in Israel," was a key agent who established contact between the defendants and Israel. "This Yale University postgraduate together with others who were sent to study in the USSR took a special course in 'subversive sciences' in the United States" during the course of which he was told, "you will receive 1,000 dollars for every Soviet scientist whom you succeed in persuading to go to the United States."

> Hence, it is understandable why on coming to the USSR and taking up his studies in the chemistry faculty of Leningrad State University, Melament showed little interest in science. His main efforts were aimed at conducting anti-Soviet and Zionist propaganda in the USSR, attempting to persuade certain Soviet scientists and specialists to go abroad. The personnel of the laboratory where Melament received his training demanded that the American behave himself. However, he continued his agitation and recruiting. It was then that the personnel and the teaching staff of the chemistry faculty submitted a statement to the Rector's Office demanding that an end be put to the activities of this postgraduate who had gone beyond all bounds.
> Failing to find like-minded people within the university, Melament continued an active search for them. This was how in February 1970 he came across Vladimir Mogilever, an engineer in one of Leningrad's research institutes.

Melament, then working on his doctorate at Harvard University, wrote as follows to *The New York Times* on May 17, 1971:

> On May 12 a Tass dispatch reported that Vladimir Mogilever, who is currently on trial with eight other Leningrad Jews in connection with their alleged participation in a plane hijacking attempt among other charges, had supposedly admitted to having established contact through me with "Israel government circles" while I was a participant in the American-Soviet Exchange for Young Scholars at the chemistry

department, Leningrad State University, during the 1969–1970 academic year.

I do not know how to react to Mr. Mogilever's purported testimony, but the simple fact of the matter is that I had no such contacts with "Israeli government circles" and that Mr. Mogilever made no such request of me.

The truth lies in a very different set of circumstances. Only a short time before his incarceration in June, 1970 Mr. Mogilever showed me his meager library of Hebrew books, and as Hebrew books have been virtually unobtainable in Soviet book stores since the 1920s, requested that I send some intermediate-level Hebrew texts to him by *open mail.*

I knew that this request did not involve either of us violating Soviet law and agreed. Such was the nature of our "conspiracy."

The Soviet allegation also implies that I had been in Israel only shortly before arriving in the Soviet Union in August, 1969. Actually, I was a Junior Year Abroad student at the Hebrew University in Jerusalem in 1963–64. I have not been in Israel since 1964.

Another similarly groundless charge, apparently unrelated to the present trial in Leningrad, was made by Soviet authorities to the effect that I had been promised $1,000 for each Soviet scientist I could induce to defect to the United States. I was never promised money or in any way solicited to urge Soviet scientists to defect to the United States or any other country.

While I do not have any direct information bearing on the validity of most of the various charges made against Mr. Mogilever and the other defendants by the Soviet authorities, the false charges made by the prosecution concerning me and the closed-door nature of the trial indicate that the case against the Leningrad Nine may be very flimsy.

For reasons that have never been made clear, Israeli authorities and official Jewish organizations in the West discouraged efforts by supporters of the defendants abroad to confront the Soviet authorities with press conference appearances of Melament, Asher Blank, Rami Aronzon, and Carl Litsman.

The other alleged proof of foreign contacts came from detailed testimony concerning overseas financing of the movement. Various defendants had received parcels containing fur coats, suits, other clothing, fabrics, and shoes from Dinerman and Company, a London overseas gift shipping firm. Because of the consumer shortage in the USSR and the unavailability of good clothing in Soviet stores, British clothing was considered valuable, and a major part of the movement's financing came from the sale of such goods. The private sale of one's own clothing, even though received by gift from abroad, is not illegal in the USSR, but a black-market business of selling clothing could be considered an economic crime. In testifying that "We understood that the parcels our people got through a British company were sent by Zionist organizations in Israel," Mogilever was at least partially correct. One way recent activist immigrants to Israel helped the movement was by mailing parcels of valuable, permissible goods, through Dinerman, to activists in the USSR. The substantial expenses were usually underwritten by Zionist groups in Israel, England, the United States, and other Western countries.

Lassal Kaminsky, the Leningrad organization's treasurer, gave extensive testimony concerning financing. Dues were paid. Kaminsky received 1,500 rubles from Vitaly Svechinsky in Moscow to pay the cost of preparing publications. On occasions, he had sold fur coats received from abroad; two, belonging to Mogilever and Vertlib, sold for 300 and 350 rubles respectively. The funds were deposited in the organization's treasury to be used for its activities. Kaminsky explained further:

> I wish to state emphatically that the English firm, Dinerman, through which many of us received parcels, is not a firm belonging to the Zionist movement, but simply a private firm to which private persons, including our relatives, apply. Very often, after receiving invitations to emigrate [vizovs], people also received parcels. Our relatives understood that emigration involves great expense and they tried to help us.

There was no dispute that a Leningrad group existed in an organized and formal sense, that it had meetings, recruited people, carried on a program, was in contact with other groups in other cities, was instrumental in organizing VKK (the All-Union Coordinating Committee), and was involved, in cooperation with Jewish activists elsewhere, in preparing and distributing a journal, *Iton*, and other *samizdat* literature. But it was equally undisputed that the goals of the defendants and of the Leningrad organization were to learn and teach Hebrew, Jewish history and culture, and to circulate information about Israel for combating assimilationism and maintaining Jewish national existence. Its other primary purpose was the political struggle for the right to leave for Israel.

Part of the definition of the crime that comes under Article 70 of the Russian Criminal Code is that the propaganda, "slanderous fabrications," or literature preparation or circulation be carried on "for the purpose of subverting or weakening Soviet authority." It was argued that this was not the group's purpose. Among the elements in Article 72 is that the organizational activity be "directed to the preparation or commission of especially dangerous crimes against the state," or that participation be "in an anti-Soviet organization." The defendants contended that the Leningrad group was not of such a character. In denying that the organization had ever aimed at undermining or weakening the Soviet system, Kaminsky said, "Really, how can such a small group of people undermine the Soviet regime if this cannot be done by all the imperialist powers taken together?" * Kaminsky, Yagman, and others flatly denied guilt under Articles 70 and 72. Yagman said: "I am profoundly surprised that some of my comrades admit they were guilty of taking part in an anti-Soviet, Zionist organization. Our organization was interested only in matters that concerned the Jewish people and the Jewish state."

Perhaps Yagman's surprise was directed at the testimony of the oldest defendant, 48-year-old Lev Korenblit, a brilliant mathematical physicist. Korenblit had grown up in a village in Bessarabia and had received a traditional Jewish education. He was the group's philosopher, if not its ideologist. His ironic, sensitive testimony mght well have been misunderstood by the younger militants as much as it doubtless was miscomprehended by the prosecution.

> I want to say something about anti-Soviet literature. During the investigation, I had an absolutely false idea of the term "anti-Soviet." I thought that anti-Soviet literature could be considered literature that calls for the overthrow of the Soviet regime. As has been dinned into me in the time that has passed since my arrest, "anti-Soviet" is any suggestion that differs from the official Soviet line, anything that does not coincide with, or is contrary to, the letter of Soviet newspaper articles. In this sense, those articles that expressed sympathy for Israel and support for its struggle for existence are really "anti-Soviet," even though the Soviet Union might not even be mentioned in them. Therefore I admit that I am guilty of distributing, preparing, and keeping "anti-Soviet" literature and I am prepared to bear punishment for this.

That was, and still is, the precise point that has escaped many of the activists both in the USSR and abroad. In a repressive state that holds

---

* A similar point was made by Shepshelovich, in his final statement at the Riga trial: "Can one say seriously that several home-made publications of an informative and educational nature can undermine the might of such a state as the USSR?"

subversion trials, and given the arbitrary nature of Soviet legal practice, it is philosophically absurd to quibble over what is or is not "anti-Soviet." To the Soviet state, any opinion or expression that differs from the official line is subversive if the state says it is. The Soviet state is challenged whenever any group asserts its rights to leave, to worship, to speak without censorship, to differ over domestic or foreign policy. Certainly a challenge to Soviet nationalities practice is an assault upon an important ideological bulwark of state power. Guilt on these charges was predetermined at the time of indictment. Lev Korenblit's exposure of the situation by the use of irony was as valuable a defense tool as the principled denials of some of the defendants that degenerated into legal sophistry.

In their final summations, the defense attorneys admitted that their clients were guilty of membership in an "anti-Soviet underground Zionist organization." They pleaded for mitigation of the sentences or the exact degrees of guilt. In their final statements, most of the defendants basically admitted the facts and raised question only about their own motivations. Essentially speaking for all, except Shtilbans, who had become a state witness, Butman said:

We never had the goal of undermining or weakening Soviet authority. Our purpose was: (1) struggle against assimilation, (2) free exit to Israel for all the Jews who wished to repatriate to their historical motherland.

We never had other goals or aims. We never read in official documents that the aim of the USSR was to force assimilation on minority groups, Jews among them, and we never considered free exit from the USSR to be in contradiction to Soviet legislation and the international commitments signed by the USSR.

My friends and I think that the future of our people lies only in our historical land—on Israeli soil. My friends and I, like many other Jews in the Soviet Union, dreamed of and prepared ourselves and our children for reunion with our people in Israel. Many of us applied to OVIR for permission to go to Israel, but we were refused, unlawfully.

I am accused of preparation for hijacking the plane for the purpose of escaping from the Soviet Union. Yes, I was preparing this action. I was aware that hijacking of the plane was a crime. The material in the indictment and the evidence of witnesses speak of this. I repeat that I don't want to speak about the essence of the charge brought against me. I would like only to explain the reasons that guided me.

I witnessed OVIR's unlawful refusal to issue visas to thousands of Jews who wanted to emigrate to Israel. I saw that, for the great Soviet Union, the fate of those Jews was not a problem, but for these

Jews, it was a tragedy, and the ruination of all their hopes and aspirations.

By this desperate act, we had hoped to move the problem from dead center. Besides, I believed that the Soviet Union—this mighty state—wants to destroy the people of Israel, my people. I considered it such a crying and moving injustice that no moral criterion could be relevant to the state of the USSR.

I am proud and happy that I belong to the great Jewish people, great, not in number, but in history, traditions, national and social ideals; a people who, after 2,000 years of banishment, realized their dreams of rebirth of their national state on the land of their forefathers.

Butman received a ten-year sentence; Mikhail Korenblit, seven; Kaminsky and Yagman, five; Mogilever, four; Dreizner, Boguslavsky, and Lev Korenblit, three; and Shtilbans, one year. The Section 189 charge was dismissed against Yagman and Kaminsky on the grounds that there was no proof they had knowledge the Era duplicator was stolen.*

The second Leningrad trial could hardly be considered a victory for the prosecution. The central thesis that "international Zionism is conducting disruptive activity" and carrying out "ideological sabotage against the USSR" remained as unproved as the assertions about the Zionist conspiracy against Hungary, Czechoslovakia, and Poland. The narrower charges regarding the defendants' activities were both proved and admitted, but the facts reaffirmed that a Jewish national movement, in the face of massive state power, had formed an underground organization to achieve its goals. In Soviet terms, this was subversive, but in terms of human freedom, it was heroic.

An analysis of the trial written on its final day by Dr. Meir Gelfand, then in Israel, explains the reaction of Soviet Jews to the proceedings. It was based upon the information released daily by the Soviet press agencies.

Why do people confess to what they haven't done? Why do they judge as criminal, actions that are not criminal? After all, thousands of people in the USSR received packages from friends and relatives in Israel through a London company. Packages from Israel are not delivered by the Soviet post office. Thousands in the Soviet Union study Hebrew; many teach it at home. People locate books about the history of their people, books about contemporary Israel, translate them into Russian from any language, so that their friends can learn about their historical homeland. Thousands record Israeli songs, yet

*Dreizner, Boguslavsky, and Lev Korenblit have served their time and been permitted to emigrate to Israel, where they now live.

similar tapes are being presented as evidence during the trial. People meet to consult on how to obtain a permit for exit to Israel, where to buy a Hebrew textbook, in what book store to find Howard Fast's book about the Maccabees. (*My Glorious Brothers* was being sold in 1956 in a German translation in the Soviet Union. Now its Russian translation is presented as evidence at the trial.) Thousands signed petitions to international organizations asking for help in emigrating to Israel. Why didn't they think that they were committing crimes? Because these activities are not criminal, just as the activities of the Leningrad Nine were not. Thousands of Jews in the USSR every day commit similar "crimes" and quite a few were permitted to leave. What is the reason for this selectivity? Why were some sent to Israel and others to jail? . . .

It is far better to lose a few hundred "criminals" and then frighten, by show trials directed against a small group, hundreds and thousands of others. It is quite coincidental that Mogilever and Chernoglaz were arrested and not those lucky enough to reach . . . Israel.

Why is it then that brave people are "confessing" uncommitted crimes? How is it that Mikhail Korenblit has become a physician plotting the poisoning of pilots? Why is it that, in December, Mendelevich confessed to having authored an article which he didn't write and whose real author has been given permission to leave for Israel? Why? Let the answer be given by him who had experienced the horror of solitary confinement for a few months. How can a human being oppose a pitiless machine which has perfected its methods of "treating" criminals during many years?

In the West, protests about the trial were widespread and vigorous. Addressing the Knesset on the last day of the proceedings, Israeli Premier Golda Meir set the tone for Israel and the Jewish world. Referring to the trial as one of "nine of our people," she said:

> the sole guilt of the Leningrad defendants is their wish to immigrate to Israel. . . . These Jews are not acting against the Soviet regime. Their only crime is the study of Hebrew, love of Hebrew literature, and reading an "underground" book such as *Exodus*. . . .
> The aim of these trials is not merely to try the accused, but to spread fear and terror among others, so that they should not dare to express their longing to immigrate to Israel. . . . The right of a Jew who wishes to emigrate to his people's homeland is a natural right which the Soviet Union must recognize. The struggle . . . deserves the support of all who seek justice and believe in human rights.

Mrs. Meir's response is counterposed by the Soviet assertion that all the USSR seeks to do is enforce its own laws. Both statements are correct; both are in error. The issue is one of Jewish rights and aspirations, and of basic human rights. But any assertion of these rights threatens a closed society and can be perceived as socially dangerous and illegal. Defense of Jewish rights means insistence on civil liberties in the Soviet Union, including the basic right to leave. Any such insistence, or assistance from abroad, although justified in terms of the Universal Declaration of Human Rights and universally acknowledged international standards, is an interference in Soviet domestic affairs. Soviet Jewish activists, the Israeli government, and Western Jewish organizations often avoid this reality. But the Soviet authorities, when they cite "interference in domestic affairs" as the reason for their refusal, fail to acknowledge that the method of treatment of their citizens violates human rights and cannot be excluded from world concern.

Such an analysis is uniquely Western. For Soviet Jews, living suspended between their knowledge of and affinity for Western freedom and their specific, surrealistic Soviet reality, the choice of political methods is ambiguous. At one extreme, the fanaticism required for the single-minded commitment to an underground movement leads to statements such as that of Butman: "No moral criterion could be relevant" to the Soviet state. Such attitudes toward methods led many Soviet Jewish activists to admire the activity of the Jewish Defense League in the United States. The JDL and its program were well known among Soviet Jews. Often, particularly in 1969-70, many felt that in the West only the Jewish Defense League was militantly concerned with their problem. But at the second Leningrad trial, a number of the defendants—some possibly to curry favor in sentencing, others possibly as an expression of sober reflection—denounced the JDL, which was the *bête noire* of the Soviet authorities. Deploring its "terrorist methods," Lev Korenblit stated that the JDL "disgraces my ancient race—the race that gave the world such men as Karl Marx and Einstein." And Kaminsky said, "We do not identify ourselves with those Zionists who organize raids on Soviet institutions, instead of going to Israel and working there for the good of their country." He continued retrospectively, "However, I now consider that our organization was not necessary. It was an error to have established it."

A year after the trial, Polina Yudborovskaya, the wife of Mikhail Korenblit, and herself an active member of the Leningrad group, tended to agree with Kaminsky.

> The main character of the movement up to the arrest [she said] was that it was made up of educated and intelligent people who were brave

but not careful. In contrast to the leadership in Riga and Moscow, the Leningrad center was much more emotional. In the Moscow center there were also educated people, but there was less emotion. Perhaps in Leningrad, among people like Butman, Boguslavsky, and Misha [Korenblit], their emotions and bravery caused them to commit errors in judgment. They took steps that weren't necessary. It was wrong to act illegally. They did nothing bad, but in Russia it may be illegal for Jews to type and distribute papers about Jewish life and Israel. Those in Moscow knew the line of separation between legal and illegal because they'd been in the democratic movement. And besides, they didn't have such strong emotions. Mogilever, Boguslavsky, and Misha had been in the democratic movement, too—they knew the difference—but the intensity of their emotions swept them away and they didn't use their knowledge and experience. In Riga there was a long Zionist experience. They understood how to work underground. In Moscow their knowledge of legal and illegal protected them. But in Leningrad we were too young in Zionism and not experienced enough for open struggle. During 1968 and 1969 we had decided to accept the ideas of Butman that we should be a Jewish repatriation movement. Our ideal was to do something for Jews in Russia, not to correct Russian life. But once this was decided, some felt we needed an organization to create order and discipline in the movement. This was probably a mistake. Then they wanted an organization in the whole USSR. They pushed for the VKK. This was debated in the other cities. Leningrad got its way, but this may also have been a mistake. Our group taught in *ulpanim*, taught literature, wrote letters, and signed them. We did both open and underground things, and this was a mistake. We knew of the risks, but did it anyway. At the time, we had no time to think of what we were doing. But it was wrong because people were endangered. The creation of the VKK, *Iton Aleph* and *Bet*—perhaps they were useful—but only the creation of literature is basic. The *samizdat* material helped Jews know of Israel and Jewish life. We had to do this or there would be no movement.

From the viewpoint of Soviet power, if there had been no plane, there would be no chance to attack. Soviet power needed the plane. It was Soviet power's idea to do this. It was a provocation from the beginning and they needed a provocation. The details of the Leningrad center and the plane were known to the KGB ahead of time. They were so emotional, there were no secrets. They made themselves open because they were so emotional. Butman thought the movement had to be bigger and bigger. He offered to teach Hebrew to everyone. He wanted everyone to read Jewish literature. The KGB could infiltrate us easily.

After the arrests, there was decentralization, but only briefly. Our task in Leningrad was to free our boys and not the movement. After the arrests, we understood there had been many mistakes. We had no strength or time for a big organization. We were afraid to make new mistakes. Our key people were arrested at once or a little later. Few leaders were left. Our concern for our boys caused us at first to want to avoid angering the KGB. We were very careful, but then we began again. New leadership developed. New young people joined the movement in protest against the arrests. If Soviet power thought it had stopped the movement, it was wrong. There were protests and demonstrations in the USSR and even in Leningrad. The KGB couldn't do anything except make new arrests. Then they arrested Boris Azernikov to show us their strength. But they frightened no one.

Boris Azernikov was born in 1946 in Kaliningrad (formerly Königsberg, in East Prussia), the son of a Russian Army Dental Corps officer. At 23, he was graduated from a medical institute as a stomatologist (oral surgeon) and, after working briefly in Siberia, was transferred to a village clinic in the Leningrad region. He quickly became active in the Jewish movement in Leningrad and friendly with some of its leadership. In early 1970, Butman, aware of Azernikov's athletic proclivities, asked him to teach free-style wrestling to members of the hijacking group in an effort to rehearse methods of seizing the pilot without endangering him. Along with Vladimir Knopov, a friend of his who was also active, Azernikov had purchased a "starting pistol" for possible use by the group. On June 15, 1970, he was on vacation in Odessa with Lev Yagman, when Yagman was arrested. Called as a witness in both the first and second Leningrad trials, Azernikov was less than cooperative with the KGB; he vigorously denied any anti-Soviet activities, and his testimony helped the defendants. Meantime, too, he was interrogated twenty-five separate times by the KGB and also taken to Kishinev as a witness but ultimately not called because he refused to cooperate. During this period, he was repeatedly threatened with arrest and kept under surveillance. In June 1971, he applied to OVIR and, upon being refused an exit permit, wrote a strong letter of protest. On the morning of August 15, 1971, he, too, was arrested and charged with violating Articles 70 and 72. His two-day trial, beginning October 6 and involving Dymshits, Butman, and Mikhail Korenblit as witnesses, appears to have been a retarded, punitive continuation of the second Leningrad trial—in this instance, reprisal against a recalcitrant witness and one whose activities were not materially different from those charged to the earlier group.

By then, political trials had lost their effectiveness as instruments of terror or reprisal. Each trial of an activist created new martyrs as well as the opportunity for new protest in the USSR and abroad. The trials did not suppress; they enflamed—like pouring gasoline on a smouldering fire.

Still, the authorities never learned—or perhaps never ceased trying. The mass political trials diminished in number, but the individual trials of Jews for other charges that were political at their heart continued. Typical was the experience of Nikolai Yavor, a mathematician. A prominent Leningrad activist, Yavor had been refused an exit visa to Israel thirteen times. On November 11, 1972, he finally received permission, but by then the education tax was in force and he was asked to pay 13,000 rubles (about $16,000) to reimburse the state for his higher education. He considered the education tax illegal and specifically inapplicable to his case, and he appealed this determination. On January 19, 1973, in a conference on his appeal at the OVIR office, he was told that if he did not leave by February 7, his exit visa would be canceled. Yavor protested the decision in the light of a prior administrative ruling by Deputy Interior Minister Shukaev that permission to leave the USSR, once granted, is valid for one year. He further demanded a formal administrative determination on his earlier appeal. He was asked to leave the OVIR office and was threatened with punishment of fifteen days in jail. (In the USSR, a fifteen-day sentence, like a sentence for "hooliganism," can be imposed administratively without trial.) The following day, when Yavor returned from work, he was arrested without notice to friends and family. He served ten days. Upon his release, he was told that the record showed he had been imprisoned for being "drunk and disorderly." Yavor does not drink. Again he objected, and his protests were supported by petitions signed by thirty-six other activists. On March 20, he was arrested again and charged, under Article 206/1, for "deliberate actions involving a serious breach of the peace and clearly expressing disrespect for society." The specification was that he had urinated in a children's playground. Meanwhile, Yavor had lost his job, as had his wife, Alla, a geologist. At the trial on April 2, 1973, the testimony stressed his obstreperous behavior and disrepect for OVIR officials as evidenced by his protests at their office. The sole other evidence against him was that of a KGB agent. He was sentenced to one year in prison camp.

Alla Yavor appealed the decision to the Supreme Court of the USSR in Moscow, which rarely intervenes in "hooliganism" offenses but which nevertheless accepted the appeal and sent the case back to the Leningrad City Court with a determination that the matter should be dismissed "for lack of culpability." * The Leningrad tribunal, apparently astonished at the appellate finding that there was no evidence to support the conviction, refused to dismiss the case, but reduced the sentence to five months—the time Yavor had already served in prison. Yavor was released on August 24, and on September 30, 1973, he and his wife left for Vienna en route to Israel. In an open letter of thanks addressed to all who had assisted him, Yavor described the Supreme Court determination as "surprising" and "unexpected" and attributed it to the desire of Soviet authorities to be responsive to Western public opinion in a period of détente. "It was the result of numerous protests of people from different countries."

* Yavor's case was the only hooliganism conviction reviewed and the only appellate determination that there was no evidence to support the conviction.

The hooliganism charge has been widely applied to Jews in Leningrad. Article 206/2, "malicious hooliganism," a section for particularly aggravated offenses and permitting heavier sentences, contains a clause covering recidivist conduct but also applies where there is "resistance to a representative of authority or a representative of the public in the execution of his duty in maintaining public order, or distinguished by exceptional cynicism or insolence." Yefim Krichevsky, a friend of Yavor's, and an activist who had been waiting for his exit visa for a year, was sentenced to two and a half years in prison in June 1973 because he fought with a restaurant cloakroom attendant who had made anti-Semitic remarks to him.

KISHINEV:
Moldavian Variations

CHAPTER 13

A month after the second Leningrad trial ended, nine Jewish defendants were tried in Kishinev, the capital of the Moldavian Soviet Socialist Republic. Like a weary, shopworn road show, the Kishinev trial displayed the same charges and some of the same witnesses, and similar results could be anticipated. Among the few differences was the locale.

A fertile, hilly country, Moldavia (formerly known as Bessarabia) has passed hands repeatedly between Russia and Romania, but none of the changes have improved the status of the large Jewish minority. In 1895, a virulent Romanian anti-Semitic league, exercising semiofficial power, commenced a policy of driving Jews from Romania. Those who could not escape to America fled eastward across the Russian border to the teeming ghettos of Tsarist Russia, and many settled in Kishinev, the capital of the Russian province of Bessarabia. But in the spring of 1903, a pogrom in Kishinev was the culmination of a vicious anti-Jewish newspaper campaign in Bessarabia that had been subsidized by the Tsarist regime. It was triggered, characteristically, by the discovery of the body of a Christian boy. Although a relative had confessed the crime, the Jews were falsely accused of having murdered the boy for Passover ritual purposes. Provincial officials, newspaper editors, and St. Petersburg police officers distributed printed broadsides announcing an imperial ukase sanctioning a bloody reprisal against Jews. On Easter Sunday, April 6, bands of hoodlums, often joined by police, demolished, looted, and burned Jewish dwellings. Jews were killed, tortured, and raped. Synagogues were desecrated. The carnage, lasting

213

three days, left more than six hundred Jews killed and wounded and over fifteen hundred ghetto dwellings destroyed. The civilized world was horrified. Leo Tolstoy charged that the Tsarist government was the chief culprit.

Still, there was little relief when Kishinev again became Romanian in 1918, at the end of World War I. During the interwar years, adjusting to the corrupt, repressive, yet lax environment of the Romanian kingdom, Jewish life in Kishinev thrived. But by 1940, King Carol, under heavy pressure from Hitler's Germany, accepted domination by the pro-Nazi Iron Guard, which immediately instituted intense anti-Semitic measures. Most Jews, therefore, welcomed the Red Army when it occupied Bessarabia on June 28, 1940. On August 2, northern Bukovina and southern Bessarabia were incorporated into the Ukraine, and central Bessarabia became the Moldavian Republic, the thirteenth of the Soviet Union republics. Three months later, Romania joined the Axis, and in June 1941, Moldavia fell to the joint Romanian and Nazi armies. At the time of the invasion, out of the 300,000 Jews in Bessarabia and Bukovina, well over 90,000 lived in Kishinev. Tens of thousands fled from the German armies, but 126,000 remained in Bessarabia as late as September 1941. The Nazis deported at least 140,000 Jews from the area, and ultimately most were murdered in the death camps. A Kishinev ghetto was recreated for those who remained, but not before the Nazis murdered 12,000 more Jews. When the Red Army reoccupied the territory in August 1944, few Jews were left to be liberated. Of those fortunate enough to have fled or to have survived deportation to Romania, many flocked to Palestine. Others straggled back to Kishinev and the Soviet Moldavian Republic.

According to the 1959 census, the 95,000 Jews in Moldavia constituted 3.3% of the total population, the highest concentration of Jews in any Soviet republic. The same census showed more than 43,000 Jews in Kishinev, or 20% of that city's total population. The census also revealed that over 50% of the Jews reported Yiddish as their mother tongue. (That figure was exceeded only in Lithuania.) Thus, Kishinev and Moldavia had among the highest concentration of Jews and Jewish cultural background in the USSR. According to Jewish estimates, there were 130,000 Moldavian Jews in 1972, of whom 55,000 lived in Kishinev. But no Jew sat in the Supreme Soviet of the Moldavian Republic, and Jews generally not only experienced the patterns of discrimination and anti-Semitism found in other parts of the

USSR, but also inherited a tragic historic memory of violence and insecurity. More than most other Soviet Jews (only the Jews of Latvia and Lithuania are comparable), they had a strong Yiddish and Zionist tradition, and many had relatives in Israel. They responded exultantly to the creation of that state and to the Six-Day War. Among younger, well-educated Jews, there was also a spirit of militancy and a desire for freedom that their anxious, frightened parents could not display.

Midway between Kishinev and Odessa is the Moldavian city of Bendery, with a population of 50,000, almost 20% of whom are Jews. Among them were two high school teachers, Yakov Suslensky, born in 1928, who taught English, and Iosif Mishener, eight years younger, who taught history. Both had Jewish backgrounds and strong Jewish identifications. Mishener, a member of the Communist Party, had graduated from medical school and worked as a radiologist, but he went on to do graduate work in history and became a teacher. The two men shared ideas, alienation from their society, and ultimately the same peril. Knowing no other way to protest the absence of freedom of speech and the disparity between Soviet practices and constitutional principles, Suslensky began writing scholarly letters of protest to the Central Committee of the Communist Party. Both men independently wrote open letters condemning the invasion of Czechoslovakia in 1968. One of the letters described the invasion of Czechoslovakia and the barbaric hanging of nine Jews in Baghdad as kindred atrocities. Mishener was expelled from the party and dismissed from his job. At the end of 1969, he wrote to the UN complaining of the violations of human rights involved in those occurrences. Shortly thereafter, Suslensky was arrested. In the search of his home, tape recordings of BBC broadcasts were found, as well as a detailed diary and copies of his letters and those of his friend. Mishener, too, was arrested, and he and Suslensky were charged under the Moldavian equivalent of Russian Article 70. At their trial at the end of October 1970, the prosecution asked for a three-year sentence for Suslensky and two years for Mishener, but the court sentenced them to seven and six years, respectively. Even in the USSR that was astonishingly severe, particularly since they were not well known and had not circulated their letters abroad or widely in the Soviet Union. Suslensky and Mishener were, as Margarita Shpilberg of Riga later described them, "lonely battlers for freedom."

In the camps at Potma, they became friendly with the prisoners from Ryazan who had preceded them, and they were soon joined by those from the Leningrad trials and later by those from Kishinev. With others, they renounced Soviet citizenship, insisted on Jewish practices, and participated in hunger strikes in support of Jewish movement objectives. Although their arrest and trial had been reported in *Khronika* and were known to Jewish activists in the USSR who, along with their fellow-prisoners, had urged their support by the outside world, Suslensky and Mishener have remained generally unknown, presumably because their travail resulted from *samizdat* activity that was not of a specifically Jewish character.

Not all Jewish dissenters in Moldavia were intellectuals like Suslensky and Mishener. Some, like Yankel Leibovich Khantsis, were simple workers. Khantsis was born in Kishinev in 1929, when the city was part of Romania, of Jewish parents of Austrian nationality. His formal education ceased at the end of the fourth grade, as Red Army troops occupied the city. During the war, he was separated from his family, most of whom died in the Holocaust. After the war, he became a truck driver, married, and had two children. From all accounts, he was a strong, stable worker and an affectionate father. In 1966, he learned that his sister had survived the war and was in Israel with a family of her own. She soon sent the Khantsis family a *vizov*. In early 1967, he applied to OVIR and was refused. Many refusals followed, but he persisted. The authorities threatened. Khantsis made multiple official complaints. In early 1970, he was fired from his job, and his driver's license was revoked. But Khantsis was stubborn. Unable to get his renewed OVIR application completed because he could not obtain a *kharakteristika* (a formal character reference from the place of employment), Khantsis went to Moscow to complain to higher authorities. The Presidium of the Supreme Soviet and the Central Committee of the CPSU refused to listen to the obstinate Jew from Kishinev. He called the Netherlands Embassy, which represented the interests of Israel in the USSR, to tell his story, and since the militia that guarded the embassy would not permit him to enter the building, he arranged to meet with an embassy secretary across the street. But instead of the official, three militia men and two dressed as civilians came up to him, beat him severely, pushed him into a car, and had him taken to a Moscow hospital. That was on June 19, 1970. Almost two months later, Khantsis was released from the hospital and on August 17 was placed on trial, charged with malicious hooliganism (Article 206/2). The trial was a closed one. His family was not permitted in the courtroom. Khantsis was sentenced to two and a half years in a prison camp in the Kirov district.

But prison did not make Khantsis less stubborn or less determined to go to Israel. He wrote dozens of indignant letters protesting his innocence, insisting on his right to leave for his homeland and excoriating Soviet injustice. The torrent of protests to President Podgorny, Premier Kosygin, Chairman Brezhnev, and other officials evoked no response, except that Khantsis was sent to Moscow's Serbsky Institute, a psychiatric hospital, which is distinguished for the number of prominent political dissenters it has found insane. But after a few months, even Serbsky despaired of Khantsis. He was certified sane and returned to the prison camp which, on April 18, 1971, paroled him to the neighboring town of Omutninsk, for forced labor in "the construction of the national economy." There he continued to insist on his rights. Finally, on August 30, 1972, a Kirov district court handed down a lengthy bill of indictment under Section 190-1 of the Criminal Code of the RSFSR. Section 190-1, a convenient catch-all for dissenters since its promulgation in 1966, makes criminal "the circulation of knowingly false fabrications which defame the Soviet state and social system." The indictment stated that from December 1970 to May 1972, Khantsis had been involved in fourteen counts of illegal activity embracing several dozen individual criminal acts. All of the criminal behavior charged consisted of writing letters to officials or making comments to fellow-prisoners and friends. The indictment summarized the long list of specific charges as follows:

> While insistently demanding an exit visa to Israel, Khantsis, from December 1970 to May 1972, systematically disseminated among citizens deliberately false fabrications, defaming the Soviet state and social system in oral and written forms, comparing it unfavorably to the state system of Israel, which he described as an exemplary one, in one of the world's most advanced states.
>
> In his letters addressed to highest party, government, and Soviet organs, he called the leaders of the party and the government fascists; and the Soviet system of management, double-faced, hypocritical, and fascistic. The Soviet state system was called unjust, vulgar, speculative, exploitative, opportunistic, and fascistic. He stated that hypocrisy, lawlessness, arbitrary rule, exploitation, and oppression of man exist in the Soviet Union. With respect to treatment of the Jewish nationality, he claimed humiliation, racism, discrimination, and abasement.

He disseminated slanderous fabrications about Soviet justice. He told
citizens and wrote in letters that the Soviet Union lacks any hu-
maneness and that innocent people are imprisoned without cause. He
alleges that he had been sentenced not for a crime, but for his belonging to the Jewish nationality.

All of this is a crime under the statute 190–1 of the Criminal Code of
the RSFSR.

At his trial, Khantsis did not deny having made the comments
attributed to him. He pleaded truth and his right to criticize. On December 29, 1972, he was given another two-year sentence for his stub-
bornness, many months of which he spent in solitary confinement. As a
result of having been beaten in prison camp, Khantsis has suffered spinal
fractures and is now paralyzed.

Within Moldavia, the Suslensky-Mishener example was noted, as was
the Khantsis case, most particularly by a group of recent university
graduates in Kishinev who had formed a Jewish movement group.
Although Kishinev, with its substantial Jewish population, had experienced sporadic Zionist underground activity, not until 1968 had a group
with close ties to other cities come into existence. Instrumental in the
formation of the Kishinev organization were two young Leningrad
engineers, 28-year-old David Chernoglaz and 22-year-old Anatoly
Goldfeld, who made the initial contact with local activists. Goldfeld,
though a resident of Leningrad, was then working at a Kishinev research
institute. The core of the group was five young men, all recent graduates in various fields of engineering from the Kishinev Polytechnic Institute, all friends, and all about Goldfeld's age: Aleksandr Galperin and
Arkady Voloshin (both co-employees of Goldfeid), Gari Kirzhner,
David Rabinovich, and Lazar Trakhtenberg. Their group was augmented by other young people, including Semyon Levit, a 25-year-old
physicist at the cancer research institute. Chernoglaz, only slightly
older than the others, was already a veteran member of the Leningrad
organization. As a 20-year-old student in 1960, he had experienced difficulties with the KGB because of his alleged authorship of a letter
describing desecration of a Jewish cemetery in Leningrad.

The group's first activities were the creation of *ulpanim* to teach
Hebrew and the distribution of literature from Leningrad. As their
samizdat activity and Hebrew instruction expanded, more Kishinev
young people joined their ranks. The organization formalized and
adopted rules of procedure. It also began planning ambitious projects

such as the organization of a summer camp for Moldavian Jewish youngsters where Hebrew and Jewish culture could be taught. Contacts were strengthened with Leningrad and made with Odessa, Moscow, and other cities. In the summer of 1969, aware of the pressing need for equipment to reproduce the Hebrew grammar *Elef Milim* (One Thousand Words) and other material, the group discussed where a photocopying machine could be found. (It was, of course, not possible to purchase such equipment legally.) Galperin learned from Rabinovich that there was an Era portable photocopier at his place of work, the Moldavian branch of the USSR Tsentrosoyuz (Central Council of Cooperative Unions) Institute of Design.

On a late Sunday evening in the summer of 1969, Rabinovich led Galperin and Voloshin to the basement where they disassembled the machine, and they carried away the parts in separate parcels. It was both dangerous and unwise to keep the Era in Kishinev. A code name —Motorboat—had been adopted for the operation. Arrangements were made to transport the machine to Leningrad where the need was greater and where the finished products could be sent back to Kishinev by the Leningrad center. Voloshin's uncle, Gerts, was a conductor on the Kishinev-Leningrad railway line, and without knowing the contents, he agreed to carry the boxes to Leningrad. In early September, Galperin called Goldfeld and told him the number of the train and the time of its arrival. Goldfeld and Trakhtenberg, who had also traveled to Leningrad, met the train, secured the boxes from Gerts, and gave them to Chernoglaz, who was waiting outside the station with transportation. Chernoglaz took the boxes to his *dacha* outside the city and then carefully transferred the machine piece by piece to the apartment of Hillel Shur, a 33-year-old engineer who possessed mechanical skill with office machinery. Shur lived with his mother and his younger sister Kreina, who, like himself, was a dedicated Jewish activist. Unfortunately, in the process of disassembling and transporting the machine, a critical part was lost. Solomon Dreizner was assigned the task of making the Era operative, and Shur was to assist. They were, however, unable to secure a new part or to fashion an adequate substitute, and the machine was never put to use.

Meanwhile, in Kishinev, the theft was discovered, and Rabinovich became the prime suspect. He was charged in an administrative proceeding and fined. KGB officials may have known what happened to the machine and been simply biding their time to catch larger fish.

By late January 1970, through Butman, Goldfeld was aware of the plans for an escape by airplane, and Galperin learned of the proposed hijacking shortly thereafter. He and Voloshin flew to Leningrad to discuss the plans with Butman, Dymshits, and others. Mikhail Korenblit came to Kishinev to discuss the Wedding plans with Galperin and advised that fifty-four tickets had to be purchased in advance to make the plan work, since they could not take the chance that others would occupy the seats. Galperin, Voloshin, Kirzhner, and a fourth activist, Isai Fishman (who soon changed his mind and withdrew from contact) agreed to go on the Wedding trip. Each raised 30 rubles for an air ticket, and Voloshin took the 120 rubles to Leningrad. Not long afterward, the Wedding plan was abandoned. None of the Kishinev organization members appear to have been aware of Dymshits's revised plans, nor did they have advance knowledge of the actual hijack attempt.

On June 15, 1970, Chernoglaz and Goldfeld were arrested along with their friends and colleagues who constituted most of the leadership of the Leningrad Center. Searches took place that day and on subsequent days in Kishinev. On July 24, Galperin was arrested; Shur was detained on August 5, and Voloshin, Rabinovich, and Trakhtenberg on August 15. Kirzhner and Levit were not arrested until November 17, but Kirzhner was both searched and heavily interrogated prior to that time.

The search of Chernoglaz's *dacha* on June 15 is memorialized by an official KGB protocol reproduced in full in *Iskhod* No. 3. The search was made in the presence of Berta Veinger, Chernoglaz's wife. Seized, among other things, were: photocopies of articles from Israeli newspapers and of letters from Soviet Jews; a 1965 article on Arab-Israeli relations from *Midstream* (an American Zionist magazine); copybook notes of Hebrew grammar; a photocopied textbook of Jewish history by Dubnov published in Petrograd in 1918; a *samizdat* (typed) book, *How I Fought for Justice;* typewritten and handwritten lecture notes on Jewish history and culture; and eight recording tapes. A search the same day of Voloshin's Kishinev apartment resulted in the confiscation of three volumes of the pre-Revolutionary *Jewish Encyclopedia,* published in Russian; Dubnov's *History of the Jews in Europe,* published in Riga in 1936; and three different editions of *Elef Milim.* A search of Shur's apartment on August 5 led to seizure of a travel brochure in English called *This Is Israel* and a 1965 Russian-language copy of the Israeli literary magazine *Ariel,* the feature article of which was "Shakespeare on the Israeli Stage."

The KGB interrogated many prospective witnesses. Galya Ladyzhenskaya, a 25-year-old Odessa graduate student, who acted as a courier for the movement, was summoned to the KGB in Odessa on November 15, 1970. It was evident from the questioning that the KGB was seeking to prove that there was a widely dispersed but centrally organized Zionist underground in the USSR. Although they knew of the VKK by now, they apparently desired to prove the interconnections between cities, particularly with Kishinev. The two-day interrogation centered on those connections and particularly on Ladyzhenskaya's knowledge concerning Galperin, Voloshin, Chernoglaz, and Goldfeld. Goldfeld had already given information that he had traveled to Odessa in the summer of 1969 at Chernoglaz's suggestion to see Ladyzhenskaya concerning OVIR matters. She provided little information and specifically denied most charges concerning the movement in Kishinev and its connections to Odessa and Leningrad. Her testimonial utility was obviously limited because a few months later she was permitted to go to Israel.

Hillel Shur's case was the most inexplicable one of the Kishinev defendants. Although an active member of the Leningrad organization, he knew no one in Kishinev and had no connections at all with Kishinev, except for the abortive effort to reconstruct the Era photocopier. On June 19, 1970, his apartment was searched, but nothing was found. On July 2, he and Grigory Vertlib addressed a strong open letter of protest to the authorities about the arrests of their friends. Thereafter, Vertlib was arrested, released, and soon given an exit visa to Israel. Efforts by the KGB to obtain responses in their interrogation of Shur were unsuccessful, and early on the morning of August 5, he was seized in his apartment, lifted from his bed, and taken to KGB headquarters. When he again refused to serve as a witness against others, he was arrested and charged with violating Articles 70 and 72. He still refused to speak. On October 1, his case was detached from that of the other Leningrad defendants and sent to Kishinev, where he was taken and jailed.

While in prison camp, after his sentencing, on October 25, 1971, Shur prepared a detailed declaration of protest to the Presidium of the Supreme Soviet. It documents at length "the tyranny of the investigating agencies," the "violations of due process of law," various "flagrant violations of Soviet law in the court proceedings," and constitutes a comprehensive indictment of the legal processes from arrest to sentencing. Among other contentions, Shur claims that the Kishinev investigators "went so far as to use physical measures against me," that

222THE LAST EXODUS

medical assistance (for an ulcer) was denied him, that he was constantly threatened with "prison and confinement to a mental hospital" and with "the arrest of my younger sister." He notes that the literature seized in searches was endorsed as material evidence of anti-Soviet activity. Also included were Howard Fast's *My Glorious Brothers,* a story of the Maccabees which was cited as told "from a nationalistic point of view," and Dubnov's books, which although formerly used in Soviet Jewish schools and still available in state libraries, are categorized as "replete with nationalistic and Zionist ideas." The books seized from Voloshin were similarly described, even though the *Jewish Encyclopedia* was still occasionally available in antiquarian book stores and was a standard work. Shur described Captain Ivanov, the senior investigator who categorized the literature as material evidence, as "not just ignorant. His ignorance is militant and takes on the aspects of hooliganism." Ivanov had ordered the destruction, as having no relevance to the case, of seized copies of *Prayers, Rites and Religious Laws of the Jewish People.* Shur commented: "A savage, barbarian act! I wonder whether Jewish prayer books have been burned since the Spanish Inquisition." Shur lists a number of other books of Jewish history and Hebrew grammar confiscated by the KGB investigators preparing the Kishinev trial, under the direction of Major Kulikov, the Moldavian KGB investigative chief.

> The law does not exist for Kulikov. [He] does everything to root out "Jewish sedition" . . . His actions reek from afar with anti-Semitism. He is ready to forbid Soviet Jews to study their language, history, and literature, and to celebrate their religious holidays. He appended the poems of Bialik, the great Jewish poet and a classic of Jewish literature, as material evidence, that is, instruments in the commission of crimes.

Shur's declaration demonstrates that the terrorization of the burgeoning Jewish national movement in Moldavia was a primary motive for the trial. The trial itself confirmed the charge. It opened on June 21, 1971, with a strong police cordon encircling the courtroom. A streetcar stop in front of the courthouse was removed, ostensibly to prevent curious Soviet Jews or foreign journalists from mingling with the queues of people normally waiting. The public was not allowed to approach the court building without a pass, and although the trial was again "public," only a few relatives were permitted to join the carefully preselected audience. Chernoglaz, Shur, Voloshin, Galperin, Goldfeld, and Kirzhner were charged with organizing and abetting the hijacking effort, with appropriating state property, and with anti-Soviet propaganda and organization. Trakhtenberg was accused of the last three charges, Levit with the last two, and Rabinovich only with theft of the Era machine. The Moldavian equivalents of the RSFSR's Articles 70 and 72 were made specific by reference to Uris's *Exodus, The Six Day War* by Randolph Churchill, *My Glorious Brothers,* and *Iton Aleph* and *Bet.* The defendants from Leningrad pleaded not guilty. Shur startled the courtroom by declaring:

> The Kishinev court is not competent to try me; I have never been to Kishinev; not a single witness to the items in the indictment relating to me is a resident of Kishinev. Not once since the time I was transferred from Leningrad to the Kishinev investigation prison have I been questioned on the case of the Era theft. Investigator Kulikov, in the presence of the procurator, proposed that I should plead guilty and be released from custody in the courtroom; otherwise I would get five to seven years' imprisonment.

After announcing that the prosecution had attempted to make a deal, he refused to cooperate in the trial and declared a hunger strike. He later amplified these remarks in his complaint to the Supreme Soviet:

> Immediately following the end of the trial, right there in the courtroom, a representative of the KGB took away from me (as from the others who had been sentenced) my copy of the indictment. Apparently the authors of the sentence and the indictment aren't too comfortable about their work, and are "shy" about handing copies of these documents to the accused, as required by the law. But not too "shy" to break the law once again, the law which they are called upon to defend.

Thirty-two witnesses testified, including Butman, Lev Korenblit, Yagman, Dreizner, Mogilever, and Mikhail Korenblit. Neither they nor the young activists from Kishinev who were called were helpful to the prosecution. The Kishinev youths came to court in blue shirts and white trousers (Israel's national colors) and wearing Stars of David. Four university students, all involved in the movement and attending *ulpanim* —Etta Bondar, Olga Treigerman, Aleksandr Zhenin, and Riva Waksman—refused to testify. A fifth university student, Yury Dorfman, told the court he was prepared to testify only in his native language, Yiddish. To applause from the "public," the procurator demanded that proceedings should be taken against them for refusing to give testimony. (On September 1, most of the recalcitrant witnesses were given sentences of six months' corrective labor plus a fine of 20% of their earnings. One was fined 60 rubles.)

The defendants were found guilty and sentenced on June 30. Chernoglaz received five years; Goldfeld, four; Galperin, two and a half; Voloshin, Kirzhner, Levit, Trakhtenberg, and Shur, two; and Rabinovich, one year. The following day, the Kishinev paper *Molodezh Moldavii* summarized the significance of the trial:

> The "ideological" brainwashing of the executors of criminal plans, such as Butman, Dymshits, and Kuznetsov, was carried out in the so-called *ulpanim*, where under the guise of studying "history," the Hebrew language (the official language of the State of Israel), as well as the geography of the Near East, individual citizens of the Soviet Union of Jewish nationality were drawn into engaging in subversive antisocialist activity. Among these persons nationalist feelings were ignited, and hatred was inculcated for all the peoples of our country. . . .
>
> The *ulpanim* were one of the spheres of the criminal activity of the accused. "In addition to studies in history," testified Voloshin in court, "and in the language that I taught, we disseminated among the students Zionist literature, which contained attacks on the policy of the Soviet Union." In the *ulpans* slanderous fabrications were spread that defamed Soviet reality and that roused vile nationalist feelings.

Since the trial, Jewish activity in Kishinev has intensified. The defendants who have served their prison time—Galperin, Voloshin, Kirzhner, Levit, Trakhtenberg, Shur, and Rabinovich—and witnesses have left for Israel, but *ulpanim* still exist in Kishinev, and so does the Jewish movement.

THE RIGA TRIAL:
Disaster for the Prosecution

CHAPTER 14

The Riga trial, which began on May 24, 1971, was a greater disaster for the prosecution than any of the other trials. More intensely Zionist and more culturally Jewish than other Soviet Jews, the Jews of Riga were steeled to adversity and better prepared for the ordeal of trial. By now, important leaders of the movement from Riga were in Israel and thus able to secure information and direct a defensive campaign in the West. None of the accused had any connection with the hijacking plans and none was involved in the theft of the Era machine. In the two Leningrad proceedings and the Kishinev trial, the prosecution was able to charge and prove acts, attempts, or advance knowledge that could be viewed as criminal in most societies. In Riga, however, the entire case was predicated upon the propagation through literature of the Zionist point of view. This was a subversion trial pure and simple, and as such it was anathema to anyone who believed in civil liberties.

The four Riga defendants, like those in the other cases, were young, attractive, articulate, and well educated. Arkady (Aron) Shpilberg, viewed by the prosecution as the ringleader of the group, was a 33-year-old design engineer, formerly a key member of the Leningrad organization who, since 1967 and his residence in Riga, had become a tough-minded organizer of the Jewish movement there. Slight, square-jawed, and prematurely balding, he was determined, forceful, and courageous. Mikhail (Misha) Shepshelovich, a 28-year-old metal worker and student of advanced physics and mathematics, was dark-haired,

226

THE LAST EXODUS

handsome, quietly intense, and reserved. A tall, large man, with dark curly hair, black-rimmed glasses, and a sad, gentle face, Boris Maftser, a 25-year-old engineer, alone of the four defendants, ultimately cooperated fully with the prosecution. In the courtroom, he exhibited a submissiveness and contriteness that augmented his beaten, puppylike appearance. The large light blue eyes, curly light brown hair, and schoolgirlish appearance of Ruta Aleksandrovich, a 23-year-old nurse, belied her stubborn, strong, intense personality. She was the focus of attention in the West.

Ruta's unusual prominence in the outside world resulted largely from the fact that her aunt, Leah Slovin (see pages 62ff.), assisted from Israel in orchestrating the defense of the Riga Four (as, inevitably, they came to be known). Her energy was awesome. In support of the movement, she traveled to Europe, England, and the United States, prodded and berated the Israeli authorities, and maintained a constant flow of information from Riga to Tel Aviv and then to the world. No other person was more responsible for world knowledge about the plight of Riga's Jews.

Leah was aided—originally from Riga, and from mid-April 1971 from Jerusalem—by her older sister, Rivka Aleksandrovich, Ruta's mother. A stout, strong-minded secondary-school teacher, Rivka had a tongue as biting as Leah's. She could communicate freely in English, whereas Leah at times struggled in that language. Rivka's departure from Riga a month before Ruta's trial began helped turn the proceedings into a disastrous propaganda rout for the Soviet regime. Apparently calculating that Rivka should be given an exit visa because of her frequent and troublesome communications to the West, the authorities found themselves confronted with both sisters energetically agitating in Israel, Europe, and America. Shortly after Rivka's arrival in Israel with her son Viktor (Avigdor), who was soon to turn 18 (an important factor in her decision to leave, since she feared that he would be inducted into the Red Army), she was off to England and then to the United States, where she told the UN, public officials, Catholic cardinals, Billy Graham, newspapers, television, and large, rapt audiences about the upcoming trial and its background.

The Aleksandroviches were a remarkable family. Their spacious home in Riga had been an "open house" where local Jews and out-of-town guests could meet, discuss Jewish matters, listen to Jewish records, and keep the important personal contacts that lubricated the movement.

Ruta's father, Yitzhak, a slight, blue-eyed man with receding light brown hair, had managed a state clothing store. He is the brother of Mikhail Aleksandrovich, a well-known Moscow opera singer before his departure for Israel. From childhood on, Ruta was intensely Jewish and became deeply involved in the Zionist movement. Her aunt Leah's emigration to Israel in 1969 gave her direct links to that country. Enrolling at the Moscow Teachers Institute in the fall of 1967, she became friendly with David Khavkin and, with other young Moscow Jews, actively participated in Khavkin's circle. Soon she dropped out of school, in part to enable herself to devote more time to her Jewish activities. By 1969, she was maintaining and broadening contacts with burgeoning Jewish movement groups throughout the USSR. She frequently traveled to Moscow, Leningrad, Kiev, Minsk, Kharkov, Odessa, and other cities as a courier and disseminator of information. She met Isai (Sanya) Averbukh of Odessa, whom she subsequently married. Sanya, full of democratic conviction and poetic passion, became a militant member of the Jewish movement.

On June 15, 1970, Ruta's twenty-third birthday, the arrests and searches began in Riga. The Aleksandrovich house and a family summer home at the seashore were searched. Hebrew books and dictionaries, Israeli postcards, copies of petitions and letters, personal correspondence—all were seized. Almost daily interrogation of Ruta followed. She intransigently refused to cooperate with the KGB. At the end of September, she wrote an open letter, "In the Expectation of Arrest," which began: "One after another of my friends are arrested and, evidently, it will soon be my turn."

> Of what am I guilty? I don't know how the charge will be formulated and what statute will come to the minds of my accusers. I only know that my conscience is clear.
>
> I shall be put on trial only because I am a Jewess and, as a Jewess, cannot imagine life for myself without Israel. I am 23 years old. My entire conscious existence has been tied with the Jewish state, and it is not my fault that up to the present I had no possibility of making use of my indubitable right—to go to my homeland, to Israel. . . .
>
> I don't know what my fate will be. I don't know how many years of life, how much health and strength the prison or the camp will take away from me. But to all who will not remain indifferent to this letter of mine, I promise that never will anyone be able to take away my conscience and my heart, I shall never betray my friends, those who today are in Israel, and those who are still here. I shall never

betray my much-suffering people. I shall never betray my most cherished dream—to live, to work, and to die in Israel.

Her turn came on October 7th. Her mother describes the event:

> Early in the morning, five KGB men entered our flat. They pushed Ruta's dog aside and ordered Ruta to come with them. To our question where they were taking her, they answered that she must be questioned and that she would be back home in a few hours. Thus she was not permitted to say goodbye to her family and her fiancé. She was hardly given time to dress, and was taken away, by two of the KGB men. At the very last moment, standing in the doorway, she told me: "Mother, if something happens, don't wait for me. Go to Israel." Those were her last words to me. I have not seen her since, nor had words from her.
>
> When she was gone, the remaining three men handed me an order for Ruta's arrest and for a search of the house. To my question why did they arrest her, Major Parushov answered that she was accused of anti-Soviet agitation and propaganda. "She did not want to give us evidence during the interrogations, so she is arrested." Later that statement was repeated by two other investigators, Korobionkov and Brovadsky.

Within days after her arrest, her fiancé Sanya Averbukh, her mother, and other Riga friends addressed a lengthy "Appeal to the Jewish People," which was the start of her defense. It concluded:

> Jewish People! You are our only support and hope. You and we are one body out of which you cannot extract a single cell without causing pain to all the others. What has happened to Ruta Aleksandrovich has already happened to many of our brethren and can, at any moment, happen to anyone of us. Let each person who considers himself a Jew raise his voice in defense of Ruta Aleksandrovich; in defense of all Jews arrested for their love for their people and their wish for an exodus to the land sacred to us, because their fate is truly our common fate.

Sanya then wrote to Israel's aged chief rabbi, Yehuda Unterman.

> By arresting my fiancée a few days before our wedding, the KGB authorities have nullified the registration of our marriage and have made impossible our wedding in the Riga synagogue. . . .
> At present, the official Soviet institutions refuse to register our marriage and thus, from the point of Soviet law, we are strangers to each other, because in neither her passport nor in mine is there a

corresponding notation. Practically, this means that we have no right either to see each other or to have any other sort of communion.

Today, we are separated from each other by impenetrable walls but hear each other with our hearts because nothing in the world can interfere with our love. We know nothing about our tomorrow. Even in expectation of arrest, we carefully keep our vow of faithfulness.

I appeal to you with the request to recognize our marriage as valid and to marry us *in absentia* in Israel, in that ancient homeland of our people, whose call has forever united our souls and has made our hearts beat in unison.

Rabbi Unterman never replied. The following spring, shortly before the trial, England's chief rabbi, Immanuel Jakobovits, agreed to marry Ruta and Sanya *in absentia,* as a part of symbolic protest against the ordeal of the trial, but the idea was discouraged by Israeli authorities.

Other efforts were made to attract attention to Ruta's case. Comparison with a parallel case was made in a BBC External Service Current Affairs Talk:

Two young girls have recently attracted worldwide attention. They share the common expectation of a forthcoming political trial. By far the better known is Angela Davis, the first Communist heroine in a long time. Less publicized is Ruth Aleksandrovich, a 23-year-old Jewish girl imprisoned in Riga. Comparisons between the two are illustrative of differing moralities and the illogical inconsistency of world public opinion. Both girls are young, Ruth Aleksandrovich at 23 is believed to be the youngest political prisoner in the Soviet Union, Angela Davis is a former instructor of philosophy and Ruth Aleksandrovich is a student nurse. Angela Davis is charged with a nonpolitical crime—accessory before the fact of the murder of a California judge. Ruth is charged with anti-Soviet propaganda, clearly the political crime of advocacy. The indictment against Angela Davis is known to her and the world public. Ruth Aleksandrovich still does not know the particulars of the charges against her, although imprisoned since last October. Miss Davis has a team of energetic and talented attorneys diligently defending her. Miss Aleksandrovich is unrepresented and incapable of securing counsel who are not Soviet agents. Angela Davis has had the widespread support, visits, and consultation of family, friends, and supporters. She continues to speak and write. No one but her KGB jailers have been able to see Ruth Aleksandrovich since her arrest. She has been denied food parcels and medicine because she wrote a Mogen David on one of the lifts in the KGB prison. She has been denied medical care although she suffers from bronchial asthma. Angela Davis's attorneys will have the right to preliminary motions and challenges to the prejudice of Cali-

230 THE LAST EXODUS

fornia judges, and unlimited challenge to the jury selection is expected to consume weeks of time. Ruth Aleksandrovich, not being informed of a trial date and having no attorney, is unable to prepare a defense. No provisions exist in Riga for challenging the judges and there are no juries. Miss Davis's anticipated trial will be public, with the massive glare of world news media focussing on every word and witness. The Soviet Union's request to send official observers to her trial was promptly granted. Miss Aleksandrovich's trial will be secret. Past precedent suggests that no news media will be permitted to cover the trial, and no observers will be allowed.

The world has been urged to demand the freeing of Angela Davis. No voices have been more insistent than those of Moscow and the world's Communist parties. Yet no one suggests that Miss Davis has suffered any violation of universally accepted human rights. Ruth Aleksandrovich, like some 350,000 other Soviet Jews, has been requesting that the Soviet Union honor their Universal Declaration of Human Rights commitment that "every person has a right to leave any country including his own." The charges against Ruth and her three young co-defendants are that they insisted on this right. She is charged with circulating literature requesting that the Soviet Union let her people go, with circulating literature about Israel, and with advocating the teaching of the Hebrew language. These activities are required to be protected as expressions of opinion and conscience under Human Rights conventions, to which the Soviet Union has adhered. Yet their exercise is punishable by seven years in Soviet labor camps. Angela Davis is not being tried for being a Communist. This is irrelevant to the charges against her. But the only crime charged against Ruth Aleksandrovich is that she is an active Zionist. We are not able to, and in any event should not, prejudge whether Miss Davis assisted in the murder of the judge. Miss Aleksandrovich proudly acknowledges that she circulated literature about Israel and requesting the right to leave Russia. She asks whether such activities can be a crime in any civilized society.

A world hardened by inhumanity, mass violence, and genocide yearns for heroes and heroines. It is uplifted by evidence of the unquenchable free spirit of others. One may raise the question as to why the plight of Ruth Aleksandrovich and her fellow defendants has not aroused as widespread public concern as the forthcoming trial of her fellow defendant Angela Davis. One may ask why world student groups have not formed "Free Ruth Aleksandrovich" committees. One may even enquire as to whether there is a double standard for freedom fighters.

At the request of the World Union of Jewish Students, Henry McGee, a UCLA law professor and one of Angela Davis's counsel, traveled to the USSR in an effort to observe the Riga trial. He was denied permission to be an observer, denied opportunity to meet the families of the defendants and even to learn the official view respecting the proceedings.

Angela Davis was ultimately acquitted in a fair jury trial. After her release from custody, she issued a statement that she would devote her time to fighting to free political prisoners everywhere. When asked to intervene on behalf of Soviet and Czech political prisoners, however, she refused, indicating that she did not think that people should seek to leave socialist countries for capitalist ones.

Fortunately, the Riga defendants were not dependent for their support upon people whose views of freedom were similar to those of Angela Davis. Protests developed from many sources. The USSR was deluged with individual appeals from well-known people in many countries whose civil liberties convictions were not equivocal. There was also protest from the U.S. State Department, members of the British Parliament, spokesmen for a number of other governments, and even the Commonwealth of Massachusetts, whose unanimous Senate resolution condemned the trial. But no protests were more worrisome to the Soviet authorities than those in Riga itself. Instead of cringing in fear, Riga Jews commenced outspoken activity. Isai Averbukh was arrested by Riga police and immediately declared a hunger strike in jail, where he fasted throughout the period of the trial. A group of young Jews who announced a hunger strike in Riga's synagogue to last until the end of the trial were barred from the synagogue and given fifteen days' imprisonment on a hooliganism charge. Others who tried to enter the synagogue to protest these detentions were also arrested. Twelve other Jews who announced their intention to demonstrate against the trial were given exit permits immediately. Many persons signed petitions that circulated in Riga.

As the trial opened, the extreme anxiety of Soviet officials became apparent. Instead of being conducted in the courthouse, the proceedings were transferred to the Fisherman's Club, a large workers' building, 20 kilometers from the city center. Approaches to the peninsular site were over a single bridge heavily guarded by police. The "public trial" charade was repeated, and admission was as selective as in previous proceedings. Fortunately, a close relative of one of the defendants managed to bring a small tape recorder into court, and the four-day trial was recorded almost in its entirely, resulting in one of the most detailed transcripts of any Soviet political proceeding.

Shpilberg and Maftser were charged under Articles 65 and 67 of the Latvian Criminal Code (the equivalents of Russian Articles 70 and 72), while Aleksandrovich and Shepshelovich were indicted on Article 65 only. The specifications in connection with Article 67 included participation by Maftser and Shpilberg in the VKK and in the formation of a Riga *samizdat* committee.* The Article 67 charges included the publication of *Iton, Your Native Tongue,* and a book called *The Biography and the Poems of a Soviet Jew,* as well as the distribution of other books and pamphlets, including the American novels *Exodus* and *My Glorious Brothers.* Among the more serious charges was the distribution of a pamphlet prepared in Israel by former Rigaites and sent into the USSR: *For the Repatriation of Soviet Jews; and Domoi* (To the Homeland), one issue of which carried the "For the Repatriation" article. *Domoi,* a four-by-six-inch thin paper pamphlet printed in Russian, began appearing in 1969. The first few issues were written in Israel by Dov Shperling and financed by Joseph Mirelman, an Israeli banker, who, having originally come from the Baltic countries, had a long-time militant interest in the fate of Soviet Jews. Its tone and content were stridently Revisionist Zionist, and some of its issues featured articles by Jabotinsky. Through January 1971, seven issues were produced. *Domoi* reached the Soviet Union in a number of ways. Some copies were brought in by tourists, some were carefully enclosed in packages of other goods mailed from European countries, and microfilms of some issues were brought in to Soviet Jewish leaders who developed the film and reproduced the pamphlet. At least one issue came to David Khavkin in that fashion; he gave the film to Ruta Aleksandrovich, who brought it to Riga, where it was reproduced. Another issue that came by mail to Ruta was reproduced, but after Maftser read it, he suggested that the copies be destroyed, since he found the contents to be "anti-Soviet." He was afraid it would be "against the criminal code," and he burned his own copy. According to Silva Zalmanson, Maftser feared that the mailed booklets of *Domoi* "could play the part of a 'marked atom.' " He may well have been correct.

The group's efforts to secure and reproduce literature took complex

* Of the other dozen or so participants in the three VKK meetings in August 1969 in Moscow, November 1969 in Riga, and June 13-14, 1970, in Leningrad (the February 1970 meeting in Kiev was aborted), the Moscow, Kiev, Minsk, Kharkov, and Tbilisi representatives had been permitted to go to Israel. The Leningrad members were in prison. Ilya Volk, a VKK member from Riga, was not criminally charged. Some of the other Riga *samizdat* committee members also were not indicted.

courses. Ruta Aleksandrovich would secure an item, in original, microfilmed, or photographed form, and bring it to Riga, where Maftser would arrange for its production. Shepshelovich had the primary technical responsibility for reproducing the *samizdat* materials. At various times, Ruta transported mimeograph equipment and a contact box from David Khavkin in Moscow. She was also involved in a complex transaction relating to the purchase, transfer, and trade of typewriters. Maftser secured mimeograph equipment and made blueprints. Shepshelovich made equipment for photographic reproduction. When his house was searched, a photo enlarger, contact box, time relays, and other equipment were seized and placed in evidence. There was no doubt (or denial) of their continuing activity in creating educational materials. The real question was one of criminal purpose and criminal intent.

Maftser pleaded guilty to the charges. Shpilberg pleaded not guilty. Shepshelovich and Aleksandrovich acknowledged the facts but denied guilt. In all, some thirty witnesses appeared, including Silva Zalmanson, Lev Korenblit, Boguslavsky, Mogilever, Altman, Dreizner, Bodnya, and Leib Khnokh.

Maftser testified first. He detailed with considerable precision his activities and those of the movement. At the conclusion of his direct testimony, he said:

> I think that Zionism is opposed to the Soviet national policy, to the Marxist-Leninist ideology, to the political line of the party and government . . . having nothing against the Soviet regime and not intending to go into anti-Soviet activities, I committed a political crime . . . I think that I should be punished according to Soviet law.

Ruta Aleksandrovich's testimony was less detailed. Although not defiant, she gave little information. At the close of her direct testimony she said:

> With the facts in the charge sheet I basically agree. That is just what I meant when I said that I plead partially guilty. But the indictment states that I acted with the aim of undermining and weakening the Soviet regime. I deny that part of the accusation as I never had such an intent. I wanted to leave for Israel. My applications were always rejected, so I tried to obtain information on Jewish culture and Israel. The only aim of my activities was to obtain and distribute that kind of information. The literature I distributed expressed a point-of view

different from the official point of view existing in the Soviet Union.
Perhaps some facts were not interpreted correctly. But this literature
does not contain any idea aimed at weakening the Soviet regime.

Shepshelovich was even less cooperative. He succinctly summarized
his position as follows:

> I do not plead guilty for the following reasons:
> (*1*) The indictment says that I went into producing anti-Soviet
> literature because of my anti-Soviet views. My views are socialist in
> the social field and Zionist in the national field.
> (*2*) The indictment says that I deliberately went into activities aimed
> at undermining and weakening the Soviet regime. I say that the only
> aim of my activities was my desire to study the history and cultural
> heritage of the Jewish people. I also wanted to know more about the
> problems of Israel and the situation in the Middle East. That interest
> in the past and present of my people to a certain degree was aroused
> by the desire of some of the Jews to leave for Israel.
> (*3*) The indictment says that the literature which I participated in
> issuing is slanderous to the Soviet regime. I say that the above men-
> tioned literature holds no slanderous material, no lies aimed at attain-
> ing certain goals. The facts mentioned in this literature are true and
> their interpretation is objective. The only aim of our publications is
> to give information about Israel to those Jews who want to know it.
> Such publications are not criminal. I do not plead guilty.

He clearly expressed his position in his final statement:

> I ask the court to take into account the following: First, I acted in
> accordance with my Zionist convictions which cannot be identified
> with anti-Sovietism. I have no anti-Soviet views. Second, I acted with
> full awareness, but I never had the aim of undermining or weakening
> the Soviet regime. I had only one aim, the awakening of the national
> self-consciousness of my people. Can anyone speak seriously of a few
> homemade publications of an informative, educational nature as un-
> dermining the might of such a state as the Soviet Union? Third, I do
> not consider the literature I issued as illegal and slanderous. I con-
> sider it, to a certain extent, critical, and I find nothing criminal in
> this. My goal is to emigrate to Israel. I had no other aim. I ask the
> court to ascertain the motivation of my actions and to make a just
> decision.

Shpilberg, the most contentious and defiant of the accused, also denied acting "with the aim of weakening the Soviet regime."

I stress that I did nothing of the kind, and that my views were never anti-Soviet. I could not have gone into anti-Soviet activities because of my national views and interests, because such activities would have turned my attention away from the realization of my ideas. It is a pity that you don't want to understand this.

Throughout the trial, Shpilberg's defense counsel, A. I. Rozhansky, conducted himself with diligence and acuity, refused to concede the guilt of his client, and courageously insisted upon fairness from the court. His was a remarkable performance, considering the generally suppliant attitudes of defense counsel and their unwillingness to be vigorous advocates. Repeatedly, he extracted admissions from witnesses that they had no direct knowledge of Shpilberg's participation in certain events. In cross-examining Silva Zalmanson, who was a generally cooperative prosecution witness, he succeeded in securing her admission that she had not been truthful in prior testimony. His final statement was comprehensive, courageous, and highly skillful. Among his points was the following:

> This is the first time in my life that I have heard that the sentence depends on the behavior of the defendant during the investigation and not on what he has done. Such an approach is absolutely inadmissable. That is not only my opinion; it is the opinion of the law. . . . While accusing Shpilberg of four charges and Maftser of seventeen, the prosecutor demands for Shpilberg a sentence four times that ˙ for Maftser. You, comrade judges, cannot follow this path. You will be committing an injustice.

Point by point, Rozhansky demonstrated that there was an absence of the requisite intent, that the evidence was nonexistent, insufficient, or biased, and he asked for a verdict of not guilty.

Prosecutor Chibisov, in his final summation, expressed clearly the political character of the trial by charging that

> International Zionism, the weapon of which the accused have become the bearers, is actively attempting to undermine the Soviet Union and the countries in the Socialist camp. . . . Nowadays Zionism has joined hands with the most aggressive imperialistic forces, including the West German revanchists and neo-Nazis, on whose hands is the blood of millions of Jews. The methods of the fascist cutthroats have been adopted by the Jewish Defense League in the U.S.A. Honest Soviet citizens of Jewish nationality indignantly reject the pretenses of all

types of defenders and, as the parents of Shtilbans, sentenced at the
Leningrad trial, state: "We need no uninvited 'defenders' from Israel."

The Riga Four were sentenced on May 27. Shpilberg received three
years; Shepshelovich, two; and Aleksandrovich and Maftser, one year.
Ruta Aleksandrovich had then been in confinement for eight months.
Under Soviet law, prisoners received credit for their pre-trial confinement. In October 1971, she, her father Yitzhak, and her fiancé Sanya
Averbukh, who had waited for her to be released, arrived in Israel. On
November 15, Ruta and Sanya were married in Tel Aviv at a huge
wedding attended by hundreds of Russian immigrants, Israeli government officials, and Israeli celebrities. As Premier Golda Meir kissed the
bride, Ruta's mother wept tears of joy and her aunt Leah whispered,
"I wish all the stories had such a happy ending."

But the Riga trial had other aftermaths. Months later, after Boris
Maftser had also emigrated to Israel, and the former Rigaites planned
an anniversary press conference commemorating the trial, Ruta Aleksandrovich refused to participate because of Maftser's presence. She
angrily declared:

> It is impossible to let Maftser assume the role of an innocent victim.
> This way we are forgetting the difference between Good and Evil,
> which is a blasphemy and lack of respect to Shepshelovich and
> Shpilberg who are suffering for their ideas. . . .
> We will have to state that in our movement there were not only
> heroes of great spirit; there were not only average people who lacked
> experience and courage to defend on a high level their ideas before
> the KGB (I think I myself belong to this group of people); there
> were also absolute scoundrels and traitors who conscientiously bought
> their forgiveness on the blood of their friends.

Maftser, by then a Tel Aviv University law student, answered questions of reporters for hours. His sad eyes, slightly stooped frame, and
expressive hands were more eloquent than his quiet, monotone responses:

> From the point of view of Soviet law, what I did could be considered
> a crime [he said]. But it is clear that the reason for the arrests was
> because the authorities wanted to intimidate us and break our move-
> ment. They simply waited for a good time and circumstances to do it.
> After the arrests and searches, the KGB had all of the literature
> that was published. They knew what had been distributed. If the KGB

allows a book through the mail, they can follow distribution. They took the literature and gave it to a special commission to read. It was summarized and phrases were taken out of context. They chose those comments most useful to them and characterized the book as they wished or needed. Literature was the basis of their accusation. They were particularly angry about *Iton*. They told me *Iton* could not be forgiven and they would find an occasion to punish us for it. It was not the book itself, but the fact that Jews were publishing a periodical.

We made two mistakes. First, we didn't listen to more experienced people who advised us to struggle only in a legal way. By using codes and secret places, we could be accused of underground activities. Second, since we were engaged in publishing *samizdat* materials, we had to look through them more carefully. There were expressions in books and articles that gave the KGB an excuse to accuse us of anti-Soviet activities. *Domoi* had a lot of such expressions. At the trial, even Ruta and Misha [Shepshelovich] had to acknowledge that they couldn't agree with the correctness of the phrases.

Aron's case is the most tragic one. He was arrested because the Leningrad defendants had given evidence against him. He was accused of his part in forming the Leningrad Center in 1966 and 1967, and then for his later role with the VKK and *samizdat*. They knew that Shpilberg was one of the eight or ten Leningrad organizers, most of whom were arrested on June 15, but they knew little of his Riga activities. Aron was not in Leningrad for the period of the acts charged there, and the literature they accused us of producing and distributing could not be easily traced to him. Under Soviet law, if you are accused of anti-Soviet acts, it is important [for the prosecution] to prove your personal connections to the literature or organization. Those connections came from what they found in Aron's apartment and from the testimony of Silva and Israil Zalmanson and me. But the proofs were weak; they could not show that Aron either made or distributed the *samizdat* productions. The evidence was simply insufficient. There was no proof of his connection to the VKK, and none whatsover of his being in an anti-Soviet organization. But then in Soviet political trials, they don't need proof.

Why did I admit everything? The KGB had much more information about me than [about] anyone else, and after a while it was pointless to deny. The main reason is simply my weak character. At first, I denied anti-Soviet activities. But then my younger brother was attacked and beaten, and I was told by the KGB that his nose was broken by my friends. It wasn't true, of course. It was only drunks. But in jail in isolation, you wonder. My wife lost her job over my arrest and friends came to her with a rumor I had given evidence against them. It was wrong, but again, it was more pressure. I was interrogated hours on end; I was hungry; I was cold; I was frightened. Then my mother suddenly died. There was nothing I could do. No way to help. After her death, I finally confessed that my activities were anti-Soviet. It's no excuse that I was weak. But I gave no facts that were not true and I implicated no one about whom they did not already know. I wish I could have been more brave.

On August 4, 1973, the last of the Riga defendants, Aron Shpilberg, was released from prison. His co-defendants, as well as his wife Margarita and his two small daughters, had already emigrated. Shpilberg did not receive his exit visa immediately. On September 23, he picketed the headquarters of the Central Committee of the Communist Party in Moscow, carrying a large placard: "Let Me Go to My Family in Israel." He was arrested, along with Roger Leddington, an Associated Press reporter who was photographing the demonstration, and the film was confiscated. Shpilberg refused to be silenced. He was permitted to leave the USSR in early October 1973.

Not everyone can be as brave or defiant as Shpilberg. Maftser certainly is not a hero. But Silva Zalmanson, who admitted as much as he did, has been treated as a heroine—in part because of her courageous final plea in the first Leningrad trial. Shpilberg and Shepshelovich were brave throughout; many others were not. In a world of confused morality, whom should we admire—the committed zealot who lies to his persecutors and remains silent in the face of questioning to further his cause, or the sensitive, weak man, who reluctantly tells his small piece of truth even though it injures a friend and a cause? To the person who accepts the twisted logic of Soviet law, one commits a crime if one is not a conforming citizen. But by universal standards of human freedom, the Soviet government belonged in the dock—not its victims, whether strong or weak.

ODESSA:
A Librarian's Ordeal

CHAPTER 15

One week after the arrest of Ruta Aleksandrovich in Riga, Raiza Palatnik, a 33-year-old Odessa librarian, was interrogated following an exhaustive KGB search of her apartment. On June 24, 1971, one month after the Riga trial began, Raiza was sentenced to two years in prison camp by an Odessa court. In the West, the two cases were regarded as similar, and, in fact, they were closely related despite the 800 miles that separate Riga from Odessa and the ten-year difference in the ages of the two women. Ruta's fiancé, Isai Averbukh, was a long-time friend of Raiza's, and during Ruth's visits to Odessa, the two women had come to know each other well in the course of discussing their social and political attitudes. Furthermore, Averbukh's younger brother Igor (Yitzhak) and Raiza's younger sister Katya were romantically attached. There is little doubt that the KGB's interest in Ruta's activities had put them on the trail of the Odessa librarian.

Odessa's Jews had not been as actively involved in the movement as might have been expected, given the fact that Odessa was at one time the city with the largest Jewish population in Russia and that even today it ranks fourth, following Moscow, Leningrad, and Kiev. The city, a large Ukrainian Black Sea port, is an industrial and cultural center and, by virtue of its beaches, a major resort. The Ukraine has historically been one of the world's most densely Jewish-populated regions. The area presently constituting the Ukrainian Soviet Socialist Republic had about 2,615,000 Jews at the turn of the century and about 2,500,000 just before World War II. The loss, despite an impressive birthrate,

239

was attributable largely to emigration to the United States. In the
area of the present Ukraine, in 1926 forty-eight cities had populations of more than 5,000 Jews, and, as late as 1959, there were
twenty-three such cities. Odessa was one of the largest. The Odessa
region had 200,000 Jews in 1926, and the city itself was 35% to
40% Jewish. Odessa had a strong pre-Revolutionary Yiddish culture
and a Zionist tradition. Its docks were noted for their Jewish workers'
organization. At the outbreak of World War II, there were an estimated 175,000 Jews in Odessa. Romanian troops besieged the city
on August 5, 1941, and occupied it on October 16. Meantime, as many
as two-thirds of the Jews had been evacuated eastward. In three days,
October 23–25, the Romanian military occupiers slaughtered 26,000
Jews and deported the rest to forced labor and concentration camps.
When the Red Army reoccupied the city in April 1944, the former
center of Jewish population and culture no longer existed. About
75,000 of Odessa's Jews perished in the Holocaust. But others returned.
According to the 1959 census, 107,000 Jews lived in Odessa. By now
more than 125,000 Jews live in the city and constitute about 17% of
the population.

There is no ready explanation of why Odessa's Jews responded less
readily to the resurgence of Jewish identification than did their brethren
elsewhere. But whatever the reason, by the late 1960s there was a
small but active nucleus of Jewish militants. In the somewhat unlikely
figure of a Jewish librarian, Odessa produced a genuine heroine of the
Jewish movement—and a highly literate one at that.

In her open letter of November 20, 1970, Raiza tells her story:

> After the last conversation with the KGB interrogator who again
> threatened me with arrest, I decided to write this letter, as I am afraid
> I will not be able to tell my friends and dear ones what has formed
> and motivated me in my 34 years.
>
> I was born in a small town of a Jewish family. Yiddish and Jewish
> traditions were taught me at home. There was no Jewish school and
> therefore I attended a Russian one. In childhood I felt myself a Jewess
> and unconsciously I looked for opportunities to express personal,
> national identification.
>
> In the eighth grade, my refusal to learn Ukrainian and insistence
> that my mother tongue is Yiddish confounded the school authorities.
>
> I was fourteen when the unbridled anti-Semitic campaign known
> as the struggle against cosmopolitanism began. I remember the at-
> mosphere of fear and trepidation in the family awaiting something
> terrible, frightful, and unavoidable. During that period I kept a

diary. Now that I reread it before destroying it so that it will not fall into the hands of the KGB, I again relive the pain and bitterness, anger and resentment.

But Stalin died. The doctors were rehabilitated. Beria and his henchmen were executed. With childish naiveté I exulted and believed that Justice had triumphed.

I entered the Institute for Librarians in Moscow. I remember the enthusiasm with which I received the condemnation of the personal cult of Stalin by the Twentieth Congress of the Communist Party. But why did they not drop so much as a hint of the physical destruction of the best representatives of the Jewish intelligentsia from 1949 to 1952? Why did they not condemn anti-Semitism which had been raised to the rank of internal policy? Why did they not open Jewish schools, theaters, newspapers, magazines?

That my belief in the liquidation of anti-Semitism was only an illusion, I began to understand when I finished the Institute and began to look for work. No one was interested in my knowledge and capabilities. The fact that I belong to the Jewish nationality closed hermetically all opportunities for work in a high ranking library. With difficulty, I managed to find work in Odessa in a minor library, where I work to this day.

Raiza then recounts that her disillusionment led her to question, and since "I found no answers in official literature, I began to read *samizdat*." She also listened regularly to foreign broadcasts. Having a strong literary interest, she was especially shocked at the 1964 sentencing of the famous Leningrad Jewish poet Iosif Brodsky to five years of hard labor as a "parasite." She "perceived this as part of a new stage of Soviet anti-Semitism. The poet was condemned on the evidence of patent anti-Semites." Like most other Soviet intellectuals, she was deeply affected by the February 1966 conviction of authors Yuli Daniel and Andrei Sinyavsky to five and seven years respectively for "slandering" the Soviet State by their writings. "What astonished me was the hypocritical, Jesuitical censure of Sinyavsky for anti-Semitism." Raiza's involvement in *samizdat* material and her opposition to literary censorship caused her to have a natural affinity and identification with those Soviet intellectuals, many of whom were Jews, who constituted the developing democratic movement. However, she continued:

In search of a solution, I began to think more and more of Israel. The prelude to the Six-Day War shocked me to the foundations. . . . The eve of the war when the Straits of Tiran were closed; the UN forces expelled; the Arab armies approached the borders of Israel, and Fedorenko in the UN said cynically, "Don't overdramatize events"; I was close to nervous exhaustion. I wanted to shout to humanity, "Help!"

Then I understood that I could have no future in the country in which I was born. . . .

I remember the unbounded pride and happiness when the reborn David again conquered Goliath. The flood of anti-Semitic curses and hysteria from the Soviet press, radio, and television forced me to feel even more strongly the unbroken bond to Israel and personal responsibility for her. I began actively to interest myself in everything connected with Israel. And friends who felt as I, discussed the possibility of leaving for Israel . . .

By now, Raiza was involved with Sanya and Yitzhak Averbukh and with other activists such as Aleksandr Chapla. Through Ruta Aleksandrovich, Galya Ladyzhenskaya, and others, there was contact with movement activity in other cities. She was elated by the Letter of the Moscow 39 in March 1970. "How sorry I was that I could not also sign that letter." She initiated a request to Israel (through Tel Aviv P.O.B. 92, the well-known post office box for Soviet Jews who wanted to go to Israel but had no address of a family member) to locate a "relative" so that a *vizov* could be sent to her. She had cast the die. Then came the KGB search and interrogation.

. . . I understand that arrest and maybe years of imprisonment await me. But I know one thing positively; my fate is tied irrevocably to Israel, and no imprisonments in Leningrad, Riga, and Kishinev can halt the struggle for repatriation to Israel.

To my regret, I do not know my people's tongue, Hebrew, but in my trial I will cry out against all anti-Semites in the Yiddish I was taught by my mother and father.

What really got Raiza into trouble was that she had a good personal library. The five-hour search of her tiny, one-room apartment on October 14 was undertaken on the pretext of looking for property stolen from nearby Elementary School 53, with which she had no connection. No stolen property was found, but enormously incriminating things were taken, such as the Universal Declaration of Human Rights, Nasser's speeches before the Six-Day War, and a *New York Times* interview of Golda Meir. In addition, Raiza's typewriter was taken as well as many Jewish *samizdat* materials such as the Letter of the 39, an open letter of Yiddish poet Iosif Kerler, an article on "Einstein and Zionism," and handwritten translations from English of articles in the mazazine *Israel Today*. Other items seized included an unofficial transcript of the Brodsky trial; Daniel's story "Strange Planet"; Sinyavsky's article "On Socialist Realism"; the "Story of One Voyage," by Larisa Bogoraz-Daniel (then Yuli Daniel's wife); and books and poems by Boris Pasternak, Osip Mandelshtam, Anna Akhmatova, Bulat Okudzhava, Aleksandr Galich, Yevgeny Yevtushenko, and other disfavored writers. Since the items taken had nothing to do with the alleged school thefts, Raiza demanded their immediate return.

The next day, the KGB interrogation began. Raiza was told that over fifty pieces of anti-Soviet and "illegal" literature were involved. She was questioned endlessly about her friends, associates, and contacts and threatened with arrest when she refused to give names. All of her friends and work associates were questioned. In the weeks that followed, the KGB kept up its interrogations and threats and promised Raiza that she would be left alone if she would reveal where she got the literature. Meanwhile, Raiza officially complained that she was being harassed because she sought to go to Israel. After days of interrogation, she announced that she would answer only in her native tongue—Yiddish. This did not endear her to her KGB questioners. On December 1, she was arrested and her room was again searched for evidence of "slanderous anti-Soviet" material. This time, the KGB took a book by the Yiddish poet David Bergelson (executed in 1952 but rehabilitated), some Soviet literary journals, and a book by Stalin.

When Raiza continued to refuse to talk, the KGB adopted a new approach. She was sent to a mental hospital for examination, but the psychiatrists reported that she was quite sane. Her sister Katya and her friend Chapla were unable to secure an attorney for her, and the investigation continued for some seven months. Katya was frequently questioned. She reports:

> Investigator Larinov demanded of me information as to how all the anti-Soviet material found during the searches had come into Raiza's possession. He reiterated many times that the KGB was aware that she was not guilty but that they wished to determine who it was who had exerted a bad influence over her. Who had given her "forbidden material" to read? Who tried to propagandize her into going to Israel? "When we know this," he said, "we will release your sister and punish those who are truly guilty, in accordance with the Soviet law."

On May 3, Raiza went on a hunger strike, which she continued until she was permitted to see her parents, who had been barred from contact with her. The KGB surrendered after five days. On June 22, 1971, the trial began. Raiza was indicted under the Ukrainian Criminal Code equivalent of Russian Article 190-1. The specification of anti-Soviet slander included the Letter of the 39, the article "Einstein and Zionism," some of the poems, some open letters by members of the USSR Union of Writers, including Lydia Chukovskaya, a well-known Russian novelist, that protested Solzhenitsyn's expulsion from the Writers' Union, and other well-circulated *samizdat* materials. Raiza pleaded not guilty, stating the material was not slanderous. The trial provoked some remarkable side effects. On the first morning, a large crowd of protesting Jews congregated outside the court house. It was the first public demonstration within memory by the Jews of Odessa. Raiza was brought to court in a Black Maria, manacled and surrounded by armed militiamen. This so aroused the crowd that on the second day, forty Odessa Jews sat outside the court house and staged a hunger strike. It was June 23, Raiza's thirty-fourth birthday. Friends carrying flowers shouted, "Happy birthday!" but were forced away by the armed guards.

Things went no better within the courtroom. Some of Raiza's co-workers and neighbors who had been severely importuned to say that she had negative attitudes toward the USSR now conceded that they had been pressured into such pre-trial statements. Three fellow-librarians testified in her behalf. No one pointed to any overt criminal act. In her examination-in-chief, much was made of the fact that Raiza did not vote in the 1962 elections and that she had once failed to work on a Soviet book exhibit. Prosecutor Tekunova called Raiza a renegade: "How did you dare renounce your Soviet citizenship! You are a traitor. You know how we deal with traitors." She described Raiza as "a very dangerous Zionist propagandist whose guilt is aggravated by the fact that she works on the ideological front." Israel was labeled "a festering boil on the healthy body of humanity."

Raiza's closing speech was proud and eloquent. (A complete transcript exists.) She spoke for forty minutes. The courtroom was silent. Some women wept. Even the KGB men sat in rapt attention. Some of what she said follows:

> Why am I being tried? I am tried because all my life I had acutely felt my Jewishness, because I dared to join the movement of the rebirth of the national consciousness of the Jews in the USSR, who wish to emigrate to Israel.
>
> I know that in the last months, the months of my arrest, quite a

large number of Jews, including some of my friends, have gone to
Israel. . . .

But eight months ago, during the searches in my home and my
arrest, the situation was entirely different. Permission for emigration
had then been granted to only a few individuals, and the authorities
were frightened by the growing lava of applications demanding emigration. These demands became more and more insistent from day to
day. Then an age-old method was tried—the method of intimidating
the Jews. This was how the arrests and the searches began in dozens
of houses in Riga, Leningrad, and Kishinev. I, too, was arrested here,
in Odessa. My arrest is one of the links in this chain. . . .

The charge does not dwell on the contents of the incriminating
literature, calling it "illegal" and "slanderous" only because it is printed
not by typography but on a typewriter. But I am profoundly certain
that neither Galich's songs nor Korzhavin's poems contain any slander.
They are talented writers, members of the Union of Writers, and they
write about what they themselves had gone through and what they
know well. They write about the lawlessness, the cruelty, and the
camps that existed in the epoch of the personality cult. But these
things did exist! Ten years ago all the newspapers wrote about them!
They were discussed from the tribunes of two party congresses! Why
then, have these subjects become forbidden today? Why is it a crime
to talk about this today? . . .

There are many Soviet writers for whom I have great love. There
are others whom I like less, and there are still others that I do not
respect at all. I think that most normal people have their own likes
and dislikes in literature and that nobody reads a writer just because
he is a Soviet writer. And nobody gets the idea of accusing a person
for his likes and tastes. Why then, in my case, should this be used
against me in the accusation of anti-Soviet views?

Among the books in my personal library, published by Soviet publishing houses, there was also literature that was typewritten and not
yet published. I collected this literature exclusively from my personal
interests and taste and pursued no other aims by this. We, the librarians, know very well what harsh conditions of censorship exist in
the Soviet Union, and how often works, which for years cannot get
published because of their ideological impurity, suddenly become most
popular and most widely read. I can give as examples the poems of
Akhmatova, the books of Platonov and Mikhail Bulgakov, published
in the sixties, and others that were published after their authors were
already dead, for example the works of the Jewish writer David
Bergelson, shot in 1952 for "anti-Soviet activity" and rehabilitated four
years later, in 1956! His book, published in Moscow in 1961, has also
been taken away from me during the search.

I have said almost everything I wanted to say in court. I have not
admitted and do not admit myself guilty of the crime of which I am
accused. The latest events in my life have absolutely convinced me

246 THE LAST EXODUS

that the rights guaranteed us by the Soviet Constitution and by laws are constantly and deliberately violated. For me personally, my trial is another proof that I am right. Seeing around me, and experiencing on my own skin, the absence of rights and lawfulness, and realizing the impossibility of restoring the trampled-upon justice, I have decided to give up Soviet citizenship, and I have written a statement to this effect to the Presidium of the Supreme Soviet of the USSR. From this day on I consider myself a citizen of Israel. I wish to add once more that I do not admit that I am guilty of anything.

I do not wish to hide behind anyone's back. I have permitted myself the luxury of thinking—and this, evidently, is not yet permitted.

At the conclusion, there was absolute silence. Then her father's voice was heard: "Thank you, my daughter. I am proud of you."

Raiza Palatnik was given a two-year sentence. Not only Jews protested. Valery Chalidze, a member of the Soviet Human Rights Committee, wired the Supreme Court of the Ukraine insisting that her illegal conviction be reversed. Lydia Chukovskaya, speaking for herself and other Soviet writers, expressed shock at the kind of literature the court had found slanderous and anti-Soviet. She tartly noted: "Observing court practices in recent years, one involuntarily comes to the conclusion that 'anti-Soviet' is gradually approximating the concept of 'anti-Stalinist.' " She was particularly outraged that two of her own anti-Stalinist samizdat letters had played a role in Raiza's conviction. She accepted full responsibility and urged a higher court reversal. "I cannot allow some other person to answer for my actions and not myself."

On September 23, the Ukrainian Supreme Court affirmed the verdict. Raiza was transferred to a woman's camp where she was the only Jew. Most of the prisoners were prostitutes, drug addicts, shoplifters, and the like. Apart from the near-starvation diet and the twelve-hour work day, anti-Semitism was rife. In December, Raiza went on a hunger strike in protest.

Katya, her green-eyed, vivacious, 23-year-old sister, quit her music studies, went to Moscow, and joined Raiza in a supporting hunger strike. She went from office to office protesting the camp administration, demanding medical care for Raiza, urging a reopening of the entire injustice. She contacted foreign newsmen, who were delighted by her striking beauty and charm. When Katya returned to Odessa, OVIR told her that an exit visa had been granted and she must leave for Israel promptly. Katya first went to the camp for a last visit with her sister.

Arriving in Israel in January 1972, she quickly arranged a trip to Europe, England, and the United States to plead for her sister's freedom. On December 1, 1972, the first day of Chanukah, Raiza was freed. With her elderly parents, she joined Katya in the Promised Land.

The saga of Raiza Palatnik and her family epitomizes the struggle of Soviet Jewry. Although the Palatnik family originally had a Jewish background, they were substantially assimilated. Neither the parents nor Raiza's brother nor Katya, the younger sister, had had any interest in Jewish affairs. Before her sister's intense activism, Katya attended a music school in cosmopolitan Odessa and was engaged to the son of a Bulgarian diplomat with whom she intended to live in Bulgaria. Raiza's primary nonconformity was literary and then democratic. But, being the daughter of a proud, stubborn people, she responded to her Soviet environment with the characteristics of her heritage. So did her sister, and ultimately her parents. Katya demonstrated these traits dramatically, in the USSR, in Israel, and then in England and the United States. In all of these countries, she carried on the struggle for her sister's freedom in defiance of government pressures, organizational advice and taboos, and with a chin-high persistence that remained undaunted until Raiza was free.

In Odessa the effect of the Palatnik trial was just the opposite of what the Soviet authorities had desired. It mobilized many of the city's Jews, increasing numbers of whom applied to go to Israel. One of them, Grigory Berman, a 26-year-old literature teacher and school principal, filed his OVIR application in the spring of 1972. He joined others in signing telegrams and petitions. The KGB interrogated him about anti-Soviet activities and the dissemination of Zionist propaganda, but he refused to answer their questions. At about that time, Soviet authorities began using the threat of military call-up as a companion reprisal to that of imprisonment in the case of many young Jews. Berman was among those who received a draft notice. Previously he had been exempt from military service. Now his exemption was canceled, and the military commissariat ordered him drafted. He refused to sign the induction notice. A prior health disqualification was ignored, and he was ordered to report without a new medical examination. Berman then told the authorities that he refused to serve, since he considered himself an Israeli citizen. He was arrested and imprisoned with another Odessa Jew, 22-year-old Yury Pokh, who had a congenital heart defect and had also been deferred until he applied to emigrate. Pokh and Berman received prison sentences of three-and-a-half and three years respectively for refusing to serve in the Red Army.

But Odessa could no longer be quieted, and neither could other parts of the Ukraine.

THE UKRAINE

CHAPTER 16

The 50 million people of the Ukraine—a vast area that includes within its borders portions of the former territory of Poland, Romania, Czechoslovakia, and Hungary—consist mainly of the largest, most concentrated national minority in the USSR. Although linguistically and ethnically related to the Russians, they have retained a fierce independence and a traditional resentment of rule from St. Petersburg and the Kremlin. Ukrainian nationalism persists, and Soviet prison camps are believed to contain a higher percentage of Ukrainian nationalist political prisoners than of any other dissenting groups. The Ukraine has also been the heartland of Jewish concentration—the Pale of Settlement, the *shtetl,* the world of Sholem Aleichem—and the scene of endemic anti-Semitism and pogroms. Yet the modern Jewish movement, despite traditions of Jewish religiosity, Yiddish culture, and political Zionism, found it relatively difficult to seed and spread in parts of the Ukraine. True, there were loosely grouped Jewish activists in Kiev, Kharkov, and Odessa, and individual activists in other Ukrainian cities, but a cohesive, effective Jewish underground did not exist as in Riga or Leningrad, and the militancy, articulateness, and high quality of leadership characteristic of Moscow's Jews did not exist in the large Ukrainian cities, despite the fact that of the ten cities of greatest Jewish population in the USSR, five—Kiev, Odessa, Kharkov, Dnepropetrovsk, and Chernovtsy—are situated in that republic.

Chernovtsy is illustrative. That city in the extreme southwestern Ukraine, earlier known as Cernauti (in Romanian) or Chernovitz, was

the capital of the Romanian province of Bukovina. Before World
War II, its 80,000 Jews constituted 60% of the city's total population.
The most recent official Soviet census recorded 36,500 Jews, but some
Jews contend that they number 70,000 and comprise almost half the
total population of 150,000. Whatever the precise facts, Chernovtsy
may still be the most Jewish city in the USSR. Bukovina, a hilly agri-
cultural area roughly the size of Connecticut, neighbors Moldavia, and,
like its sister territory, it was ruled by Turks, Habsburgs, and the
Romanian kingdoms. At the time of the Red Army occupation in
June 1940, more than 300,000 Jews occupied the Romanian provinces
of Bessarabia and Bukovina. Although many Jews fled into interior
Russia with the advance of the German armies in July 1941, 58,000
Jews still lived in Chernovtsy when the Nazis and Romanian troops
arrived. Murder and deportation followed. But in accord with Romanian
custom, the mayor of Chernovtsy began selling exemptions from deportation, and the corrupt, sometimes relaxed Romanian occupiers
showed less than the expected genocidal predisposition. Despite a
savage crackdown later, many Jews were permitted to attempt to emigrate to Palestine during the mid-war years, and Chernovtsy became
not only a haven for many Jews but a point of departure for the Holy
Land. By August 1944, when the Red Army reoccupied the city, there
were still some Jews in Chernovtsy, and others returned from the deep
Soviet interior.

Life under Soviet rule was not conducive to the maintenance of the
formerly flourishing Jewish religious and secular institutions. By 1959,
only two small synagogues remained. In that year, there was a widely
publicized educational trial (the term for a nonjudicial form of public
indoctrination) in the Philharmonic Hall of Abram Schecter, the Jewish
community's *mohel* (circumciser). The authorities billed it as an evening of Jewish culture, and the thousands who attended were regaled
with a polemical public exhibition vilifying Schecter and condemning
the barbaric, unsanitary ritual of circumcision. Capping the evening,
two expatriates from Israel told in horrendous detail how cruel and
reactionary life in that country was. Since the Schecter affair had been
shortly preceded by the trial of Jews arrested for "drinking alcohol in
public places" (the synagogue) and circulating Zionist propaganda—
the religious ritual recitation of *"L'shanah habah b'Yerushalaim"* (Next
year in Jerusalem)—it took courage to display affirmative Jewish
feeling. Still, Chernovtsy became the scene of an early, unpublicized
trial, foreshadowing those to come.

The trial of Lilia Ontman—apparently on the basis of her Jewish activity—took place in Chernovtsy on January 8, 1970, and thus preceded the hijack arrests by six months and the trial of Raiza Palatnik in Odessa by a year and a half. All that is known from the sparse accounts is that Lilia Ontman was born in 1937, was married, had an adopted son and a younger sister who was a medical student, and that she had often applied to go to Israel to join her aged father who lived there. She was arrested as a consequence of an incident or incidents at an OVIR office, where, she was alleged, after OVIR officials refused to permit her to emigrate, to have announced that she no longer considered herself a Soviet citizen. It was contended that she refused to take back her identity card and ignored a written summons to pick up her OVIR documents. Following her arrest in October 1969, no lawyer in the area could be found to defend her, but she finally secured Moscow counsel. Mrs. Ontman defended herself by demanding the right to leave for Israel under the Soviet Constitution and the Universal Declaration of Human Rights. She also charged that her trial was part of an anti-Semitic campaign. Evidence against her consisted of two letter appeals she had written to the Women's International League and the UN Human Rights Commission. Both were confiscated by Soviet authorities and neither has been published in the West. Other young Jews who were called as witnesses against her refused to cooperate with the authorities, and a group of young militants demonstrated at the courthouse when the verdict was read. Mrs. Ontman was sentenced to two and a half years in prison camp for anti-Soviet calumnies and insults (presumably under Article 190-1). Her sister was expelled from medical school, and her son was placed in a children's home. After the completion of her sentence, she was permitted to emigrate to Israel. Still, nothing has been made public about this early trial, although its central features would appear to parallel the other publicized proceedings.

Similar silence concerning another trial in Chernovtsy is somewhat easier to comprehend. Dr. Yury (Chaim) Rennert, a 48-year-old radiologist, was sentenced to five years in prison camp in March 1971, for allegedly attempting to bribe an OVIR official for an exit visa. Dr. Rennert, a bachelor, had been seeking since 1965 to join his mother and sister who had been permitted to emigrate to Israel in that year. After Soviet troops had occupied Chernovtsy in 1940, the Rennert family was exiled to Siberia because the father was a successful bourgeois clothing store owner. Returning to Chernovtsy at the end of the war, Rennert was admitted to medical school, and then practiced as a radiologist in Chernovtsy hospitals, where he was well liked and successful. But after 1965, with the remnants of his family in Israel, he persisted in applying to leave and visited the OVIR office with stubborn frequency. In late 1969, he received indications that his application was finally being favorably considered. One day, while Rennert sought to verify this, the OVIR chief called in a subordinate who, pointing to a brown envelope on the table, declared, "This man tried to bribe me." Despite his denials, Rennert was immediately arrested. Details of the trial are extremely scant. It appears that Rennert admitted the offense, but friends of his who subsequently arrived in Israel contend that the KGB beat and tortured him. Several conclusions can be drawn: The trial was staged to discourage the Jews of Chernovtsy from applying to go to Israel. Although the offense charged was not political, the criminal law was utilized in a political way for a political purpose. If there was a bribery attempt, it can be understood in light of the maddening frustration of a man persistently denied the right to be reunited with his aged, half-blind mother and his last living sibling. Finally, bribery of officials is so commonplace in the USSR that when it is punished, it is rarely treated with such severity without ulterior motive.

In contrast to the Rennert case was the treatment of Yefim Potik of Chernovtsy, who was arrested on March 15, 1973, at the railroad station at Brest on the Polish border, while en route to Israel. Potik was charged with attempting to offer a hundred-ruble bribe to a customs official so that he could take with him the family's Zimmerman piano which his daughter played. Given the ambiguity of regulations over what goods people leaving the USSR are permitted to take, and the lack of even-handed administration, bribery of border officials is not unusual. One of the few apprehended, Potik received a three-month sentence and was then permitted to join his family in Israel.

The Rennert and Potik trials arose directly as a consequence of misguided efforts to expedite the process of departure. The entire exit procedure in Chernovtsy has been consistently fraught with human tragedies. At least two such cases resulted in formal complaints to the UN Human Rights Commission, which completely ignored the appeals. On May 16, 1971, Ulrikh Gait, formerly of Chernovtsy, wrote:

> On February 2, 1971, I received an exit permit to leave for Israel with my family: my wife Rosa and son Mikhail. We had completed

all the required formalities. We had returned our apartment, paid the
fee of 900 rubles per person for Soviet documents, received the exit
visa stamped on our passport, received the entry visa to Israel from
the Netherlands Embassy and the transit visas for Austria and Hungary. All that remained was to buy our railroad tickets.

Just before our departure date, I was called to OVIR in Chernovitz,
to Colonel Yefymov, who told me to return all my visas, though they
had been granted in strict accordance with the law, and to take back
Soviet papers. I returned the visas, but refused to accept Soviet
documents.

Then I complained about OVIR in Chernovitz to OVIR of the
USSR in Moscow, to Colonel Ovchinnikov, who promised that the incident would be settled and that we would soon be permitted to leave.
But when I returned to Chernovitz, Yefymov told me that Ovchinnikov
had no authority over him and that he handled problems by himself.

Meanwhile, our economic situation had become catastrophic. All
our belongings had been packed and removed for shipment. For one
and a half months we were all unemployed and unable to earn money
for food.

Yefymov tried to persuade me to remain in the USSR, but met
with my determined refusal. On March 23, he advised me to leave
alone and my wife and son would come later. Because I thought that
once out of Russia, I would be better able to fight for their right to
join me, I agreed. But more than seven weeks have passed and my
family is still not permitted to leave.

Their situation is desperate. With no work, no money, and enforced
separation, they are on the verge of collapse.

On May 11, after trying for weeks, I succeeded in reaching them
by telephone. My wife could not stop crying, and my son said that if
they didn't let him leave, he will commit suicide. My son has not
worked for six months, for as soon as he presented his documents,
he was fired.

In the name of humanity, I plead that you use the influence of your
high authority with the Soviet government to let my wife and son
join me.

On July 9, 1971, Rita Gluzman, a Tel Aviv University student and
a former resident of Chernovtsy, desperately presented this story to
Mrs. Rita Hauser, the U.S. representative to the Human Rights Commission, who was attending an international conference in Tel Aviv:

Rita and Yakov Gluzman were schoolmates at the university, in
Chernovitz where both were born. Yakov was the first to leave
Chernovitz, going to Moscow to study biology. Rita (then Shapiro)
followed, attending the university in the city of Gorky to study chemistry. In 1969, they were married in a religious ceremony, as well as
the civil one required for registration with the authorities.

Almost immediately afterward, the Shapiro family received permission to leave for Israel, which they had been seeking for twenty years. The permit included the father, mother, Rita, and her younger sister Miriam. None of their efforts to add the young husband, Yakov, succeeded. OVIR officials told them that to do so they would have to cancel their permission and make another request. Finally, Yakov insisted to Rita, "Go first with your family, and I will follow. Certainly they will not refuse me permission to join my wife." And Rita, pregnant, left Russia in January 1970 with her family.

Twenty-two-year-old Yakov left his studies just a few weeks before he would have received his second degree and went to work as a carpenter in a small town near Chernovitz in the hope that as a simple worker it would be easier for him to receive an exit permit. For months he was neither refused nor given an affirmative answer.

Meanwhile, Rita had a son she named Elan. She also returned to the university to complete her studies.

On July 2, 1971, she received a cable from Yakov that the Soviet authorities had refused him permission to leave.

Mrs. Hauser took an interest in the Gluzman case, as did others, and soon Rita was invited to the United States to tell her story. Seeking the release of her husband, she testified before a U.S. Congressional Subcommittee on Foreign Affairs in November 1971. Meanwhile, Ulrikh Gait busily circulated petitions to mass media in many countries, hoping to have his wife and son join him. Ultimately, both the Gait and Gluzman families were reunited, largely as a consequence of their energetic personal efforts. But Chernovtsy remains a city lacking concerted Jewish leadership and thus the support of the Jewish movement, both within the USSR and in the West.

Lvov, a city of nearly half a million near the Polish border, was once the home of almost 125,000 Jews and was an important center of Jewish culture. Long a part of Polish Galicia, it was incorporated into the USSR in 1940, during the partition of Poland. At least 100,000 Lvov Jews died in the Holocaust. When the Red Army entered Lvov in July 1944, only 827 Jews were left alive in the city, and only 9,000 could be found in Galicia where half a million had lived. Some Lvov Jews survived in the concentration camps and some had successfully fled east or fought in underground partisan units. The few who returned were augmented by others, from rural areas and even Siberia. The 1959 Soviet census recorded 25,000 Jews in the city, and according to recent estimates, there are 40,000. But the one synagogue in Lvov was closed on November 5, 1962, after a campaign in which it was vilified as a center for black marketeering, drunkenness, and intrigue with American tourists and Israeli Embassy officials, both groups of whom were charged with being espionage agents. In the same year, the *shohet* (ritual slaughterer) and a synagogue elder were sentenced to death for profiteering and black marketeering. Given such a history, it is little wonder that the Jews of Lvov were timid.

Still, some were never intimidated. In 1949, two university students, Leonid and Ludmilla Reznikov, prepared a pamphlet advocating a struggle against anti-Semitism in the USSR. They were arrested. Leonid received ten years in prison camp, Ludmilla was sentenced to eight, and her father, who had protested his daughter's arrest, also received ten years' imprisonment. Their convictions were annulled and they were rehabilitated in 1958. Leonid became chief engineer of the Lvov electrical plant. When word reached Lvov at the end of 1968 that some Jews were applying for permission to go to Israel, the Reznikovs applied, and in May 1969, they sent a letter to the Supreme Soviet relinquishing Soviet citizenship. Refused an exit permit, they applied again and this time publicly renounced their citizenship. Leonid resigned his job to expedite receipt of permission. They then wrote a public appeal to the government of Israel asking that the matter of their treatment be raised in the United Nations. On March 1, 1971, with their 13-year-old son, they managed to enter the British Embassy in Moscow to ask for help. After being taken by British Embassy car to the Netherlands Embassy, they were arrested, interrogated, and then released. The following month, along with a handful of other families, they were permitted to leave the country.

By late 1971, numbers of Lvov families were applying. Pressures were great. Officials in the Lvov office of OVIR were both nasty and venal. An engineer-polygraphist who emigrated in June 1972 describes what was required when application for an exit visa was made:

> When we received our forms from OVIR, if we filled them out ourselves, the officials would find some technical fault in them and refuse to accept the documents. They would recommend a lawyer, out of a list of a few names. If we retained one of these men privately and paid him what he asked in an "unofficial" way, our forms were processed. When we applied, someone immediately came to our apartment to see when it would be "free." We had to bribe everybody: the members of the house committee for the certificate that we had re-

turned the apartment and paid for repair; the officials at the luggage department to get our goods packed; and finally, the customs official. This was the normal practice in Lvov. Nobody would dream of refusing to pay. When we received permission, time was short and the procedures long. Departure could not be postponed. A Jew had nobody to complain to about bad service. We took no chances and paid whatever was asked.

In Lvov, there was no organized Jewish movement and few brave souls like the Reznikovs. In Moscow, Riga, Leningrad, or other cities, the militancy of the movement would have precluded possibilities of widespread bribery, and if efforts to obtain bribes had taken place, they would have been widely publicized by *samizdat* and in overseas telephone calls, long before they could have been institutionalized.

Although Jews in Ukrainian cities that had formerly been part of Romania or Poland were relatively inactive, those in some major urban centers were early and continuously committed to the movement. Foremost were the Jews of Kharkov, an industrial center in the northeastern Ukraine with a population of 1,250,000, including an estimated 125,000 Jews. Kharkov's Jewish population had grown rapidly after the Bolshevik Revolution, as they left the *shtetl*, the Pale of Settlement, and the border areas and moved to the large interior cities from which they had been largely excluded during the reigns of the tsars. Economic and educational opportunity led many to become technologically skilled and to contribute to the burgeoning industry of the area. But the early Zionist movement was destroyed in the 1920s; the ideological, revolutionary Communists were liquidated in the 1930s; the remnants of Yiddish culture were annihilated in the late 1940s; the war and German occupation claimed large numbers of victims; the few religious Jews were wholly intimidated by a well-publicized public educational trial of the ritual of circumcision as early as 1928; and, in Stalin's last days, whoever was left with overt, identifiable Jewish feeling was subject to prison camp.

Typical was the experience of Yefim (Chaim) Spivakovsky. Born in 1927 into a once-wealthy Ukrainian merchant family, Spivakovsky was evacuated from the Ukraine with other Jewish children in World War II. During that period, his Jewish national consciousness was awakened by Leah Slovin, a young Riga refugee who attended the same school, and by some others. After the war, Spivakovsky sought to enter law school but was barred by a quota system for Jews, and he enrolled instead as a student of economics at Kharkov University. A small, wiry, intense man with fiery black eyes, he reacted vigorously when, in 1948, Ilya Ehrenburg, the famous Soviet writer, stated in *Pravda* that Soviet Jews had no connection with, and should display no attachment to, the newly formed State of Israel. Spivakovsky, then 21, wrote and signed a letter of sharp disagreement. For the next two years the KGB shadowed him and interrogated him about his accomplices. In November 1950, he was arrested for having disseminated Zionist propaganda and sentenced by administrative commission (without a trial) to ten years' imprisonment. He was in forced labor in the Kolyma prison camp in Siberia for five years and eight months. In camp, he became friendly with Vitaly Svechinsky and other political prisoners. Returning to Kharkov in 1956, he married a non-Jew and, as the time became more propitious, began reading and circulating *samizdat* materials and quietly identifying with what was to become the democratic movement. By the early 1960s, he began to contact Zionist-minded friends whom he had known either in prison or during the wartime evacuation. In mid-February 1968, while working as an economist in an instrument factory, Spivakovsky was summoned by the KGB for interrogation, but the officials appeared to be more interested in his democratic activities than in his Zionist connections. Yet, within a few months, Zionist activities were to claim a major part of his time until he finally managed to get an exit visa in March 1971. His connections with Svechinsky in Moscow and friends in Riga led to his serving on the VKK, to the KGB search of his house on June 15, 1970, to continuous contact between Kharkov and other cities, and to Kharkov's greater involvement in the Jewish movement.

Heartened by news that exit visas were being issued, a number of Kharkov Jewish movement people, including Spivakovsky and his friend Aron Bogdanovsky, had applied to OVIR in 1969. As far as they knew, no Jews had left Kharkov for Israel since the end of World War II. But Bogdanovsky, a chemical engineer whose mild, quizzical expression hardly gave notice of his mulish determination, was not only an important movement leader, but also plagued the OVIR office with his persistent visa requests. On September 12, 1969, the unexpected happened. Bogdanovsky received permission to emigrate—but not to take much of his personal library with him. An obscure regulation was found allegedly prohibiting volumes written before 1946 from leaving the country. Bogdanovsky appealed this decision and filed a complaint with the Ministry of Culture castigating the high-handedness and red tape. After he had made all preparations for departure, permission to leave was withdrawn. For months he tramped from ministry to department, to bureaucrat and judicial official, submitting complaints, pleas, and detailed arguments, all demonstrating that he had meticulously obeyed the law and that the officials were constantly breaking it. In an open letter of March 13, 1970, he asked the highest judicial authorities to curb this "flagrant disregard of the law." They did not do so, but OVIR reissued his exit visa and, in July 1970, Bogdanovsky became the first Kharkov Jew in a quarter of a century to receive permission to go to Israel. For the USSR, it was a mistake. In Israel, he organized telephone communication with Kharkov and Moscow and defied the slow-moving Israeli government office on Soviet Jewry by maintaining contact with his friends and publicizing their cases in the West. There was much to keep him busy.

Among the brightest stars in the Kharkov resistance was the young activist Leonid (Yona) Kolchinsky. Born in 1952 of conforming Jewish parents, he is a strikingly handsome six-footer. In school he won judo championships and was also a boxer and swimmer. He wrote poetry and was an excellent student, especially in mathematics and linguistics. But by his sixteenth birthday, he had spoken openly on behalf of Daniel and Sinyavsky and publicly condemned Soviet intervention in Czechoslovakia, and because he was persuasive to other students, the high school authorities expelled him. His relationship with his worried mother was ruptured, and he sought friends who shared his dissenting views. He found them in Spivakovsky, Bogdanovsky, and Alex Volkov, a 33-year-old concert pianist and professor of music at the Kharkov Conservatory and his wife, Lena Volkov, an electrical engineer. The Volkovs, in effect, became his foster parents. Called to the Soviet recruiting office the day he turned 18, Kolchinsky was found to be in excellent health and was rated immediately eligible for service. He declared that although he was not a pacifist, he did not regard the USSR as his motherland, but rather Israel, where he was prepared to enter the military. In May 1970, he went to the Netherlands Embassy in Moscow to arrange for a *vizov* and then renounced his Soviet citizenship. A *vizov* soon arrived, but his mother told the authorities that he had no relatives in Israel, and OVIR denied him a visa. In September 1970, Kolchinsky again (this time with the Volkovs) renounced Soviet citizenship. He declared to the Supreme Soviet that it was his duty to protect his homeland, Israel, and that he could not bear any responsibility for his former Soviet citizenship since he could not support the policy of the USSR in the Middle East. He executed a power of attorney before a notary permitting Lena Volkov to process his efforts to emigrate to Israel. On October 14, he sent a declaration to the Ministry of Defense (with a copy to the president of Israel) announcing that he would consider any pledge of allegiance or induction into the Soviet Army as a mere formality. That day, while he was at the Volkov apartment, a squad of police officers cut the telephone wires, raided the apartment, beat up Kolchinsky, and arrested him for hooliganism for arguing with the notary. He was summarily given twenty days in jail. As soon as he was released, he and the Volkovs issued another renunciation of citizenship. But on December 28, 1970, Kolchinsky was inducted, protesting the compulsion.

From Spivakovsky and from Leonid Rigerman in Moscow, Bogdanovsky learned the news about Kolchinsky, who, even as he was being inducted, wrote to Israel's President Shazar and the chief rabbi of the Israeli Army, Shlomo Goren (now Israel's chief rabbi), reiterating his loyalty to Israel. In the army, he barraged his commanders with explanations of his position and complaints about army practices. One such statement, addressed to General Yepishev, chief of the Political Department, and transmitted by telephone from Spivakovsky and Bogdanovsky, read:

It is as hard for me to imagine myself worried about the military capacity of the Soviet Army as it is to imagine myself as a soldier in this army. But I have respect for law, a trait characteristic, to my regret, of only a very few, except for Zionists and democratic Russians. Otherwise, I would not be in the USSR and certainly not in the army. It is this trait that compels me to present this report to you, under paragraph 103 of the Army Disciplinary Code. . . .

I sent a declaration of renunciation of citizenship to the Supreme Soviet. In this declaration, I expressed hope that not for long would I have to bear this citizenship that fails to arouse in me any feeling other than disgust, and that the people who must handle this matter, those who value their Soviet citizenship, would not permit this citizenship to lie on someone as a yoke and a shame. . . .

The fact that, knowingly, one forces someone to serve in a hostile army is hard to classify other than as an act, not so much against the one who suffers from it, but as an act against the army and the state itself. . . .

I did not present this report before because I was not completely certain that such an incredible act as my induction into the Soviet Army was purely anti-Soviet in its purpose. My induction did not arouse in me anti-Soviet feelings, as did my imprisonment. Quite the opposite; the induction pushed aside anti-Sovietism and aroused contempt and even compassion for the superpower that must draft, to defend itself, a stranger who cannot feel toward it any kind feelings whatsoever.

He asked to be sent to the Chinese front, where he could be regarded as politically reliable, since China was hostile to his homeland, Israel. On March 25, 1971, some fifty of his friends in Kharkov, Moscow, and Odessa, all leading activists, sent an open letter of protest to Soviet officials about Kolchinsky. Meantime, on March 2, a dozen activists, including Spivakovsky and the Volkovs, became the first from Kharkov to receive permission to join Bogdanovsky in Israel. They immediately increased the agitation for Kolchinsky. On a weekend leave from his unit, Kolchinsky joined a Moscow hunger strike. In June, he committed the unpardonable political sin of refusing to vote in an election and was joined by a number of young Jews from Kharkov, all of whom regarded themselves as Israeli citizens. In the summer of 1971, Valery Chalidze, a member of the Soviet Human Rights Committee, to whom Kolchinsky had given power of attorney when the Volkovs left the USSR, again petitioned the USSR defense minister. It was all to no avail. Kolchinsky had to serve two years in the army. In January 1974 he was given permission to go to Israel.

When, in March 1971, the first group of Kharkov activists were permitted to leave for Israel, Aleksandr Gorbatch, a 35-year-old building engineer, assumed leadership. He served fifteen days in jail for leading a protest about trials in other cities. Arrested in Moscow, he went on a hunger strike and was returned to Kharkov, where he was force-fed. He was then charged with an economic crime—being engaged in private enterprise—and was taken to a small Ukrainian town for trial. The Kharkov contingent in Israel quickly publicized his plight, noting that the charges were in fact based on the contention that Gorbatch was guilty of parasitism—not working at an officially registered place—a crime that can result in five years' imprisonment. (An eye disorder had caused him to leave his post, and he had been forced to find brief temporary jobs, leading to the charge against him.) Meanwhile, Gorbatch had been subjected to lengthy KGB searches and interrogations (which had uncovered a substantial collection of Jewish *samizdat* materials) and violations by the authorities of Soviet criminal procedure laws. In May 1971, Israel's Knesset enacted a law permitting the grant of Israeli citizenship to Jews who sought to become Israeli citizens but who were prevented from achieving this status by virtue of their involuntary detention elsewhere. Equipped with Gorbatch's power of attorney, Bogdanovsky immediately applied for his friend—a petition believed to be the first under the new law. Although seventy-two witnesses were called at Gorbatch's trial on July 15-16, 1971, none could confirm that he had violated any law. Still, he was found guilty and sentenced to pay a fine of 400 rubles. Some months later, Gorbatch was permitted to leave for Israel.

Yuli Brind, a 42-year-old metal engraver, did not get off so easily. His father was a well-known professor of dermatology and his mother was also a physician. Brind graduated from a technical institute in machine construction but worked for many years as a milling machine operator, and more recently as a master engraver. In the months before the Six-Day War, he wrote letters to various newspapers attacking their hostile, inaccurate accounts about the Middle Eastern crisis. In early June 1967, he sent *Pravda* a letter (never published) entitled "Take Your Hands Off Israel," which condemned the domestic and foreign policy of the USSR and particularly Soviet support for the Arab states, which he likened to the 1940 pact with Nazi Germany. That letter, and one criticizing Kharkov officials for their failure to memorialize Tractorny Zavod, the local site where the Nazis slaughtered thousands of Jews in World War II, led to his extensive interrogation by the KGB. He was asked to write a retraction, but he refused. Both he and his father were threatened, but Brind was adamant. The incident seemed to have passed. The USSR has a five-year statute of limitations on alleged criminal offenses of this category. But in early 1972, Brind spoke at a meeting commemorating the thirtieth anniversary of the Tractorny Zavod slaughter. He also took a pro-Israel position at an officially sponsored meeting condemning Israeli activity. In March 1972, the KGB advised him he was under suspicion of anti-Soviet slander. He was arrested on March 24 at the OVIR office and ordered sent to a mental hospital for psychiatric examination. For Soviet dissenters, the possibility of long commitment to mental institutions is even more fearsome than detention in a prison camp, since they are subjected to

physically and psychologically debilitating drug therapy as well as
more subtle methods designed to break their will.*

Brind was neither the first nor the last Jewish activist so confined.
But he went on a hunger strike in the hospital, and letters from him
smuggled to the UN Secretary General and the Human Rights Commission resulted in telephone calls of inquiry from prominent European
and American psychiatrists to the doctor in charge of his case. As a
consequence, Brind's mental status was reevaluated and the hospital
psychiatrists concluded that he was of sound mind and therefore only
a political criminal. After his release from the hospital, he was tried,
on June 1, 1972, not in a courtroom, but in the factory where he
worked, in a proceeding open only to selected fellow-workers. The
evidence against him consisted largely of his five-year-old expressions
of opinion and his more recent protests concerning neglect of the site
of a Jewish massacre which had included members of his own family.
He was sentenced to two and a half years of imprisonment under the
Ukrainian equivalent of Russian Article 190-1 (anti-Soviet slander).
He alone of Kharkov's Jewish activists received a prison-camp term.

Brind's imprisonment did not quiet Kharkov's more militant Jews;
neither did the continuation of harassments and arrests for hooliganism
nor the fact that some activists received exit visas. Agitation continued
and was heightened when Kolchinsky was discharged from the army in
November 1972. Only a few days after his release, he and several
friends were arrested to prevent their joining demonstrations in Moscow. In the winter and spring of 1973, the group bitterly denounced
Soviet emigration policy in a letter to *The New York Times* and
publicly appealed to Henry Kissinger and New York's Mayor John
Lindsay for exit-visa assistance, charging that they had been discharged
from jobs and otherwise harassed because of their applications to go
to Israel.

In Kiev, whatever salutary effects, in terms of intimidation, the
Kochubiyevsky trial might have had from the regime's viewpoint had
since worn away. In the spring of 1970, in a letter to Golda Meir, ten

---

* This method of social control for nonconformity, widely used by Soviet
authorities in recent years, has been aptly characterized by Aleksandr Solzenitsyn:
"The incarceration of free-thinking healthy people in madhouses is spiritual
murder, it is a variation on the gas chamber, but is even more cruel. The torture
of the people being killed is more malicious and more prolonged. Like the gas
chambers, these crimes will never be forgotten."

Kiev Jews signed the first collective application for Israeli citizenship ever prepared by Soviet Jews.

> Mrs. Meir. We petition that all of us who have signed this letter should be granted Israeli citizenship. Having made this decision we thus give you the right to defend our interests and to undertake any measures directed at our speediest departure to Israel.

There was no reply and, for over a year, no recognition of the growing number of citizenship requests.

On September 26, 1970, according to *Iskhod* and *Khronika*, Semyon Shulimovich Shmurak, one of the signers of the letter, had

> submitted an application to OVIR requesting permission to emigrate to Israel. That evening he was stopped outside his home. With cries of "Stop that! I know you! Don't try it on! I'll show you!" an unknown man began waving his fists at Shmurak. Two policemen immediately appeared, took Shmurak by the arm and led him to the police station. There it turned out that Shmurak had "used obscene language and attempted to assault citizen Yampolsky." He was then taken to a preliminary-detention cell and on September 28 tried "for petty hooliganism." The only witness was a man whom Shmurak had never seen before. He told the court, however, that Shmurak had done everything of which he was accused. The sentence—fifteen days' imprisonment—"is not subject to appeal."
>
> "And so," Shmurak wrote, "I was not at the rally at Babi Yar on September 29, 1970, and I celebrated Rosh Hashanah in a cell."

In early 1971, however, Shmurak, Anatoly Gerenrot, who had been the Kiev representative to the VKK, and other leaders of the movement in Kiev received permission to go to Israel.

In August 1971, eight Jewish leaders received fifteen days' "administrative detention" for refusing to disperse after declaring a one-day hunger strike at Babi Yar on Tisha b'Av, the traditional Jewish day of mourning for the destruction of the Temple in Jerusalem. But a month later, on September 29, when over 2,500 Jews from various parts of the USSR gathered at Babi Yar for a ceremony commemorating the thirtieth anniversary of the massacre, the police did not interfere. Previously the Babi Yar commemorations had been the focal point of organization for Kiev's Jews, but after the intense arousal of feeling stimulated by the first Leningrad trials in December 1970 mobilized many Jews to apply to leave, the OVIR office in Kiev became a meeting place for like-minded militants to make contact. But a major turning point occurred as a result of the events that began at the Kiev synagogue on February 19, 1972.

A tradition had developed among Kiev's Jews. Every Saturday at noon, near the synagoguge, Jewish youths sang, played guitars, and indicated their Jewish solidarity. On Friday, February 18, word was received that there would be arrests at the synagogue the next day. Nevertheless, about thirty people gathered outside on Saturday. A small crowd of drunken workers and several KGB plainsclothesmen also came, as well as a militia (police) officer named Filenko.

When the young Jews arrived (the synagogue was already full of elderly people who were praying), the crowd started to shout: "To Babi Yar with them! Where are trucks? Crush them!" At about 1 p.m., police vans arrived and, with the aid of the drunkards and KGB men, they seized Jews. Five were soon released, but four were arrested and taken to police headquarters, where they were ordered to write "an explanation." Instead, they wrote a protest to the city prosecutor, complaining about "drunken hooligans who, together with officer Filenko, dragged us here." Although the protest was officially accepted, the four were charged with "hooliganism." The mob leaders were not.

The next day, all four were tried separately before a judge, his secretary, and a major of the police. The charge was that the head of the synagogue (who was not there) had complained that they disturbed the religious service and "cursed in an unknown language" (presumably Hebrew). They were sentenced to fifteen days "for an attempt on the life and health of workers of the militia."

The Jews maintained their solidarity in prison. When they were ordered to shave their beards, they refused, saying that they were religious Jews, and they were shaved by force. They then went on a three-day hunger strike.

The next Saturday, February 26, there were about a hundred Jews outside the synagogue. When the militia drove them away, they went to the party committee headquarters. Four more people were arrested, including 56-year-old Vladimir Barboy, a professor of chemistry and long-time Zionist who had spent ten years in prison camp in his youth. (Even before Professor Barboy applied for an exit visa, the KGB advised him not to do so since he would never receive permission to leave. He was offered, instead, chairmanship of his department at the university and a higher salary. He refused. After he applied, he lost his job.) The four were sentenced to fifteen days for hooliganism.

Many Kiev Jews cabled a protest to President Podgorny. After that Sabbath, the authorities spread rumors in Kiev that the Jews had organized demonstrations demanding that they be given the Palace of the Ukraine for their synagogue, that Jews going to Israel be permitted to take with them any amount of gold, that there be created in the Ukraine a Jewish Autonomous Republic, with Kiev as the capital, and that Jewish schools and theaters be opened throughout the Ukraine.

On Saturday, March 4, only twenty young Jews gathered outside the synagogue. Three were arrested and sentenced to fifteen days. On March 11, the police cordoned off the synagogue area and refused to allow anyone to approach the building. The repressive tactics were effective for some months, and the synagogue gatherings ceased. But almost all of those arrested received their visas, and by late spring the emigration flow from Kiev became much heavier. Militancy again appeared to be the only effective way of lubricating the sluggish, unwilling wheels of OVIR bureaucracy.

The 1972 synagogue arrests, instead of deterring the Jews of Kiev, consolidated the movement, and when the second group of activist leaders departed for Israel, still others took their place. Most were articulate young engineers and scientists who had been persistently refused permission to leave. These activists, in constant touch with Kiev "alumni" in Israel, have utilized the whole arsenal of protest— public appeals, hunger strikes, petitions to and meetings with authorities —to publicize their being held involuntarily in the USSR. Characteristic of the demonstrations was this report in the final issue of *Khronika*:

> Babi Yar, 7 September [1972]. A group of Kiev Jews attempted to lay a wreath and flowers on the gravestone of Babi Yar in memory of the eleven Israeli sportsmen murdered in Munich. Participants in the ceremony of mourning were met by rows of policemen and KGB men in civilian clothes (among them KGB "operatives" Smirnov and Bryukhanov from the Kiev regional department—already well known to many Jews—and others who have often taken part in various police actions against Jews, in particular at the Kiev synagogue).
>
> Persons who approached the memorial with flowers or refused to "disperse" were detained. In all, twenty-seven people were detained; five of them were fined 25 rubles and eleven were sentenced to fifteen days' administrative arrest on the basis of false testimony by witnesses, and a different "corpus delicti" was invented for each person. Arrested were: Yury Soroko, Basya Soroko (his wife), Simkha Remennik, Zinovy Melamed, Mark Yampolsky, Yuli Tartakovsky, Dmitry Dobrenko, Vladimir Vernikov, Vsevolod Rukhman, David Miretsky, and Yan Monastyrsky.

Following an objection by the procurator responsible for ensuring legality in places of confinement, B. Soroko was released one day before her term expired in view of the fact that she and Yu. Soroko have a child who is a minor. The police tried to disperse their friends and relatives when they gathered outside the prison. Yu. Soroko and Z. Melamed were driven straight from prison to the offices of the Kiev regional KGB, where a KGB officer called Davydenko "chatted" with them in threatening tones. He declared that "circumstances had changed," that the KGB had now "had its hands untied," and that the next time their term of imprisonment would be far longer.

But the activity continued. Mark Yampolsky, a mathematician and jazz drummer, came to the United States on a visit after receiving an exit visa to Israel. There, in the spring of 1973, Yampolsky conducted an extended hunger strike in front of the Soviet Embassy in Washington, D.C. Others continued to agitate, awaiting either arrest or an exit visa. On April 20, 1973, an appeal to Mrs. Meir and "the Jewish Communities of the Free World" stated:

We appeal to you now because we have come to the conclusion that the Kiev branch of the KGB is holding us in the USSR as hostages, candidates for a new anti-Jewish trial.

By blackmailing people, the KGB workers are feverishly seeking false witnesses who would agree or who can be forced to slander us. . . . Some of us, Basya Soroko and Zinovy Melamed, are refused exit visas on the fabricated argument of having had access to some secrets in their work. We are vainly trying to prove the groundlessness of this argument.

The refusal to Aleksandr Feldman is based on his military service, in spite of the fact that he served as a private in a construction unit that was not engaged in any secret project. . . .

We are constantly subjected to psychological terror and more. The authorities arbitrarily throw us into prison. Yury Soroko, Zinovy Melamed, and Aleksandr Feldman were imprisoned three times and Basya Soroko and Yuli Tartakovsky were imprisoned once. Tartakovsky was forced out of his job and an attempt was made to induct him into the army.*

* Feldman, a 26-year-old activist, had been seeking a visa since early 1972. Arrested many times for his involvement in demonstrations and protests, he had received repeated fifteen-day hooliganism detentions. On October 18, 1973, he was again arrested, this time for malicious hooliganism, allegedly for bumping into a woman carrying a cake. The charge was believed to be a pretext and a punitive reprisal for his extreme militancy. He was sentenced to three and a half years for this crime on November 23, and his appeals were denied. His conviction is the harshest of the recent prosecutions of Jewish activists.

In Vinnitsa, a growing industrial center in the central Ukraine with 25,000 Jews in a total population of 150,000, there is little evidence of intellectual ferment or oppositional tendencies. As recently as March 1973, a 50-year-old Jew, David Kosarovsky, was stabbed to death in the Vinnitsa market when he sought to prevent three Ukrainians from stealing furs brought to the market by Jewish merchants. The police certified the cause of death as a heart attack, refusing to take testimony of eyewitnesses to the murder. Having lived through decades of official lawlessness and anti-Semitic discrimination, local Jews were too frightened to protest. For any Jewish activism to arise, let alone flourish, in such an atmosphere would be remarkable. Yet the renaissance of Jewish national identity produced, even in Vinnitsa, some Jews who applied to emigrate to Israel and a few who were brave enough to express their feelings openly. One such person was Isak Shkolnik. Unlike most Jewish activists, he was neither a college student nor employed in intellectual pursuits, but a mechanic in an automation equipment plant. Born in 1936 to a family of traditional Jewish background, Shkolnik had been a laborer, miner, and factory worker since his youth. He had also taught himself English, was widely read, had a long-time interest in Israel, and was studying Hebrew on his own. Like many others, he listened to news broadcasts of the Voice of America, BBC, and, when possible, Kol Israel and Radio Liberty.

In 1967, six Englishmen came to Vinnitsa to install equipment the USSR had purchased for a local chemical plant, Khimkombinat imeni Sverdlova. During the year and a half they worked in the area, Shkolnik made their acquaintance, despite KGB warnings not to be too friendly to foreigners. He practiced his English and invited them to his home, even to a birthday party for his infant daughter. On one occasion, he assisted them in photocopying the description of some equipment that had to be ordered from England, going openly to the Engineering Society Club in Vinnitsa and securing permission for this task. He also gave them a roll of film taken at a party they attended. Some years later, all of these seemingly innocent relationships were to become exceedingly sinister.

When news reached Vinnitsa in 1971 that Jews were securing exit visas to Israel, Shkolnik, along with a few others, indicated his desire to emigrate. But the lack of a *vizov* prevented his making application. In late June 1972, his *vizov* arrived by post from Israel but, like others sent earlier, Shkolnik never received it. Instead, on July 3, he was arrested, and when his home was searched, some damning evidence was found. It included a business card reading, "Howard Braverham, Propane Spencer & Co," photocopies of the Hebrew grammar *Elef Milim Aleph*, some old copies of American magazines, a U.S. five-dollar bill, a Japanese-made transistor radio, some letters from England and Canada, as well as postcards and photographs with English inscriptions.

Shkolnik was charged under the Ukrainian equivalent of Russian Article 190-1. The anti-Soviet slander alleged was pro-Israel remarks made in conversation by Shkolnik and his fellow-worker and friend Mikhail Mager, at an anti-Israel factory indoctrination lecture many months earlier. The local paper attacked Shkolnik and Mager in an article entitled "The Poisonous Fangs of Zionism." Mager was also arrested but subsequently released. Six months passed. For reasons seemingly as legally inexplicable as the first action, the charges were changed to the Ukrainian equivalents of Russian Articles 64 (treason) and 70 (anti-Soviet propaganda). Specifically, Shkolnik was accused of having been a traitor to the USSR and of having acted as a spy for Great Britain by passing secrets in 1968 to the English engineers. The British Foreign Office quickly denied the charges, and Mr. Braverham expressed incredulity. The indignation of Westminster and Whitehall was minuscule and tempered compared to that of the Shkolnik family, faced with the possibility of a death sentence. Shkolnik's wife Feiga was advised that her husband's trial would be a closed military one and that the former Vinnitsa prosecutor, Nikolai Makarenko, was available for the defense. She was further advised that, with luck, Shkolnik might receive only fifteen years.

In bewilderment, Feiga Shkolnik wrote to Roman Rudenko, procurator-general of the USSR:

> I don't know how the investigation could have reached such a terrible conclusion, but I am certain that my husband did not and could not commit an act that could be regarded as treason to the fatherland. He is blamed for his good knowledge of the English language and his acquaintance with foreigners, who came to our country as tourists or on missions. He always met openly with them, in places where there were many people; in our home, at the birthday party for our daughter. At these meetings many of our acquaintances and relatives had always been present. He is also blamed for visiting exhibitions organized by foreign states in our country, such as "Popular Education in the USA," "Communication Media in the USA," etc. Why, then, had these exhibitions been organized at the time?

Following receipt of this letter, the claim that Shkolnik was a British spy was dropped and the specifications were modified to charge him with being an Israeli spy who had collected information in his head to communicate to Israeli officials after he received an exit visa. Although his remarkable prescience was said to have commenced some years earlier, before Vinnitsa Jews were securing permission to leave, Shkolnik was accused of being both diabolically clever and possessed of a remarkable memory.

The trial, which lasted from March 29 to April 11, 1973, took place in a brick factory commandeered for the occasion and was guarded by a Red Army detachment. Members of the family were not permitted to approach closer than 100 yards from the site. At least forty-six witnesses were called. The prosecutor's only documentary evidence appeared to be the KGB-confiscated *vizov,* seized because "his criminal intentions were known." One other allegation was considered important to the prosecution. On May 26, 1972, Shkolnik had been part of a group saying goodbye to a Vinnitsa couple, Mr. and Mrs. Mark Charnis, who were leaving for Israel. This was viewed as evidence of his guilty mental preparations for espionage. Most witnesses testified to conversations allegedy held with the defendant in which he had expressed interest in the work that they did. To avoid the death penalty, Makarenko, the defense counsel, apparently persuaded Shkolnik to plead guilty to collecting information in his head. Late in the trial, Feiga Shkolnik again wrote to Rudenko and sent copies of her letter to, among others, U.S. Senator Henry M. Jackson of Washington, whose fame had by now spread to this remote Ukrainian city:

> Since March 29, in the town of Vinnitsa, the military tribunal of the Prikarpatski military district has been in session. Sitting in the dock is my husband, Isak Rafaelovich Shkolnik. In the words of his counsel, the court is objectively trying to establish his guilt. What, in essence, is the basis of his crime? According to his counsel, the collecting of information of national importance, with the aim of passing it abroad, to Israel. What has been established? No country recruited him. Nobody gave him instructions. The court is not accusing him of that. The information was passed nowhere, nor to anybody. There is not a single document which substantiates the facts about the collection of information. Where then did my husband, in fact, store the information thus collected during the fifteen-year period since the day he started military service? In his head, it appears. From his head it had to find its way to Israel. From his head it found its way to the investigation records and he collected it, not for the sake of curiosity

but with the aim of passing it onto that country about which he has been dreaming since he has been thirteen years old. And by what means did he collect this information? He had talked with different people—for example, with construction workers who had previously served in the ranks of the Soviet Army. Who then bears the greater responsibility? The one who talked in contravention of his oath or the one who asked the questions? It appears that they could blurt things out because of the simplicity of their minds, but he being ten times cleverer, according to the words of counsel, could give them the necessary questions. Anyone can understand the absurdity of such an accusation. Even if he asked these questions, how could he possibly know that the corresponding information constituted a state secret? Even the investigating department had to utilize all its ingenuity in order to prove the importance of these pieces of information. In which direction, in general, did they apply their expertise? Bits of information which he stored in his head which subsequently found their way to the interrogation record. And what kind of terribly important information could he have collected, bearing in mind that he has not even had a secondary technical education and that he understood such matters at about the level of a tenth-grade pupil? What do they want to punish him for? For espionage which did not and could not exist? Or for too openly desiring to leave for his historic homeland, Israel.

Shkolnik, "for his repentance," received only ten years in prison camp. There was immediate pressure to discourage him and his family from appealing. After sentencing, when Feiga Shkolnik attempted to discuss the case with her husband, the guards separated them. Makarenko persisted in refusing to appeal and was discharged by Mrs. Shkolnik and the prisoner's father. When the distraught wife went to Moscow and, with the aid of activists there, located an attorney willing to process the appeal, Makarenko suddenly agreed to proceed, and letters were produced from Shkolnik himself stating that he wished Makarenko to continue to act for him. The Moscow lawyer was refused permission to see Shkolnik since Makarenko was still counsel. The family, however, categorically rejected him and appealed to the Vinnitsa Collegium of Lawyers and the chairman of the Military Collegiate of the Supreme Court of the USSR, charging that Shkolnik was being hidden by his jailers to prevent proper representation; that he had been forcibly coerced to sign letters approving Makarenko, "whom we do not trust"; that they doubted "the legitimacy of the actions of the prison administration and of Attorney Makarenko," who has "no right to lead the defense." They insisted that "the attorney from the

Moscow Collegiate should act as counsel for the defense." Their appeal was denied and they were not permitted to see Shkolnik to ascertain his true wishes. Access was available only to Makarenko.

The desperate wife then appealed to Leonid Brezhnev and the Presidium of the Supreme Soviet:

> The court recognized that Shkolnik had not been recruited and was not an agent of any intelligence service, that he had not transmitted information to anyone, and that, consequently, he had not caused any real harm to the country and could not have caused it.
>
> My husband is a technically illiterate man and has no special education. He simply was unable to differentiate what information is important and what is a government secret. . . . Not a single one of the witnesses who had testified against him had been called to account for making public a state secret. . . . The testimony given by my husband was self-slander. These expressions suddenly appeared half a year after the beginning of the investigation. In support of this view is the statement by Makarenko that if Shkolnik would make evasive statements in court, the death sentence would not be given. . . .
>
> There is no other proof, except his own testimony. The conviction of my husband is a tragic misunderstanding and I beg you to repeal this cruel sentence.

Meanwhile, international interest had been aroused. The International League for the Rights of Man appointed a distinguished French attorney to attend the appeal as an international observer, but the Soviet government refused to issue him a visa. On July 2, the Soviet Supreme Court reduced the ten-year sentence to seven years. Justice had triumphed in the Ukraine.

MINSK:
Military Militants

CHAPTER 17

In the fall of 1971, an extraordinary wedding occurred in Tel Aviv. Among the many hundreds in attendance were Israeli cabinet ministers and Knesset members; young college students and grizzled pioneers whose memories encompassed more than half a century of the blood and toil that built the state; kibbutzniks and intellectuals; Arabs in ceremonial dress and new immigrants from various countries, notably the USSR. The occasion was the marriage of 43-year-old Anatoly Rubin, recently of Minsk, and 24-year-old Karny Jabotinsky, the grand-daughter of Vladimir (Zev) Jabotinsky, the brilliant writer, soldier, and founder of Revisionist Zionism. Rubin, a physical education therapist who had spent seven years in Soviet prison camps, had been the principal leader of the Jewish movement in Minsk. His marriage to the Israeli medical student symbolized the uniting of half a century of Jewish struggle.

Jabotinsky, born in Odessa in 1880, committed his talents as a journalist, foreign correspondent, and organizer to the creation of the Zionist movement. He organized a Jewish self-defense corps in Odessa in 1903; Jewish battalions to fight with the British against the Turks in Palestine in World War I; a Palestinian self-defense unit in Jerusalem in 1920 (for which the British sentenced him to fifteen years, only a brief period of which he served); a new Zionist world-wide party; illegal immigration into Palestine during the 1930s; and the technique of direct action which culminated in the underground liberation army—the Irgun. Although Jabotinsky died in 1940 and thus never saw either the Irgun or the Jewish state, his adoring disciples viewed him as the Garibaldi of the Jewish Revolution. His oratorical gifts, facile pen, and example of direct action left a legacy that constituted the single most powerful inspiration to the Jewish movement in the USSR. Jabotinsky was a passionate Jew. He was also very Russian. His most consuming passion was a Jewish state which would be inhabited by large numbers of immigrants from the USSR.

To Anatoly Rubin and to the activists of the Soviet Jewish movement, Jabotinsky was the prophet, the example, the inspiration. Like her grandfather, Karny, the daughter of the late Professor Ari Jabotinsky of Technion University in Haifa, was a passionate intellectual with an overwhelming commitment to the cause of Soviet Jewry. It was little wonder that their wedding was an unparalleled social and political event in the year that the first large wave of Soviet Jews reached the homeland, thus realizing Jabotinsky's dream.

Minsk, from which Rubin came, is the capital of the Byelorussian Soviet Socialist Republic (White Russia) and is the center of a circle that encompasses, within its 300-mile radius, one of the historic heartlands of modern Jewish life. Within such a circle around Minsk are such historic Jewish centers as Warsaw, Lublin, and Białystok in Poland, Kovno and Vilna in Lithuania, Riga in Latvia, Kiev, Lvov, and many other major Ukrainian cities; Moldavia and Bukovina; and, somewhat farther away, to the northeast, Leningrad and Moscow. Byelorussia, long a backward, poverty-stricken land of farms, forests, and lakes, now is a rapidly industrializing republic of 10.5 million people. It includes a number of cities with Jewish populations of 15,000 to 30,000, such as Gomel, Mogilev, and Vitebsk. Minsk, its 900-year-old capital, has doubled in size in a quarter of a century; its population is now close to 1 million. It is a computer and science center and the home of automobile, truck, and tractor plants and of many higher educational institutions. Minsk experienced a phenomenal increase in Jewish population in the late 19th and early 20th centuries, but the urbanization of Byelorussia was accompanied by widespread peasant hostility, often expressed in intense anti-Semitism. Just before the outbreak of World War II, the Jewish population of Minsk was officially said to be close to 90,000, and some commentators have claimed that there were several hundred thousand Jews in the city and its surrounding areas. Minsk had Jewish theaters, Yiddish newspapers, and, up to the 1930s, dozens of synagogues and religious institutions.

The Germans captured Minsk on June 28, 1941, after a three-day bombardment that leveled much of the old city. Many Jews fled to the east before the approaching Wehrmacht, but at least 40,000 remained when the city was occupied, and their travail was among the worst suffered in the war. The Nazis set aside two areas as ghettos, and two old forts encircling the city were prepared as reception centers for the "resettlement" of German, Austrian, and Czech Jews who were transported to the starving ghettos in the fall of 1941. There had been considerable organized Jewish resistance to the Nazis in Byelorussia, and 2,278 Jews were executed at once for "sabotage and terrorist activities." Still, continuous Jewish partisan activity took place in the heavily forested areas although Jewish units often found the White Russian partisans as hostile to them as the Nazis. The Minsk ghettos also had a well-organized underground to which the Nazi occupiers responded by killing 20,000 Jews in November 1941 in an effort to crush the "resistance." In July 1942 alone, 11,000 Jews were slaughtered, and by the end of that month the German commandant reported that 55,000 White Russian Jews had been liquidated in ten weeks. The "final solution" for the Jews of Minsk and White Russia was thorough. Between 125,000 and 200,000 Jews met their death in Minsk in 1941-44. Not only Jews were the victims of the Nazi occupation, however. Perhaps a quarter of the Byelorussian people, Jews and non-Jews alike, were slaughtered. The infamous Katyn Forest massacre occurred near Minsk.

With 80% of the city destroyed, postwar rebuilding in Minsk was designed to create a new city, and Jews by the thousands flocked back to assist in the process. Although the official 1959 census figure for Jews in Minsk was 40,000, the present Jewish population is at least 70,000. But the city has no Jewish theater, newspaper, or cultural life, and only one small, shabby synagogue.

This was the environment in which Anatoly Rubin grew to manhood. Born in 1928, he was 13 when the war broke out, and his entire family was killed in the ghetto during the war. Arrested and sentenced in 1946 to five years in a labor camp as a consequence of his Jewish partisan activities, which were officially viewed as "Zionist," he was freed after a year and received specialized higher education in rehabilitative medicine through physical education and ultimately had the responsibility for 600 beds in a Minsk hospital. It was in Minsk that the postwar Soviet anti-Semitic campaign began in 1948 with the Stalin-ordered murder of Solomon Mikhoels, the great actor who had been the head of the Yiddish State Theater and chairman of the wartime Jewish Anti-Fascist Committee.

Rubin was already interested in Jewish history and culture and for the next decade attempted to meet this concern in a city cowed by the Black Years of Soviet Jewry. In 1957, he traveled to the International Youth Festival in Moscow "in order to see Israelis with my own eyes." From Israeli delegates and from Soviet Jewish youths in attendance, he secured Jewish literature, Mogen Davids, and Israeli material. That summer, a sports delegation returned to Minsk from Warsaw with additional books on Israeli and Jewish subjects. A small group of young people formed around Rubin to discuss Jewish affairs and to distribute literature about Israel and Zionism. In December 1958, Rubin and seven other Jewish youths were arrested for "organizing a Zionist cell." Rubin was charged with having connections with the Israeli Embassy. The Minsk newspapers virulently attacked the defendants for "smuggling cancer microbes" inside counterrevolutionary Zionist literature transported from the sports meeting in Poland. Rubin spent six additional years in Soviet labor camps. When released, he was more determined than ever that emigration to Israel was the only answer. On returning to Minsk,

> I already had connections with friends from Riga, Moscow, Leningrad, and other cities whom I had met in the camps. I traveled frequently to those cities to obtain information and literature. In Minsk we began copying the literature and distributing it. We secured tapes and records which were also circulated. We listened regularly to VOA, BBC, Deutsche Welle, and Kol Israel. In spite of the fact that I was constantly watched, I maintained contact with our group, but their number was limited because I didn't want to cause them to be followed. Around each of these friends, other groups formed.

Activity in Minsk was not limited to young people. In December 1968, Leopold Solomonovich Grinblat, a middle-aged electrical engineer, was tried on charges of "Zionism." The prosecution's case appears to have consisted of the fact that a map of Israel, and a biography of Israel's first president, Chaim Weizmann, published in Israel in Yiddish, were found in Grinblat's possession. No details of the trial are available. We know, however, that the Grinblat prosecution was designed to crush the resurgence of Zionist sentiments among Minsk Jews. It failed in its purpose. Rubin relates how, following the trial, the small activist groups increased their *samizdat* distribution, although they still proceeded cautiously.

In 1969, the KGB decided to get rid of the Jewish activists and began to allow them to leave from several cities. I was one of those permitted to leave. I was told clearly at OVIR, "It is better to get you out of here to Israel than to poison the minds of our youth." I left in May 1969. At the train station, dozens of Jews came to say goodby. Some accompanied me to Moscow, from where I left for Vienna. After they saw that I wasn't arrested but allowed to leave in spite of the fact that I had been under KGB surveillance, they began to be more active. From Israel, I sent them records, literature, and letters. Their groups began to grow.

While in Moscow, before leaving, I got activists there in touch with my friends in Minsk. These contacts remained afterward. Due to the contact between Minsk, Moscow, and Riga, the Minsk group began writing petitions and hunger-striking before the Ministry of the Interior. They organized classes for the study of Hebrew.

Rubin's explanation of the growth of the movement in Minsk is modest. Ernst Levin, who subsequently became an important Jewish leader in that city, said: "Tolya was the *madrikh* for all of us." *

The Minsk group, although small in number, was an early, energetic one. Its representative to the VKK was 23-year-old Isak Zhitnitsky, the son of a prominent artist. Grigory, Inda, and Israil Reshel were also extremely active. At the age of 22, Israil Reshel became well known throughout the USSR as the composer of *"Kakhol v'Lavan"* (Blue and White), the Soviet Zionist anthem about the national colors of the State of Israel: "The blue and the white, like a song, like a dream; the blue and the white, of hope and peace." Reshel, an expressive, thickset youth, with round, rimless eyeglasses perched precariously on his nose, wrote song after song in Russian and Hebrew, which he joyfully sang to groups of young Jews in various cities in the USSR. He and Zhitnitsky, like Rubin before them, knew and became well known to young activists in Riga, Moscow, Vilna, Kiev, and Leningrad. By the spring of 1970, collective letters had been sent and circulated demanding the right to leave. At the time of the first Leningrad trial, along with Jews from Moscow, Riga, Kharkov, Vilna, and Kiev, nineteen from Minsk joined in a mass appeal. Ten of them sent a separate protest. Twenty-six prepared and circulated a strong petition of protest against the

* Tolya is the Russian diminutive of Anatoly. *Madrikh* is the Hebrew word for leader-teacher.

Kishinev trial. When local officials sought to prevent the continuation of *ulpan* classes in Minsk, forty-seven Jews vigorously denounced the effort to prevent their learning Hebrew. In midsummer 1971, five hundred signed a petition requesting the right to leave. In March 1971, when activists in other cities had begun again to receive visas, Minsk's young militants were among those who received permission. Israil Reshel, who was among them, carried a letter he had received just before departure:

> Leperous, stinking *Zhids!* Get out! Leave quickly! Don't stink here among honest Soviet citizens. Hitler struck you too gently—you who sold your souls.

It was little wonder that Semyon Zorin, who arrived in Israel at about that time and who had been a partisan commander during World War II, declared that "most of the Jewish community of Minsk wishes to go to Israel." Whether or not Zorin was accurate, many Jews applied in the face of heavy official pressure against such a course, reprisals against applicants, and widespread refusals of permission. By the summer of 1972, Ernst Levin, the 35-year-old former executive of the Minsk Engineering Society who had lost his job because of his Jewish activism and had become a Hebrew teacher, indicated that about a thousand Minsk activists had left but that four thousand applications (which are made by families) were still being held at OVIR. Levin and his wife Asya, a sociologist who had also lost her job, were denied an exit visa, ostensibly because his brother in Leningrad, with whom he had no contact, was working as a physicist in a field of optics alleged to be secret employment. Asya's younger sister Larisa and Larisa's husband Yakov Schultz, a physician, had been permitted to leave and constituted a continuous link to Ernst Levin and other activists.

As each wave of activist leaders received permission to leave, Minsk, like other cities, continually had the problem of developing new leaders and new links in the USSR and abroad. The departing class of 1969 (for example, the Slovins, Shperling et al. in Riga; Khavkin and Kazakov in Moscow; Rubin in Minsk) was replaced by young militants who either were arrested or received permission to leave in the class of 1971. As they departed, others, like Ernst Levin, took their places and developed their own contacts and channels of communication. Each new group of leaders became accustomed to official harassment, questioning, and arrest. Levin was arrested several times in connection with demonstrations. When, unexpectedly, he was told by OVIR that he would be permitted to go to Israel in late summer 1972, Minsk developed a remarkable new leadership that was unlike that in any other city. It included a group of middle-aged, high-ranking military officers and a 67-year-old Jewish artist. These men became the principals in KGB Case 97, sometimes called "the Jewish Officers' Plot." For six months, from late 1972 to late May 1973, there was a widespread investigation and interrogation of at least 155 Minsk Jews and of activists in other cities with the avowed official purpose of demonstrating a massive Jewish conspiracy against the regime. Vigorous pressures from abroad aborted the potential trial.

The first premonitions that a major trial might be in the offing occurred in the summer of 1972. Colonel Lev Ovsishcher, born in 1917, a twenty-five-year veteran of the Red Army, a wounded hero of the Battle of Stalingrad, with fifteen orders and medals, was reduced to private and denied his pension because he applied to go to Israel. In early December 1972, he wrote to President Podgorny:

> The only reason for the refusal is my former service in the Soviet Army, although I was transferred to the reserves in September 1961— more than eleven years ago. It is known that in present circumstances of the development of science and technology, any new invention loses its novelty and practical value after five to seven years. Second, any secrets which were once known by me have at one time or another been shared by the Soviet command with the great Soviet "friends," the Chinese, the Albanians, the Indonesians, and so on. All this has been known overseas for a long time. Third, I am 55 years old, no longer fit for army service, and my only wish is to take part in the peaceful work of rebuilding the ancient homeland of my ancestors. Fourth, if someone needs outdated information, it is not necessary to look for someone who is leaving the USSR to obtain it.

Ovsishcher further complained that his correspondence was intercepted and censored and that his freedom of movement was severely restricted. His friend, Lieutenant Colonel Naum Alshansky, was similarly demoted to private in the reserves, deprived of his pension, and told he would never be permitted to leave. Alshansky, who had been decorated thirteen times for bravery, declared that he and Ovsishcher "were subjected to a moral execution." He added, "I have been doomed to starvation. Perhaps I should put on my medals and ask for alms."

On November 29, 1972, 67-year-old former Red Army Major

Gedalia Kipnis and his devoted wife, having received an exit visa, were on the first leg of their trip to Israel when they were detained at the Polish border city of Brest. Removed from their train, Kipnis was arrested and returned to Minsk. He remained in isolated confinement for almost half a year until Case 97 was discontinued. Kipnis was charged with "activity undermining the Soviet regime by spreading slanderous fabrications."

Two days after the Kipnis arrest, the home of Colonel Yefim Davidovich was searched and literature received from Ernst Levin before he left was seized. On December 8, 1972, Davidovich was charged with anti-Soviet activity. Thus, Case 97 began. Of all the prospective defendants, Davidovich was the most interesting and certainly the most articulate. Born in Minsk in 1924, he joined the Red Army when the Nazis attacked. His parents, three younger brothers, and seventy-eight relatives were trapped in the Minsk ghetto and exterminated. Davidovich was commissioned and fought throughout the war, being wounded five times and decorated on fifteen occasions. He commanded Soviet units that captured Prague toward the war's end, by which time he was a 21-year-old major. In the postwar period, he graduated from the Frunze Military Academy, the Soviet West Point, and became a career officer. By 1966, he was a full colonel, in command of a model regiment of the Byelorussian Military District. That year he suffered the first of three serious heart attacks, the last of which resulted in his retirement from service in 1969.

A loyal Communist, Davidovich remained a member of the Central Committee of the Byelorussian Communist Party until October 1972, although from the spring of 1970 his official internal protests about anti-Semitism in Byelorussia constituted the first signs of his disenchantment and the regime's distrust of him. Although his Jewish interests were known to his fellow-officers and a handful of Jewish friends, he did not openly identify with the movement. It was not until a letter of December 19, 1972 to Party Chief Leonid Brezhnev, which was publicly released, that Davidovich openly assumed major leadership of the Jewish struggle. In that document he stated:

> On December 1, 1972, the workers of the KGB made a search of my house. I was held in the KGB prison for twenty-four hours. During the search, they took away copies of letters sent by me in the spring of 1971 to various Soviet bodies and to the organs of the Soviet press. These letters had been provoked by the unrestrained anti-Semitic orgy

in the press which led to bloody crimes in Minsk: the murders of Professor Mikhelson, of the brother and sister Kantor (students), and of the 16-year-old schoolboy Grisha Tunik. The anti-Jewish atmosphere was later inflamed even more after an explosion in a radio plant. Only the urgent measures taken by the Commission of the Central Committee of the CPSU headed by Commissar Ustinov prevented worse happenings.

In my letters, I called upon the Soviet mass communications media to refrain from publishing anti-Jewish and anti-Israeli material of local and foreign origin, and called upon the Soviet press to join actively in the struggle against anti-Semitism. I received no reply to my letters. In addition to the copies of the letters, the confiscated documents included a short resumé of my two-and-a-half-year campaign in connection with these letters, as well as many other documents concerning Jews, Jewish history, and anti-Semitism. Some tapes of Jewish songs and melodies were also taken.

On December 8, 1972, the senior investigator of the KGB, I. I. Nikiforov, presented me with a formal charge sheet which stated: "The documents sufficiently established Davidovich's activity with the intent of undermining the Soviet regime by having spread, for many years, slanderous fabrications vilifying the Soviet government and society, as well as the production and distribution of literature of this nature, and the illegal possession of firearms." . . .

All my life, with all my strength, and with my blood, I always defended and strengthened the Soviet regime. All my letters and personal notes contain the truth and only the truth. Is telling the truth an anti-Soviet act?

There is no memorial at Babi Yar or at the Minsk ghetto where 200,000 Jews were murdered. For many of us, their blood is not cheaper than that of the 200 Frenchmen from Oradour, the 160 Czechs from Lidice, and the 149 Byelorussians from Katyn, where great memorials have been erected.

My serious illness forced the KGB to release me from prison under a signed obligation not to leave the city. Detectives have surrounded my house and follow me step by step whenever I am able to leave for a walk. They follow the members of my family, my friends, and my acquaintances. In the sick minds of the organizers of this "operation," the impression was evidently created that I had been preparing terrorist acts of major proportions: the murder of all the sportsmen of the USSR, setting fire to all the homes for the aged in Byelorussia, placing hydrogen bombs in the Komarovsk market, the murder of the chairman of the Municipal Council and replacing him with Ben-Gurion. And with the TT 1941 model pistol with eight rusted bullets found in my possession I was supposed to be preparing to expand the Israeli borders from the Nile to the Euphrates, the annexation of Byelorussia to Israel, as well as effectuating all the designs of the Elders of Zion contained in the Protocols—the establishment of

Jewish mastery over the entire world. All of this is not so funny as it is sad. The anti-Jewish hysteria under the slogan of anti-Zionism continues.

Neither the twenty-four hours spent in the KGB prison nor the interminable interrogations are helpful to my physical condition. After interrogations of this type, my wife brings me home only half alive. Her selflessness and extensive medical experience enable me to function, but with great difficulty. My wife, incidentally, is not Jewish. . . .

You understand that during one of the KGB interrogations, or after one, I shall die. My death will not bring laurels to anyone. Willingly or unwillingly I shall become a martyr, a victim of anti-Semitism.

By January 7, 1973, Colonel Davidovich was appealing to veterans' groups and the Jewish people throughout the world.

The threat of judicial reprisal looms over me—reprisal for telling the truth, for struggling against anti-Semitism.

My complaints to the higher bodies of the Soviet Union have remained unanswered. . . .

The "investigation" is continuing and a court trial is being prepared. For forty days, scores of KGB agents have kept my house under siege, have dogged the footsteps of members of my family, my friends and acquaintances. Day and night they do not take their eyes off me, as if I were a dangerous criminal. . . . But the "criminal" is bedridden . . . and is kept alive only by injections.

I have committed no crimes nor had I any intention of committing any. . . .

The material confiscated from me by the KGB . . . contains only facts of anti-Semitism known to the entire world. . . . I have also cited scores of examples of unpunished anti-Semitism . . . committed not only by members of the Black Hundreds but also by officials.

The passing over in silence and the distortion of the truth about the Jewish people, its great history and its contribution to world civilization, is also a direct act of anti-Semitism.

When I . . . spoke about the great sons of the Jewish people, I was told that this was Zionist propaganda. My "crime"—not a feeling of national exclusivity, but elementary human dignity . . .

I am tied to my people by the trenches in which the Hitlerites buried old women and babies. In the past—rivers of blood; in the present—the malignant weeds grown from racist seeds, the hardiness of prejudices and superstitions. The struggle against these carriers of prejudices and superstitions, whether they are "individual" anti-Semites and hooligans or highly placed officials, is the duty of every honest person. I wrote and spoke the truth and there is an attempt to present it as "slanderous fabrications."

Meanwhile, other Minsk Jews who had received permission to leave were detained as witnesses, questioned, and informed that they could go only if they testified to the existence of an underground Zionist organization in Minsk. Refusal to cooperate would mean that they, too, would be included in the charges. Davidovich, heart condition and all, refused to be silent. On February 10, 1973, he directed an open letter to the Communist parties of half a dozen European countries:

> The exhausting investigation of "Case No. 97" is continuing . . .
> My letters to Brezhnev and the Procurator-General of the USSR Rudenko were unanswered. The officials sent these letters to Minsk—to the very organizations about which I complained. I think that neither Brezhnev nor Rudenko has even seen my letters. The war veteran, the 68-year-old Jewish painter Gedalia Kipnis, is spending his third month in prison. I am under house arrest. . . . Dozens of Minsk Jews are called for questioning. Former combatant officers Lev Ovsishcher and Naum Alshansky are threatened that their status will be changed from "witnesses" to accused because of their desire to go to Israel . . .
> More than 100 years ago Heinrich Heine wrote: "The modern history of the Jewish people is tragic, but if someone will try to write about this tragedy, he will be laughed at. This is more tragic than everything else." Today, the Soviet poet Y. Yevtushenko writes, "Even the ragged whore yells at the old Jew: 'Zhid.' " The endless baiting of the Jewish people in the press; . . . the anti-Semitism of the officials of various ranks; all these actions are not only left unpunished but have become a kind of fashion, a norm of "good behavior," an evidence of loyalty. I openly wrote and spoke about this tragedy. During Heine's time, people were laughed at for this. Today a person is declared a criminal, put in prison, or declared abnormal and placed in a psychiatric clinic. . . .
> Although the people who are repressing me are indeed sitting under Lenin's portrait, they are violating in the gravest way his ideas and theories. . . . Only the strong voice of progressive public opinion—Jews and non-Jews, veterans and anti-fascists, Communists and non-Communists, people of goodwill—will be able to stop the ruthless machine of death, to prevent in Minsk the conducting of a shameful anti-Jewish trial.
> As far as I am concerned, whatever will happen to me, I will repeat till my last breath the words of one of the first revolutionaries of Russia, Radishchev:
>> "I am the same one as I was and will be all my life—
>> Not an animal, a tree, a slave—but a man."

The investigation broadened to include interrogation of Jews in Vilna and Riga. Davidovich wrote again to Brezhnev. This time he

MINSKMilitary Militants283

insisted that a journalist, Vladimir Begun, be prosecuted under Article 123 of the Soviet Constitution for instigating national antagonism by his recent article defaming the Jewish people in a Byelorussian magazine:

> The *Protocols of the Elders of Zion* are innocent babble compared with Begun's article. Julius Streicher, the chief ideologue of the anti-Semitic Third Reich, would have envied Begun if he had not been hanged by the sentence of the International Tribunal. . . .
> As far as Jewish culture is concerned, Begun considers it a major subversion, an invasion without arms. He considers the very opportunity to develop a Soviet Jewish culture, to have a Jewish press and publications, a national theater, to be "an act of subversion" and writes: "Jewish culture is reactionary and pursues goals of subversion and sabotage." One cannot help remembering Hermann Goering's Thesis No. 2: "When I hear the word 'culture' I reach for my gun." . . .
> Yet a trial is not being prepared for him. I will be tried. . . . Case No. 97 is an immoral act of unheard-of violation of the elementary norms of human dignity, of the basis of Communism and morality. . . .
> I am waiting for a just decision and an answer.

He received no reply. Friends from abroad began telephoning Davidovich. By now, former Captains Boris Alouf and Iosif Kuchmar and former Major Solomon Poliachek were involved and appeared to be likely defendants. Poliachek, a neighbor of Davidovich, was questioned six times. His 17-year-old-son Robert suffered a nervous breakdown, attempted to slash his wrists, and was placed in a psychiatric hospital. In a telephone conversation, Davidovich declared that the regime was preparing "a very serious, major anti-Jewish trial. As Beria said, 'Just let us have the man; we will find the crime.' The goal is to scare the Jews. I don't believe that Moscow is aware of the true situation. Even if they know that something is cooking in Minsk, they know about it only from KGB reports. It is essential to let Moscow know." He called for massive protest in the West: hundreds of letters and telegrams; the involvement of leaders of governments, scientists, intellectuals, veterans. "We can't wait. We have to stop our trial now, and this can be done. Once the trial begins, it is too late." Davidovich suffered another heart attack. As soon as he had recovered sufficiently, he wrote again to Brezhnev, this time including President Podgorny, Premier Kosygin, and Procurator-General Rudenko:

> I have repeatedly written to you that this case has no more moral or legal grounds than the Dreyfus or Beilis cases, or the case against the

physicians, the "murderers in white coats." Because of my protests
against the arbitrariness of the anti-Semites and against anti-Semitism,
the KGB of the BSSR chose me as one of the chief accused.

April 1, 1973 marks the fourth month that my exhausting investigation has been going on. In essence, this is deliberate murder of a
gravely ill person who, because of his state of health . . . is in need
of absolute calm and for whom any physical exertion or the slightest
emotion of a disturbing nature can be fatal.

After almost every interrogation by the KGB, I was revived by
first aid and intensive heart-care units. . . . I was in the hospital for
twenty-four days. . . .

The KGB interrogations will evidently be renewed. . . . They are
conducted on the fourth floor of a full-size building without an eleva-
tor, and they last many hours each day. Every interrogation is a real
threat of death.

By then, although Moscow remained silent, public opinion in the
Western world was aroused. Busily stimulating protest everywhere, the
Minsk alumni in Israel provided details of the latest indignities and
KGB questioning as learned from frequent telephone calls and coded
letters from friends and relatives left behind. In a letter to American
Jews, they wrote: "We appeal to you to stop this terrible action. Make
demonstrations of protest against the harassment of the Minsk Jews
during Brezhnev's visit! Appeal to President Nixon to raise the question of Kipnis and Davidovich before the Soviet authorities!"

The shape of the trial seemed clear. There would be at least five
defendants. Some fifty other Minsk Jews would be called as witnesses.
Some were believed to have agreed to testify on condition they would
be freed to go to Israel. Witnesses from Riga, Vilna, Khabarovsk, and
Mogilev would prove that the conspiracy was widespread. The KGB
was even using statements of a few Minsk Jews in Israel, who wished
to return to the USSR, to demoralize those who insisted on an exit
visa. On May 8, Davidovich again addressed an appeal to the leaders
of Israel, war veterans' organizations, and Jewish communities throughout the world. He reviewed the current developments of Case 97, the
slanders in the mass media, the intimidated and bribed witnesses.

The KGB tries to split people, to force them to make false statements
against each other and thus to finish their case preparation, so we
can be imprisoned before Brezhnev's visit to the United States. This
will allow emotions to cool. The world is inclined to forget. There is
no time left. We appeal to you: "Do not stand idly; the village is
burning!"

On May 28, Gedalia Kipnis was released from prison. The following day, Colonel Davidovich was called to the KGB and told that the file on Case 97 had been closed. The Byelorussian Supreme Court had ordered the action under a criminal procedure article permitting dismissal where "the acts committed had lost their socially dangerous character or the persons had ceased to be socially dangerous." Some Jews were told that the evidence was too flimsy, others that the case had been dismissed "because of the excellent war records of the accused and not because of any evidence of innocence." Nonetheless, connection between the Minsk trial and Brezhnev's June visit to the United States to secure trade, strengthen détente, and achieve most-favored-nation status for the USSR seemed too great a coincidence to be lightly discarded.

To dozens of Minsk Jews, including Gedalia Kipnis and his wife, who were permitted to leave for Israel in June 1973, it mattered little what the reasons were for the sudden abandonment of a major trial. Those left behind—Davidovich, Ovsishcher, Alshansky—were gratified that they could avoid prison camps for the time being. But for men committed to the right to leave, the Soviet Union was one vast prison camp, and the sweetness of their victory was tinged with a continuing bitterness.

SVERDLOVSK:
The Perils of Speaking Out

CHAPTER 18

Yekaterinburg, the site of the murder of the last of the ruling Romanovs in 1918, was renamed in 1934 for a Russian Jew who had served on the executive committee of the Bolshevik Party and as a chairman of the central executive committee of the Congress of Soviets during the period when the Bolsheviks seized and consolidated power. Dying of typhus at the age of 34 in 1919, Yakov Mikhailovich Sverdlov entered the pantheon of Bolshevik heroes; had he lived long enough he might have joined his brother Venyamin as a victim of Stalin's purge of Old Bolsheviks in the 1930s. His reputation, alone of the Jewish leaders of the Revolution, has survived the twists and turns of Soviet historiography.

The city that bears his name lies on the eastern slope of the Ural Mountains, 1,200 miles from Moscow. Even at that distance, Sverdlovsk experienced the turmoil, discontent, and alienation that resulted in the contemporary Jewish movement. Two important trials of Jewish activists occurred there. The first, in June 1971, involved Valery Kukuy, an engineer; the second, in August 1972, was of Vladimir Markman, also an engineer and a close friend and colleague of Kukuy's. Both men were sentenced to three years in prison camp solely for their leadership in the Jewish effort to go to Israel.

Sverdlovsk is a city of over a million persons. With a Jewish population in excess of 25,000, it is the largest Jewish city in the Russian Soviet Federated Socialist Republic (RSFSR) after Moscow and Leningrad, yet, unlike the Western cities, it has had almost no Jewish culture, history, or religious experience. Even among Soviet citizens, Sverdlovsk is referred to as a Communist city, and it is often described as the place where the Iron Curtain was forged. Known as the Pittsburgh of Russia, it is the major steel and industrial center in the Urals, with an enormous growth rate since the Bolshevik Revolution. Jews who came to this city worked as skilled engineers and technicians in the industrial plants, a process accelerated by evacuation to the interior during World War II and the postwar search of Jewish young people who, unable to secure admission elsewhere, entered Sverdlovsk's universities. Jews tended to assimilate with and marry non-Jews. Thus, Sverdlovsk's Jews—technocrats, intellectuals, Communist enthusiasts—were uprooted from traditional background and knew neither the Yiddish language nor Jewish culture. Kukuy and Markman grew up in this atmosphere. The small wooden house that had once served as the city's only synagogue was attended by a handful of old people until, in 1961, it was torn down to make place for a garbage dump.

During the post-Stalin thaw, a handful of university students, most of them Jewish, began discussing problems of Soviet life. Their intellectual interest and their distaste for the grossness of Soviet bureaucracy stimulated an interest in freedom and thus attracted them to what became the democratic movement. Although numbering approximately forty in a student body of 12,000, they provided both student leadership and intellectual ferment in the otherwise culturally barren industrial center. (They described Komsomol members as "dull, careerist boy scouts.") As early as 1955, Ilya Voitovetsky, a student slightly older than the others, had formed a group that was interested not only in the new wave of free thinking that followed Stalin's death but also in national questions. With Boris Eidelman, a medical student, and a few other young Jews, Voitovetsky began to learn Yiddish and discuss Israel, the Sinai campaign of 1956, and other Jewish issues. After their group was broken up by KGB threats and warnings, Kukuy, Markman, and their friends, in 1958-59, occasionally met for animated conversations on the streets or to read the *samizdat* literature that was beginning to mushroom among young Soviet intellectuals.

Born in Moscow in 1938, the second son of a professional violinist, Kukuy came to Sverdlovsk at the age of 4. Shortly thereafter, his parents separated, and his mother remarried. Although he studied civil engineering, Kukuy had strong interests in literature and music and was a chess master, a boxer, and a writer. Having no background in

Jewish culture, no knowledge of Yiddish or Hebrew, no religious training or impulses, he still identified as a Jew and was intensely hostile to
anti-Semitism in any form.

In 1964 he married a dark-haired, blue-eyed chemical technician
who had been born in a small Byelorussian town and whose family had
moved to Sverdlovsk when she was 6. Ella had as little Jewish background as Valery. Indeed, although her mother was Jewish, her father
was Russian, and her internal passport identified her as of Russian
nationality. Kukuy became a senior planning engineer of the Sverdlovsk Planning Institute but continued to meet with university friends
who shared his interests. His Zionist convictions grew with the growth
of the movement. The process is described by his wife and some of
his friends, now in Israel:

> We became Zionists because we began questioning the Soviet regime
> —the Soviet system. We came to feel ourselves Jews from the dem-
> ocratic movement, from being negative toward the regime. We wanted
> to know who we were. Until after the Six-Day War, no one we knew
> in Sverdlovsk talked about going to Israel. It was like wanting to go
> to the moon. But after 1967, we learned for the first time from people
> in Moscow that it was possible to go to Israel. We heard of a Jewish
> movement. We saw our first Zionist literature—books by Jabotinsky.
> We were amazed that our point of view agreed with his. We listened
> to Kol Israel, but it wasn't useful at all, since you couldn't find out
> anything from it. Radio Liberty, Voice of America, and BBC kept
> us well informed. We read the *samizdat* literature of the democratic
> movement. More and more, we talked of Israel and our Jewish na-
> tionality, but not until the first Leningrad trial did we do much more
> than talk and read *samizdat,* and not until March 1971 did our group
> apply for exit visas.

Actually, in 1967, Boris Eidelman's mother and brother had succeeded in going to Israel and had sent him a *vizov.* By 1967, too,
there was contact with the small Zionist circle in Moscow, and a trickle
of Jewish *samizdat* materials began to reach the few activists, who
were working in small groups independent of each other. Some, like
Eidelman, who had been born in Moldavia, whose father had spent
five years in prison camp, and who himself had been imprisoned at the
age of 18, were both highly politicized and Zionist. Others—physicians,
teachers, engineers in good positions, without extensive experience of
acute, crude anti-Semitism—were more assimilated and less severely
alienated. Still, there were incidents, such as the murder of an entire
Jewish family of seven by persons who took money that had been

collected to build a synagogue and left a note: "Strike Down the Yids!" Such events, coupled with the anti-Israeli, anti-Zionist, crudely anti-Jewish official propaganda preceding and following the Six-Day War, inevitably led to a Jewish consciousness that ultimately, by 1970-71, for many supplanted the lingering hope that the USSR could become a decent place to live.

Meanwhile, in 1968, the KGB had detained Kukuy and searched his apartment (although Ella didn't learn of the incident until 1971). Twenty-seven pieces of literature were seized, including such subversive items as Pasternak poems with Biblical themes and Albert Camus's speech accepting the Nobel Prize. This incident was to play an important role in Kukuy's trial in 1971. Charged with Article 190-1 (anti-Soviet slander), Kukuy was specifically indicted, among other charges, because he had "from 1964 to 1970" asserted orally that there was no freedom of speech and no democracy in the USSR and because he had prepared typewritten copies of *samizdat* reports of the trials of Brodsky, Daniel and Sinyavsky, Galanskov and Ginzburg, and Pavel Litvinov, as well as material defending them. But it was neither the 1968 incident nor his obvious, long-term sympathy with the democratic movement that led to Kukuy's arrest.

By the time of the widespread arrests of Jewish activists in the summer of 1970, a group of Sverdlovsk Jews had begun to learn Hebrew and to circulate Jewish *samizdat* documents. By late fall, if not before, Kukuy had copies of *Iton Aleph* and *Bet*. On December 26, 1970, ten Sverdlovsk Jews signed a sharply worded protest against the Leningrad hijacking trial directed to Soviet leaders as well as to the president of Israel. They denounced the death sentences as a return to Stalinism and characterized the hijacking attempt as one of desperation engendered by the unlawful closing of opportunity for the exercise of human rights. Kukuy was the first to sign. The other signers were Yuli Kosharovsky, a radio engineer, and Vladimir Aks, a metallurgical engineer, both 28 years old; Dr. Eidelman; 29-year-old Boris Rabinovich, also a physician; Markman, and four other students or young activists. Voitovetsky and several others were not asked to sign because they had applied to go to Israel and it was feared that signing would jeopardize their chance to leave.

Brought into the KGB office for lengthy questioning, the signers were threatened with arrest and told they would never be permitted to leave Russia. Kukuy defied the authorities. Ella Kukuy explains:

The KGB was frightened. They wanted to stop the movement at its beginning. The threats were prophylactic measures. During February and March 1971, Sverdlovsk witnessed a battle between the KGB and Jewish activists. Some of us went to Moscow and demonstrated with the Jewish movement there. On February 21, 1971, *Uralsky Rabochy,* a Sverdlovsk newspaper, printed a major article attacking Valery and Yuli Kosharovsky as traitors. It spoke of Valery's 1968 questioning. The paper tried and convicted them of many vile deeds. Then, Valery's coworkers staged a meeting branding him as anti-Soviet and asking the KGB to bring criminal proceedings. On March 17, Yuli Kosharovsky was arrested for hooliganism and detained twenty-seven days. On March 20, the apartments of the ten signers were searched. The KGB ransacked our apartment for eight hours, holding us captive in one room. They found nothing but *Babi Yar* by Kuznetsov, a typed copy of *The Heart of a Dog* [a 1925 satire on Soviet bureaucracy] by Mikhail Bulgakov [a famous Soviet writer, now disfavored and rarely printed], and some letters from relatives in the West. We had carefully gotten rid of any Jewish *samizdat.* But they arrested Valery. Later, I asked the KGB why they singled him out. I was told because his name was first on the letter and they needed to make someone an example. I'm proud of what he did, but we all did the same things.

Boris Rabinovich was also arrested on a charge of Zionist propaganda and agitation and questioned, not only about the Sverdlovsk activity but about contact with Ruta Aleksandrovich and the other Riga activists. He was released, and ultimately all of the signers except Kukuy, Kosharovsky, and Markman were permitted to go to Israel.

Kukuy's trial, which took place June 15-16, 1971, during the same month as the trials of the Kishinev defendants and of Raiza Palatnik, is interesting in part because—even by Soviet standards—it is so bereft of evidence. An informal transcript of the proceedings was prepared by Kukuy's family and by the witnesses themselves. The trial was conducted in a small courtroom seating only fifty people. Both the judge and State Prosecutor Zyrianov had been involved in the trial of Andrei Amalrik, the democratic writer and social critic, in November 1970. (Amalrik had also been charged under Article 190-1, and he, too, had received the maximum sentence possible—three years.) * In addition to the state prosecutor, Kukuy also faced a public prosecutor, a Jew named Dobrynin, who worked in Kukuy's plant, but whom the defendant did not know. Kukuy protested this, sensing correctly that

---

* Vladimir Aks has described Article 190-1 as a charge made when there is no crime; "according to 190-1, you can even accuse a table."

Dobrynin's role would be to affirm how good life was for Jews in Sverdlovsk. The court refused to hear defense testimony from Aks, Rabinovich, and Kosharovsky. Apart from references to Kukuy's possession of *samizdat* materials in 1968, the other specifications were (*1*) that Kukuy had committed oral slander that Jews were discriminated against in the USSR, were the victims of anti-Semitism, and that USSR policy toward Israel was hostilely one-sided: (*2*) that he typed and/or distributed slanderous anti-Soviet material such as *The Heart of a Dog* and the articles found in *Iton Aleph* and *Bet* and in *Iskhod*.

The most damaging evidence was that of Kukuy's older brother Anatoly, a Party member who teaches international affairs and the history of the Soviet Communist Party at a technical school. He gave the KGB a pre-trial statement that Valery (toward whom he had been hostile for many years) had expressed anti-Soviet Zionist thoughts and had a typewriter on which he copied literature. He had learned this from their mother, who lived with Valery. Anatoly did not appear at the trial, but his statement was put in evidence. Both the mother and Valery denied these charges. The other nine witnesses, who included Markman, claimed that the KGB had secured pre-trial statements from them by threats and had falsified or misconstrued them. All denied knowing that Valery had committed any criminal acts.

Only a neighbor named Prutkin linked Kukuy to the distribution of *Iton*, and he seemed embarrassed to have done so. The KGB had secured the incriminating material when Prutkin "returned" a copy of *Iton* to the Kukuy apartment at the very moment a KGB search was being made. That fortuitous coincidence for the prosecution caused some Sverdlovsk Jews to suspect that Prutkin was a provocateur, even though he subsequently cooperated with the activists in preparing the informal transcript of the trial.

Kukuy denied the charges in a long, dignified, carefully reasoned statement and in his eloquent final remarks.

The prosecutor's demand for a three-year sentence was confirmed by the court.

There was intense reaction to the sentencing of Kukuy. On July 16, Dr. Andrei Sakharov and Valery Chalidze, members of the Soviet Human Rights Committee, pointed out in a letter to the Supreme Court of the RSFSR that at the trial "an unusually wide range of topics was scrutinized" that had "no relevance to the substance of the indictment" and that "it is doubtful whether a thorough study of them could have been made without detriment to the examination of the case, in the two days the hearing lasted."

> It is strange that the court was indifferent to the fact that the wit-nesses directly accused the [pre-trial] investigator of having created an atmosphere during questioning such that they, the witnesses, had been compelled to give testimony to the investigator's liking. All the witnesses who appeared at the trial repudiated, directly or indirectly, the testimony they had given during the pre-trial investigation. The court simply took the view that they had altered their testimony in order to mitigate the fate of the accused . . .
>
> Only one witness enjoyed the complete trust of the procurator and the court: V. Kukuy's brother Anatoly. In the words of the procura-tor, this witness was a member of the Communist Party and had recently been awarded a Jubilee Medal, and it was therefore doubtful whether such a man would give false testimony. This was obvious discrimination based on party membership and on the possession of medals: it is clear that everyone, irrespective of party membership and medals, has the right to a court's trust, until the opposite has been *proved.* In this particular case, such discrimination against witnesses led to the conviction of Valery Kukuy solely, in fact, on the basis of the testimony (read out in court) of his brother [who was absent].
>
> The classification of materials alleged to have been circulated by V. Kukuy is also strange. Thus the prosecutor stated that he had superficially familiarized himself with the story *Heart of a Dog.* . . . The law does not state that the prosecutor's superficial acquaintance with the materials of a case is sufficient to constitute grounds for a successful appeal, and so it now depends on the Supreme Court whether Bulgakov will once again [as under Stalin] be judged to be anti-Soviet.
>
> The atmosphere of strangeness even affected counsel for the defense: after substantiating his conclusion that there was nothing in the actions of V. Kukuy which constituted a crime, he asks the court . . . to lighten the sentence.

In letters to the Supreme Court and the UN Human Rights Com-mission, forty-six Moscow Jews charged that the trial was in flagrant violation of law and was "one more piece in the pattern of persecution of Jews who wish to go to Israel." A group of Sverdlovsk Jews, in-cluding Ella Kukuy, Aks, Markman, Kosharovsky, and Voitovetsky, described the trial as "another link in the long chain of repression and persecutions, in violation of all Soviet laws and international obliga-tions." In an open letter to *Izvestia,* prompted by their "outrage" over "the wave of anti-Jewish trials," they declared (August 8, 1971):

. . . not a single witness gave the prosecution any material that could serve as a basis for a verdict of guilty. Nevertheless, by crudely distorting the utterances of one of the witnesses, and by using the testimony of others, *given under threat and dictated* by the investigator Kirinkin, the court sentenced Kukuy to the maximum terms of imprisonment provided. . . .

We are profoundly convinced that all these trials, without exception, have been staged and played with one purpose only—to intimidate the Jews of the Soviet Union, who had already expressed their desire to go home, to Israel, and particularly to frighten those who intend submitting documents for this purpose. The vileness of the means is really justified by this aim. The aim and the means are worthy of each other.

We appeal to you . . . to all whose concept of justice, lawfulness, and humanism has not lost its essence in the dark times of the Stalin personality cult—to raise your voice of protest . . .

In September 1971, despite the courtroom presence of Dr. Sakharov, some two hundred Moscow Jews, and a delegation from Sverdlovsk, the Supreme Court affirmed Kukuy's conviction—"a strange and monstrous act," according to his defenders. That same month, a group of Sverdlovsk activists, their number increased despite the fact that many other Sverdlovsk Jews had left for Israel and Kukuy was in prison, complained to the KGB that they were being harassed by "a large staff" of KGB agents that "occupies itself with us." They charged that they were being persistently shadowed, hounded, and victimized by "false and dirty rumors spread with the permission and participation of officials." They claimed that the KGB had sent them a crude provocateur who claimed he was a representative of the World Zionist Organization from Israel. They denounced the KGB for the Kukuy trial frame-up and claimed "we are being blackmailed by evidence invented against us, and criminal charges." They concluded:

We are confused. Is it possible that the huge apparatus of the counter-intelligence of the KGB has no other cares besides the invention of imaginary enemies of the Soviet regime? We assure you that we do not deserve such attention. We do not belong to any organization, we are not engaged in anti-Soviet propaganda, we do not commit terrorist acts. We only want to go home. This desire of ours ought to be protected by the state in which we live, because our right to it is guaranteed by the legislation of the Soviet Union. If this state is not able to ensure the defense of our rights, then at least protect us from persecution.

294   THE LAST EXODUS

> We cannot be bent, we cannot be broken. We are Jews and we
> want to live in a Jewish state. We join our brethren in Georgia, in
> their courageous and desperate appeal: "Israel or death!"

The appeal was to no avail. A new victim had been selected:
Vladimir Markman. Born in 1938, Markman had grown up in Sverdlovsk, and at 18, when called into the army, had been assigned to a
KGB unit. During his service, an officer made an anti-Semitic remark
that led Markman, a strong, agile young man, to strike his superior before the entire unit. He was arrested, but when he proposed to defend
his action before the military tribunal on the basis of exposing anti-
Semitism in the KGB, the charges were dropped. After demobilization,
Markman studied engineering at the university and in time became
director of a group in the State Project Institute. After the letter of
December 26, 1970, he was forced to resign his job and, with others,
was interrogated and searched. A reluctant and noncooperative witness
in the Kukuy trial, at its conclusion he took the unprecedented step of
instituting a legal proceeding against the investigative team and the
members of the court who, he asserted, had falsified and distorted his
pre-trial testimony. He demanded that they be criminally charged, but
the case was dismissed, and Markman appealed without success. Meantime, virtually all of the original group of Sverdlovsk activists, including
Ella Kukuy and her child, had left for Israel, except for Kosharovsky,
who now worked in Moscow as a warehouseman, and Markman. Both
men allegedly could not receive exit visas because they had been
involved in secret work involving security clearance. Kukuy gave Markman his power of attorney, and Markman now committed himself to
securing his friend's release from prison. Much of the KGB's efforts
seemed directed at establishing that the Sverdlovsk group, and now
Markman, were closely linked to the Moscow activists then being led
by Vladimir Slepak, Viktor Polsky, Vladimir Prestin, and others.

Markman persisted in his struggle both to receive permission to
leave and to assist Kukuy. His wife, Genrietta Kisina, the daughter of
a loyal, retired KGB official, had lost her job as an accountant because
of their activities, and their 7-year-old son developed a series of ail-
ments resulting in his persistent hospitalization. In early spring 1972, a
Sverdlovsk newspaper accused Markman of connections with "Zionists" who during World War II participated hand-in-hand with the
Nazis in killing people in the death camps. A local TV program con-

demned him. A "public opinion meeting," convened at his new place of work, petitioned "the competent organs" to prosecute him for his Zionist activities. Markman reported each event to his Sverdlovsk friends in Israel, with whom he kept in close contact by telephone. Ilya Voitovetsky, Vladimir Aks, and Ella Kukuy maintained the communication and distributed the information to mass media, including Kol Israel's Russian-language section, which in turn broadcast the information back to the USSR.

On April 12 and 13, 1972, in a telephone conversation with Ilya Voitovetsky, who had called him from a railroad siding telephone in Beersheba, Markman sought to read his answer to the Sverdlovsk newspaper attack, but the call was constantly interrupted and disconnected, and Markman, in great frustration, utilized some choice language. The Soviet telephone operator complained to the police authorities that he had insulted and abused her. On April 29, Markman was arrested at the Sverdlovsk railway station, and for several days his friends did not know where he was. When it was revealed that he had been criminally charged, protests were issued in Moscow, Vilna, and Kishinev and by his friends in Israel. His wife Genrietta sought to secure competent Moscow counsel and a number of attorneys agreed to serve, but the Moscow Collegium of Lawyers advised her that no one could be made available for this purpose out of their membership of well over a thousand attorneys. (The Moscow activists labeled this a violation of the Criminal Procedure Code and "a flagrant violation of constitutional and human civil rights.") Genrietta Markman was advised that if she returned to Moscow on her husband's affairs, she would be sent to a mental hospital. Fifty activists from Moscow and Kishinev testified to her sanity and condemned this new harassment in a letter to the UN Human Rights Commission. Claiming that the charges were "invented," Mrs. Markman appealed to Golda Meir and asked assistance in securing a competent lawyer for her innocent husband, who had meanwhile been granted Israeli citizenship. On July 17, to protest the denial of legal defense, Mrs. Markman and activist friends from Moscow and Kishinev went on a hunger strike in the reception room of the Central Committee of the Communist Party. Despite sporadic arrests of participants, they continued the strike until July 24.

On August 8, 1972, Markman's trial began. A portion of the official court record of Sverdlovsk District Court Case No. 2–231 is available. Prosecutor Zyrianov again presented the case for the state as he had in the Kukuy and Amalrik trials. The defendant was represented by legal counsel made available just before trial. He was accused of violating Article 190-1 as well as Article 74 (propaganda or agitation for the purpose of arousing hostility or dissension of nationalities) and 206 (hooliganism). The latter charge was based on "using obscenities and insults, expressing open disrespect and showing an offensive attitude toward the workers of telephone communications." The Article 74 charges were dismissed for lack of proof at the conclusion of the evidence. The hooliganism charges were supported by the testimony of the telephone operator that when his connection to Israel had been continually interrupted, Markman had banged on the receiver, cursed, and called the long distance operators "fascists." For that offense he received a one-year sentence. His principal crime, however, was that, like Kukuy, he had asserted that Jews were persecuted in the USSR, which denied democracy, freedom of speech, and individual freedom to its citizens while disseminating untruths through its press. Various amplifications and variations of this theme constituted the specifications of crime. Specifics included the December 1970 letter, the various collective protests over the Kukuy conviction, a collective letter in April 1972, and telephone conversations with friends in Israel, all of which subsequently appeared in foreign radio or newspaper reports, thus constituting anti-Soviet slander. Markman admitted the letters and statements but denied that they were slanderous and asserted that his comments were true and that he was entitled to such expression of opinion.

Leonid Zabelyshensky was a chief prosecution witness, since he was present on April 12–13 when the telephone coversation with Voitovetsky took place. His pre-trial protocol had supported the state's position, but two weeks before the trial, Zabelyshensky issued a formal protest to the Sverdlovsk prosecutor, the substance of which he repeated in court. He charged that on May 24 he had been detained by investigating officers on the pretext that he had failed to answer a summons—which was never produced—that he was then interrogated about Markman, was told that because of his "bad behavior" he would be formally charged under Article 190-1, and was placed in a cell overnight. He continued:

On the next day, May 25, from 10 a.m. until 2 p.m., I was interrogated as a witness in Markman's case by Pushkariov. During the interrogation, he also insulted and attacked me crudely. At the end of the interrogation, I was again taken into custody. By the end of that session it had been thirty hours since I had had anything to eat.

During the interrogation, I was shivering, as the cell in which I had been detained from the moment of arrest until the interrogation was not heated in spite of the very cold weather. Besides, I could not sleep because of the vermin in the cell. The 26th of May I spent in the cell expecting another summons to the investigator. Only on the 29th, Monday, was I summoned to an investigator in whose study we had a long talk. Then, at approximately 1 p.m., they said that they would not detain me any longer . . .

It has recently become clear that as a result of all the above, there was a phrase in the record of the interrogation that Markman had used obscene expressions. I did not say that during the interrogation, as it was not true. Lack of attention when reading the record before I signed it (now it is absolutely clear to me) was caused by over-strain, the result of a sleepless night, severe trembling from cold, and the use by the investigator of forbidden methods of conducting an interrogation.

In the light of all the above, I state my protest against the illegal actions of the investigator Pushkariov and insist that criminal proceedings be instituted against him.*

The other prosecution witnesses did not support the prosecution's case. Nevertheless, despite various minor irregularities and the absence of evidence, Markman received a sentence of three years in prison camp.

Now only Kosharovsky was free to protest. In late August and early September 1972, he organized a detailed, scholarly appeal to the RSFSR Supreme Court which he signed along with more than sixty Moscow activists. It analyzed at length the evidence, the corruption of witnesses, and the atmosphere of prejudice in which the trial was held:

V. Markman did not admit his guilt in court. He had impressive reasons for this, as confirmed by the circumstances of the case. First, the verdict passed over in silence (in our opinion deliberately) the fact that V. Markman had for over a year and a half been waging a difficult struggle, the struggle for emigration to Israel—a struggle that is founded on law. All the letters, telephone conversations, and personal conversations dealt with this concrete question . . . To find

* Since then, Zabelyshensky has suffered from continuous harassment by the Sverdlovsk authorities. A 32-year-old computer scientist, he had been a faculty member in calculation technique at the Ural Polytechnic Institute but was discharged on November 25, 1971 for applying for a visa to Israel. Unable to find any employment in his own or related fields for over a year, he worked as a loader, milkman, and railway station porter, and finally secured a more suitable job, but was dismissed for "loafing." He appealed the dismissal. On October 23, 1973, he was arrested for "parasitism" and on December 20, after a four-day trial, received a six-month sentence under Article 209 of the Criminal Code for "leading an antisocial [parasitic] life."

him guilty it was necessary to establish that the information he delivered orally or in writing had been deliberately false and that at the moment of delivering it Markman knew it was false. This was not established. . . .

In our time, one cannot throw an innocent person behind bars without violating the law. If there are violations, this means that there will be protests. If there are protests, this means that there is a possibility to see slander in them, which is a pretext for other trials. The chain is endless; it will not bring glory to its creators, nor will it bring good to the USSR. It is necessary to end it now, without delay. Markman's trial in Sverdlovsk took place in an atmosphere that made an objective investigation impossible. The circumstances of the case show that there is no judicial foundation for the charge. A Jew has been convicted who uncompromisingly defended his right to emigrate.

Genrietta Markman and their son Baruch were given permission to emigrate to Israel, which they did in the summer of 1973. In a letter to a Detroit family who had been supportive of her after her husband's sentencing, she wrote her appreciation for the assistance, noting that letters sent her from Detroit to Sverdlovsk had not been received.

My last year in Russia was very hard. Even now I have nightmares that they are coming to arrest me. Our little son . . . suffered very much after his father's arrest. To go through an interrogation by the KGB and constant surveillance by the military regime can break a healthy and strong man—imagine what it can do to a mere child who sees and observes everything that is going on. But now for my son and me all of this is in the past. . . .

What happened to my husband is that one of the foremen of the camp stole his warm boots. In Krasnoyarsk, where the weather is 50 below, it is impossible to survive without boots. My husband wanted to resolve this in a peaceful way, but the foreman started a fight. My husband, thank God, is strong and courageous; he knocked his teeth out and beat him up.

He could not write about those things; he told me about it when we were saying goodbye to each other. . . .

He tries to keep up his courage. He is constantly busy . . . learning English, although he has no way of learning Hebrew. It would be of great moral support to him to write him in English since he can receive unlimited amounts of letters. You probably will not receive an answer since he is permitted to write only twice a month, and then only to his immediate family. . . .

While saying goodbye to each other, I asked him if he would do all this over again, knowing how much struggle he would have to endure to go to Israel. He answered, "Yes, definitely. The only thing is I feel so sorry for you and our son."

ROSTOV-ON-THE-DON:
A Cantankerous Quixote

CHAPTER 19

Group trials, such as those in Leningrad, Riga, and Kishinev, did not take place after June 1971—perhaps because, by then, it had become virtually certain that reaction in the West would be hostile and criticism widespread. The sporadic trials of individual activists in various cities cannot be explained in terms of their important movement leadership or even in terms of the salutary deterrent effect stemming from their prosecution. In more instances than not, the most important leaders have been permitted to go to Israel rather than sent to prison camp or—as in the case of the most prominent Moscow activists, who have been denied exit visas—they have been threatened and harassed but remain unprosecuted and ostensibly protected by their very prominence. Even the most obtuse Soviet official should have learned by now that political trials have not had their desired repressive effect, and since such proceedings are rarely reported in the Soviet press, any public education value to be derived is minimal at best. Why then have political trials continued? Perhaps because of the essentially irrational, petty pique of the frustrated Soviet legal bureaucrat driven to near-madness by the persistent activist brinkmanship of some of the stiff-necked Jewish militants. The farther such officials are from Moscow, where sensitivity to Western journalists and diplomatic representatives is greatest, the more likely a trial becomes.

A notable example of this thesis was the almost suicidal courting of legal disaster by Lazar Lyubarsky of Rostov-on-the-Don. Lyubarsky's stubborness exceeded even that of Yakov Khantsis (see pages 216–

18). His articulate ingenuity in defying officialdom surpassed Hillel Shur's (see pages 221–23). For two and a half years, Lyubarsky was the nemesis of his opponents. In many ways, he was the arch-prototype of Jewish audaciousness and simple, principled bravery.

Although Rostov is not nearly as far from Moscow as is Sverdlovsk, it is more of a backwater. Its three quarters of a million inhabitants are more closely associated with the people of the southeastern Ukraine, which it borders, and the backward Caucasus to the south than with the Great Russians. Situated on the Don River, Rostov is in the historic heartland of the Don Cossacks, and despite its recent industrialization it is not frequently visited by foreign correspondents or tourists, nor is it under the constant political surveillance of the distant capital of the RSFSR. Its 20,000 Jews have not engaged in any consequential Jewish movement activity. Yet in Lazar Lyubarsky, Rostov produced a lonely, quixotic battler for Jewish rights.

Lyubarsky was born in 1926 in Beltsy, Moldavia. At 18 he was inducted into the Red Army. He attained the rank of captain and remained in service until 1948. After receiving a degree from the Odessa Institute of Communications Engineering in 1953, he began to work as a power station engineer in a small city in the northern Caucasus. By then, he was teaching himself both Yiddish and Hebrew. Nevertheless, he advanced professionally and remained a member of the Communist Party, which he had joined in 1946. Subsequently, after moving to Rostov-on-the-Don, he became a chief engineer in the Rostov Institute of High Tension, with responsibility for power system and station design. But his interest in Jewish matters led him, beginning in the 1950s, to travel extensively to establish contacts with Jewish communities in places as remote as Dagestan, Georgia, Central Asia, and Moldavia, to visit synagogues that still functioned and Jewish cemeteries everywhere, and to meet with the last few Soviet rabbis who asserted a Jewish national identity. A cantankerous, persistent, itinerant chronicler of the Jewish people, Lyubarsky kept copious notebooks of his findings and became known to those Jews everywhere who subsequently formed the heart of the Jewish movement.

His idiosyncratic hobby apparently passed unnoticed for many years. But in March 1970, Lyubarsky suddenly asked that his security clearance be canceled. He was promptly expelled from the party and reduced in rank in the military reserve from captain to private. In August, he applied for an exit visa to Israel. Soon, suspected of complicity with Leningrad, Riga, and Kishinev defendants, he was questioned about his connections with those arrested in the summer of 1970. On September 19, 1970, he and his father-in-law, Iosif Pevzner, wrote an open letter to *Pravda* denouncing the Jews who had participated in the government-staged press conference in Moscow in March. The letter indicted the government for systematically depriving Soviet Jews of cultural and educational possibilities and destroying Jewish national life. As for the "distinguished" participants, Lyubarsky contemptuously concluded, "we see no difference between you and those thugs with 'vodka and onion' against whom the heroic units of Jewish self-defense were created in the dark years of Tsarism."

Nine days later, under the pretext of investigating the Leningrad hijacking case, the KGB conducted a six-hour search of Lyubarsky's apartment and confiscated twenty-four tape recordings of Jewish songs, art books in Hebrew, song books in Yiddish, Hebrew Bibles and prayer books, a *Hagadah* (the formal liturgy of Passover), Jewish histories, and other items. That same day, the Rostov KGB opened Criminal Case 18868—an investigation of Lyubarsky's violation of Article 190-1. The ordeal had begun. Mismatched as the adversaries were, Lyubarsky gave as he received. Denounced at work; his application to leave rejected by OVIR; persistently questioned in pre-trial investigative proceedings by the KGB in connection with the trials that were to take place in Leningrad, Riga, and Kishinev—Lyubarsky responded in January 1971 by writing to President Podgorny that there would have been no criminal cases if Jews had been permitted to exercise their legal right to leave. "It is too late for the Exodus to be stopped by imposing hardships and sacrifices," he warned Podgorny. The following month he wrote again, complaining of OVIR's denial of his exit visa and of the national policy it reflected:

> Sometimes the desperate striving for individual Jews to leave for Israel to study Jewish culture lands them in a mental hospital or in the dock. However, their desire to emigrate to Israel is only made stronger by this (the individual backsliding of weak-willed and unprincipled persons cannot be taken seriously). . . .
> The desire of the Soviet Jews to go to the State of Israel, which is in process at present, will enter world history as a page of a self-sacrificing struggle for self-preservation, and it will always be studied by succeeding generations with empathy and a sense of mutuality and relatedness.

It is the sacred duty of the Soviet Union to assist this historical movement.

In a letter to the KGB on March 22, 1971, Lyubarsky insisted that his confiscated material be returned and requested KGB assistance in securing a visa. On April 13, he addressed V. A. Smirnov, the Rostov public procurator:

Since this is the week of Passover, the festival of Jewish national liberation, I request for the second time that you return to me the materials required for the observance of the historical traditions connected with this festival: the Bible and the Hagadah . . .

These materials were confiscated from my apartment, illegally, in the course of a search conducted on September 28, 1970, in connection with the so-called Leningrad Case, with which I had no relationship whatsoever, as was proven by the results of the search.

On April 21, he filed a case in the People's Court, charging that Smirnov had in his possession personal belongings of "Jewish national culture," which had not been returned to Lyubarsky and which were necessary for holiday observance. Smirnov, Lyubarsky alleged, refused to return the articles and declared that no harm would be done since the same Jewish holidays occurred each year. That "deliberate act completely destroyed our family observance of Passover," "profoundly offended my national dignity," and was a "profanation of the ancient and holy festival." By the "intentional lowering of the honor and dignity of a person," this "insult" violated Article 131 of the Criminal Code. The same day, appealing to Podgorny and Rudenko, Lyubarsky requested the return of his seized articles, demanded an exit visa, and insisted that the public procurator, Smirnov, be prosecuted. On June 6, he protested to Smirnov that the KGB possessed a Hebrew letter he had written to Israel many weeks before the search in September 1970 and demanded "an explanation of this violation of the secrecy of correspondence." And on the same day, he wrote to a Soviet theoretical magazine protesting the cancellation of a Yiddish play and contending that it illustrated the forced absence of Jewish theater art in the USSR.

Nelly, Lyubarsky's 20-year-old daughter by a first marriage, now wrote President Podgorny insisting that she had a right to an exit visa despite the rejection of her father's application. That same day, Lyubarsky again addressed Podgorny "about the persecution to which my

family and I have been subjected for almost a year by the organs of
the KGB and by the procurator." He reviewed the fruitless investigative efforts to link him to the Leningrad, Riga, and Kishinev defendants,
the searches, interrogations, and harassments, and rhetorically asked
what had been established. Only "that I have an unshakable desire to
go to Israel with my family."

> Why, then, shouldn't the misunderstanding and the label ascribed to
> me as "suspected of a criminal offense" be finally corrected, and
> why shouldn't my pardon be begged for such lengthy and great
> sufferings to which my family and I have been subjected? . . .
> Why is the entire correspondence of my family, including the
> outgoing mail, daily subjected to constant examination, in violation
> of the secrecy of correspondence guaranteed by the state, as I have
> repeatedly established in the Procurator's Office?

That month, in a complaint to Procurator-General Rudenko, Lyubarsky insisted that Rostov officials be prosecuted for illegally seizing and
reading his mail and advised the chief law enforcement official that
previous complaints to Smirnov and to the Lawyers Association in Rostov had been unanswered. He sent several more letters, petitions, and
appeals in July 1971. Then on July 28, the criminal case was discontinued—an almost unprecedented event. The official document makes
a preliminary finding, after an extensive recitation of the defendant's
acts, that "on the basis of Article 190-1, Lazar Moiseyevich Lyubarsky
committed a crime," but the actions "have lost the character of being
socially dangerous." Under Article 6 of the Criminal Procedure Code,
a criminal case may be terminated because of a change in the situation,
such as acts losing their socially dangerous character, or the person's
ceasing to be socially dangerous. Some of Lyubarsky's seized materials
were returned to him, but others were maintained in the file of Case
18868.

When Lyubarsky received the formal papers advising him that the
case had been discontinued, he protested immediately and asserted
that he had committed no illegal acts and that "there have not been any
changes in my actions or thoughts" before, during, or since the criminal
case.

One week later, Lyubarsky and a friend, Moscow activist Vladimir
Prestin, were arrested on the street in Moscow and taken to the police
station, where they were searched without a warrant and their documents and papers were taken. They were faced with a preliminary

charge of minor hooliganism and black marketeering, but both refused to sign the charge sheet, protested the illegality of the seizure, and were finally released.

In September 1971 Lyubarsky again insisted to Smirnov that everything seized in the September 1970 search be returned. The failure to do so is "an open act of racial discrimination on your part, aimed at depriving me and my family of the opportunity to live a Jewish national life." In light of the onset of the Jewish high holidays, failure to respond would cause him to "expose the anti-Semitic essence of your decision." For the next ten months, Lyubarsky missed few opportunities to decry the abuses of Soviet power or insist on his rights. On July 18, 1972, he was arrested again. Confiscated this time were albums of his photographs of obscure Jewish synagogues and cemeteries and four notebooks recapitulating in detail every interrogation and conversation with officials. But now a new charge was added to Article 190-1: Lyubarsky was accused of divulging state secrets under Article 75-1. This act provides that making available classified information to an unauthorized person without intent of treason or espionage is punishable by from two to five years. The facts were simple: Four years earlier, Lyubarsky, while designing a power station, had a dispute with an accounting department chief about the cost estimate of a proposed design. To verify his contentions, Lyubarsky took the classified design blueprints to the departmental head, who was authorized to see only the unclassified cost estimates. Learning of the incident, the Institute administrator ordered Lyubarsky to return the plans to their depository and reprimanded him for negligently removing the plans from their authorized place.

The formal investigation lasted six months while Lyubarsky was held incommunicado in prison. His wife, Dr. Galina Pevzner, sought to engage a Moscow attorney, and she found a willing counsel, but the Moscow Collegium of Lawyers refused her the right to retain him. Moscow activists vigorously protested this refusal to the UN and to the International Association of Democratic Lawyers. Finally, an honorable, competent Rostov attorney, Olga Kamynina, was retained. During the investigation, the KGB interrogated more than fifty people in Moscow alone, and similar questioning occurred in other cities. Clearly, the questioning had nothing to do with the technical classified information charge against Lyubarsky, nor was it closely related to the long-standing anti-Soviet slander allegations. The authorities were trying to establish an all-Union conspiracy in which the peripatetic, persistent Lubarsky was thought to have played a key role. Vladimir Slepak, a leading Moscow activist, was interrogated for two days in mid-August 1972. Prestin, Viktor Polsky, Roman Rutman, Valentin Prussakov, and other important Moscow Jewish leaders were interrogated during the same period. Interviews with them subsequent to their harrowing questioning elicited the information that, apart from persistent inquiry about the time, place, and circumstance of any Lyubarsky contact, interest centered on the inception and method of organization of collective letters, particularly those that were signed by people in a number of cities; how such appeals reached abroad; how contacts were maintained between cities; how literature was created and distributed; how and by whom organization and arrangements for overseas telephone calls were accomplished. Despite the anxiety provoked by the interrogations, no additional charges were brought, and some of those questioned were permitted to go to Israel.

Lyubarsky's trial opened on January 31, and ended on February 2, 1973. Because it allegedly involved state secrets, it was an officially "closed" trial. All other proceedings in the courthouse were canceled and the building was heavily guarded. Only Lyubarsky's wife, daughter, and counsel were permitted to be present. Not a word about the trial appeared in the Soviet news media. Foreign news releases were brief and uninformative. Details of the trial are therefore difficult to secure. The official verdict protocol containing the details of the charges, the evidence, and the court's conclusions reveals nothing that could be easily regarded as criminal. At the request of Lyubarsky's attorney, Ms. Kamynina, Polsky, Prestin, and the Goldshtein brothers (Grigory and Isai from Tbilisi) traveled to Rostov to testify for the defense, but they were not allowed to enter the courtroom. (They, along with other Rostov Jews, went on a hunger strike outside the courthouse.) Called as a witness, the accounting department head, Vladimir Movsesyan, refused to testify that he had ever been shown the classified document, or that he could recall any violation of secrecy, or that the document shown him was involved in the four-year-old conversation. The Soviet slander charges were supported solely by evidence of acts that in July 1971 had been declared to have lost their socially dangerous character. What caused them to become dangerous again was never stated. The evidence included Lyubarsky's many letters, his notebooks, and some tape recordings of foreign radio broadcasts. Lyubarsky denied all criminal activity, and no witness testified to having heard him make any anti-Soviet comments. Attorney Kamynina appears to have done her best and asked for dismissal of all charges, but Lyubarsky received four years, two for each charge, running consecutively rather than the usual concurrent sentences.

Thirty-two Vilna Jews held a supportive hunger strike during the trial. So did groups in Moscow, Leningrad, and Kharkov. Foreign legal observers, including three members of the British Parliament, were refused Soviet visas. Protests against the "judicial persecution" of Lyubarsky occurred both during and after the trial in the USSR and abroad. Once the inexorable process began, however, it could be neither stopped nor reversed—but it could have been avoided if Lyubarsky had been less contentious, if Smirnov had been less spiteful, less bigoted.

The Lyubarsky case dramatically illustrates significant aspects of the Jewish struggle and of the Soviet response to dissident behavior. Nothing could be clearer than that Lyubarsky compulsively courted disaster. A stubborn, principled Jew, made of the stuff of the Old Testament prophets, he is very much like contemporary nonconformist civil libertarian individualists anywhere. But there is a specifically Soviet quality to his dogged, daring behavior—a quality one finds as well in Andrei Sakharov, Vladimir Bukovsky, and other Soviet democratic nonconformists, who, while insisting on legality and civil liberties, recklessly disregard their own safety. How does this happen in brilliant, otherwise rational people? One possible explanation relates to the tension and psychological stress of Soviet life for the principled intellectual. After years of guarded conversations, of surreptitious reading and discussion of forbidden documents, of secret, hidden, nonpermitted thoughts, shared intimately and partially, if at all, with one's closest confidants, of walking the elusive line of legality, and finally, of open but carefully circumscribed struggle, there is a palpable, maddening emotional exhaustion, a "combat weariness" that paralyzes the normal instincts of self-preservation and leads one down the perilous path of martyrdom. This is admirable and understandable but mad. It is the ultimate logic of a tightly repressive, strangulating society. It has happened to the best of men who, at some point, no longer give a damn about themselves, their safety, or perhaps their effectiveness. Their point of no return is the mental hospital, the prison camp, exile—or emigration.

The regime also displays a kind of madness. To attempt a rational explanation of official behavior in the Lyubarsky case, or in most political trials of dissidents, is an exercise in futility. Decision making is secret and often arbitrary, capricious, and decentralized. There is constant tension between the dissidents who seek some kind of Soviet legality—a rule of law, a reasoned restraint, an acceptance of what the Western world calls "due process"—and those in authority, some of whom are convinced believers or malevolent and petty bureaucrats. Since this conflict is not openly debated, it cannot really be resolved. Instead, there is an ebb and flow, a silent debate, or an undulating, unseen struggle, the outcome of which is uncertain. As a result, no one can logically explain or predict who will be prosecuted, or why and when.

Although defense counsel in most trials submissively betray their clients and their legal responsibility, some attorneys, in frighteningly constricted circumstances, have exemplified principled commitment to their clients and to the law. Many prosecutors and judges, knowing full well that their victims are innocent of any real crime, seem to do no more than persecute them cynically; but others, the heirs of endemic anti-Semitism, appear to believe that there is a massive Zionist conspiracy and that Jews are both diabolically clever and pervasively evil. In all societies there are politicians who rationalize repression, illegality, cruelty, and violations of human rights in terms of the overriding exigencies of the society. They identify their goals with the welfare and safety of the state. But given a half-century of mind-boggling brainwashing propaganda and a legal structure that circumscribes the parameters of nonconformity so sharply that a generalized critique of petty bureaucrats is the only form of "self-criticism" permitted, it is inevitable that Soviet judges, prosecutors, or KGB men see opposition as treason and regard a natural interest, identification, and desire for contact with one's national brethren or coreligionists as illicit, subversive conspiracy.

A VARIETY OF VICTIMS

CHAPTER 20

According to conservative estimates, there are more than 10,000 political prisoners in Soviet labor camps, including persons convicted for religious offenses, nationalist advocacy, or violations of the subversion sections of the criminal code—anti-Soviet slander, propaganda, and organization—as well as persons sentenced, irrespective of the criminal code section, for demonstrations or for *samizdat* activity. (In addition, many are sentenced for crimes such as "hooliganism" or "parasitism" or for various kinds of economic crimes when the true gravamen of their offense is political nonconformity.) Although a large number of the prisoners are Jews, many of the Jewish political prisoners have been sentenced for offenses that are not connected with strictly Jewish issues, and among the democratic dissidents, a large percentage are of Jewish origin.

Information about previously unknown political prisoners becomes available when those inside are released—particularly if they are given permission to go to the West—and they tell about their prison experiences. Boris Kochubiyevsky, for example, reported, after his arrival in Israel, that Jews from Kharkov—including Vladislav Nedobora, Arkady Levin, and Vladimir Ponomaryov, engineers who held responsible positions in scientific enterprises—had been tried in secret and given three-year sentences for sending letters to the UN condemning his trial and the trials of others. It is difficult to believe that other Kharkov Jews were unaware of the fate of these men or failed to report it upon their arrival in Israel. Yet, for reasons that have yet to be explained, the details had not been released in Israel and their cases had remained unpublicized by spokesmen for the Jewish cause. The trial of these Jews from Kharkov had been fully reported in *Khronika*. They were part of the "mainstream" democratic movement—supporters of the Action (or Initiative) Group for the Defense of Civil Rights, which is discussed in greater detail in Chapter 23. The Action Group first came into prominence on May 20, 1969, with the appearance of an open letter to the UN Commission on Human Rights requesting an inquiry into the Soviet violation of the right to hold independent opinions and to propagate them legally. Members of the group pointed to various political trials, including those of Kochubiyevsky and of other Soviet Jews who had demanded permission to emigrate to Israel. The group's identified supporters included Nedobora, Levin, Ponomaryov, and five other engineers from Kharkov. On June 12, 1969, the regime sponsored meetings that condemned the signers. Genrikh Altunyan, a former Red Army major, military academy professor, and Communist Party member, who at the time was working as an engineer, was the leader of the group and the first arrested. He was tried on November 26, 1969, and sentenced to three years. On November 27, Nedobora's apartment was searched and he was arrested a few days later. Levin was arrested on December 2, and Ponomaryov on December 6. Nedobora and Ponomaryov, tried in March 1970, were accused under the Ukrainian equivalent of Russian Article 190-1. Among the defamatory statements in the *samizdat* documents they were accused of disseminating were "Jews who wish to go to Israel are persecuted," "A policy of undisguised chauvinism is conducted in the USSR," and "Human rights are violated." The prosecution frequently alluded to the defendants' criticisms of the Kochubiyevsky trial. In his final statement, Nedobora said:

> How am I to love my country? I could not learn to love my country with closed eyes, a bowed head, and sealed lips. I find that a man can be of use to his country only if he can see her clearly; I think that the time for blind declarations of love has passed . . . I believe that we have come after others in order to do better than they did, so that we should not fall into their errors or be a prey to their illusions and superstitions.

The two men received three-year sentences. At Arkady Levin's trial, which began on April 24, the charges and the result were the same. Other signers of the appeal, friendly witnesses, and the family of the accused, many of whom were Jews, were dismissed from employment and subjected to other forms of harassment, but not persecuted. Like Nedobora, many of those who were tried or harassed in 1969–70 still thought of the USSR as their country—an imperfect, often cruel one, but a country to which one showed love by criticism, not by obeisance or departure. Therefore, the three Kharkov Jewish dissenters, although known in the West through *Khronika,* received neither attention nor support.

There are various reasons why other cases have remained obscure or unknown. Most obvious is the fact that Jews in small or distant communities, or those who struggle in lonely ways, have no contact with the democratic or Jewish movements, let alone with the West. Neither their existence nor their fate becomes known. That is exactly the kind of isolation the Soviet regime intends. No groups may exist except those sponsored by the regime. Any nonpermitted organization is regarded as anti-Soviet. Any nonofficial contact between cities is viewed as subversive, and contact with the outside world is not only discouraged, it is regarded as heretical. But such an explanation does not answer the question of why so little is known about a Jewish trial in Tashkent or Samarkand.

With a population of 1.4 million, Tashkent, the capital of the Uzbek SSR, is the largest city in Soviet Asia. Its 60,000 Jews experienced blood-libel anti-Semitic riots in 1962, and its considerable Muslim population has been particularly subject to the official anti-Israel propaganda that has been rife since the Soviet Union's strong advocacy of the Arab position in the Middle East. World War II, and the huge population displacement from the Western borderlands, brought to Tashkent large numbers of Jewish refugees from the Baltic states, the Ukraine, Moldavia, and Byelorussia; it carried the virus of anti-Semitism and an old malignancy in new form—the charge of Jewish wartime shirking. Tashkent was the locale of many scurrilous wartime "jokes," the butts of which were Jews. When the war ended, tens of thousands of Ashkenazi Jews who had fled eastward remained in the Soviet republics of Central Asia where they met, mingled with, and sometimes married the Oriental Jews who already resided there. These Jews, particularly those of Uzbekistan, are referred to as Bukhari Jews from their centuries of living in the Emirate of Bukhara. Although most commentators, until recently, approximated their strength at 80,000 to 100,000, the Bukhari

Jews estimate their numbers as high as 200,000 to 250,000. The majority dwell in Tashkent, Samarkand, Bukhara, and Khiva—major cities of the Uzbek SSR—but many also live in the Tadzhik, Turkmen, Kazakh, and Kirghiz republics.

Bukhari Jews probably were settled along the "Silk Route" for millennia, and their presence amid the Persian-Islamic civilizations of their area for a thousand years is beyond dispute. Their culture reflects that of the surrounding peoples, and their fervent religious practices, like those of the Georgian Jews, are orthodox and (in Ashkenazi eyes) relatively unsophisticated. They first encountered Ashkenazi Jewry after their area was annexed to the Russian Empire in the 19th century, but not in large numbers until World War II. Like the Georgians, many Bukhari Jews are messianic Zionists, some of whose grandfathers emigrated to Palestine (and particularly to Jerusalem) more than half a century ago.

Samarkand, an ancient city some 200 miles southwest of Tashkent, is the second largest population center of Uzbekistan. It has about 25,000 Jews, largely Bukharis, and its recent Jewish history appears to be similar to that of Tashkent.

There is little indication of a Jewish repatriation movement among Bukharis or of any attempts they may have made to secure exit visas until the fall of 1971. They did not begin to secure such visas until the spring of 1972, but by that summer, numbers of Bukharis were securing permission to leave and, in 1973, they constituted a disproportionately large percentage of the Jews arriving in Israel. There had been no organized, open Jewish movement in Tashkent. From all accounts, OVIR had refused even to accept applications until the fall of 1971. The Bukharis did not organize petitions, write letters, or circulate *samizdat* materials. It was up to the displaced Ashkenazi Jews to create whatever struggle would appear. One, Yakov Soloveichik, had appealed to the UN as early as May 1970, complaining of anti-Semitic discrimination, pro-Arab attitudes, and the miseries of his existence and begging to be assisted to any "non-socialist country." Perhaps because it was not a Zionist outcry, Soloveichik's letter was never made public in the West.

But that could not have been the reason for our limited knowledge about the trial of Emilia Trakhtenberg, a 40-year-old librarian from Samarkand, who is now serving three years in a prison camp. Born in Kiev, she was sent to Samarkand at the outbreak of World War II.

Her father, an artist, and her mother, a doctor, remained behind and died at Babi Yar. She graduated from a pedagogical institute and became the head of a children's library in Samarkand. In a letter she wrote anonymously to Premier Kosygin in March 1970, she described the oppressed circumstances of Soviet Jews, stated that freedom for Jews exists in the West, and argued that Soviet Jews should be able to emigrate to Israel. As a consequence, the prosecutor opened a criminal file. After she wrote another anonymous letter, to Foreign Minister Andrei Gromyko, in February 1971, investigators and handwriting experts implicated her, and she was charged under the Uzbek equivalent of Russian Article 190-1. Her opinions were regarded as so abnormal that she was forced to undergo a sanity hearing. Since she was found sane, she was sentenced to three years in a forced labor camp for "systematic dissemination of deliberate lies, vilifying the Soviet state and social system." In sentencing her, Judge E. I. Doduyev stated, "Trakhtenberg had everything except a feeling of gratitude for the Soviet people and its government." A report of the Samarkand People's Court trial appeared in a Tashkent newspaper under the heading "We Will Not Be Slandered." It said "the contents of her letters were so disgusting that criminal proceedings were started." The writer reported that Emilia Trakhtenberg's sentence was received by enthusiastic courtroom applause and cries of "Too little!" and "Not enough!" Yet someone in Samarkand or Tashkent noted the newspaper account and related it and a few details of the victim's background to Moscow, where they were telephoned to the West, and *Khronika* was able to report the trial. But because there was no regular contact between Moscow and Samarkand, additional details were not available.

There is no absence of dissidents in the Uzbek SSR, however. Leaders of the extremely militant Crimean Tatars live there, and the trials in Tashkent of General Piotr Grigorenko and the Moscow educator-editor Ilya Gabai, human rights advocates who rendered major support to the Crimean Tatar movement, were fully reported.

There is less news of a similar, more recent trial in Tashkent, perhaps because of *Khronika's* suspension. The only source of information is an article in the Tashkent newspaper *Pravda Vostoka*, January 14, 1973, which, under the headline "Slanderers," reported the trial and sentencing of Yakov Kaufman and Boris Kim for defaming the USSR. Kaufman, an engineer and geologist who held a high position in a Tashkent institute, was said to have "yielded to the influence of Zionist anti-Soviet propaganda and found himself in the captivity of Zionist theories." He had previously been fined 200 rubles for arguing with his subordinates and slandering the Soviet Union in pamphlets and letters. At the trial, "specialists" in international relations, history, and economics were called to testify that Kaufman's views on the position of the USSR in the Middle East and on the Soviet nationalities policy "vilified Soviet reality." His "slanders" were contained in various letters to public officials and newspapers and apparently in *samizdat* pamphlets. His co-worker, 40-year-old Boris Kim, was sentenced for sending anonymous, critical letters to Soviet organizations in Moscow and Tashkent. Under the headline "New Jewish Prisoner of Conscience," Western Jewish publications mentioned Kaufman briefly, but they did not mention Kim at all.

Alma Ata, the capital of Kazakh SSR, is 400 miles due east of Tashkent and only a few miles north of the border with the Chinese province of Sinkiang. A city of about 750,000 inhabitants, it has a Jewish population of about 10,000, of whom Bukharis constitute the largest element. Except that it is even more remote from the West than neighboring Uzbekistan, Kazakhstan's contemporary Jewish history is similar. As far as is known, there was no Jewish movement in Alma Ata, and only one Jew had persistently applied for an exit visa— Arnold Finger, a politically unsophisticated draftsman with a wife and two children. Finger was not a Zionist activist, and his travails, as well as those of his in-laws, would never have come to light except for the dogged persistence of his father, Chanan Finger, a Tel Aviv electrician.

The story began in 1939 in Poland, where Chanan Finger, then 23 and serving in the Polish Army, was transferred, with his unit, to the Polish Ukraine. The collapse of Poland under the Nazi onslaught and Soviet occupation led to his discharge from the army at Lvov. One of his siblings had emigrated to Canada prior to 1939; the five others, his parents, and fifteen nieces and nephews were murdered by the Nazis. Finger married a Polish-Jewish woman in Lvov in 1940, and shortly thereafter, Soviet authorities transferred them to Siberia. In September 1941, Chanan and Zura Finger were permitted to move to Kazakhstan, where his only child, Arnold, was born in 1943. When Arnold was four months old, Chanan was arrested for alleged Zionist activities and sentenced to ten years of hard labor in a northern Siberian camp. Two months later, his young wife Zura was arrested for attempting to steal groceries and sentenced to two years' imprisonment. Later evidence indicated that Zura, left with a six-month-old baby, no work, and a husband in a Siberian camp, entered a store begging for bread and the anti-Semitic shopkeeper cried "Thief!" Arnold was taken into the home of a childless local woman, a Jewish doctor, whose Ukrainian husband had been killed in the war.

At the end of the war, Chanan was released and rehabilitated and was returned under guard to the Polish Army in Cracow. He sought in vain for his wife and son among Polish citizens repatriated from the USSR. In 1949, he emigrated from Poland to Israel, and for the next fifteen years, he devoted everything he could save from his electrician's salary to the effort to find his son.

Chanan Finger's search was rewarded in 1964, when the Soviet Red Cross notified him that Arnold was alive and living in Alma Ata, and he secured a visa to visit his son. The overjoyed young man began the long process of attempting to join his father in Israel. Meanwhile, Arnold married an Alma Ata Jewish schoolteacher. The family first applied to OVIR in 1966, but the local head of OVIR, Serotov, refused the application. For five years, Finger persisted. Each time, Serotov told him that no Jew would ever be permitted to leave Alma Ata for the West. All appeals to higher authorities were fruitless, as was an effort to emigrate to his only other relative, the uncle in Canada. Both father and son persisted, although no other Jew from Alma Ata had ever been successful in securing a visa or had even been known to apply. In December 1970, Finger's mother-in-law and her husband, Abraham Levinson, were arrested for a currency violation, and in April 1971, Arnold Finger was charged with criminal complicity, apparently on the ground that he and his wife had accumulated some funds for their emigration to Israel. Chanan Finger tried again and again to assist his son. With the advice of the Soviet human rights expert Boris Tsukerman, now a resident of Jerusalem, he secured competent Moscow counsel. Some attention was drawn to the case from the unremitting efforts to secure journalistic interest in the West, and there was intervention with Soviet diplomatic officials in the United States. Charges against Arnold Finger were dropped and in April 1972 he and his family became the first Jews in Alma Ata to receive an exit visa to Israel. But for a tenacious, stubborn father in Israel who was able to elicit the assistance of activist friends, there is little doubt that Arnold Finger would have served time in prison like others from remote Jewish communities in the USSR.

Many trials and political prisoners have remained unknown outside the USSR because those involved had little or no connection with the Jewish movement and thus did not receive the benefit of the mass media exposure available in the West. Prisoners or persons on trial became better known if they had advocates abroad or because friends had previously emigrated to the West, usually to Israel, and they in turn were able to reach the media. Jewish organizations in Western countries received most of their information from Israeli authorities who had been assigned responsibility for Soviet Jewry, but these authorities had little interest or enthusiasm for Jewish defendants and prisoners who were not Zionists. Thus, Western Jewish sources gave no attention to the trials at Ryazan and Bendery (see pages 135 and 215) until the victims displayed prison-camp solidarity with other Jews of Zionist commitment. Even then, it was the continuing, principled support of Jewish activists in the USSR and of the activist emigrés that secured publicity and support for those prisoners, despite the reluctance of the Israeli authorities.

Another case in point concerns the Leningrad poet Anatoly Radygin. Born in 1934 of a Jewish mother but designated Russian on his passport, Radygin became a Soviet naval officer after graduating from the Leningrad Higher Nautical College and subsequently was captain of a fishing boat in the Soviet Far East. He edited a poetry anthology, *The Salt of the Ocean,* which was published in 1962, and became a member of the Writers' Union, but in September of that year he was arrested while attempting to escape to Turkey by swimming the Black Sea. He was sentenced to ten years under Article 64 (betrayal of the homeland). Like other intellectuals in the prison camps, he was a troublemaker, and he was mentioned with other "friends and comrades" by Anatoly Marchenko in his memorable book on Soviet prison camps, *My Testimony.* In the fall of 1971, while in Vladimir prison, where he had been sent for organizing escape efforts, Radygin decided to leave for Israel after his release. He sought to have his name and nationality legally changed to that of his mother, whose surname was Shulman, and when that was denied, he went on a three-week hunger strike. Finally released in September 1972, he remained under administrative surveillance in Tarusa, in the Kaluga region, 100 miles south of Moscow, still attempting to leave the USSR for Israel, but now the recipient of some concerned attention in the West. Radygin and his wife were permitted to emigrate to Israel in July 1973.

Another category of persons whose plight remains wholly or incompletely publicized consists of those who, despite their victimization, are felt to have moral blemishes. Among such cases are those in which the prisoner was accused of economic offenses or where there may have been culpability that compromised the victim's status as a prisoner of conscience—for example, Chaim Rennert (see page 251). An interesting symbiosis has developed between the original reporters of news— the Soviet Jewish dissidents—and the Western purveyors—the Israeli authorities and the Jewish-establishment organizations. The Jewish activists, at times puritanical and censorial, see their movement in the highest moral terms, cannot permit its heroes and martyrs to have the human frailties that are inevitable among any group of people, and regard those who are less than heroic with the KGB, such as Boris Maftser, as virtual traitors.

Some publicists in the West, with their finely toned public relations sensitivities, cannot tolerate the whole truth. For them, heroes have no warts, and they are worried that Soviet external propaganda organs may document the less noble aspects of a case. Such a conflict between what constitutes good public relations and the demands of truth was the source of considerable embarrassment in the Leningrad hijacking case, when it subsequently became clear that the image created was not consistent with the facts established.

A classic example of the problem is the case of Ilya Glezer, which should have been an ideal one from which the stuff of movement martyrs is made. Glezer is the only Moscow activist to have been made the victim of a Soviet political trial for his Jewish activity. A distinguished biological scientist, Glezer, born in 1931, was well known in the USSR and abroad for his research and internationally published writings on the pathomorphology of the brain. The early stages of his harassment by the authorities were documented and publicized, but his trial in August 1972, which resulted in a three-year sentence, was barely reported, and few efforts have been made since then to publicize his victimization or to secure his release—apparently because Glezer was considered to be a homosexual.

While at the Institute for Brain Study of the Moscow Medical Academy, Glezer developed mathematical methods of brain research and organized the USSR's first department of research with an electronic microscope. He nonetheless left after an anti-Semitic campaign and worked in the Psychiatric Institute of the Medical Academy of Sciences and lectured at Moscow University. But in 1970, he again lost his position over issues involving his Jewishness. After applying to go to Israel in January 1972, he was arrested on February 7. The KGB seized some *samizdat* material, his typewriter, and letters he had written (most of them anonymously) to Soviet newspapers, government leaders and institutions, and foreign embassies, accusing the USSR of anti-Semitism. He was charged under Article 70 with having disseminated anti-Soviet propaganda. Almost immediately, seventy-two Soviet Jews petitioned the KGB for his release, and somewhat later, sixteen British neuromedical specialists came to his defense in a letter to *The Times* of London. On August 22, after a two-day closed trial, unattended even by his mother, Glezer was given a three-year sentence for anti-Soviet propaganda, slander, and "other crimes."

The next day, *Pravda,* in an unusual, detailed first-page article, reported the event, the first "news" that the proceeding had taken place. The article claimed that Glezer admitted his crimes of writing anonymous, "dirty, anti-Soviet letters"; that he had been incited by hearing "the lying transmissions of Kol Israel" and "become infected with the poison of the most rabid and unrestrained Zionism"; that he was seen "in shady places where he exchanged whispers with all sorts of dregs of society and moral monsters." Glezer also was accused of "preaching a hostile, anti-Soviet morality, including matters of the family and marriage." Then came the *coup de grâce.* Glezer was described as "a morally corrupt person who has left two wives" and who "indulged in immoral and unnatural habits." His "dissoluteness and sexual deviations, punishable by the Soviet Criminal Code," having been exposed, were admitted. These "shameful, vile facts of this pseudo-intellectual, amoral type" were said to be characteristic of the "renegades" supported in the West. The process of investigation caused "other figures from Glezer's surroundings, such as his friend Vladimir Slepak and other adherents of the Israeli paradise" to come to the surface. Not only Jewish activists but also diplomatic observers viewed the diatribe as ominously pointing to an imminent arrest of Slepak, but that did not occur, nor was any campaign mounted on behalf of Glezer. The only protest was a letter to *Pravda* signed two weeks later by the prominent scientists Venyamin Levich and Aleksandr Lerner and other Moscow Jews. The letter decried the *Pravda* attack, likening it to the ways of the Stalinist secret police and noting that it evoked "the most somber associations and serious concern." Then there was silence. Given the sexual prudishness and straitlacedness of Soviet society, it seems as if Glezer's sexual nonconformity made him the most vulnerable target in Moscow of the regime's repressive attitudes. Certainly his political behavior was far more benign than that of dozens of unprosecuted Moscow activists who were permitted to go to Israel or who still continue to demonstrate, protest, and defy the regime. Glezer, the undefended victim, may be but one of many Jewish prisoners whose personal lives or chargeable behavior make them seem less than perfect heroes.

Of all those charged and convicted, there are also many who face lengthy criminal investigations yet, like the Case 97 defendants in Minsk (see page 279), are inexplicably released. Soviet Georgia, for all of its Zionist agitation, has had few Jewish prisoners. An exception is Boris Davarashvili of Tbilisi who, on June 16, 1972, was sentenced to prison for seven years for the nonpolitical crimes of hooliganism and assault and battery. His family, having applied to go to Israel, had received permission in February 1972. Davarashvili went to Moscow to make the arrangements that are required for departing families.

> In the GUM department store, he met a friend and told him that he was leaving. A Russian overheard and called Boris a traitor for going to a fascist country. Boris answered that in his opinion, he was leaving a fascist country for a democratic one. A fight broke out, causing the Russian to be hospitalized with a brain concussion, and Boris was arrested. For one month he was held in a Moscow prison where he went on a hunger strike. Then he was sent to a mental hospital for observation. After two months in the hospital, he was declared sane.

The Davarashvili family is in Israel, but 45-year-old Boris is in prison.

Others, less hot-tempered but more political, have escaped such a fate. As early as January 26, 1970, a group of Jews appeared at the Georgian Ministry of Internal Affairs with a petition to leave the USSR. An altercation ensued, in which a particularly vocal role was played by Veniamin Zhaneshvili and Abram Danilashvili. Warned by the authorities to cease their agitation, they persisted and were arrested on July 9, 1970. Shortly thereafter, another Georgian Jew, Semyon Burshtein, was arrested in Sukumi. The three men were held for some time and then released. The details have never become publicly known. Subsequently, other Georgian activists were arrested during the course of demonstrations but quickly released. The comparatively relaxed attitudes of Georgian officialdom may be the best explanation for this as well as for the relative ease with which Georgian Jews have secured permission to emigrate.

The most protracted legal encounter occurred with the Goldshteins, a Tbilisi family of Ashkenazi background. Grigory Goldshtein is a physicist, his brother Isai is a prominent mathematician, and Isai's wife, Elizaveta Bykova, is also a physicist. The Goldshteins first applied to emigrate in 1971, but they were refused permission, as so many other scientists have been, because they had been engaged in "secret work." (The definition of classified work has been both broad and arbitrary.) The Goldshteins had resigned their jobs in security classifications, as had many others, in an effort to avoid such a categorization, but this was to no avail. In late 1972, an administrative procedure involving commissions of inquiry became available in some installations where classified jobs existed, to determine if the "secret work" classification was warranted. A closed hearing concerning the Goldshteins did not admit them or their evidence, and they were informed that their classi-fication had not changed even though the director of their institution told them that "none of us consider that you have any knowledge or are in possession of any secret information." Those Soviet Jews who were persistently refused permission to leave for that reason derisively began referring to themselves as "secretniks." In an open letter to scientists throughout the world in February 1972 about "the tragic situation of the 'secretniks' who are striving to repatriate to Israel," the Goldshteins declared: "We find ourselves between the hammer of a despotic authority which will not allow us to leave and the anvil of a commission of inquiry whose members, out of sheer personal terror, are prepared to sign a false finding declaring us to be in possession of secret information." They protested anti-Semitic newspaper and maga-zine articles. They vigorously and openly supported Colonel Davido-vich and the Minsk activists; traveled to Rostov for the Lyubarsky trial and went on a hunger strike outside the courtroom with Polsky and Prestin; appealed to the U.S. Senate and UN Secretary General Kurt Waldheim to free Silva Zalmanson; led protest delegations to Georgian officials and newspaper editors objecting to the featuring of information about those Georgian Jews who had found life in Israel disappointing and wished to return to the USSR; and were involved in numerous collec-tive letters and other social action insisting on the right to leave. After the murder of Israeli athletes at the Olympic Games in Munich

in September 1972, they renounced their Soviet citizenship because of
Soviet support for Arab terrorists.

On February 10, 1973, the Goldshteins' homes were searched and
the usual melange of movement items—Hebrew tape recordings, songs,
and grammars, Jewish *samizdat* materials, and letters to and from
Israel and the West—were seized, as well as fourteen copies of the UN
Declaration of Human Rights. Shortly thereafter, the two brothers were
charged with violating the Georgian equivalent of Article 190-1, principally by having written protest letters, particularly the one on the
Munich massacre. Placed under surveillance but not taken into custody
as the investigation continued, they protested the search and charges
as a "provocation" and refused to come in for KGB interrogation. This
was unheard-of defiance. Isai Goldshtein compounded the offense by
writing as follows to the editor of the "Amazing Stories" column in
Izvestia:

> Comrade Koryagin! An amazing thing happened to me on the night
> of the 10th of February: I arrived home from Moscow at 1 a.m. and
> was met by six angry men (apart from my mother-in-law and, nat-
> urally, my wife).
> "Where have you been until now?"—asked the oldest of them.
> "I am sorry," said I. "The plane was late. Am I allowed to go to
> the toilet?"
> "You are, but only under guard, and just in case you don't know,
> a search for provocative slanderous materials defaming the Soviet
> regime is being conducted in your apartment."
> I tried not to show my amazement and went to the toilet, accom-
> panied by a shy young man, and then ate a cold meatball given me
> by the trembling hand of my mother-in-law. I inquired what kind of
> "provocative slanderous materials" against the Soviet regime were
> being confiscated. After long hours of diligent work, they gave me
> the protocol of the search. The confiscated materials were as follows:
> my passport, a few copies of the text of the Declaration of Human
> Rights, two copies of the recently published Moscow book by Bol-
> shakov, *Zionism in the Service of Anti-Communism,* receipt for pay-
> ments for inter-city telephone conversations, postcards, and so on. All
> this, naturally, had no connection with what had been written in the
> order for the search. After carefully packing all the "evidence" into
> a house-bag obligingly lent by me, Kvashali and his companions left,
> apologizing to the witnesses and not forgetting to apologize to me and
> my family.
> A whole week has passed since then, and the confiscated things
> still have not been returned. I am graciously ready to acknowledge
> the apologies I received, just as is my brother in whose apartment

something very similar happened. It is said in Solomon's tales: "The unpious run when nobody follows them but the pious are quiet as a lion." We are quiet indeed, but we do need these things, especially the passport.

Do you like our amazing story, Comrade Koryagin? How do you think it is going to end?

More seriously, the Goldshteins appealed to the first secretary of the Georgian Commmunist Party "to prevent a shameful page being written in the history of Georgia—an anti-Semitic process. Allow us to repatriate to Israel and to take with us fond memories of Georgia."

On April 4, after refusing to reply to a summons to answer charges under the equivalent of Article 190-1, the brothers were detained. They refused proffered legal counsel and went on a hunger strike. Elizaveta asked the Netherlands Embassy in Moscow for diplomatic protection and their release since both her husband and brother-in-law had received Israeli citizenship. On April 6, 1973, although their passports were retained, they were released and restricted to Tbilisi, when they agreed to report for further questioning. Activists in the USSR and Jewish organizations abroad protested their arrest. On June 2, they were formally charged under Article 190-1 because in their letter concerning the Munich affair they had claimed that the murders could have been committed with arms that the USSR had supplied to the Palestinian organizations which underwrote the terrorists. Out of jail and untried, the Goldshteins remained under investigation. The pending charges did not deter them from filing a civil claim for 1,600 rubles against the postal authorities for failing to deliver forty international registered letters, or from protesting to the U.S. Congress about their uncertain status.

The commitment to mental hospitals of those who stray outside the established parameters of conformity is often viewed as a greater sanction than the political trial. Many Jews have been the victims of such detention. Unlike the political trial, where a modicum of procedural forms is followed, irrespective of the lack of practical effect it may have on the results, commitment for insanity occurs without the participation of the accused and without the formal safeguards that are associated with a criminal proceeding. Because, theoretically, no punishment is involved, commitment is for an indeterminate period. The inmate has no protection against drug therapy that can produce organic change or against psychotherapy that is designed to achieve submissive conformity rather than the relief of symptoms or the increase of self-understanding.

Among the Soviet Union's prominent articulate dissidents who are now, or have been, held in mental hospitals are such heroic figures as Major General Piotr Grigorenko, Vladimir Bukovsky, biologist Zhores Medvedev, mathematician-philosopher-poet Aleksandr Yesenin-Volpin, poet Natalya Gorbanevskaya, mathematician Yury Shikhanovich, philologist and collective-farm chairman Ivan Yakhimovich, artist Viktor Kuznetsov, fine arts specialist Viktor Fainberg, and electrician and Action Group leader Vladimir Borisov. Members of the Jewish movement also have been so detained. Some, such as Yesenin-Volpin, have been released and thus can tell about their experiences.

Among the earlier mental hospital inmates were Yulia Vishnevskaya, a Moscow poet, and Ilya Rips, a Riga mathematician, both born in 1948. After having been apprehended during the trial of Natalya Gorbanevskaya, Vishnevskaya, a democratic activist since her middle teens, was committed in 1970 to the Serbsky Institute in Moscow with a diagnosis of "creeping schizophrenia." Shortly after her release, she was permitted to migrate to Israel. Rips, a mathematical theorist, was declared insane and hospitalized after a self-immolative political demonstration over the Soviet invasion of Czechoslovakia. A book he wrote while in the hospital has been hailed as a significant contribution to mathematical theory. His family and he were permitted to leave for Israel after his release from the hospital.

An early Jewish movement activist, Girsh (Grisha) Feigin, a Riga engineer and Red Army reserve major born in 1927, was forcibly placed in a psychiatric hospital in Riga after he publicly returned his war medals and renounced Soviet citizenship in protest against Soviet policy toward Jews. "Normal people do not renounce government decorations" was the official explanation for Feigin's commitment. Feigin had made twenty-four applications for an exit visa to join his mother and sister in Israel, and had been repeatedly refused, but he was permitted to leave after international protest.

Some Moscow Jewish activists have been committed after participating in political demonstrations. In April 1972, Ilya Belau, 27, was hospitalized because of his "bad behavior" following a melee between hundreds of young Jews and the militia outside the synagogue on the first night of Passover. In September 1972, among thirty-one young Jews arrested at a protest demonstration outside the Supreme Court against the education tax, at least one protester, Aleksei Tumerman, was forcibly confined in a psychiatric hospital. It was the fourth such experience for the 30-year-old leader. A long-time activist in both the democratic and Jewish movements, Tumerman, a friend of Bukovsky's, was a link between the two groups. After Tumerman's fourth hospitalization, his mother was told that he would be released and the family would be permitted to leave the country if they ceased all agitation. In a *samizdat* statement, Tumerman indignantly refused the proposition, and a few months later, he was released both from the hospital and from the country.

Sergei Gurvits, a 27-year-old Moscow physicist who had been dismissed from the Institute of Nuclear Physics after he applied to leave for Israel, was placed under psychiatric observation because he wore a *kipah* (the traditional Jewish skull cap) to a meeting of physicists. The psychiatrist assigned to the case viewed Gurvits as "sick in the head" for wearing a skull cap.

After being served, in the spring of 1972, with documents requiring him to register for military service, a prominent Moscow activist, Viktor Yakhot, who worked as a research physicist at the Nuclear Physics Institute of the Academy of Sciences, refused to register on the ground that he had renounced his Soviet citizenship when he applied to leave for Israel. Arrested and forcibly taken for a psychiatric examination on April 28, Yakhot steadfastly refused to answer the psychiatrists' questions without the presence of a representative of the international psychiatrists' organization or the International Red Cross. He advised both bodies of his position in an open letter. He, too, was ultimately permitted to go to Israel.

Not so fortunate was Yan Krilsky, the son of an engineer who managed to emigrate with the details of Yan's experience. Young Krilsky was arrested in 1970 at the age of 18 in a factory altercation resulting from anti-Semitic comments. During a KGB interrogation, he was asked, "If the USSR and Israel were at war, for whom would you fight?" When he responded, "Israel," he was threatened with a criminal charge of counterrevolutionary activity. His prosecutors claimed that only an insane person would respond in the way he did. His attorney persuaded Krilsky's parents that psychiatric treatment was preferable to ten years' criminal imprisonment. Krilsky was institutionalized as a "schizophrenic" for his "militant Zionism." When last visited by his mother, he was in a ward for the criminally insane, where he was receiving injection therapy and subjected to physical restraints.

Perhaps the most ironic of all the cases involving psychiatric hospital

324

commitments is that of 26-year-old Kiev psychiatrist Semyon Fishelevich Gluzman, who was sentenced to ten years under Article 70 because he was a *samizdat* activist and—though this did not figure among the formal charges—he had criticized the detention and compulsory treatment of social critics in special psychiatric hospitals. Gluzman was one of the authors of the devastating *samizdat* document *An In Absentia Psychiatric Opinion on the Case of P. G. Grigorenko,* which was based on the medical record of the illustrious human rights leader. Andrei Sakharov stated that "Gluzman was sentenced for his professional integrity" and he appealed to psychiatrists throughout the world to "speak up in defense of their young colleague" and to "demand without delay the initiation of an internationally based investigation into all the evidence on the use of psychiatry for imprisoning dissenters."

TACTICS OF
CONFRONTATION

CHAPTER 21

In the struggle of the last half-decade between the Jewish movement and the Soviet government, the opposing forces could hardly have been more disparate. One one side stood Soviet power, with its awesome array of army, police, KGB, publishing and mass media monopoly; its control of movement, travelers, journalists, communications, and transportation; its capacity, through party and factory, to harass, isolate, persecute, and make unemployable; and finally, its courts, prison camps, and insane asylums. The mismatched adversary was a despised, stubborn, stiff-necked remnant of a people, led by a handful of brave, able fanatics and using the slingshot of words against the Goliath. Certainly the movement began, cohered, and grew from self-education and *samizdat*. It was bound together by singleness of purpose—the desire to leave—and was reinforced and further unified by the trials that had been designed to destroy it. But ultimately, its unique success and its ability to maintain a continued momentum arose from its highly creative sense of confrontation politics. Every act was designed for a specific purpose or audience: first, to inform and support fellow-Jews in the cities of the USSR; next, to cause the recipient or target to respond, be influenced and affected, even if minimally; and finally, to reach an unseen army of supporters in the outside world—mobilized by the friends who left Russia—eagerly telephoning, writing letters, sending packages, coming in on tourist trips, and producing headlines, television programs, parliamentary or congressional support, and a variety of pressures, pushes, demonstrations, boycotts, screams, shrieks, and other noises that had unnerved and discommoded Soviet power to an extent that no one could have predicted. The letters, petitions, and collective appeals, once essential to the creation of the confrontation and then necessary to its maintenance, ultimately became valuable in that they permitted the signer to engage himself in a moral act.

The tactics of confrontation politics had to be as ingenious as the constrictions of Soviet society would tolerate. Political demonstrations in the USSR are as rare as labor strikes, despite the provisions of Article 125 of the Soviet Constitution which provides that "The citizens of the . USSR are guaranteed by law: (a) freedom of speech; (b) freedom of the press; (c) freedom of assembly, including the holding of mass meetings; (d) freedom of street processions and demonstrations." Mass meetings, street processions, and demonstrations were unheard of during the Stalin period and were both rare and hazardous thereafter, unless they were organized by the authorities. The few that did occur involved only a handful of protesters who would gather at a public place, surreptitiously carrying rolled-up banners, or cardboard posters wrapped in packing paper, which would be unfurled for a few minutes before the police intervened.

Every December since 1965, in Moscow's Pushkin Square, a demonstration has marked Constitution Day. One protesting the arrest of the writers Yuli Daniel and Andrei Sinyavsky was held under the slogan "Respect the Constitution." At another, on January 22, 1967, about thirty young men and women displayed signs that protested the arrest of some intellectuals who had defended Sinyavsky and Daniel ("Down with Dictatorship. Release the Arrested!") and the recent promulgation of Article 190-1 of the Russian Penal Code. The protesters were quickly arrested and some were later sentenced to prison camp. At more recent meetings, surrounded by hordes of police, KGB men, and plainclothed security officers, a few participants silently bared their heads.

At noon, August 25, 1968, in Moscow's Red Square, eight people protesting, by a sit-down, the Soviet invasion of Czechoslovakia four days before, carried small Czech flags and banners reading "Long Live Free and Independent Czechoslovakia," "Shame on the Occupiers," "Hands Off Czechoslovakia," "For Your Freedom and Ours." As the banners were unrolled, a whistle blew and from all sides of the massive square KGB plainclothes men rushed toward the small group shouting, "They're all Jews!" and "Beat up the anti-Sovietists!" They tore the banners from the demonstrators and beat some of them badly. The protesters sat quietly until they were carried away amid anti-Semitic epithets and jeers. Subsequently, Pavel Litvinov, Larisa Bogoraz-Daniel, Vadim Delone, and two others were criminally charged, and Natalya Gorbanevskaya and Viktor Fainberg were sent to insane asylums. Other spontaneous demonstrations against the Czech invasion in various parts of the USSR were responded to similarly. Most, however, were simple, isolated acts such as the attempted self-immolation of Ilya Rips. The contrast between these events and the contemporaneous demonstrations in the United States against the war in Viet-Nam is too striking to ignore.

Most insistent about their constitutional rights have been the Crimean Tatars, some 350,000 persons descended from the intermarriage between the Golden Horde and indigenous Turkic tribes. These Tatars had lived along the Crimean coast for hundreds of years until Stalin uprooted and deported them *en bloc* during World War II. Remnants still live in Uzbekistan and other Soviet Asian republics. Despite their geno-cidal treatment, they have produced a rich body of *samizdat* ma-terials and have persistently reiterated their rights and their claim to their ancestral lands. No other Soviet people have so persistently petitioned the authorities. Their appeals have contained tens of thousands of signatures. One to the Twenty-third Party Congress was signed by 120,000 people. By the mid-1960s, the Crimean Tatars had embarked upon the use of demonstrations to further their cause. The participants were subjected to arrests, administrative detentions, and political trials. On August 27, 1967, more than 2,000 Tatars assembled in Tashkent were dispersed by military forces. Two days of demonstrations led to the arrest of 130, twelve of whom were sentenced to up to three years of imprisonment on charges of fomenting mass disorders and resisting the authorities. Since then, the Tatars have intransigently petitioned, demon-strated, assembled, been dispersed, and arrested *en masse*. In Moscow, eight hundred representatives of the Tatars were escorted under guard back to Central Asia. On June 6, 1969, at Moscow's Mayakovsky Square, a Crimean Tatar demonstration protesting, among other things, the arrest of their great supporter General Piotr Grigorenko, resulted in the detention of those involved.

Another displaced and persecuted Soviet minority has been similarly militant. The Meskhetians, who number about 200,000, had lived for centuries in southern Georgia. In the 16th century the Meskhi-Georgians adopted the Turkish language and were converted to Islam. Like the Crimean Tatars, they were deported to Central Asia by Stalin during

World War II and have not been permitted to return. They, too, have refused to surrender their claim to their ancestral lands and have vigorously insisted upon their right to return. On July 24, 1968, 7,000 Meskhetians converged at Government House in Tbilisi, where they were provoked, beaten, and assaulted by police and army detachments but refused to be dispersed until they achieved an audience with the authorities. Since then, their leaders have been arrested and their meetings broken up, and some, finally, are seeking the right to migrate to Turkey.

In the face of this recent history and the example it has set, the Jewish movement commenced an unprecedented series of demonstrations that have continued in their variety and intensity, not only showing no sign of waning, but displaying an unabated audacity. These demonstrations and the confrontations they have provoked have provided material for their supporters in the Western world. The first such planned action had a specific target—the Twenty-fourth Congress of the Soviet Communist Party, which was scheduled in Moscow from March 29 to April 7, 1971. Foreign party delegations were expected to arrive throughout the month of March, and the focus of world press attention would be on the capital. In February, a petition to the UN and to Western governments had garnered the signatures of 1,185 Jewish families comprising 4,056 persons from Moscow, Leningrad, Georgia, Latvia, Lithuania, the Ukraine, Byelorussia, Moldavia, and even Tashkent, Bukhara, the Urals, and Siberia.

Heartened by this, by the outcry over the Leningrad trial, and by the Letter of the 39, Jewish activists planned a sit-in for February 24, 1971, at the Reception Center of the Presidium of the USSR Supreme Soviet. Twenty-four Jews submitted a statement signed by thirty-two people, raising a series of questions concerning the right of emigration and the procedures followed by the government. They demanded an audience. For six hours, the Jews sat and were told they could not be received since no members of the Presidium were available. At 5 p.m., the reception room closed and cleaners appeared. The Jews refused to leave. The administrator of the office, A. S. Dumin, demanded that they go but later asked them to nominate a representative to negotiate for them. They refused to budge. At 7:30 p.m., Dumin returned to announce that the Presidium would consider their questions and give reasoned answers by March 1. The group dispersed. No one was arrested. On March 1, government officials, including the OVIR head, received the original thirty-two signatories, augmented by eight more people. Over one hundred Jews waited outside. An official reply assured them that the question of emigration would be considered for each person individually; OVIR would assist in obtaining *kharakteristikas* (references) from places of employment, and applications could be submitted without this requirement. Furthermore, the authorities would investigate why the post office was remiss in delivering *vizovs* that had been sent to applicants and application forms that had been mailed to them. Another crisis had passed without incident.

The hunger strike is a political action technique that Soviet dissidents utilize extensively. In a country that has known periods of extreme deprivation and food shortage, it is a particularly dramatic device. On March 10, 1971, one hundred fifty-six Jewish activists from eight cities went to the Presidium to dramatize, in a way that would secure international attention, the refusal of Soviet authorities to permit emigration. (Fifty-six of them came from Riga, where ten days earlier they had demonstrated before the Latvian Council of Ministers.) They assembled in the reception room and delivered a document to the Secretariat demanding an audience. When no conference was scheduled, they all signed a statement declaring a hunger strike in protest "against our forcible detention on the territory of the USSR." That afternoon, Western correspondents came to interview them but were removed. At 5 p.m., the room was darkened and the Jews were asked to leave. They remained at benches along the walls. Various officials engaged them in heated exchanges, but they did not move. Then they began to read aloud from the Old Testament Book of Exodus. At 7 p.m., the lights went on again, and a police commandant ordered them to leave. No one stirred. At 7:30 p.m., 450 helmeted police entered the room. They cordoned off the demonstrators in small groups and began moving them from the benches. The lieutenant general of the Moscow police entered and gave the Jews two minutes to leave or face "the full severity of Soviet law." Resistance seemed pointless. The group left, but some immediately telegraphed President Podgorny that the hunger strike would continue.

The next day, they reassembled at the Presidium, but after delivering a statement, marched through the streets to the Ministry of Interior. There they rejected offers of reception with officials on an individual basis and insisted that the entire delegation be seen. After a protracted argument, including various counterproposals and their insistence that they see Colonel General Nikolai Shchelokov, the minister of interior affairs, he appeared. He spoke at length to the group, answered questions, and promised strict adherence to "Socialist legality." He also promised that a special representative would be appointed to examine each rejection, but he maintained that there could be no principle of free emigration. "We must decide the fate of each one separately. We cannot permit a mass emigration to a country at war with our Arab friends. Policy and state principles are more important than individuals." Other high officials from OVIR and the KGB spoke to the group. At 4 p.m. on March 11, they disbanded and none was arrested. They had won an unprecedented victory. That month, more than a thousand Jews were permitted to leave, and by that summer, most of the strikers also received permission.

On March 25, 100 Moscow Jews again went to the Presidium and tendered a petition signed by 213 persons demanding that the Jews held without bail in Leningrad, Riga, Kishinev, Odessa, and Sverdlovsk be released or that open trials be held at once. Having been told that this issue was within Procurator-General Rudenko's jurisdiction, forty-nine of the group went to his office where, after being politely received, they waited two hours and then discovered that the door was locked. Two more hours passed. The door opened and a group of police entered followed by a psychiatrist known for certifying political dissidents as insane. The police forcibly led the Jews from the room into waiting police vans and ambulances manned by husky orderlies. Several were taken to psychiatric hospitals, but most were placed in a drunk tank in the central jail, where they were kept overnight and denied telephone facilities and food. Many were interrogated that night or the following morning. The women in the group were fined and the men were held in detention a number of days. Ten of their leaders were given a fifteen-day administrative sentence for "hooliganism." In prison, eight of the men went on a hunger strike that lasted for twelve days. The other two fasted the entire time. One, Mikhail Zand, was carried from the jail on a stretcher. Among those who were sent to a psychiatric hospital, one, a distinguished, non-Jewish dissident painter, Yury Titov, remained incarcerated for months.

The demonstrations had emboldened the activists. After March 1971, there were few intervals when they did not undertake some form of overt, public protest. There were individual hunger strikes by particularly aggrieved persons. At times, large delegations of Jews from other republics would come to Moscow to press their demands by sit-down strikes or by hunger strikes at party headquarters, government offices, or the post office, and always accompanied by petitions and appeals. During June and July 1971, delegations from Georgia, Latvia, and Lithuania, often supported by similar action by their colleagues at home, engaged in at least a dozen demonstrations. Many filled the drunk tanks; many received administrative sentences. The groups were frequently detained or sent back by bus or train to their communities, under guard. Some were held at airports and train stations and prevented from leaving for Moscow. Still the protests continued, and Moscow was their focal point.

In Moscow, a new group of leaders developed who were to provide continuity and endurance during the years ahead. By the early summer of 1971, most of the prominent earlier activists had been given permission to leave or were in prison. In some cities, their replacement was a problem, but in Moscow, with its large Jewish population, there were many articulate, vigorous people—in particular, highly trained engineers and scientists who, on the ground that they had participated in work involving secret, classified material, were denied exit visas and prevented from leaving for a period of time ranging from two to five years. Having been demoted or lost their jobs, these talented, highly educated, bitterly frustrated individuals devoted their energies and talents to the movement.

Vladimir Slepak has been prominent among those involved in virtually all important Jewish activity since early 1970. Born in Moscow in 1927, he is a bulky, bearded man with a warmth, intensity, and integrity that have won him the respect of the diverse elements that make up the Jewish movement. After receiving a degree in radio-electronic engineering from the Aviation Institute, Slepak worked in the planning and use of control equipment for TV tubes for seventeen years and became the chief of laboratory at the Scientific Institute for TV Research, where his job was the development of electronic impulse apparatus. During that time, he signed a conventional classification agreement. But it was from his later position at the Geophysics Trust that he was discharged in March 1970 when he requested the character reference that was to accompany his emigration application. Although he later secured other employment in planning nuclear magnetic resonance, he has not worked regularly since September 1971.

Slepak's numerous applications to OVIR were denied on the ground of his having been involved in "secret work." Meanwhile, he signed most of the important petitions, beginning with the Letter of the 39, and was jailed after participating in the major demonstrations. The KGB searched his apartment on June 15, 1970 and interrogated him constantly in connection with most of the political cases during the three years after that. Slepak is a marked man. His wife, Maria, a highly trained radiologist, has also been unemployable since 1971, although her medical skills are in great demand. She and their eldest son, Aleksandr, born in 1951, a former laboratory worker at the Psychiatric Institute, have participated with Slepak in his activities and, like him, have been constantly harassed and interrogated. In February 1972, the authorities threatened Slepak with a criminal charge of parasitism, despite the fact that it was they who forced him out of his last job at the Institute of Organic Chemistry of the Russian Academy and despite his continued self-employment tutoring physics and mathematics. He was assigned to work as a porter at Moscow Concrete Factory 23, but this directive was reversed under appeal. Although he has spent substantial periods of time in jail, been the object of press vilification, and been labeled a traitor and threatened consistently with long-term imprisonment, Slepak remains a stalwart leader and example to the movement. He signs petitions, leads demonstrations, speaks to foreign newsmen and tourists, telephones and writes to outside contacts, and appears at the Moscow synagogue on Sabbath afternoons when Jews maintain their window to the West by their physical presence.

Slepak's friend Viktor Polsky has been equally indomitable. Born in Moscow three years after Slepak, Polsky studied physics and engineering and worked for eleven years in the same plant as Slepak. After receiving his doctorate in photo electronics, he taught at the Institute for Energetics before becoming chief of a laboratory doing research in nondestructive tension. During those years he also signed the routine secret work form. After applying to go to Israel, he was demoted, then forced to resign his position. Neither he nor his wife, Elena, an electrical engineer formerly employed at the Institute for Communication Research, has had regular employment since early 1971. Polsky is a determined red-headed, trim-bearded man, with blue eyes that peer from rimless glasses. He writes and speaks crisply and asserts his authority forcefully. As early as January 14, 1970, Polsky sent an open, critical letter to *Pravda* in response to a group of letters from "loyal" Jews condemning Israel:

Nobody has yet succeeded in assimilating the Jews throughout the 2,000 years of their homeless history, when there was no Jewish state. This will succeed still less now, when the Jewish state exists and is a center of attraction for all Jews who have kept their national pride and dignity.

Since then, he has written or signed dozens of letters and petitions. Like other veteran movement leaders, he has been involved in every form of political action and has been repeatedly arrested, imprisoned, questioned, kept under surveillance, and harassed. But Polsky has neither faltered nor equivocated.

For as long as four years, Slepak, Polsky, and other seasoned activists —Vladimir Prestin, a 39-year-old electrical engineer; Pavel Abramovich, a 34-year-old radio engineer; and, in Moscow alone, some hundred others, each distinguished in his field—have, on the grounds of "internal security" or "state interest," been refused exit visas. Even men as internationally renowned in science as Venyamin Levich, a 50-year-old member of the Academy of Science and a world-famous specialist in theoretical physical chemistry; Aleksandr Lerner, a 60-year-old professor of cybernetics formerly at the Institute of Control of the Academy of Science; David Azbel, 62, a professor of chemistry; and Aleksandr Voronel, a former professor of physics and head of department at the Research Institute for Physical Measurements, have been unemployed and refused exit permission, yet others inexplicably have been permitted to leave.

Typical of the techniques used by the Moscow group was a two-week hunger strike conducted in June 1973 by seven scientists in the apartment of Aleksandr Lunts, a 49-year-old mathematician and specialist in medical cybernetics, who was formerly at the Institute of Electronic Computers. Remaining in constant telephone communication with the West throughout their fast, the men issued statements, saw foreign newsmen, and explained the reasons for their action. The youngest participant, Anatoly Libgober, 24, formerly a graduate student in abstract mathematics, received his exit visa during the hunger strike, which was terminated after appeals from prominent persons in the West. By October 1973, two of the other hunger strikers also were permitted to leave.

Jewish activists cannot always agree on tactics. They must try to guess the Kremlin's next move and assess Israel's role and the responses

of Western governments, most notably the United States, in a period
of "détente." They must weigh media interest and Jewish community
morale and, above all, take advantage of the main chance when it
presents itself. Sometimes there is bitter acrimony within the movement.
Rather than indulging in the Russian penchant for philosophic generalizations, the Jewish leaders generally have learned to focus on individual cases in Western-media style. Some, including Slepak, have
noted that this tactic, which has been utilized "in order not to give
Soviet authorities the opportunity to create a 'global answer' by some
device like the 'education tax' operation," has its dangers.* Some particularly skillful and prominent activists, writes Slepak—persons "who
have the means, the opportunity, and the energy for making self-publicity
a full-time job—are constantly in the public eye, and the outside world
concentrates on them to the exclusion of the general issue. By granting
permission to leave to a deliberately blown-up person, the authorities
can, at low cost, obtain a period of euphoria in the West and crush
those left behind." It is not surprising that such fears exist and are the
subject of constant argumentation.

When a few democrats or Crimean Tatars raise banners of futile
protest in Red Square, or if one of them immolates himself in solitary
fashion, they do so essentially out of deep moral compulsion—because
they feel they have no choice. If their actions are publicized in the West,
so much the better—but that is not their main goal. Jewish movement
leaders, however, have insisted that their cause is most effectively
furthered by being fully and faithfully reported and responded to in the
West. They commit their acts of resistance not only out of moral conviction but also to evoke reaction and response. Of Soviet dissent movements, only the Jews have had a large, structured, well-financed, internationally distributed, strategically placed lobby in the West—world
Jewry. Yet, Soviet Jewish activists, both within and outside the USSR,
have, at times, severely criticized Western Jewish organizations for un-
responsiveness, inefficiency, inadequate commitment, and stupidity.†
The Soviet regime, however, has viewed the relationship between Soviet
Jews and the world Jewry with an anxiety bordering on paranoia. Many
Soviet citizens believe the charges of an international Zionist conspiracy

* When application of the education tax was abandoned, some in the West
saw that as a softening of the Soviet hard line.
† The facts and reasons behind this censure are so complex that they require
detailed development, which is not possible here.

which are documented in Soviet propaganda and in political trials by descriptions of the links between Soviet Jewish activists, the State of Israel, and world Jewry. The exaggerated, lurid, and at times incredible tales of conspiracy spun by Soviet mythmakers have a basic core of reality—namely, the sense of solidarity between Jews in all countries and their willingness to give time, money, and energy (and often, influence and power) to the cause of the Soviet Jews. But Soviet authorities and propagandists overstate this to so great an extent that their credibility is destroyed; and their attitude, dangerously reminiscent of Tsarist and Nazi anti-Semitism, reinforces the collective Jewish memory of pogroms and death camps and strengthens the determination of the Jews to see to it that never again will any of them, anywhere, be the victim of a holocaust.

By the summer of 1971, the outside world had become sufficiently aware that the remarkable sit-down and hunger strikes of February and March constituted a new, daring dimension of the struggle of Soviet Jewry. The original tentative, anxious response to these events was replaced by much more systematic support, much of it encouraged and stimulated by the activists who had left Russia and were now prodding and pushing the Israeli government and organized world Jewry. It was these activists and activist allies in Israel, the United States, the United Kingdom, and other Western countries who set up the telephone networks, mail, and tourist channels that reported and supported the movement. Thus, when on September 16, 1971, ninety-three Jews presented a list of demands to the Central Committee of the Communist Party, this information was quickly relayed to the West. "We demand," said the petition:

(1) that OVIR cease requiring *kharakteristikas,* which are an unnecessary burden;
(2) that the postal authorities deliver letters, packages, and *vizovs* to the addressees and without delay;
(3) that answers to requests for visas be given promptly and that there be reasoned replies;
(4) that there be no further massive extralegal persecution such as demotions, unlawful dismissals from work, and academic expulsions in violation of the Human Rights Declaration, of people who ask to emigrate to Israel;
(5) that exit permits should be granted to those submitting applications, more than a month prior to the date of exit;
(6) that a member of the Politburo receive us.

The group were told they would be received the following day, the 17th. The dissenters returned, but, unable to meet with officials of sufficient authority, they protested, and on September 20, a five-man delegation including Polsky and Boris Orlov met with a group of Soviet leaders from the Interior Ministry, OVIR, and the Party Central Committee. The meeting was lengthy, the argumentation extensive, and the concessions minimal. A full report was communicated abroad. No arrests occurred, but a little more than a month later, when ninety-two Jews again protested to the Central Committee in an operation co-ordinated with trips abroad of Kosygin and Brezhnev to Canada, Denmark, and France, all ninety-two were arrested and thrown into drunk tanks. Sixty-two were released after six hours and the rest were interrogated for several days.

Other tactics were employed. An International Congress of Surgeons, meeting in Moscow, was sent the message, "We Jews of Moscow appeal to the participants of this Congress convened to discuss important problems of the health of man." After details of their plight had been described, the message continued: "The cancer of prejudice has not been cured in the USSR. We ask you all to lift your voices in defense of the rights of Soviet Jews to return to their historic homeland." Some delegates were contacted, and Yuli Nudelman, a Moscow physician, was arrested.

On Rosh Hashanah, Simchat Torah, and other Jewish holidays, large crowds gathered outside the synagogue. When some of the participants were arrested, others marched and signed petitions protesting against police brutality.

International Human Rights Day, celebrated each December 10 by member nations in commemoration of the UN adoption of the Declaration of Human Rights, is not recognized in the USSR. When a large number of Jews went to the UN Information Center in Moscow on December 10, 1971, to deliver a petition asking assistance in enforcing their right to leave, all were arrested. Similarly, because the authorities were highly sensitive to contacts by Soviet citizens with foreign officials, the KGB detained persons who demonstrated outside embassies or who tried to deliver petitions to official representatives of foreign governments.

No other event elicited as much activity as the news that President Richard M. Nixon would visit the USSR in the spring of 1972. As soon as his visit was officially announced, people from virtually every Jewish center in the Soviet Union began sending detailed letters to the president—pathetic in their confidence that the president would hear, respond, and intervene in their behalf and in support of principles of human rights that the United States represented for them. Requesting individual and collective audience with him, they advised the president that "we are convinced that your visit will not accomplish its aim if, in your negotiations with the government of the USSR, you do not touch upon the question of the unhindered emigration of Jews from the USSR to Israel." Women appealed to Mrs. Nixon. Relatives of prisoners implored the president to intervene in behalf of their loved ones. Detailed accounts were sent of recent arrests, police violence, and anti-Semitic outbreaks at synagogues in Kiev and Moscow, and similar interferences with memorial services at Babi Yar and Rumbuli.

Shortly before President Nixon's arrival, Polsky, Slepak, Prestin, Abramovich, Lerner, and Roman Rutman issued a statement to the press:

> In order to facilitate contacts with the president or members of his delegation, we, Jews signing this letter, scientists and specialists living in Moscow and long unsuccessful in obtaining permission to emigrate to Israel, have formed an information committee for the occasion of the president's visit. We are ready to apprise him objectively concerning the situation of the Jews mentioned above so that the representation to the president on this question may be based on facts and correct data.

While Soviet Jews were feverishly preparing for the Nixon visit, Soviet authorities were making other preparations. According to *The White Book of Exodus:**

> Lists of Jews to be sent to military camps were confirmed, prison locations were chosen and cells prepared for Jews who were to be kept silent during the visit with disregard for laws, declarations, and conventions. Lists were checked of the telephones that were to be disconnected during the president's visit.

* *The White Book of Exodus* is a 54-page *samizdat* document containing dozens of letters of appeal relating to President Nixon's visit as well as newspaper reports, eyewitness accounts, descriptions of court actions, and a dramatic commentary, compiled and edited by a group of Moscow activists in the late summer and fall of 1972 and smuggled to the West in the spring of 1973. The compilers noted that the book was "devoted to the difficult and dramatic period of *aliyah* [emigration], when the hope of many Soviet Jews seeking repatriation to Israel was linked with the visit to the USSR of the president of the U.S.A."

Special cars were provided around the clock for surveillance of the apartments of Jews. . . . Crowds of agents openly shadowed Jews and their wives. . . .

In the second half of April and the beginning of May, activists who had applied for exit visas to Israel were summoned to the office of military registration and enlistment. . . .

Most of the call-ups were for retraining exercises at military camps. Since military instruction of persons leaving for Israel can hardly be included among the aims of the Soviet Army, most of those summoned refused to report to the military offices. They perceived in the call-up to military service a device to expose them to military secrets and thereby create a pretext for denial of exit permits as well as a means for removing them from Moscow in the period of May-June 1972—for President Nixon's visit. . . .

All those summoned sent written statements of refusal to engage in military service. Militia and military officers searched day and night for the men who had been called up, breaking into their apartments and into those of their relatives and acquaintances.

Many were asked to sign statements pledging that they would not commit "anti-public actions" during the visit. Most refused. Beginning May 19, telephones were disconnected. All of these repressive steps were communicated to Mr. Nixon. Three days before he arrived, a full report was delivered to the U.S. Embassy in Moscow. On May 22, the president arrived. Early on the morning before, without explanation or charges, police officers took Slepak, Polsky, Orlov, Rutman, and others from their apartments to prisons in towns many kilometers from the capital. They were held incommunicado until after President Nixon left the country and then were released with no explanation other than that their confinement had been preventive. Others, such as Prestin, were arrested on the street, charged with offenses such as "pestering a woman," and given fifteen days' imprisonment. Further, "In railway stations and airports, militia and agents of the KGB challenged Jewish-looking people traveling to Moscow. In some cases, tickets were not sold to Jews. In one instance, a gentile husband was permitted to take a plane, leaving his Jewish wife in the airport. The president's visit was going according to plan." The Soviet press reported that at an official banquet at the Kremlin, Mr. Nixon said, "We have learned to respect each other. . . . Let us raise our glasses." And the editors of *The White Book* noted: "The president of the great democratic country, after a hard day of negotiations, made a touching speech at the banquet about the triumph of the principles of peace and justice. We imagined how everybody nodded his head."

Mrs. Nixon visited schools and subway stations, Moscow University, the circus, and the GUM department store. "Letters addressed to the president's wife continued to arrive," says *The White Book*. "Certainly the people's belief in good is inexhaustible." Among the letters was one from Maria Slepak describing how her husband and eldest son had been seized and taken away without a word. Their telephone had been disconnected. KGB cars shadowed her every move and five automobiles waited outside her apartment.

On May 30, President and Mrs. Nixon concluded their official visit. "The prisoners of Cell No. 4 of the Kolomna prison ended their hunger strike of protest." Those preventively detained were released. Telephones remained disconnected. The Voice of America and Radio Liberty remained jammed as they had been for the entire visit. All of this was made known to the president. To this date, there is no indication that he ever raised any question with Soviet leaders.

Demonstrations and arrests continued. When sit-down protests over the education tax imposed in August 1972 took place, arrests occurred. When Israeli athletes were murdered in Munich by Arab guerrillas, protests outside the Lebanese Embassy in Moscow resulted in the detention of some thirty persons, including Andrei Sakharov. Picnic celebrations of the twenty-fifth anniversary of Israeli independence resulted in the arrest of the participants. Each reprisal stimulated a new response; each response triggered a new reprisal. Replacing their husbands and sons who were in detention, or expressing their own strong convictions, women began conducting sit-down protests and hunger strikes. They, too, were arrested. In the two-year period from the summer of 1971 to the summer of 1973, over one hundred demonstrations involving some thousands of Jews took place. Many hundreds were arrested and served time in jail totaling thousands of days. Some activists spent almost as much time in jail as out. Remarkably, though, no political trials resulted from these demonstrations, and except for a hard core of scientists and a few public personages, most activists ultimately secured permission to leave for Israel. It was as if a gray area of permissiveness was tolerated—if the actor was prepared to pay the price of police confrontation and up to fifteen days in jail.

Of all the confrontation tactics, none was as devastating and indigestible to the Kremlin as the renunciation of Soviet citizenship by Jews and the assumption by many, after the spring of 1971, of Israeli citizenship. To a state as ideological in its rhetoric as the Soviet Union, the very intention of seeking to leave the workers' paradise was an affront. For large numbers of people to publicize such a desire was humiliating and for them to renounce their Soviet nationality was intolerable. It bespoke more eloquently than boxcars full of glowing propaganda the failure of the highly vaunted Soviet nationalities policy and the inability of the society to produce the level of contentment that was implicit in its stated utopian goals. Such persons must be perverted malcontents, seduced and deluded by bourgeois blandishments. The failure was theirs, not that of the Communist state. For such people to prefer the nationality of a reviled, degenerate enemy like Israel aggravated the indignity to the point of national disgrace. Yet a veritable epidemic of such acts occurred.

The first publicly known case of Jewish renunciation of Soviet citizenship was that of the Moscow writer Vitold Kapshitser, on May 31, 1967, the day before the outbreak of the Six-Day War. The next was that of young Yasha Kazakov two weeks later. Neither act became widely known until Kazakov publicly announced his defiance almost a year later. But then the idea began to spread slowly. In Riga, Ruta Aleksandrovich smuggled out a renunciation to Israel through a departing friend, Ephraim Tsal. David Drabkin in Moscow and Mendel Gordin in Riga did the same. In the spring of 1969, Ruta's aunt, Leah Slovin, delivered the renunciation to Shaul Avigur, then the head of the Israeli government office responsible for all matters concerning Soviet Jewry, but Avigur refused to publicize the statement. Leah then wrote Avigur concerning Ruta: "Her renunciation of Soviet citizenship was thought through thoroughly. The example of Yasha Kazakov confirms that such renunciations can be effective. The sad experience of my friends Drabkin and Gordin when their declaration of renunciation could not be published in the world press because of the position of the Israeli Ministry of Foreign Affairs makes me address you." She asked Avigur what Israel would do if Ruta sent her renunciation to the Supreme Soviet. "Will you cooperate or at least not hinder the publication of her renunciation in the world press?" Avigur refused to answer. Leah found an attorney prepared to attempt a presentation of the issue to the World Court. She wrote to the Israeli Foreign Ministry and to Avigur asking for the text of Gordin's renunciation which they were known to have. She was refused although she asserted that "the attempt to invoke an international law to help people who renounce their Soviet citizenship on the ground of their desire to live in Israel can substantially aid Gordin and can inspire the desired response in the whole world and Soviet Jewry."

Despite the danger of reprisals from the Soviet regime and the cold, censorial silence of the Israeli authorities, Soviet Jews continued to renounce. In February 1970, Dora Koliaditskaya brought a law suit in Moscow, with the assistance of Boris Tsukerman and Valery Chalidze, seeking the right to change her residence and nationality to that of her husband who lived in Israel. The court rejected her application. A few months later, ten Kiev activists, including Shmurak and Gerenrot, petitioned Prime Minister Golda Meir to grant them Israeli citizenship. "Having made this decision, we thus give you the right to defend our interests and to undertake any measures directed at our speediest departure to Israel." There was no response, but an Israeli government spokesman stated that citizenship could be granted only when an immigrant to Israel was physically present in Israel. In the USSR, some Jews countered by noting that once they applied to leave and received permission, their Soviet citizenship was taken and they thus became stateless. Some, like Aron Bogdanovsky of Kharkov, argued prior to the first Leningrad trial that the accusation of treason against the defendants was groundless since those Jews accused were not Soviet citizens under the USSR Citizenship Law of 1938.

The legal confusion over citizenship status was an inevitable consequence of unique provisions in both Soviet and Israeli nationality law, but the real motivating force for the striving by Soviet Jews to shed USSR nationality and adopt that of Israel was an intense expression of their political alienation from the Soviet Union coupled with their powerful identification with Israel. Since Article 15 of the Universal Declaration of Human Rights provided that no one should be "denied the right to change his nationality," they felt justified in urging upon the Israeli government the same grant of citizenship it made to all Jews emigrating to that country under Israel's Law of Return, arguing with some persuasiveness that they should not be discriminated against since their inability to be present physically in the country was not the result of their lack of intent. The poignancy of their position was made more dramatic at the time of the Leningrad trial in December 1970.

Although the Israeli government was unsympathetic to these appeals from the USSR, their lobbyists in Israel found a supporter in Dr. Binyamin Halevi, a Knesset member and former Supreme Court Justice. On December 28, 1970, he introduced a bill permitting the government

to grant citizenship to a person otherwise entitled who was unable to
secure citizenship because his emigration to Israel was prevented despite
his desire to settle in the country. After strong initial opposition, Mrs.
Meir dropped her objections and an amendment to Israel's Nationality
Law incorporating these concepts was adopted on May 17, 1971. Government support of the measure was mustered by agitation in the USSR
itself, such as a cable made public by seventeen Moscow Jews who
stated, "We are relinquishing the citizenship of a country which forcibly
detains us because we consider ourselves citizens of a country which
is our historic and national homeland. Israel is a country whose citizenship we seek, while Soviet citizenship is something thrust upon us, and
we shall not remain citizens by force."

Once the new law became known in the USSR, a flood of applications
was sent by telephone, letter, and word of mouth. The Israeli authorities moved slowly, acknowledging none of the requests and refusing to make public the names of any persons to whom the grant was
given. Applications from prominent activists such as Mikhail Zand were
expedited with assistance from people in Israel, but for most, the waiting was protracted and, since they had generally simultaneously renounced Soviet nationality, uncertainty about their status was painful.
Questions about the Israeli government's conduct respecting citizenship
grants engendered a bitter controversy in the USSR and in Israel. In
November 1971, Knesset member Halevi filed formal parliamentary
inquiries about the matter. On December 9, the government conceded
that only fifty-eight citizenship certificates had been issued, although by
then many hundreds of Soviet activists had requested citizenship.

On December 19, it was learned that the defendants sentenced in
the various Jewish political trials, who were collectively referred to as
"prisoners of conscience," were to begin a hunger strike on December
24 (the first anniversary of the Leningrad death sentences), renouncing
Soviet citizenship and requesting a grant of Israeli nationality. However
disconcerting this would be to the Russian camp authorities, its effect
in Israel was tantamount to a cabinet crisis. At least two of the prisoners
of conscience, Yury Fedorov and Aleksei Murzhenko, were not Jews,
and several others had antecedents that, in terms of a religious definition
of their Jewishness, were questionable. Since the grant of citizenship, if
made at all, had to be confined to persons who were "Jews" within the
meaning of the Nationality Law, the Israeli government could not consider grants to "non-Jews" or in questionable cases without directly

conflicting with the religious bloc. Furthermore, some of the well-publicized prisoners had requested citizenship long before, and their hunger strike could be seen as a reproach to the government of Israel as well as to the USSR. The government issued an appropriately conciliatory and evasive statement, but on December 24, the hunger strike began and friends in Jerusalem simultaneously released a full statement from the prisoners. Among other things, they demanded "official registration of our Israeli citizenship, in connection with which we have today sent applications to the Presidium of the Supreme Soviet of the USSR and to the Embassy of the Netherlands. Since from now on we consider ourselves Israeli subjects, and as we do not wish to be together with people who stained themselves with Jewish blood in the years of the Second World War, we demand to be transferred into a camp for foreign subjects." The appeal's first three signatories were Kuznetsov, Fedorov, and Murzhenko. Among the others who signed were defendants from the Ryazan and Bendery proceedings who had not been sentenced in "Zionist" trials and whose names and plights had not been released to the public by Israeli authorities. When the prisoners' statement was released in Israel, those names were excised from the press release.

As if this were not trouble enough for Israel, the Netherlands Embassy in Moscow, representing Israel's interests in the USSR, began to be inundated with requests for certificates of Israeli citizenship for those who believed the grant had been made, for assistance from those who wished to apply, and for diplomatic protection from those who already held Israeli citizenship. Since no lists were ever published indicating what applications had been received or granted, the Dutch could not easily be criticized for their reluctance to become involved in the process. The matter became particularly heated and the activists unusually frustrated by the spring of 1972, when many who had requested citizenship almost a year before had still received no word, let alone the precious certificates.

One of the methods of repressing the Jewish movement was for Soviet military authorities to induct activists into the Red Army. Most had already served, having been officers, technically subject to recall, but only when their entire unit was recalled. Among those who received induction notices were younger scientists like Gavriel Shapiro, Mark Nashpits, Viktor Yakhot, Mikhail Kliachkin, and Pavel Abramovich (who, at 33, was considerably older than the others). The poet David Markish (son of the famed Yiddish poet Perets Markish, who had been murdered on August 15, 1952) was another activist harassed in this fashion. These men, and dozens of others, had renounced Soviet citizenship and claimed Israeli citizenship—and thus invulnerability from the Soviet draft. But they had no proof that Israel had granted them citizenship. Their friends in Israel urgently requested Prime Minister Meir and Knesset leaders that their Israeli citizenship be confirmed by public announcement, including broadcast over Kol Israel, with specification of the numbers of the citizenship certificates. They further asked the Israeli government to "transmit these certificates to the recipients" so that "they may be given the full protection of the state." But despite the urgency, no compliance with the requests occurred. The Israeli Foreign Office responded to inquiry from Knesset members by asserting that since the Soviet Union would not acknowledge the grants of Israeli citizenship, there was no point in exacerbating the situation by testing the issue. The only concession it would make was to send copies of the certificates, when granted, to the recipients in the USSR, by registered mail. But almost no one ever received them when sent in this manner.

In mid-June 1972, when Shapiro and Nashpits were arrested in Moscow for failing to report for military service, their supporters demanded that, since they were Israeli citizens, Israel should ask the Netherlands Embassy to defend their interests or at least to make official inquiry about them as it would for any other Dutch or Israeli citizen who was arrested. But the Israeli government refused to ask the Dutch to assist. By then, more than a year after the law had been passed, only ninety-two Soviet Jews had been granted Israeli citizenship although many more had applied. The arrest of three Kharkov activists at the end of June 1972 led to a request for the protection and visit of the Netherlands consul, since those arrested had been granted Israeli citizenship. When there was no response, Aron Bogdanovsky stated, "My friends and I are weighing presenting legal charges against the prime minister of Israel and her ministers for abandoning our brothers, who are in detention in the USSR and who hold Israeli citizenship." Israel failed to act, but the Kharkov detainees were released promptly. Shapiro and Nashpits, who were formally charged under Article 198-1 with "evasion of training courses or musters," secured vigorous overseas support. Shapiro had married a U.S. citizen,

Judy Silver, on June 8, 1972, after a brief, tumultuous courtship that was widely reported in America. Urging intervention, the energetic new Mrs. Shapiro promptly and personally pleaded the case to journalists and to government leaders in a number of countries. Meanwhile, the two defendants were tried, and they pleaded, among other defenses, that they held Israeli citizenship and were no longer Soviet citizens; but neither was assisted by Israel or the Netherlands Embassy in securing a certificate to be used in evidence. Each received a one-year sentence of corrective labor (but without imprisonment) and a fine. Shapiro's term was commuted on October 23, 1972 and he was permitted to go to Israel with his bride. (Not long afterward, the couple were reported to be separated.) Nashpits was also released from prison, before his full term expired, but he was not permitted to leave the country.

The greatest collective act of renunciation of Soviet citizenship occurred in September 1972, at the time of the Munich Olympic massacre, when more than one hundred Moscow Jews sent their renunciations of citizenship to the Supreme Soviet in protest against the USSR's failure to condemn the murder of Israeli athletes and police brutality toward those who demonstrated at the Lebanese Embassy in Moscow.

The political effectiveness of the citizenship issue is difficult to measure. Soviet Jews regarded it as a major confrontation device and justified it under both international and Soviet law and practice. Israel, after recognizing the right by statutory amendment, was markedly unenthusiastic about its utilization. Soviet authorities publicly ignored the issue and refused comment. But all adults leaving the USSR after September 20, 1970 for "capitalist countries" were required to pay 500 rubles for compulsory citizenship renunciation. Thus, there was official involvement in the citizenship issue—and the issue became one of more than academic interest, since a Jewish couple securing permission to go to Israel had to pay 1,000 rubles for shedding an undesired Soviet nationality as a precondition to departure.

By the summer of 1973, when several hundred Jewish emigrants to Israel had asked to return to the USSR, the Soviet press took the opportunity to state that its nationality could not be taken lightly: "USSR citizenship is not membership in a table tennis club that may be acquired, surrendered, and reacquired at will." In August 1973 it was reported that the Soviet nationality law would be amended and clarified.

Of all the forms of protest emanating from the Jewish movement, perhaps the most remarkable came from the prison camps. Most Jewish prisoners of conscience were originally sent to camps in the Potma area, about 500 kilometers east of Moscow. What life was like for them has been detailed in documents smuggled out of confinement and in statements some of them made after they were released. A characteristic description is found in an appeal on behalf of those still confined, by seven who are now in Israel (Ruta Aleksandrovich, Arkady Voloshin, Lilia Ontman, Raiza Palatnik, Lazar Trakhtenberg, Mikhail Shepshelovich, and Hillel Shur):

> We sat behind barbed wire only for one or two years, but even during this relatively short term we felt that we were being physically extinguished. Hard labor, terrible food, the lack of even the most elementary medical assistance, as well as systematic punishments in the form of being transferred to a punishment cell or deprivation of food, were sufficient to bring a healthy prisoner to a state of complete physical exhaustion and lead a sick one to his grave. Proof of this is the death of Yury Galanskov in a Mordovian camp. He was unable to withstand the conditions under which he was held for almost six years, even though he had only one more year to serve. At the age of 33, at the height of his strength, he died because he had not been given basic medical aid.
>
> The terrible conditions of life, the slave labor, and inhuman punishments, however, do not fully describe the tragic situation of Jews who are political prisoners. There is also anti-Semitic hounding of people. Taunts by KGB agents and guards, blows and insults from prisoners who had collaborated with the Nazis, place the prisoners of Zion in a particularly difficult situation. The imprisoned Jews can complain only to the local administration; their complaints do not leave the camp without first being scrutinized by the local officials. And these officials, themselves filled with zoological anti-Semitism, punish the victim of the crime and not the pogromists. In their attitude to the Jews, there is full harmony between the camp administration and the Nazis. We are certain that the prison officials and the convicted collaborationists feel free to express their base instincts because anti-Semitism is encouraged by the higher authorities.
>
> The Soviet regime has learned that the convicted Jews continue their struggle for their right to go to Israel even in the camps. It was decided to "break these people," and intolerable conditions of life and of work were created for them. The Soviet authorities and the camp administration do everything possible to conceal from the public the true situation of the prisoners of Zion, keeping them in a state of complete isolation and conducting their dark deeds behind an iron curtain that has been erected around the concentration camps. It has

already become a rule that imprisoned Jews are constantly deprived of visits due to them in accordance with Soviet laws so as to exclude the possibility of any information about their situation seeping out.

In spite of the efforts to seal off news of the camps, word of the condition of the prisoners did reach the West. A few visitors were allowed, and despite the close guarding, some were able to communicate what their loved ones told them. Written messages and even *samizdat* documents were sometimes smuggled through the barbed wire. Even the later transfer of many of the prisoners to camps in the more isolated area of Perm failed to stop the leakage of information. We know that the 1971 hunger strike at Potma beginning on the anniversary of the Leningrad convictions was repeated in 1972 at both Potma and Perm. We know that, although they are forbidden to do so, the prisoners have continued to study Hebrew in *ulpanim* organized in the barracks and that they study Jewish history and culture from smuggled *samizdat* books. We know that they manage to celebrate the Jewish holidays, build a *sukkah*, find substitutes for a Passover ceremony. We know that some prisoners attempt to wear a *kipah* in their dormitories. We also know of anti-Semitic incidents involving guards, some of which involve physical brutality, and that there are protests to the authorities about such abuses and that some of these protests, like other *samizdat* documents, are smuggled out of the camps. Characteristic was an appeal to the UN by Lassal Kaminsky, Arkady Shpilberg, Lev Korenblit, Mikhail Korenblit, Arkady Voloshin, and Lazar Trakhtenberg, which reads, in part, as follows:

> On the morning of August 4, 1972, prisoners at Camp No. 17 of the Dubrovlag, when they were taken out to work, unwittingly witnessed a scene of characteristic cruelty. The prison guards, led by Captain Bakaykin, dragged a prisoner, Hillel Shur, out of the watch-house and pushed him into a special car. His hands were handcuffed behind his back and on his face the white traces of lime could be seen. . . .
>
> Jews are detained with Nazis who occupy all the leading posts in the concentration camps. It is a paradox that the same persons who killed our relatives during the war against the Nazis are now again giving us orders—this time in Soviet camps. Is this not an affront to the memory of the Soviet Jews massacred by the Nazis?
>
> The camp administration, with the full support of higher authorities, creates intolerable conditions for the Jews by a wide variety of methods. These include sending people to particularly hard labor without taking into consideration their state of health, denying dietetic food to the sick, and depriving them of the possibility of buying

even that small quantity of products a prisoner is allowed under camp regulations. . . . Even the wall newspaper is used for hounding Jews. In it are anti-Semitic articles and remarks of the Nazi servants. Fault finding is intensified and punishments become more frequent and harsher. The cruelest measures are used, such as putting people into punitive isolation cells and placing them on punitive rations which physically undermine the health of the prisoners.

The following are only a few examples of recent cases: On July 9, twelve Jews were transferred to newly established political camps in the northern Urals under severe climatic conditions. During a search that preceded this, a textbook for learning Hebrew, *Mori,* and a Pevsner dictionary were confiscated from Grilius and Mendelevich under the pretext that these were foreign publications. In this way, Jews are deprived of the possibility of studying their own language or of having a Jewish calendar; neither Hebrew textbooks nor calendars had ever been published by the Soviet state.

When Levit, Shpilberg, and Kirzhner were in Dubrovlag hospital in November 1971, the director of the operative unit of Zone No. 3, in which the hospital is also included, stated that he would not allow correspondence with relatives in the Yiddish language . . . six letters in Yiddish from Trakhtenberg's wife have been withheld under the pretext that they were being translated; a letter from Shpilberg's wife in Yiddish has been confiscated and so have been a number of other letters from relatives. It is forbidden to wear a skullcap inside a building . . .

On July 26, 1972, Trakhtenberg was put into isolation for five days because he had given up his lower sleeping berth to a former prisoner in Nazi concentration camps, Lev Korenblit, and not to a Nazi collaborator as had been demanded by Sr. Lt. Zenenko, who expressed his anti-Semitism in this manner. For the same reason, Lev Korenblit was deprived of a visit from his relatives.

For having defended Trakhtenberg and Korenblit, Arkady Voloshin was put into an isolation cell for ten days on July 31.

Shpilberg was deprived, on August 7, 1972, of the right to receive the one yearly food parcel permitted and of buying food products for a month because he had "insulted" the foreman, Kadolich, during working hours on July 28. Shpilberg's "misdemeanor" consisted of having stated that he refused to listen to anti-Semitic insults from Hitler's *"Polizei"*—foreman Kadolich and storekeeper Stepanov. . . .

Mikhail Korenblit had repeatedly asked for but not received medical assistance and, in spite of grave illness has not been sent to a hospital. On the morning of August 11, 1972, he fainted, and on the next day, Sr. Lt. Zenenko reprimanded Korenblit for "endlessly" requesting medical assistance. On Zenenko's order, Korenblit was sent, on August 14, 1972, to dig trenches.

These are only a few of the most recent examples of how the KGB and the administration of the camps treat the Jews.

What is perhaps most remarkable is the solidarity of the prisoners and their evident concern for each other. Thus, a group of her fellow-prisoners appealed to the world to free Silva Zalmanson and conducted hunger strikes on her behalf. Each such activity increased their own jeopardy. When a comrade was abused or punished, the political prisoner gave of his own meager stock of strength, or food, or hope to provide support and solace for the other. Out of degradation came courage, and out of misery came the camaraderie of the wretched. The prison camp, more than any other Soviet institution, became the training school for a domestic fraternity of the unafraid—for those who, having lost all else, would not lose their dignity and their belief in the ultimate triumph of the goals for which they suffered. If, for some brave men like Piotr Yakir and Viktor Krasin, the horror of a renewed detention, when much of their adult life had already been spent in prison, proved too much, for others, the camps steeled them and gave them courage to face any adversity. Only death or permanent departure from the country could halt a movement whose time had come.

THE RIGHT TO LEAVE

CHAPTER 22

The Jewish movement, unlike other dissident movements in the USSR, has had a single, undeviating goal—the right of Soviet Jews to leave the Soviet Union and go to Israel—and that insistence has been rewarded to an extent that would have been viewed as incomprehensible only a few years ago. An exodus to Israel has been permitted—an exodus of the last large group of Jews, other than those in the United States, left in any part of the world. In scope and political importance, the Jewish migration dwarfs that permitted for any other Soviet minority.* Yet it cannot be defined with precision, and no systematic survey of exodus experiences has been undertaken. Nevertheless, certainly fairly reliable generalizations can be made.

Despite a broad similarity of experience, there are far greater variations than one would surmise—variations in terms not only of the time when individual Jews sought to leave but also of geography. The possibilities of leaving, the administrative procedures applied, the explicit OVIR contacts, the broad community response differ sharply from one Soviet republic to another, and often between cities within a republic. People in large cities have had different experiences from Jews in villages or small towns. Depending on time or place, the character of the individual applicant also may have dictated the type of official response— his military status or the extent of his education, whether or not he was an activist or a scientist, young or old, married or single, and, if

---

* More Jews left the Soviet Union in 1972-73 than did all other Soviet citizens in the previous forty years (except for the mass deportations during World War II).

married, whether to a Jew or gentile. Throughout the entire period and irrespective of the locale, the authorities have responded with an uncertainty, ambiguity, and undependability that would not have been expected by anyone who was conditioned to the notion that something so fundamental as emigration should be subject to administrative standards and predictability, to a rule of law. In the USSR, administrative whim and caprice seem to be present far more markedly than might be anticipated elsewhere.

The Soviet Union does not release *official* statistics of the number of Jews who have left the USSR, either in gross amounts or by analytical breakdown; neither does Israel, which regards the information as subject to military censorship. Both governments "leak" information to news sources or issue politically motivated announcements to meet domestic or external political needs. Further complications are the facts that the emigration process is initiated by a *vizov* sent from abroad, that *vizovs* are not sent to individuals but to family units, and that their form does not indicate whether a *vizov* includes the recipent only, the recipient and his wife, or the recipient, his wife, and their children. Similarly, since an application to OVIR can include minor children aged 15 or under, a family of five might apply for two OVIR applications, and the children might be included with either husband or wife. Although semiofficial Israeli and Soviet releases indiscriminately mix invitations, applications, exit visas, and numbers of persons leaving or arriving, we can assume, as a rule of thumb, that one *vizov* represents 2.7 persons, on the average, and we can judge within relatively narrow ranges how many Soviet Jews have actually left.

From 1948 to the Six-Day War in 1967, about 6,000 Soviet Jews were permitted to emigrate, strictly on a family-reunion basis. That figure includes those who left during the relatively heavy migration that took place in the first five months of 1967, just prior to the Six-Day War, in response to Premier Kosygin's Paris declaration in December 1966 that "if any families wish to come together or wish to leave the Soviet Union, for them the road is open and no problem exists here." In 1967, according to the Jewish Agency, 1,412 Soviet Jews came to Israel—virtually all of them before June 5; 213 came in 1968; 3,033 in 1969, including the first group of Jewish activists; and 999 in 1970, following a repressive crackdown.*

* The Jewish Agency, a semiofficial agency created by the Israeli government, is concerned, in part, with the absorption of immigrants into Israel.

In March 1971, the Soviet government suddenly decided to let more Jews go. In the first two months of that year, it had permitted about 180 Jews to leave, but 1,025 were said to have departed in March, and subsequently, acknowledging that it had granted 1,150 visas for the first quarter of 1971, the Soviet Union stated that this figure represented 1,400 persons.* By the end of May, Israeli Prime Minister Golda Meir announced that 6,000 Jews had arrived in Israel from the USSR in the first five months of the year.† November and December 1971 witnessed a dramatic rise in emigration; 600 to 1,000 persons arrived in Israel each week. Some days, two planeloads of emigrants left the Jewish Agency-sponsored transit facility at Schönau Castle, near Vienna. In 1973, the Soviet Union belatedly acknowledged that in 1971 it had issued 10,240 exit visas, totaling 13,905 persons, almost 1,000 more than the Jewish Agency's figure of 12,923. Yet according to the UN-sponsored Inter-Governmental Committee for European Migration (ICEM), as well as newspaper reports from both Moscow and Jerusalem and totals made available to members of the Knesset, at least 15,000 Jews left the Soviet Union in 1971.

The figures for 1972, like those of 1971, also are the subject of dispute. Israeli sources stated that 31,652 Soviet Jews arrived in Israel in 1972, whereas the Soviet Union acknowledged that there were 28,000 (but also stated that 44,446 Jews left in the two-year period 1971-72). The pattern established in November-December 1971, of approximately 2,500 Jews per month, continued through 1972-73. The number was not constant; there were slow periods in the midsummer (presumably attributable to the fact that OVIR workers were on summer vacation) and high points at the end of the year (which some have attributed to OVIR's need to meet a quota and stay on the Soviet "plan"). Just before and during the U.S. presidential election of 1972, more than 4,500 Jews a month were permitted to leave.

On his visit to the United States in June 1973, Leonid Brezhnev stated that 68,000 Jews had left the USSR for Israel since 1948, and almost simultaneously, Louis Pincus, a Jewish Agency executive, stated that 62,600 Soviet Jews had arrived in Israel from the beginning of 1968 until May 31, 1973. Assuming that there were 6,000 immi-

---

* The discrepancy is typical. Were there 1,205 (180 plus 1,025) or 1,400 emigrants in the first quarter of 1971?

† But the Soviet figure for the first six months was 3,750 visas, or approximately 5,000 persons.

grants in 1948-67, the Soviet and Israeli totals differed by only 600.

Brezhnev provoked a justifiable storm, however, by asserting that OVIR had granted 95% of all Jewish applications.* How many Soviet Jews had *applied* to leave was obviously a much more sensitive issue for the Soviet government than the number who went to Israel, which was susceptible to corroboration. Israelis had only one source for determining application statistics—the number of *vizovs* that had been sent from Israel to the USSR. Here they, too, were on touchy ground because of their own inconsistent, irreconcilable figures and their policy of censoring such information. As of April 1970, Israeli sources stated that 80,000 *vizovs* had been sent, yet one year later, despite the fact that there was an enormous upsurge in the request for invitations and only comparatively few successful applicants, the official Israeli figure remained at 80,000. At the beginning of 1972, a semi-official statement indicated that 80,000 *vizovs* had been sent from Israel from July 1968 through December 1971; and in August 1972, the figure 80,000 was again released, this time designating *new vizovs*.† After the Brezhnev statement of June 1973, however, Israeli sources stated that 178,000 *vizovs* had been sent from January 1968 to the end of May 1973 and that at least 116,000 *vizov* recipients still remained in the USSR, thus belying Brezhnev's assertion that 95% of all those seeking to leave had been granted permission. When coupled with the information that 6,500 invitations had been sent in May 1973 alone, it seemed more likely that, in recent years, an average of 40,000 to 50,000 invitations have been forwarded annually. Israeli sources also insisted that 95% of those who received *vizovs* applied to OVIR. Jewish Agency sources in September 1973 placed the number of OVIR applications at 6,000 per month and the number of applicants waiting for visas at 100,000.

What is the truth? In August 1960, Golda Meir stated that 9,236 Soviet Jews had *applied* for exit visas and been rejected. By 1965, some Israeli authorities claimed that half a million Soviet Jews wished to leave for Israel. Shortly after the Kosygin speech in December 1966, sources friendly to Israel reported that 50,000 applications had been made. In the spring of 1970, Israel declared that 80,000 families com-

---

* Brezhnev's statement that out of 61,000 applications 60,200 exit visas were issued in 1972 obviously referred to the five-year period.

† At least one-third of the new *vizovs* had been sent to families with one or more persons with university training.

prising 200,000 people had applied to OVIR from the beginning of
1968 through March 1970. Some estimates in 1971 placed the number
of Jewish applicants as high as 350,000. In April 1972, it was asserted
that 7,000 applications a month were being made, yet at virtually the
same time, Soviet officials released detailed statistics claiming that
there were only 258 applicants in Moscow, 50 in Leningrad, 119 in
Kiev, and 124 in Soviet Moldavia. By May 1973, Jewish sources stated
that there were 170,000 applications and that Jews were applying at
the rate of 5,000 per month. Obviously, only OVIR knows how many
Jews have in fact applied to leave for Israel. But Soviet statements in
September 1973 that 1,300 Jews granted exit visas in the preceding
year had chosen not to emigrate are probably as reliable as Brezhnev's
statement that 95% of those who apply have their requests granted.
Since *vizovs* are sent repeatedly to the same family when permission is
not given, and since such detainees apply again and again, thus skewing
the figures, it seems likely that at least 200,000 *vizovs* had been sent
as of the end of 1973, that the overwhelming majority of those invited
had applied to OVIR, and that a substantial number of those who
have attempted to leave the USSR in recent years have been denied
permission.

Some observations by Soviet Jews are both perceptive and revealing.
In the late summer of 1972, for example, after being in Israel for many
months, Alex Feldman, a former Kiev engineer and activist leader,
wrote, in a penetrating article on the exodus called "500 Days of the
Sixth *Aliyah*":

> Statistical analysis of immigrants from the Soviet Union during the
> last eighteen months indicates a division into three distinct groupings.
> The first includes those territories that were annexed to the USSR
> prior to the outbreak of World War II, such as Lithuania, Latvia,
> western Ukraine, western Moldavia. 44.7% of all immigrants came
> from these areas. Next came Georgia, which accounted for 34.6%.
> Finally, the major population centers of the USSR—Moscow, Lenin-
> grad, the eastern Ukraine (Kiev, Kharkov, Odessa), and Byelorussia-
> Minsk—are responsible for the remaining 20.7%.
>   As we look at the situation in the first area, we get the impression
> that the authorities were interested in getting rid of the Jewish popula-
> tion. Those who applied (a new word has been added to the Russian
> language at this time—*podavanti* [appliers]) were granted exit per-
> mits rather quickly. The only exception was a small group of people

who had access to secret or sensitive matters, either in reality or according to the authorities. The annexed territories had many people with strong Zionist leanings; however, most of those have already departed. Those who are leaving now are motivated by somewhat different considerations—a desire to reunite with relatives who are already in Israel, a striving for a different life, and last but not least, a wish to keep up with friends and neighbors. One might say that the desire to leave has become the norm in these territories.

As a rule, these people have a great number of friends and relatives in Israel; they are aware of the advantages and drawbacks of various absorption centers, and they know what things are worth taking and what should be left behind. It is obvious, therefore, that they are quite sensitive to the negative manifestations within the absorption process. The pace of *aliyah* from this sector will be determined by the speed and success of the solutions of absorption problems in Israel.

The same problems will strongly influence the *aliyah* from Georgia, as well as the recently initiated modest movement of Jews from Bukhara. One of the principal reasons for the exodus of Jews from Georgia today is the existence of strong familial-patriarchal ties between the Georgian Jews in Israel and the Georgian Jews in Georgia.

The second reason is the acute deterioration of relations between Georgians and Jews. The absorption of Georgian Jews is further complicated by their social level. The Georgian Jews are primarily employed in the service fields. In Israel these professions—including tailors, shoemakers, barbers, drivers—are not greatly needed. When this difficulty is related to the natural desire of the Georgian Jews to live together, it increases and magnifies the already existing basic difficulties of the absorption process.

Thus, in summing up, one might say that in the two groupings discussed above, the majority of Jews wish to leave, and the majority of applicants receive exit permits.

The situation is somewhat different in the third grouping. Although a much smaller number succeeded in leaving, their departure proved the possibility of emigration to many thousands. However, the main point is simply that, for the first time in over fifty years, tens of thousands of Jews have developed a vital direct link with Israel, since thousands of their relatives, friends, and coworkers now lead a new life in the land of their ancestors. It is difficult to overestimate the significance of this fact, and it far outweighs the dry arithmetical calculations that are based strictly on the percentages of those who left and of those who stayed behind.

Among the Jews of this grouping who strive for emigration, up to 40% are people with a higher education. . . .

One may well ask, "And what will happen to those Jews who do not intend to go to Israel?" Let Theodor Herzl answer: "Those who are undecided will be worse off, both here and there!"

Writing at almost the same time in Moscow, the physicist Viktor
Yakhot attempted to answer the same questions:

> What is causing thousands of Soviet Jews to abandon the places they
> have lived in for years, to depart for Israel? In each individual
> instance a person is guided by his own feelings, thoughts, and aspira-
> tions. Nevertheless, it is possible to draw some general conclusions. . . .
>   Although life in Israel is not as secure as in other countries, it is
> to Israel that the Jews are going. This is primarily a movement of
> Jews to Israel, not from the USSR. From this it follows that the
> movement is not based on anti-Sovietism. . . .
>   The Jews in the Soviet Union may be divided into two main
> groups, each of which has its specific characteristics. . . .
>   The first group is comprised of the Jews of Georgia and the Baltic
> region, where a large section of the Jewish population has applied
> for exit papers. The second group is comprised of the Jews of Russia
> and the Ukraine, from which there are only rare instances of persons
> leaving or expressing the desire to leave. Of the 30,000 Jews who
> have left in the last two years, approximately 25,000 are from
> Georgia and the Baltic. This is about 20% of the Jewish population
> of those republics. The absence of exact data does not permit us
> to give a substantiated figure for those who have applied and not yet
> received permission to leave from those regions, but it is probably
> at least as many.
>   On the other hand, the 5,000 to 10,000 who have left from Russia
> and the Ukraine comprise only about 0.5% of the Jewish population
> living there. Little more than that have expressed the desire to leave.
>   Although these are only rough estimates, it is enough to conclude
> that the Jewish people of Georgia and the Baltic region are striving
> to leave, whereas there is no similar striving on the part of the Jews
> of Russia and the Ukraine.
>   If we look at how Jews live in those areas, we shall see that it is
> the Jews of the Ukraine and Russia who encounter the most diffi-
> culties in everyday living, while the Georgian and Baltic Jews do not
> have most of the problems facing the others. It would seem paradox-
> ical at first glance that one group is leaving a relatively "good" life,
> while the other is remaining despite hardships. The professional
> qualifications of the majority of Georgian Jews are not such as to
> permit them to expect to improve their standard of living over what
> they had in the USSR. They are aware of this. They are also aware
> of the fact that in the USSR they are one of the most affluent
> groups of the population, while this will not be the case in Israel—
> others will be wealthier. Anyone who knows the psychology of the
> Georgian Jews is aware that this is not an unimportant factor for
> them.
>   Nevertheless, they are leaving. Why?

Georgian Jews have no reasons for wishing to be repatriated other than national feeling. The Georgian and Baltic Jews have a deep sense of Jewish identity. They have never forgotten their Jewishness. They have never aspired to contribute to the cultures of other peoples at the expense of their own national identity.

It is noteworthy that nearly every one of the Jews of Transcarpathia, a small region in the Ukraine, has applied for exit permission. It is also noteworthy that many of them are religious and honor Jewish laws and traditions.

On the other hand, the Jews of Russia and the Ukraine, having escaped from the Pale, built themselves an idol—education. They achieved this, and stopped being Jews and feeling like Jews. . . .

Now dissatisfaction has arisen with the chosen idol: as is always the case in history, it did not turn out to be adequate. For the nth time, the Jews failed to assimilate. It is not that Jews who desire to assimilate in the USSR are hindered from doing so—but the process is very slow even where conditions are conducive. The reasons for this are probably to be found somewhere in the irrational, otherwise it is impossible to explain why the Jewish people, never very numerous, still exist. . . .

A sense of Jewishness precedes the decision to go to Israel, although different people arrive at this feeling in different ways. But it applies to all Jews who are leaving for Israel—the Jews of Russia, the Ukraine, the Baltic, and Georgia.

We see then that there is a direct connection between the feelings of national self-awareness and the desire to live in Israel. The latter does not exist without the former.

This does not mean that everyone who feels he is a Jew must decide to leave, but it is natural that as the number of people who go to Israel rises, so does the number who wish to do so. This process will be slower at times, faster at other times, depending on external conditions, but it cannot be stopped.

Feldman's and Yakhot's statistics on the composition of those who leave vary sharply with each other and also differ from Israeli sources.

According to the Jewish Agency's figures for 1971, 80% of the immigrants came as family units. Of the total, about 22% were under 14 and another 10% less than 19 years of age. Thus, almost one-third were school-age children. Only 8% were over 65 years of age, but the largest single group (43%) were between the ages of 49 and 64; thus, slightly more than half of the immigrants were older than the period of maximum economic productivity. Only 17% of the total were between the ages of 19 and 48, the period of maximum economic utility. Many observers, however, question these figures, which were prepared for fund-raising purposes abroad. On February 11, 1972, "informed sources" stated that for 1971 the age group percentages of the new-comers were: 1-18 years, 33⅓%; 19-28 years, 15%; 29-48 years, 28%; 49-64 years, 16%; and 65 and above, 7⅔%.* Other figures released at approximately the same time state that 55.3% of the new immigrants were nonworkers—22.3% children under 14, 16.7% high school and university students, 9.3% nonworking housewives, and 7% pensioners—yet 55% were said to be skilled and professional workers.

In March 1972, Soviet officials noted that two-thirds of the Jewish immigrants were "aged people and women," but statistics for 1972 from Israeli sources produced a different picture: 20% of the immigrants were stated to be under 12 and 39% between 19 and 45 years of age. Israeli statistics for the period January 1972 through March 1973 showed that 25% of all immigrants were under 19, and figures reported in October 1973 indicated that 50% of the immigrants were under 30. The true age distribution most likely parallels a normal population cross section without heavy distortion in terms of either youth or age.

Israel's Absorption Minister Natan Peled was quoted as saying that "68% of all immigrants from the Soviet Union are professionals and/or college graduates." More accurate would seem to be statistics for 1972 categorizing 27% of the immigrants as professionals and figures released in June 1973 showing that, out of 41,898 immigrants from January 1972 to May 1973, 5,407 had university degrees. Some figures for the eighteen months from January 1972 through June 1973 show 1,807 engineers, 879 physicians, 832 teachers, 324 musicians, 299 economists, and an unstated number of mathematicians, physicists, and other pro-fessionals.

The figures on where Soviet Jews came from also showed marked discrepancies. The same "informed sources" referred to above stated that for the period through 1971, half of all Jews came from "annexed territories such as Lithuania and Latvia, 30% from Soviet Georgia, 10% from main cities like Moscow and Leningrad." Yet other reports in late 1971, of which the following is typical, indicate that "about 60% of those leaving are Georgians . . . 20% more were said to be from the former Baltic states and 15% were residents of the Ukraine. The rest of the country accounted for the remaining 5%, meaning that

* Are we dealing with 17% or 43% between 19 and 48 years of age? More likely the latter.

Jewish intellectuals in the major cities of Moscow and Leningrad were not participating in the outflow."

It seems clear that the heavy preponderance of immigrants from Georgia and the Baltic states in 1971 was reduced in 1972, when, according to Israeli sources, 37% of the immigrants came from Georgia and 25% from the Ukraine. In 1973, the number of Georgians arriving in Israel dropped even more sharply.* Nevertheless, probably almost 30% of the total number of Jews coming to Israel during the period 1968-73 were from Georgia, and they constituted a substantial exodus of the Jewish population of that republic. Beginning in the spring of 1972, a large number of Bukhari Jews were permitted to emigrate. About 2,000 came to Israel in 1972 and a larger number arrived in 1973. Thus, despite the confused, inconsistent reports, it seems probable that about one-third of emigrating Soviet Jews were from Oriental backgrounds. The exodus from the Baltic states decreased proportionately but still remained high, as many of those wishing to leave were permitted to depart. By 1973, the Ukraine, Byelorussia, and the RSFSR accounted for a higher percentage of the total.

It is fair to say that whatever the disproportion had been on a geographic basis, or based upon such considerations as economic nonproductivity, by mid-1973 the character of Jewish emigration had begun to approximate the percentages of Jewish population, age, and occupation distribution for the USSR as a whole. By then, the desire to leave had spread into all segments of the Soviet Jewish population and portended a continuing, expanding desire for exodus. As they saw that others were able to leave, Jews who had hesitated to apply became less reluctant to do so.

Additional trends should be noted. One is the dilution of the intense Zionism that had been the primary motivation for departure from the USSR and had caused what Yakhot described as negligible emigration to other countries. This shift is rapidly accelerating. Again, it is difficult to measure, and Israeli figures are distorted. In the two decades prior to the Six-Day War, apart from major population transfers negotiated by the USSR in bilateral agreements with other nations—Poland, for example—very few Soviet citizens were permitted to emigrate. Because there was no realistic hope of leaving, no large-scale efforts were made by Jews or others to emigrate from the country. There were isolated

---

* Unofficial figures released as of the end of September 1973 stated that Georgians constituted only 16,000 out of a total of 80,000 new immigrants, or about 20%.

cases of family reunion—between 1953 and 1960, for example, 55 Soviet citizens were permitted to join their American spouses. Nonetheless, substantial evidence exists that many Soviet citizens hoped to escape from the USSR and go to the West, most particularly to the United States. (The number of Jews among them was considerably larger than their proportion to the total Soviet population.) Some were motivated by a desire to rejoin family; others were seriously disaffected from the Soviet regime and/or positively preferred the ways of the West. But the number of Soviet applicants for visas to the United States and other Western countries was small and the number granted was negligible. The Jewish movement, by its nature, was not concerned with stimulating such emigration even though, in its rhetoric, it adopted the universal human right to leave. Israeli support, and thus the support of Jewish establishment organizations, was not for the abstract right to leave but for the right to leave for Israel. Furthermore, once the pattern of granting exit visas to Israel was established in 1971, a Soviet Jew could get permission to leave for Israel more easily than for another country. This led a number of non-Jews, or people whose claim to Jewish ancestry was doubtful at best, to secure permission to leave for Israel on the basis of a *vizov* sent from a "relative" in that country. Once beyond the borders of the USSR, some of those who did not wish to go to Israel proceeded to their real goals—London, Paris, or New York, for example. There were few such persons before 1972. By then, however, some Jews with exit visas for Israel decided to go elsewhere, once they arrived in Austria. In that year, at least 223 chose not to go to Israel, despite the indoctrinating atmosphere provided by the Jewish Agency at Schönau. They were transferred to Rome, where they were assisted by the United HIAS (Hebrew Immigrant Aid Service, a Jewish-American social service organization that has been aiding Jewish immigrants, principally to the United States, for more than half a century).* In the first two months of 1973, 117 Soviet Jews went to United HIAS in Rome, usually from the Jewish Agency in Vienna, and as of June 1973, over 800 Soviet Jews were waiting in Rome under HIAS aegis for transit papers to the United States, Canada, the United Kingdom, Australia, and Latin America.†

* Israel acknowledges that in 1972, 303 Soviet Jews never arrived in Israel but went to Western countries instead. That figure includes those who arrived in Vienna first and those who went directly from the USSR to other places in Europe.
† The figure of 117 does not include those who managed legally to leave the USSR directly for London, Paris, or other centers.

None of the foregoing figures included Jews who first went to Israel and then decided to leave. By 1971, some Jewish movement activists had made such a choice, although in some cases they continued to maintain contact with Israel and even had apartments there while working and living abroad. (Among them were Viktor and Rakhel Fedoseyev, who worked for Radio Liberty in Munich; Yulius Telesin and Ilya Zilberberg, who wrote, taught, or worked in England in support of the democratic movement; and Vitold Kapshitser, who wrote in Rome.) Israel claimed that only 0.5% of all emigrants, or about 70 persons, left for other countries in 1971. It asserted that in 1972 only 28 Soviet Jews emigrated from Israel to the West via HIAS. If that is true, a much larger number must have left without HIAS protection. In the first three months of 1973 alone, 125 Soviet Jews left Israel for the West with HIAS assistance. The number had become so large by September 1973 (HIAS stated it was 500), that HIAS, under intensive pressure from Israeli authorities and the Jewish fund-raising apparatus in the United States (the principal source of its funds), agreed not to extend assistance to Soviet Jewish emigrants who seek to immigrate to Western countries after first coming to Israel. The Jewish Agency, in announcing the HIAS agreement, said that aid would be discontinued because Israel cannot be considered a "country of distress." By April 1973, Israeli authorities acknowledged that 4% of Soviet Jews were leaving Israel for other countries—which meant that at least 1,200 Soviet Jews a year would be left without Jewish community assistance in resettling in countries of the West.

Although the great majority of Soviet Jews who wish to leave still have settlement in Israel as their main motivation, an increasing number seek to come to the United States. That is understandable both because many Jews from the USSR have relatives in the United States and because American society has long attracted Soviet citizens who are oriented toward Western ideas of freedom. In 1971, out of a total of 330 Soviet citizens who settled in the United States, 214 were Jews. On September 30 of that year, the attorney general of the United States announced that he would exercise his parole authority under the U.S. Immigration and Nationality Act to permit Soviet refugees to enter the United States on a priority basis without their fitting the technical-preference categories of the act. The Department of State expanded its representation list so that more than 500 Soviet Jews were included among those whom the U.S. government actively sought to assist. In 1972, of

453 HIAS-assisted persons who entered the United States, 209 did so under the parole authority. The 1973 figures appear to have been at least double those of 1972. A Department of State letter of April 20, 1973 to Senator Edward M. Kennedy acknowledged that the U.S. representation list, which contained only the names of Soviet citizens refused an exit visa at least once, included "currently some 2,200 immigrant visa cases pending at the American Embassy in Moscow. Some of these cases include an unknown number of dependents, so that the total number of persons involved could be as high as 9,000." An estimated 60% of these applicants were Jewish. If there is relaxed Soviet permission for Jews wishing to come to the United States, thousands a year can be anticipated.

Much more attention has been paid to the relatively small number of Jews who arrive in Israel and subsequently desire to return to the USSR. They have been the subject of intensive interviews by newspapers, radio, and television. The sad plight of many of them huddled together for months in a Vienna tenement slum has aroused both pity and bewilderment. Making much of this pathetic group, Soviet propaganda has asserted that thousands of Jews seek to return to the USSR. Novosti Press Agency, the USSR official overseas publishing house, has printed hundreds of thousands of copies in several editions of a 64-page booklet entitled *The Deceived Testify—Concerning the Plight of Immigrants in Israel*. The cover shows a Jew wailing at Jerusalem's Western Wall. Its pages are filled with dozens of letters to Soviet relatives and newspapers bemoaning the fate of the expatriated victims and lamenting the horrors of Israeli life. Some statements are included from those who have been allowed to return to the USSR. This is but a fragmentary hint of the vast outpouring of propaganda within the USSR, often in the form of testimonials, deprecating Israeli life and the tragic fate of those who chose to leave their Soviet homeland.

Without question, many Soviet Jews have found it extremely difficult to adjust in Israel. The subject of their absorption problems, their ability to adjust to Israeli life and Israel's ability to adjust to them, and the suitability, skill, and sensitivity with which Israeli officialdom has faced the problem is far too lengthy to discuss here in detail. Certainly there are high levels of discontent, and articulate, militant, activist Soviet immigrants have expressed their dissatisfactions vigorously both within Israel and to their friends and relatives in the USSR. The difficulties of Israeli life are no longer a secret to many would-be immigrants. Even though they may wholly discount Soviet propaganda, they are hard put to ignore what friends and relatives tell them. Still, Viktor Polsky mirrors the opinion of many Soviet Jews who wish to leave for Israel:

> I know how bureaucratic and blind the Sochnut [Jewish Agency] can be. I know how insensitive and stupid the Misrad Haklitah [Ministry of Absorption] is. I know we may have difficulty getting a proper job, or having as high a living standard as we do in Moscow, but I prefer the worst Sochnut official to the best of the KGB. I'd rather deal with the least sensitive bureaucrat from Klitah than with any OVIR person.

In late 1973, despite exaggerated Soviet claims, there were about 250 Soviet Jews in Vienna, and perhaps another 50 to 100 in other parts of Europe, hoping for entry visas back to the USSR. Many had waited in a condition of extreme poverty and statelessness for up to two years. Perhaps another 100 had been admitted back to the USSR, and then only when they had recanted sufficiently so that they could be useful propaganda tools for the Soviet Union. But Soviet officials realized their great public relations value, and on August 21, 1973, the USSR Council of Ministers passed a decree offering economic benefits to those who voluntarily return to the Soviet Union. Other legislation easing the restoration of Soviet citizenship was under consideration. The problem of the returnees becomes particularly painful to the advocates of Soviet Jews when their numbers include formerly important Soviet activists. One such person is Luba Bershadskaya (see page 107), an early militant. After almost two years in Israel, she left, disillusioned and bitter. While living in Brussels, allegedly waiting for a visa back to the USSR, she was said to have written a bitter polemic, published in the USSR as "Invented Homeland," in which she complained that Israel is more bureaucratic and less compassionate than the USSR. "Free speech is a false conception. You can shout but it doesn't get you any place," she stated. "Two years in Israel did to me what labor camps failed to do in ten. . . . Americans must stop aiding Soviet Jewry, and instead help my brethren in Israel." In private correspondence, however, she denied that she desired to return to the Soviet Union. She claimed that Soviet authorities misappropriated and misrepresented her comments about her experience in Israel. Now in the United States, she is allegedly seeking to return to the USSR. She is denounced everywhere, displaced, adrift, and isolated.

We have noted who leaves and for what destination. Despite ambiguities and unpredictability, it appears as if the probability of getting permission is enhanced, not weakened, by the extent of activism and the amount of foreign attention paid to a case. Certainly there have been periods of time—before and during a Communist Party congress, before a U.S. presidential election, during important debate on U.S. congressional legislation that concerns the USSR—when Soviet authorities have, with unseemly haste, attempted to rid themselves of some of the most militant spokesmen of the Jewish movement. They have gone out of their way to insist, with threats, that leaders of the democratic movement, or prominent dissident artists, apply to leave, even though the prospective applicant had not made up his mind to depart. In this category are the poet-mathematician-philosopher Aleksandr Yesenin-Volpin, now at Boston University and the poet Iosif Brodsky, now on the University of Michigan faculty. Both Valery Chalidze, the physicist and Human Rights Committee specialist, and Zhores Medvedev, the noted biologist and social critic, after being permitted to leave on speaking and study visits to the United States and England respectively, had their citizenship withdrawn and thus were effectively exiled. But while many are permitted to leave, others are not, despite the utmost persistence. An explanation of this seemingly inconsistent policy is found in a letter of April 1973 addressed by one hundred Soviet activists to the United States Congress. They point out that the departure of persons who have no higher education and qualification—including many persons from Georgia, Central Asia, and Moldavia, and of workers in the service fields who do not occupy significant places in the Soviet hierarchy—is solved relatively easily, that some persons with higher education in the humanities receive exit permits, but that qualified specialists in the exact sciences and technical studies, university professors, persons who occupy administrative positions, and leading actors and journalists are almost guaranteed a refusal.

In short, the system of detention of Jews is based on the selectivity principle. The authorities explain this selectivity to those outside the borders of the USSR by stating that the emigration of the detained persons may, allegedly, harm the security of the state. . . . Yet an unbiased analysis, which we have been demanding in vain, of each concrete case of prevention from emigration would undoubtedly show the complete noninvolvement of the detained persons in matters of state security. Aside from this, persons who have applied for an exit visa are automatically excluded from the life of the society and become useless for the society.

What is the real reason that the authorities are issuing permanent refusals and detaining thousands of other people in the country for years and years? Why . . . are these people subjected to repressions? Why are they and their families deprived of the possibility to live and work normally? The authorities themselves understand, probably, that the emigration of these people cannot harm the state's security. It is clear that the country's economy cannot suffer because of their emigration, since the Jews constitute a rather small percentage of the general number of specialists. The real aim of such a selective policy is to create a wide enough category of the so-called "refused ones." Their tragic fate is to serve as a frightening example for the many thousands of Jews who want to, but do not dare, start applying for emigration. No one, regardless of his qualifications, age, or sex, knows beforehand what his fate will be.

Small in number, but particularly tragic in consequences, are the family hostage group, about whom the regime is consistently intransigent. The best known of these cases involves Polina Epelman, former head of the pharmacy department of a Leningrad hospital, and her 11-year-old daughter Yulia. Polina is a remarkable woman—stylish, attractive, intelligent, and determined. Although she was not politically involved at first, in the course of her struggle to leave the USSR and the consistent refusals, she became a leader of the Jewish movement in Leningrad. She and Yulia remained as wave after wave of her friends departed. Her crime was that her husband left the USSR without permission in February 1971, and she has been held hostage for all his sins. Mikhail Epelman, a mathematician whose deep feelings are masked by his quiet manner and thoughtful, deep-set eyes, was formerly on the faculty of Leningrad University and is now a professor at the University of the Negev in Israel. Like his wife, he was not involved in the Leningrad Jewish movement, but when an opportunity came to travel abroad, he quietly made plans not to return, "in order to escape living in a society where it was not possible for me to live my life as a Jew. I could not live another week in a country whose government blindly supported Arab regimes seeking to destroy my people." He did not tell his wife because he "did not wish to make her an accomplice" to his escape. Polina sought to join Mikhail as soon as he wrote that he was in Israel, and a *vizov* was sent her, but she met strong resistance at every step. Her husband was accused of being a traitor and of being insane; she was pressured to divorce him; the KGB harassed her; at work, she was reviled as the wife of a traitor and ultimately lost her job. Still she persisted. Her many applications for an exit visa were rejected, and all of her appeals to Soviet leaders were fruitless. No formal statement of reasons was ever given, but she was repeatedly told that she and Yulia would not be allowed to leave because Mikhail had left the country without authorization. She insisted to no avail that this was illegal and that it was punishment directed at her and their child for acts they had not committed. Petitions to the UN and to the Red Cross remain unanswered.

In September 1971, Polina Epelman wrote President Zalman Shazar requesting Israeli citizenship. There was no reply. Finally, Mikhail Epelman formally applied on behalf of his wife and child, and the minister of the interior granted them citizenship. A certificate of citizenship was issued, but although Polina wrote that it was of the utmost importance that it be delivered to her, she did not receive it for more than a year. Meanwhile, she utilized every avenue available. In her letters to her husband, she wrote: "No refusals and delays will stop me. To fight, fight and fight for my legitimate rights—this is what my life consists of now, Mikhail! Do everything you can to liberate me and Yulia." Epelman did. He traveled to the United States, to England, France, Sweden, and Switzerland. He interceded with the U.S. Congress, heads of state, eminent newspapermen, public figures. His hunger strikes in various Western capitals elicited Western sympathy but no Soviet response. He prepared and filed petitions to the Soviet government, Israeli authorities, and the UN, but Polina, on inquiry in Leningrad, was simply told that Soviet authorities had again rejected her appeals, and the UN sent its usual form letter stating that the petition would be referred for study to the UN Commission of Human Rights.

Since the Soviet Union's many denials of Polina's applications clearly violated provisions of the Universal Declaration of Human Rights—the right to leave (Article 13) and the right to change nationality (Article 15)—Epelman invoked the little-known Convention on the Nationality of Married Women, which had been ratified by both the Soviet Union and Israel more than a decade before. This convention, whose purpose is "to promote universal respect for the human rights of married women," was designed to "give effect to the principle laid down in Article 15 of the Universal Declaration of Human Rights by safeguarding the free will of the wife." To implement these purposes and give meaning and effect to the convention, the contracting states agreed in Article 10 that:

> Any dispute which may arise between any two or more contracting states concerning the interpretation or application of the present Convention, which is not settled by negotiation, shall, at the request of any one of the parties to the dispute, be referred to the International Court of Justice for decision.

The Soviet Union, in ratifying the convention, made no reservations concerning Article 10, as did some ratifying states, thus clearly accepting the *compulsory* jurisdiction of the International Court. This is the only known instance in which it is possible for a state to litigate human rights claims on behalf of its citizens against the Soviet Union in an international forum. Epelman pointed out to the Israeli government in a formal request for action that "it is clear . . . as a matter of international law, my wife and daughter, as citizens of Israel, are entitled to the protection of the government of Israel." In petitions, he called upon world leaders to protect the human rights of his family and, "in the interest of the maintenance of amity between nations, and particularly between Israel and the USSR," to intercede in their behalf so that a World Court hearing might be avoided. He noted:

> Their health, their morale, indeed their very lives dictate prompt and expeditious action on the part of civilized world public opinion and on the part of whatever common humanity the Soviet government shares with the rest of the world community.

But Israel, the only government authorized to bring the case in the World Court, refused to do so, and even refused to send a formal diplomatic letter of protest. Polina still languishes in Leningrad.

Even an *attempted* escape can be viewed as an act of treason, punishable by death, as the first Leningrad trial so graphically illustrates. The 1927 Criminal Code of the USSR provided that family members of a deserter were punishable by five to ten years' imprisonment if they knew of the deserter's intention to flee and failed to inform the authorities. Although Article 58 has been repealed, the Soviet government still imposes upon family members an obligation to denounce a person who tries to exercise his basic right of freedom of exit. The idea of collective criminal responsibility for family members is anathema to any civilized legal system, yet it is precisely this attitude that has been involved in the detaining of Polina and Yulia Epelman as hostages in punishment for Mikhail's repatriation to Israel.

The Epelman case is not the only one of its kind. Almost identical is the experience of Viktor Yoran (formerly Apartsev), an internationally known cellist, who fled the Soviet Union for Israel in November 1969. His wife, Stella Goldberg, a concert pianist, and their young son Aleksandr, have been refused permission to leave Moscow to rejoin Yoran in Israel. Like Polina Epelman, Stella Goldberg has applied to OVIR on numerous occasions only to be refused orally on the illegal grounds that her husband is a traitor. She, too, applied to President Shazar for Israeli citizenship and received no reply, but after a formal application to the minister of the interior and the renunciation of her Soviet citizenship, she and Aleksandr were granted Israeli citizenship. Yoran, meantime, secured outside assistance while in England and the United States on concert tours. Yehudi Menuhin, the famous violinist, interceded directly but unsuccessfully with Soviet authorities on behalf of Yoran's wife and child, and Soviet authorities have been unmoved, thus far, by letters to Leonid Brezhnev and the Soviet Composers Union signed by Leonard Bernstein, Claudio Arrau, Zino Francescatti, Nathan Milstein, Pierre Fournier, and other musical luminaries who asked the Soviet Union to show magnanimity and humanity by allowing the family to reunite in Israel.

The lengths to which the policy is extended are illustrated by the case of Mark Nashpits, a 25-year-old Moscow oral surgeon, and his mother, Ita. When Mark was 8, his father, Chaim, abandoned his wife and child, escaped from the USSR, and settled in Israel. There he married again and had more children. His wife and son in Moscow neither knew he would leave nor maintained contact with him in Israel. But when Mark Nashpits became active in the Jewish movement, he was denied an exit visa for himself and his mother because of his father's "traitorous acts" of sixteen years before. Nashpits called on his father to explain the circumstances publicly, and the elder Nashpits did so, asking Leonid Brezhnev, "In such a case, is the son responsible for the deeds of his father?" To the Soviet state, the answer was clear: He *is* responsible. The deterrent effect on a potential defector is considered so important that the sins of the father will be visited upon the son, the parent, the wife, and the small child, and none shall leave.

Such a draconian exertion of state power may be shocking in its raw virulence, but petty nastiness sometimes plays an important part as well, as in the case of the famous dancer Valery Panov. When the 34-year-old star of Leningrad's Kirov Ballet and his non-Jewish dancer wife, Galina Rogozina, 22, applied for an exit visa early in 1972, Panov was immediately dismissed from the ballet company and his wife was reduced to the corps de ballet.* They have not danced since then. A Panov who did not dance was of no utility to the Soviet state, and clearly, Panov did not constitute a security risk, so the only basis for denying him a visa while keeping him idle was the embarrassing loss of Soviet prestige in a great artist's decision to emigrate. Panov has been repeatedly harassed, threatened, and arrested on charges of hooliganism since the day he applied to OVIR. In May 1973, he was jailed for a week in a cell full of cripples and amputees. His telephone stopped working and his mail and telegrams from abroad were no longer delivered. An Honored Artist of the Soviet Union, he now, according to observers, "is being transformed into a desperate, cornered animal by KGB harassment." Thousands of European and American dancers and other artists have signed appeals and petitions, but to no avail. Personal appeals to Soviet leaders by Arthur Miller, Tennessee Williams, Paul Newman, and other famous persons, and private conversations with diplomatic officials by Laurence Olivier, have had no effect. No reason so spiteful as loss of face could be given the Panovs. The only stated excuse has been that Galina's mother failed to give permission for her to leave the country. In late September 1973, Panov received permission to go if he would leave his wife in the Soviet Union, and Galina was told she would then be reinstated in the ballet company. Panov's answer was, "I prefer to die rather than to leave her." On November 2, 1973, the Panovs began a hunger strike to protest the authorities' refusal to let them leave, but the strike failed.

Irrational though it may seem, the lack of parental permission has been a stumbling block for some Jews who wish to emigrate. Even for mature adults, OVIR requires a consent signed by parents. Many an applicant has been refused an exit visa because an elderly parent is unwilling to see a grown child leave the country. Although OVIR does not always insist upon the parental signature requirement, some

---

* Two earlier stars of the Kirov Ballet had defected to the West—Rudolf Nureyev, who left the troupe in Paris in 1961, and Natalya Makarova, who quit in London in 1970.

of the most heartrending cases have involved precisely this tug between generations or, even worse, a fierce battle over minor children. There is, of course, a reasonable basis for preventing one parent from depriving the other of custody or visitation privileges with a child by taking the child out of the country. But it is another matter to treat the application to leave for Israel as a political crime that renders the applying parent unfit to have custody and thus to prevent emigration by the simple expedient of taking the child from his parent. Yet this has repeatedly occurred.

In Kiev, a Mrs. Bernshtein had custody of her 10-year-old daughter by a first marriage, and she and her second husband, a building engineer, had a child of their own. When they applied to go to Israel, her first husband, who had not seen his daughter in years, filed an action for change of custody, and it was granted. In Tashkent, their 15-year-old daughter was taken from the Kaziev family and placed in a children's home when they received an exit visa for Israel. In Minsk, the grandmother of 3-year-old Elena Matsevich refused to permit her daughter (the child's mother) to go unless the family left the little girl behind. Sofia Dembina, 30, a Moscow galvanization engineer, divorced her husband in 1967 when their son Yury was 3. Dembin remarried three times thereafter, failing to see the boy and renouncing all parental duties, yet after Dembina became a Jewish activist and applied to go to Israel with her son, all her visa requests were denied because her former husband refused to give consent. Finally, under official prodding, he filed a suit to change custody based upon his former wife's activities. Riva Levina of Vilna is in an almost identical plight, as is Ari Lyudmirsky of Leningrad.

Solomon Dreizner, one of the defendants in the second Leningrad trial, was released from Potma on June 15, 1973, after serving his three-year sentence, and upon his release, he applied to go to Israel. He had been divorced in January 1967. His former wife, who lived with their 10-year-old daughter Ilona, immediately petitioned the court to deprive Dreizner of all parental rights, although it was conceded that he had continued to support the child. She argued that he was a criminal who had betrayed his country and thus was not a fit father. The Leningrad educational authorities joined her petition since "the upbringing of a child should be in accordance with devotion to the motherland and the Communist attitude toward society. Dreizner is unable to educate his child in accordance with Communist morals and correct devotion to the motherland as he is prepared to desert the country which brought him up and gave him higher education." The court granted the petition. Dreizner departed for Israel in October 1973, stripped of all parental rights.

A case that has stirred thousands of Soviet Jews and their supporters abroad is that of 14-year-old Marina Temkin. Marina's appearance is hauntingly evocative of Anne Frank, the Dutch-Jewish girl whose beautiful life and early death have come to symbolize the innocence and goodness of the millions of children who died in the Holocaust. Her father, Dr. Aleksandr Temkin, 43, a professor of physics and mathematics, was employed at the Institute of Petroleum-Chemical Synthesis until he applied for emigration in February 1972 and was dismissed from his work. Her mother, Maya Raiskaya, is a child psychiatrist employed at the Academy of Pedagogical Sciences, and Maya's mother is the chief psychiatrist at a Moscow District clinic, a member of the Communist Party, and a former deputy in the Moscow Soviet.

Interested in Israel, identified with the Jewish movement, and friendly with many intellectual activist leaders, Temkin learned Hebrew and taught it to his precocious daughter. Marina, a student at Moscow's special French-language school, and more mature than her pig-tailed appearance would suggest, also became involved in the Jewish repatriation movement. She began wearing a Star of David and enjoyed observing the Jewish holidays. The mother, however, out of genuine conviction or because of anxiety about her professional position and opportunity for advancement, opposed the heavy emphasis on Jewish culture and the intense attachment to Israel. She stressed loyalty to the Soviet regime and reiterated Soviet official condemnation of Israel. Like thousands of other successful Jewish professional people who had achieved a position of status in Soviet society, she found the perils of dissent and dislocation unattractive. The tensions in the family deepened, and after Temkin received *vizovs* and prepared an application to OVIR, a crisis developed. Maya Raiskaya began divorce proceedings on the grounds of "the dangerous influence of the respondent on his minor daughter, in connection with his decision to leave for Israel together with his daughter." A divorce was granted on May 23, 1972, and custody was given the mother, although this was a formality since the couple continued to share an apartment with Marina. The next day, Temkin submitted documents to OVIR for himself and Marina stating that his ex-wife opposed the child's departure. Under

Soviet family law, judicial bodies take into consideration the wishes of children Marina's age in determining custody. Marina indicated that she wanted to accompany her father to Israel. OVIR took her position into consideration and on October 19 granted permits to Temkin and Marina to leave for Israel. The following day, Temkin paid the 900 rubles required for an exit visa, including 500 rubles for compulsory renunciation of Soviet citizenship. Marina was included in his documents. Both had been granted Israeli citizenship and managed to secure their Israeli citizenship number. On October 23, however, OVIR called him back to advise that he must leave without Marina because her mother had protested. A struggle then began which in its intensity, bitterness, and tragedy reflects in microcosm the conflict between opposing views in Jewish life in the USSR today. Marina joined her father in persistently and eloquently insisting on their right to leave for Israel, while the mother joined the state in defending her parental right to raise her daughter as a loyal Soviet citizen.

Father and daughter left the apartment to stay with friends until their exit visas were secured. Several weeks later, after a preliminary court hearing at which neither father nor daughter was present, custody was reconfirmed in the mother, and Moscow police detained Temkin and his daughter at the mother's behest, holding them for seven hours before Marina was returned to her mother. Temkin appealed the determination that he was restricted in "participation in the upbringing of his daughter," but he continued to live in the same apartment with his former wife and Marina, who by now was seriously alienated from her mother. Both Temkin and Marina meanwhile addressed appeals abroad protesting their enforced detention in the USSR. Meanwhile, too, Maya Raiskaya sought the assistance of psychiatric coworkers, school officials, and others in an effort to persuade Marina of the folly of the course she had taken. It was wholly counterproductive.

Two days before the court appeal, Temkin, Marina, and some Jewish activist leaders held a press conference with foreign newsmen to elucidate their position. Marina said:

> My mother is doing everything to prevent me from going to Israel with papa. She treats me as if I were a thing, as if I were her property and not a human being who already has her own convictions. Now something terrible is menacing me: they want to deprive me of my father. . . .
> I told my mother that I am not going to live with her, that I shall

go to Israel anyway. She threatens to give me to the state, so that
I should be forced to give up this wish, like a criminal. Who will be
able to protect me if my father is deprived of parental rights? I shall
be entirely in her hands. That will be terrible! I can be put into a
corrective home only by force. I shall escape and return to my father.
I swear this.

My father and I are Israeli citizens. I am wearing a Mogen David
—the ancient symbol of my people. I have left the Pioneer organization and I shall never again put on a Pioneer tie. Everyone must
understand that I am not a Soviet schoolgirl, but an Israeli girl; and
the judges must also understand this. Our situation is becoming more
and more difficult, from trial to trial, which my mother wins only
because we want to go to Israel. In two days a trial will take place
that will decide our fate.

In a statement explaining the importance of the upcoming trial,
Aleksci Tumerman, one of Temkin's friends, pointed out that the "essence of the matter" consisted in the protection of Marina from "a
forcible re-education intended to coerce her to renounce her Jewishness
and to drum orthodox Soviet views into her."

The hardships that will fall on Marina's shoulders if her father is
deprived of his paternal rights—for a 14-year-old adolescent will be
no less harsh than incarceration in a detention camp for an adult.
Therefore, today Marina Temkin is in need of protection by the
world public, just as any other Jew subjected to judicial persecution
for his national convictions.

On January 17, 1973, the court deprived Temkin of his parental
rights, reciting "the antipedagogical and antisocial behavior" of the
father which, it found, "traumatizes the girl and has a pernicious effect
on her mental state and moral outlook." Temkin appealed this decision,
too, and father and daughter continued their campaign to leave for
Israel, publicly renouncing Soviet citizenship and requesting Israeli
diplomatic protection. On February 19, 1973, police officers came to
the apartment and seized Marina, and for weeks, her father and paternal grandmother were unable to locate her. At the end of March, however, Marina managed to call her father to say that she had been
forcibly taken to a Pioneer youth camp on the Black Sea for "re-education." Her letters to him had been intercepted and she had been unable
to make contact. Temkin flew to the camp to see Marina, but they
were permitted only a brief interview. The court appeals continued.

The regional court upheld the district court's finding and, finally, on July 23, the Supreme Court of the RSFSR again affirmed the lower court rulings. The string had run out. Marina remained in a semimilitary re-education place of detention. Temkin appealed to Dr. Benjamin Spock, the well-known American pediatrician and radical. Temkin also petitioned the authorities to prosecute those who abducted Marina on February 19, and he made constant appeals. In October 1973, he was detained by the police and threatened with prosecution for parasitism as well as with a trial concerning ownership of the apartment. Marina remained in the Pioneer camp in Georgia while Maya Raiskaya continued ministering to the psychic health of Soviet children. Finally, in November 1973, Temkin ceased his struggle and left for Israel, and in December Marina was returned to her mother in Moscow. Whatever the competing equities between parents may be, the child is the unwitting victim of such a struggle.

Does the divisiveness of the Temkin family reflect the condition of Soviet Jewry? No one seriously doubts that hundreds of thousands of Soviet Jews wish to leave for Israel or the West. Nor can there by any question that some Jews who have "made it" in Soviet society not only lack the inclination to leave their secure lives but are annoyed by and fear the effects the Jewish movement may have upon their own security. Some observers note that the intense resurgence of Jewish national feelings, with their primary loyalty to Israel, has made all Jews suspect to the Soviet power structure, thus threatening the position and prospects of even the loyalists. Of the approximately 3 million Soviet Jews, a large number remain passive, but even those in distant villages know of the Jewish struggle. For some, it is a source of inward pride; for others, it invokes fear.

Many Soviet citizens, particularly among the well educated, discount completely the propaganda of their own mass media. Thus, Soviet Jews cannot be expected to credit the horror stories officially released about conditions for Soviet immigrants in Israel. But by now, there has been sufficient confirmation of adverse conditions in Israel from more credible sources, such as the enormous flow of letters from friends and relatives who have left, to make most Soviet Jews more realistic about the experience in Israel. No longer do they quite so blindly believe that Israel is a loving land of opportunity and freedom. Some no longer wish to leave, while others revert to their earlier dreams of

America. But the more realistic perspective about Israel does not diminish the ardor of most Jews who still want to leave the USSR. It reinforces their reasoned determination and limits the frustration and disenchantment that inevitably accompany such a major dislocation.

What the future holds for Soviet Jews in terms of their continued ability to leave the USSR is problematic at best. It depends upon many variables outside their control. Among them is the question of the solidity of U.S.-Soviet détente. An important reason why Jews have been permitted to leave has been the desire of Soviet leaders to place no unnecessary obstacles in the path of improved relations with the United States. The relationship between the USSR and the Arab world is another notable consideration. Arab states have vigorously objected to the Russian policy of permitting Jews to go to Israel, to augment its manpower and reinforce its reservoir of skilled scientists and technicians. The Yom Kippur war of October 1973, however, did not result in any curtailment of the number of Jews allowed to leave, although the Soviet Union branded Israel as the aggressor, pledged its total support to its Arab allies, and directly stimulated what could only be construed as an effort to bleed Israel to death. On Monday, October 8, the first OVIR work day after the war began, Moscow reports stated that an unprecedented number of Jews were given exit permission. That week, 1,500 Jews were allowed to leave, and most of them immediately involved themselves in Israel's problems. In October 1973, while war in the Middle East was raging, 4,200 Jews received exit visas for Israel. The conflict, far from discouraging emigration, heightened both requests and grants of permission. (At least 35,000 Soviet Jews were permitted to go to Israel in 1973.) Nothing could have solidified Jewish determination and unity more than did the Yom Kippur attack on Israel. And the diplomatic opposition to Israel, the big-power pressure upon the Jewish state, the oil boycott—all reinforced Jewish loyalty, full support for Israel, and the conviction that whatever the gripes and discontents, the survival of Jews as a people depends upon the survival of Israel as a nation.

The actions of other states can also affect the flow of immigration. When Austrian Chancellor Bruno Kreisky vowed, in the face of threats from Arab terrorists in September 1973, that he would shut down the Schönau transit center, he caused grave concern about how this would affect the flow of emigration. Schönau had long been an uncomfortable anomaly to the Austrian government, requiring the assignment of large numbers of Austrian military and police security men, as well as special extraterritorial privileges for armed security guards of the Jewish Agency. Kreisky's choice of timing in announcing termination of the facility was extraordinarily unfortunate; it demonstrated the fragility of forecasting the future of emigration and the variety of factors that could affect it. By early November, Schönau was shut down after having received, in recent years, more than 72,000 Jews in transit from the USSR to Israel.

If absolutely free emigration were permitted, we can surmise that, over a time, a high percentage of Soviet Jews would leave—perhaps as many as two-thirds. If present Soviet ground rules do not change, it is possible that half a million Soviet Jews will leave by 1980. But 2 million or more will not. Today, even in the countries of the Arab world, after a quarter of a century of brutal repression and a simultaneous willingness to permit all Jews to leave, thousands of Jews remain. For some men, apparently, a loaf of bread and a roof over one's head are more reassuring than the uncertainties of freedom.

JEWS AND DEMOCRATS:
The Ambivalence of Friends

CHAPTER 23

Despite its focus on the Soviet Jews, this book has not suggested that the Jewish movement was unaffected by its environment or without effect upon it. Quite the contrary. The Jews are not the only Soviet people involved in tumultuous change, nor are they the only ones who display tenacious bravery and creative defiance. Indeed, although theirs is the most successful dissent movement in the history of the USSR, it is a relative latecomer. A part of, and inseparable from, the Soviet condition, it carries the unique imprint of the Russian historical experience.

It is in Moscow that the relationship between the Jewish movement and the democratic dissenters is most evident and intertwined. Many of Moscow's Jewish movement leaders were democratic activists before they turned their intelligence and energy to the Jewish effort to leave the USSR. They still have ties of comradeship to friends and colleagues with whom they struggled for as long as a decade, and since an estimated 60% to 70% of the democrats are Jews or are married to Jews, they have social or family ties as well. (The rate of intermarriage between Jews and non-Jews among Moscow's intellectuals is very high.) Since Moscow's dissenters are few in number, most of that city's veteran protesters and social critics have known, or known about, each other for many years. Lastly, the democrats have supported the Jewish movement, creating a solidarity remarkable for two groups that have diverse and at times even divergent goals.

377

Nevertheless, Zionists in the USSR, being members of what is essentially a national movement, generally have not been committed to the civil libertarian universalism that is characteristic of the democrats. The Jewish activists have deliberately refused to criticize the Soviet regime, arguing that they are not concerned with the state of freedom in the Soviet Union, about which they have little optimism, and that their only goal is to leave.

Committed as they are to major change in the USSR, some democrats have regarded this as a betrayal by erstwhile comrades and decried the excessive chauvinism of Jewish rhetoric. They perceived that if the Jews were successful, many intellectuals would, by leaving the Soviet Union, weaken the human rights movement. Yet at meetings of the democrats in the fall of 1970 to determine whether support should be given to the Zionist struggle, Vladimir Bukovsky, among others, argued that since (1) the Jewish movement was one of the most important parts of the broader human rights movement, (2) the right to leave was a fundamental human right, and (3) the struggle for national dignity, in the Soviet context, was integral to any fight for human freedom, the democrats must fully support Jewish efforts to leave for Israel. The position carried and has been followed consistently since that time.

Outside of Moscow, interrelationships have been weaker and less meaningful. In areas of long-time Zionist conviction such as the Baltic states, or of strong Jewish tradition such as Moldavia, or of messianic, religious Zionism such as Georgia, there were few connections between the Jewish movement and the handful of liberal intelligentsia. Even in Leningrad, the Jewish movement, rooted in the embers of Zionist conviction, was neither closely tied to nor strongly supported by the democrats, although Jewish activists had been sympathetic to and peripherally involved in the libertarian cause. It was in the Ukraine that the greatest stress might have occurred between the two groups, yet it did not. Many Jews regarded the Ukrainian people as pogromists and Nazi collaborators, and they feared the vigorous Ukrainian national movement might be reactionary and racist. The Ukrainians, in turn, had since 1917 seen the Jews as Russifiers, agents of the Bolsheviks, and a foreign people opposed to the restoration of Ukrainian dignity. Yet it was a Kiev-born writer, Anatoly Kuznetsov, who in his book *Babi Yar* spoke against the sin of genocide. And no expression of true brotherhood has been more moving than the stirring address of Ivan Dzyuba at the Babi Yar commemoration on September 29, 1966: *

> Babi Yar is a tragedy of the whole of mankind, but it happened on Ukrainian soil. And therefore a Ukrainian must not forget it any more than a Jew. Babi Yar is our common tragedy, a tragedy for the Jewish and the Ukrainian nations. . . . Today in Babi Yar we commemorate not only those who died here. We commemorate millions of Soviet warriors—our parents—who gave their lives in the battle against fascism. . . .
>
> Are we worthy of this memory? It seems not, if even now various forms of hatred of mankind are found among us, and one of them that form which we call by a weak, banal, yet terrible word, anti-Semitism. Anti-Semitism is an international phenomenon; it has existed and still exists in all societies. Sadly enough, our society is also not free of it. There might be nothing strange about this—after all, anti-Semitism is the fruit and companion of age-old barbarism and slavery, the foremost and inevitable result of political despotism. To conquer it in entire societies is not an easy task nor can it be done quickly. But what is strange is the fact that no battle has been waged against it during the postwar decades, and what is even stranger, it has often been artificially nourished. . . .
>
> As a Ukrainian, I am ashamed that, as in other nations, there is anti-Semitism here, that these shameful phenomena, unworthy of mankind—phenomena which we call anti-Semitism—exist here.
>
> We Ukrainians must fight in our midst against all forms of expression of anti-Semitism, disrespect toward the Jews, and misunderstanding of the Jewish problem.
>
> You, Jews, must fight in your midst against those among you who do not respect the Ukrainian people, Ukrainian culture, the Ukrainian language, those who unjustly see a potential anti-Semite in every Ukrainian.
>
> We must oust all forms of hatred of mankind, overcome all misunderstandings, and achieve a true brotherhood within our lives. . . .
>
> The road to a true and honest brotherhood lies not in self-oblivion, but in self-knowledge; not in rejection of ourselves and adaptation to others, but in being ourselves and respecting others. The Jews have a right to be Jews and the Ukrainians have a right to be Ukrainians in the full and profound, not only the formal, meaning of the word. Let the Jews know Jewish history, Jewish culture and language, and be proud of them. Let them also know each other's history and cul-

* Dzyuba, a 42-year-old literary critic and writer from Kiev and a leader of the Ukrainian national movement, was sentenced to five years in prison camp in March 1973 because he had advocated the national rights of the Soviet peoples. In November 1973, suffering from tuberculosis, he was pardoned after making a somewhat ambiguous recantation.

ture and the history and culture of other nations, and let them know
how to value themselves and others as their brothers. . . .
This is our duty to millions of victims of despotism. This is our
duty to the better men of the Ukrainian and Jewish nations who
urged us to mutual understanding and friendship. This is our duty to
our Ukrainian land in which we live together. This is our duty to
humanity.

Among those who have heeded Dzyuba's plea is Avram Shifrin,
a former Soviet lawyer, who spent ten years in Soviet prison camps,
where he developed close friendships with Ukrainian dissenters. "The
one place where there is no discrimination in the Soviet Union is in
the camps," Shifrin has said. "There, all pull together." Since he was
released and emigrated to Israel, Shifrin has been as emphatically active for Ukrainian rights as he was for Jewish rights.

A similar attitude exists within the human rights movement. The
trials of Daniel and Sinyavsky, Ginzburg and Galanskov, Pavel Litvinov,
Bukovsky, Piotr Grigorenko and Ilya Gabai (to name only a few) have
been struggles for freedom of expression, right of assembly, the rights
of minorities, freedom from arbitrary detention in psychiatric hospitals.
The participants and the principals have been indiscriminately Jews and
non-Jews. Daniel, Ginzburg, Litvinov, and Gabai are Jews, the other
four are not, but they have worked together; they share the same convictions and have suffered the same fate. On October 20, 1973, Gabai,
a 38-year-old former editor at the Institute of Asian Peoples—schoolteacher, poet, script writer, and veteran dissident who had been jailed
after demonstrations following the arrest of Ginzburg and Galanskov,
and had served three years in prison camps following his arrest in
Tashkent with his friend Grigorenko—leaped to his death from a
Moscow building. He was both a democrat and a Jew.

On May 20, 1969, members of what came to be called the Initiative
(or Action) Group for the Defense of Civil Rights sent a letter to the
UN Commission of Human Rights requesting investigation of the multiple violations of the basic freedoms of Soviet citizens. Among its
signatories, who represented the basic core of mainstream democrats—
Jews, Russians, Ukrainians, and Crimean Tatars—were Piotr Yakir
(historian), Viktor Krasin (economist), Anatoly Yakobson (translator), and Tatyana Velikanova (mathematician), all of Jewish descent.
They described themselves as:

people who are bound together by certain common opinions. All of us—believers and nonbelievers, optimists and skeptics, people of Communist and non-Communist persuasion—are united by the feeling of personal responsibility for that which occurs in our country, by the conviction that recognizing the absolute worth of the individual is the basis of normal life in a human society. This also forms the basis of our efforts to defend human rights. We see social progress primarily as the progress of freedom . . . Our task is to provide opposition against lawlessness and despotism.

Of the original members and their larger number of supporters who signed the series of documents prepared by the group, many—including Viktor Krasin—found themselves under arrest or in psychiatric hospitals within the following year. Others, like Yakobson, mathematician Yulius Telesin, and poet Yulia Vishnevskaya, left for Israel, while the mathematician Aleksandr Yesenin-Volpin, the artist Yury Titov, film producer Yury Shtein, and linguist Yury Glazov emigrated to the West. Though decimated, as veteran members were sentenced in a series of political trials, the group continued, drawing support from new sources.

The Initiative Group is believed to have been the primary impetus behind *Khronika,* although the first issue of that essential, reliable, courageous journal appeared a full year before the Initiative Group made its first public appearance. And although the group's public protests diminished in intensity, *Khronika* continued to appear. Assiduously investigating *Khronika* for more than two years, the KGB opened a criminal file, Case #24, and interviewed hundreds of people throughout the USSR, with the sole purpose of extirpating the journal. After Piotr Yakir was arrested on June 21, 1972, the Initiative Group publicly declared that Yakir's public activities "originate entirely in the idea of the de-Stalinization of our society," that his "sole aspiration was to further its democratization," and that his further imprisonment was "perhaps the culminating point" in the "tactical campaign of creeping but systematic repressions which the regime has been conducting for several years now in an attempt to stifle the democratic movement." More important than protesting against the arrest, argued the group, was "to adapt the life and methods of struggle of every democrat, and consequently of the entire movement, to the reality of the present. . . . To preserve people and to preserve *samizdat,* to preserve and strengthen the movement for democratization—that is the chief aim today, that is the best answer to the arrest of Yakir."

Viktor Krasin was arrested on September 12, 1972, for the third time, after having returned from exile only the year before. He and Yakir were held in prison until they were broken. (Yakir had spent most of his adolescence and early manhood in prison.) They publicly recanted at their trial in August 1973 and received three-year sentences. Krasin's first wife and three sons had earlier been permitted to emigrate to Israel. Shortly after their trials, both men were released from prison, in an unusual display of official leniency, and, their sentences reduced to three years of exile, permitted to take up life outside of Moscow.

Among those arrested after the detention of Yakir and Krasin were the mathematician Yury Shikhanovich; Irina Belogorodskaya, an engineer; and Garik Superfin, a literary critic. All five are Jews. The arrests had their desired effect. *Khronika* stopped publication. The twenty-seventh and last issue, dated October 15, 1972, was published in English translation in the West in March 1973.

Khronika clearly reflected the strong links between the Jewish movement and the other human rights activities in the USSR. News about Soviet Jews occupied an important part of its pages. It first reported the case of Boris Kochubiyevsky, the Ryazan trial, and various acts of anti-Semitism. It told of the early movement protests and *samizdat* publications, of the beginnings of organized efforts to establish the right to leave. It first detailed the arrests in Leningrad and Riga and the trials that followed. Issue 17 (December 30, 1970) contained a section on "Persecution of Jews Wishing to Emigrate to Israel" (based extensively on issues of *Ishkod*) and fully reported the first Leningrad trial. In Issue 18 (March 5, 1971), there was an extensive new section entitled "The Jewish Movement for Emigration to Israel." This, as well as reports of political trials, major demonstrations, and the appearance of *samizdat* publications, continued to occupy prominent space in all future issues.

Although *Khronika* was the "Journal of the Soviet Civil Rights Movement" and a reflection of the mainstream democratic activists, Jewish movement items constituted almost 20% of its space from the spring of 1971 until the last issue. It reported news of other dissidents; national groups such as the Ukrainians, Baltic peoples, Crimean Tatars; religious or extrajudicial persecutions, the prison camps, censorship and suppression of writers, psychiatric hospitals, Soviet Human Rights Committee work, the activities of Solzhenitsyn, Amalrik, Bukovsky, and Sakharov.

Khronika objectively placed the Jewish movement in a perspective much more difficult to achieve in the West. From it, one could see clearly that the Jewish movement was the only human rights activity in the USSR that partially succeeded in achieving its limited objectives. Tactically, organizationally, and in terms of courage, it was remarkable. It came to involve a relatively large number of persons—never as high a proportion as the Crimean Tatars, but far more than the small but influential democratic movement and many more, relatively, than the Ukrainian nationalists could muster. In terms of intellectual capacity, articulateness, and accomplishment, the quality of its leadership is perhaps higher than any other contemporary liberation movement anywhere. The Soviet prisoners of conscience—Jewish and non-Jewish —are among the most able people in the USSR. Unfortunately, the Soviet Union devours its best citizens, and a high percentage of its intellectual and moral elite is in prison camps or psychiatric hospitals or has left the country.

Why do these men and women display such reckless defiance, knowing that they will suffer, at best, social ostracism and economic deprivation and, at worst, the horrors of prison camps and insane asylums? Why do talented and privileged artists, writers, and scientists commit acts they know may destroy them? Why do brilliant young people plan to hijack a plane? It is more than the simple searing truth that such people must be free. Years of caution, speaking in whispers, dodging surveillance, smuggling literature, snatching for breaths of information from Western radio, newspapers, books, or tourists, years of censored mail, tapped telephones, bugged apartments, surreptitious meetings, and constant fear have taken their toll. The dissidents must speak out, regardless of the consequences. They must retrieve their human dignity at any cost. Psychologically, they have come to the end of the line. They cease calculating the personal risk. They become politically suicidal.

From a distance, their bravery seems admirable but insane—because they have abandoned the instinct for self-protection. Ultimately, that happens to most of the best of them. And if they aren't tried and sent to prison, or broken, or permitted to leave the country, they simply must get away—to a country *dacha,* for example—until their emotional equilibrium can be restored, so they can fight on, another year and another and another, until there is a fundamental change in the USSR or until they finally despair and surrender or leave or die.

The desperation in their acts can be fully understood only by a person who speaks with them, amid their tribulations, in their own country. It is some understanding of their plight that causes their few knowledgeable Western admirers to love them with a deep loyalty and commitment, to be pledged to their cause and become totally absorbed in their defense.

The Soviet Committee on Human Rights well illustrates the relationship between the Jewish movement and the mainstream democratic movement. On November 4, 1970, the committee came into existence with a brief, highly legalistic statement of its principles and purpose: (a) "advisory assistance to state agencies in creating and applying safeguards for human rights," (b) "creative help" for persons requiring such assistance, (c) "the furtherance of legal education," (d) "theoretical investigation and constructive criticism of the present state of legal safeguards for individual freedom in the Soviet system." The committee declared that it was "guided by the humanitarian principles of the Universal Declaration of Human Rights," but noted that it proceeded from "a recognition of the specific character of Soviet law" and took into account "the practical difficulties facing the state in this area" and Soviet "traditions which have evolved." Its founding members were Academician Andrei D. Sakharov, Valery Chalidze, and Andrei N. Tverdokhlebov.

Sakharov, one of the most eminent Soviet scientists and three times named a Hero of Socialist Labor, the highest award the state bestows, had been expressing critical views since the early 1960s. At first, he made such comments only within top scientific circles, but by 1966, he was signing public statements. In 1968, he wrote a widely circulated *samizdat* manifesto—broadly humanitarian, libertarian, and freethinking—which was published in the West as *Progress, Co-existence and Intellectual Freedom.* Noting that "in the highest bureaucratic elite of our government, the spirit of anti-Semitism was never fully dispelled after the 1930s," he declared it was "disgraceful" to allow "another backsliding into anti-Semitism in our appointments policy." He observed and condemned many civil liberties violations in political trials, including the principal trials of Jewish activists.

Chalidze, a physicist of Georgian-Polish origin, was already renowned for his broad grasp of theoretical jurisprudence, his editing of the *samizdat* journal *Obshchestvennye Problemy* (Social Problems), and his effective volunteer advocacy in human rights test cases. Tverdokhlebov, a highly regarded nuclear physicist who had worked at the Institute of Theoretical and Experimental Physics, had written protest letters and various *samizdat* documents.

The committee also named two "experts": Aleksandr Yesenin-Volpin, a brilliant, stormy mathematician, philosopher, and poet; and Boris Tsukerman, a physicist and legal expert, who like Chalidze had distinguished himself for his studies of the law of human rights and his theoretical and practical jurisprudential activity.* The committee also named two "correspondents," "in recognition of their significant contribution to the cause of advocating human freedom": Aleksandr Solzhenitsyn, the famous novelist, and Aleksandr Galich, a poet and writer who had become an extraordinarily popular, although officially disapproved folk singer and author of ballads. In May 1971, another member was elected, Igor Shafarevich, a 48-year-old mathematician-corresponding member of the Academy of Sciences and a Lenin Prize winner.

With its intervention by lawsuit, petition, analysis, and protest of violations of human rights by the regime, this small galaxy of intellectuals presented a formidable challenge to antilibertarian state repression. Of the group, Tsukerman and Galich were Jews, and Yesenin-Volpin, half-Jewish. Chalidze was married to Vera Slonim, the granddaughter of Maksim Litvinov, the noted Jewish foreign minister of the USSR from 1929 to 1939. Vera, her cousin Pavel Litvinov, and other relatives had become important participants in Moscow's democratic-intellectual group.

At the protest before the Supreme Court following the death sentences imposed in the first Leningrad trial in December 1970, Sakharov met Yelena Bonner, a half-Jewish pediatrician, who is a relative of Eduard Kuznetsov, one of those who originally received a death sentence. She and Sakharov, a widower, were married soon thereafter. Yelena was one of a circle of Moscow Jewish democratic intellectuals that included, among others, Yury Shikhanovich and Tatyana Velikanova. The Velikanova sisters were a small but significant part of the democratic movement: one was married to Sanya Daniel, the son of Yuli and Larisa Bogoraz-Daniel; another was the wife of Andrei, the son of Piotr and Zinaida Grigorenko. Thus, the Soviet Committee on Human Rights—a fundamental part of the democratic movement—included, among its members, experts, and correspondents, a considerable num-

* Yesenin-Volpin is the son of the popular Revolutionary poet Sergei Yesenin, who before his 1925 suicide had been married to the dancer Isadora Duncan.

ber of persons who were Jewish or of Jewish background or who were married to Jews. But even more important is that in terms of natural sympathy, family, and friendship, the human rights movement is bound inextricably with Jews and their cause.

The committee was in the forefront in the defense of Jewish activists when they faced political trials or other forms of state repression. On May 20, 1971, it appealed to the Supreme Soviet "about the persecution of Jewish repatriates." It condemned the upcoming trials in Leningrad, Riga, and Kishinev, charging that the defendants' "only aim" had been to "protest against the unlawful refusals to give them visas for repatriation." In adopting the Jewish movement's own self-description as a repatriation movement, it condemned any criticism of its ultimate goals, noting that "the repatriates are sometimes even accused of egotism by those who are concerned with the defense of human rights in our country." It requested pardons for those who were convicted in the first Leningrad trial. It also stated:

> The unlawful actions of the authorities in preventing the free departure of people from the Soviet Union, and the free repatriation of Jews to Israel in particular, have in the past few years aroused active protests on the part of repatriates. They have protested against unexplained and legally unjustified refusals to issue visas, against legally unjustified delays in the examination of applications, and against the exaggerated, cumbersome procedure for the submission of applications.
> One unlawful action involves other unlawful actions: the authorities are forced to interfere unlawfully with these expressions of protest. At the same time, official propaganda distributes hostile and unfounded information about the idea of the repatriation and of Zionism. The press presents Zionism as a reactionary (almost fascist) political movement. In fact, Zionism is no more than the idea of Jewish statehood, and one can only admire the stubbornness of an ancient and persecuted people which, in the face of very difficult conditions, has revived a state that disappeared long ago. It is precisely this revival, and the removal of the consequences of dispersion that have been so tragic for the Jewish people, that is the aim of Zionism.

The defense of the right to be a Zionist was characteristic. Also characteristically, Sakharov, in an open letter to the U.S. Congress in September 1973, wrote that he considered it his duty to express his view on "protection of the right to freedom of residence within the country of one's choice":

If every nation is entitled to choose the political system under which it wishes to live, this is true all the more of every individual person. A country whose citizens are deprived of this minimal right is not free even if there were not a single citizen who would want to exercise that right.

But as you know, there are tens of thousands of citizens in the Soviet Union—Jews, Germans, Russians, Ukrainians, Lithuanians, Armenians, Estonians, Latvians, Turks, and members of other ethnic groups—who want to leave the country and who have been seeking to exercise that right for years and for decades at the cost of endless difficulty and humiliation.

You know that prisons, labor camps, and mental hospitals are full of people who have thought to exercise this legitimate right. . . .

For decades the Soviet Union has been developing under conditions of an intolerable isolation, bringing with it the ugliest consequences. Even a partial preservation of those conditions would be highly perilous for all mankind, for international confidence and détente.

In view of the foregoing, I am appealing to the Congress of the United States to give its support to the Jackson Amendment, which represents in my view and in the view of its sponsors an attempt to protect the right of emigration of citizens in countries that are entering into new and friendlier relations with the United States.

The Jackson Amendment is made even more significant by the fact that the world is only just entering on a new course of détente and it is therefore essential that the proper direction be followed from the outset. This is a fundamental issue, extending far beyond the question of emigration. . . . The amendment does not represent interference in the internal affairs of socialist countries, but is simply a defense of international law, without which there can be no mutual trust. . . .

There is a particular silliness in objections to the amendment that are founded on the alleged fear that its adoption would lead to outbursts of anti-Semitism in the USSR and hinder the emigration of Jews. . . . It is as if the emigration issue affected only Jews. As if the situation of those Jews who have vainly sought to emigrate to Israel was not already tragic enough and would become even more hopeless if it were to depend on the democratic attitudes and on the humanity of OVIR. . . . As if the techniques of "quiet diplomacy" could help anyone, beyond a few individuals in Moscow and some other cities.

The abandonment of a policy of principle would be a betrayal of the thousands of Jews and non-Jews who want to emigrate, of the hundreds in camps and mental hospitals, of the victims of the Berlin Wall.

Such a denial would lead to stronger repressions on ideological grounds. It would be tantamount to total capitulation of democratic principles in the face of blackmail, deceit, and violence. The consequences of such a capitulation for international confidence, détente, and the entire future of mankind are difficult to predict.

Sakharov's outspoken statements, and the strong support given him by Aleksandr Solzhenitsyn, led to vigorous, official threats against both men in August and September 1973. It was little wonder that important Jewish activist leaders quickly rallied to their support—Drs. Venyamin Levich, Aleksandr Voronel, Boris Einbinder, Aleksandr Temkin, Mark Azbel, and Boris Orlov among them. In an open letter, they wrote:

> . . . there are times when a man's silence makes him an accomplice in the crime. The persecution of Andrei Sakharov and Aleksandr Solzhenitsyn in the USSR today is such a situation. We cannot be silent.
>
> We decided to leave Russia because we feel that our place is not here; but we cannot be indifferent to Russia, her people, and her culture. If there were an enemy who hated everything Russian and who would like to destroy everything that is beautiful about Russia, he would begin with Solzhenitsyn and Sakharov. Any great country would be proud of these people, but only Russia, continuing her ancient tradition, devours her best sons.
>
> The goal of the newspaper persecution . . . is to frighten those who think differently, and to prepare public opinion for future repression. But if the repression includes Sakharov and Solzhenitsyn, the USSR will return to the darkest hours of its history . . .

Other Jews in Kiev and Novosibirsk in a public declaration referred to Sakharov as "an example of true patriotism, humanity, and the highest moral principles." Solzhenitsyn, however, had not displayed as warm sympathy for the Jewish cause as had Sakharov and was not as loved and admired by many Soviet Jews. Indeed, some suggested that his intense Russian nationalism and special form of religiosity cloaked anti-Semitic feelings that appeared in poorly concealed form in some of his writings. Such a view was expressed in November 1972 in a lengthy critical essay by Mikhail Grobman, an artist who had emigrated to Israel. Grobman was promptly answered from Moscow by Natan Faingold, an artist and engineer, David Azbel, a chemist, Vitaly Rubin, a Sinologist, and Mikhail Agursky, a writer and cybernetician, all prominent Jewish activists. They sharply protested against "the slanderous and definitely untrue accusation of anti-Semitism" and labeled Grobman's article "an attack on the honor of the Jewish people and of Israel which we, striving to emigrate there, hold especially dear." Support of Solzhenitsyn and the unity of the dissent movement were perceived to be of the utmost importance.

The ambivalence of Soviet Jews who also have strong emotional ties to the struggle for freedom in the USSR is clearly exemplified by Larisa Bogoraz. Born in 1929 in the Ukraine of assimilated, professional Jewish parents, she spoke Ukrainian from childhood yet experienced anti-Semitism early, without understanding her own Jewish origins. During World War II, suffering from the group libels of Jewish "cowardice" and "profiteering," she felt impelled to "declare demonstratively, with a show of pride: 'I am Jewish.' But the pride was only for my courage—see, I'm not afraid to admit this shameful fact of my biography." After the war, she began studying philology and met and married the writer Yuli Daniel, but as the Black Years of Soviet Jewry descended, found that, because of anti-Semitism, neither she nor her husband could get jobs in the Moscow region. The Daniel family, which had strong Jewish identity and connections, was particularly harassed, and many family friends were arrested. That, she says,

was when the active self-determination of Jews began—at least, in my generation. Some tried to find normal grounds for being considered Russians, or at least to register their children as Russian by nationality. Others . . . registered as Jews out of a feeling of protest. Very many experienced a flush of national pride—and not infrequently in an exaggerated form ("Jews are the most intelligent, the most capable, the most talented"). I had always found this sort of argument for national pride, whether by Jews or great Russians, alien and incomprehensible . . .

The misfortunes of the Jews played a negative rather than positive role in my self-determination as a Jew. The logic of my thinking was approximately as follows: "You want me to remember always that I am Jewish. You want me to feel Jewish no matter what! Well, I won't! You can put me down in one or another square, depending on the inscription in my passport—you won't provoke me by that. I am I, for myself—and no squares!" . . .

Among the people whose values are the same as mine, I no longer observe the same indefiniteness, the same attempts to place themselves outside the Russian people, regardless of the nationality of their passports. . . .

I see disintegration and confusion in my circle. . . . I doubt that Israel can become my spiritual homeland—for that I would have to be changed completely.

But I would not like this fate for my children and grandchildren.

I'd like them to know their nationality by blood and by spirit—and
to be recognized by it, by that nationality, to belong, and not be
beggars asking for alms.

After the trial of her husband and Andrei Sinyavsky in 1966, Larisa
became intensely involved in many facets of the dissent movement. She
was tried for participating in the Red Square demonstration against
Soviet interference in Czechoslovakia in 1968 and spent four years in
exile at hard labor in Siberia. After her return to Moscow and a new
life, she again left Moscow and lived with exiled Anatoly Marchenko, the author of *My Testimony*, a classic prison-camp chronicle.

For many, Larisa Bogoraz has come to symbolize the very soul and
conscience of Soviet freedom fighters. Those who know her well speak
of a beauty of the soul that radiates from her once-vivacious face, her
graying hair, her exile-reddened hands. In her presence one feels a
searing vitality that was well expressed in her statement to her judges
explaining why she had participated in the Red Square demonstration:

> I love life, and I value freedom. I fully realized that I would be risking
> my freedom, and it was something I didn't want to lose. But I was
> faced with the choice of acting or remaining silent. Had I remained
> silent, it would have meant giving support to an action that I cannot
> condone. It would have amounted to the same thing as lying. I do
> not consider my course the only right one. But for me it was the
> only possible one.

How does Larisa respond now to her Jewishness?

> Who am I now? Whom do I feel myself to be? Unfortunately, I do
> not feel like a Jew. I understand that I have an unquestionable genetic
> tie with Jewry. I also assume that this is reflected in my mentality,
> in my mode of thinking, and in my behavior. But this common
> quality is as little help to me in feeling my Jewish identity as similarity
> of external features—evidently, a more profound, or more general,
> common bond is lacking, such as community of language, culture,
> history, tradition; perhaps, even, of impressions, unconsciously ab-
> sorbed by the senses: what the eye sees, the ear hears, the skin feels.
> By all these characteristics, I am Russian.
>
>   I am accustomed to the color, smell, rustle of the Russian land-
> scape, as I am to the Russian language, the rhythm of Russian poetry.
> I react to everything else as alien. . . .
>
>   And nevertheless, no, I am not Russian. I am a stranger today in
> this land. . . .

For Larisa Bogoraz, who prizes freedom as she does the air she breathes, the world is her home, but Russia is where she must live. As her friends leave, one by one, what will become of her? And what will become of her baby boy, the son of Anatoly Marchenko?

The Soviet Human Rights Committee is decimated. Yesenin-Volpin, who received a *vizov* from Israel, teaches mathematics at Boston University. Chalidze, exiled by the authorities, writes in New York City. Galich seeks to leave. Yelena Bonner Sakharov's children, deprived of further higher education in the USSR, have been invited to MIT, and Sakharov himself has been asked to teach at Princeton. Boris Tsukerman was an early emigrant to Israel.

A former research physicist in spectral analysis at the Moscow Institute of Science, Tsukerman, a pudgy, owlish-looking man of 47, speaks with maddeningly enigmatic slowness, compelling his listeners to hang onto every word lest they miss a gem of insight. His encyclopedic knowledge of Soviet law made him the legal expert of the democratic and Jewish movements. He pioneered in initiating lawsuits under the Postal Convention for damages for failure to deliver mail, and he is perhaps the only person in the USSR to have won a court victory in such a case. He started legal actions, filed official protests, wrote letters objecting to a varied list of official abuses, ranging from demands that *Izvestia* be prosecuted for criminal defamation for a 1968 article condemning the liberal, brief-term Czech foreign minister, to defense of the right to worship of a Christian community in a structure of their own. Finding legal protection for "ancient literature," he challenged the Customs Department's failure to deliver Bibles by mail. Confronting OVIR in court, he fought for the right of Jews to leave. He insisted on academic freedom, decried censorship, and always found a forgotten law, a statement by Lenin or another authority to support his position.

Tsukerman applied to OVIR at the end of November 1970, and permission was quickly granted. He had plagued the Soviet authorities for years, and they were delighted to see him leave. His subtle, formal, understated sense of humor was more irritating than the militant rhetoric of his friends. "I applied to OVIR as a matter of principle," Tsukerman said. "I expected it to be rejected, so naturally it was accepted. Once granted, I went immediately. Russian literature and culture are very dear to me, but I never felt Russia was my motherland. I am a Jew, and Israel is my motherland. I came for spiritual reasons." He arrived in Israel on January 27, 1971.

In Israel, Tsukerman continues to struggle quietly and effectively for human rights and the rights of Soviet citizens to leave. His efforts to compel Israeli authorities to take seriously grants of citizenship to Soviet Jews, and to provide them with the protection international law affords, are almost as annoying to Israeli authorities as were his activities in the USSR to Soviet officials. His wife Shura, a former instructor of Russian literature at the University of Moscow, is a devout Christian believer. In Moscow, their mixed marriage had presented few problems; in Israel, it has created considerable complexities. In the USSR, neither found any contradictions in working simultaneously for the rights of Jews to leave and for civil rights and liberties for all who wished to stay. In Israel, the authorities treat such interests with a considerable degree of coolness.

This singleminded focus on Zionist objectives creates acute discomfort for Jews who are both democrats and Zionists. Some resolve it by not leaving the USSR, others by settling in more open Western countries. Long before they leave Moscow, this conflict is understood by some, and ambivalence and uncertainty as to what their course should be are more common than might be expected.

Roman Rutman is among the friends of Larisa Bogoraz who chose to leave for Israel and ultimately succeeded. From the summer of 1971 to November 1972, when he, too, received permission to leave, Rutman held an unofficial position in the Jewish movement that had been filled previously by Mikhail Zand, among others. He constituted a continuous link to the democrats, acted as a treasurer and money manager for Jewish movement purposes, and helped produce samizdat documents. Like Tsukerman and Zand, Rutman was a sophisticated, cosmopolitan Moscow Jew, a universalist and believer in freedom—Western style— as well as a Zionist of strong conviction. His background is typical of those whose democratic and Jewish feelings merge and separate, meld and fragment.

Born in Kiev in 1934, Rutman was the son of a state factory accountant. When World War II began, the family was evacuated eastward across the Urals to Omsk, where Roman graduated from the Polytechnical Institute in applied mathematical theory. After four years of work in Omsk, he moved to Moscow in 1960 to do postgraduate study at the Academy of Science. The theory of automation control became his specialized field. He received his doctorate and wrote some fifty scientific works in his specialty, many of which were published outside the USSR. Rutman is a short man, with a large head, sensitive hands, and small feet. Owlish eyeglasses dominate his mobile face. He speaks in slow bursts of great intensity. Describing his intellectual metamorphosis, he says:

> I grew up without any religion, but very Jewish. When I was a child, Yiddish was occasionally spoken at home, particularly when my grandparents were present. But Russian was my language, and it is the language and Russian literature that have bound me to Russia. My library is Russian. I speak it well. I write poems and songs in Russian. When articulation is so important to one's life, one feels crippled in any other tongue. Yet as a Jew, somewhere I knew that I was always a stranger. Always alien—a person of lower caste. And then I began questioning things so early. By the time I was twelve, I was politically serious. And by the time I was in university, my doubts and disaffection, although inside me, were great. Then came the Khrushchev speech in 1956, and I knew that what I'd heard on foreign radio broadcasts, and had been thinking, was true. My first serious trouble was in 1959, when Vice President Nixon visited the USSR. I made contact with an American student. I was investigated and questioned by the KGB for four months. It was a serious sin to have contact with the outside world.

In Soviet terms, Rutman was a great success. He had been chief of the laboratory in the Institute of Machinery of the Academy of Sciences and a lecturer at the Institute of Radio Engineering. By Moscow standards, he had a large apartment, a *dacha*, and an automobile. But he also was a democrat and was passionately devoted to a freedom he had never experienced. For a long time he had been a close friend of Larisa Bogoraz-Daniel, and when Yuli Daniel and Andrei Sinyavsky were arrested, Rutman was among those who protested. When Ginzburg and Galanskov were tried, he joined others in mute objection in the snowy subzero cold outside the courthouse.

> We believed then. We believed so strongly that somehow right would prevail—that things could be changed, even in Russia. And then there was the camaraderie of our group. Our sense of unity and our moral correctness and even superiority. And then Czechoslovakia and our impotence against this horror. This was a terrible shock and an awakening. Had we been fooling ourselves? How many people really cared? Did enough people really want a democratic, humane country, or would Russia be what it had always been—one of absolute state power, with no tradition of popular independence? There are too few

Larisas—she is the soul of the movement, but who hears her voice
or that of Tolya [Marchenko]? And then came the renewed brutality.
The new repression.

In 1969, Rutman visited Larisa in exile in Siberia. Now he had irrevocably cast the die as far as the KGB was concerned.
When had Rutman become involved in the Jewish movement?

Not until after the Six-Day War did I even consider going to Israel.
In 1965, I had read Uris's *Exodus* and had identified with the Jewish
struggle and felt a sense of pride in my people. But after the 1967
war, this feeling was enormously strengthened, and after Czechoslovakia I despaired of change in the USSR. My friends were the same
and I continued to share their feelings, but by now I was married to
Elena, and our son Sergei [Elena's by an earlier marriage] was growing up disbelieving everything he heard in school, not belonging to
his society. Where did he fit? Could he ever grow up a free, accepted
person in Russia? In early 1971, we applied to OVIR for a visa. You
know the rest.

The rest was a series of protests, arrests, KGB harassment, petitions,
detentions—the characteristic, intense travail that became the way of
life of the dissident activist. First the instructorship was lost. Then the
job. The Rutmans "ate their car," and the money from that and other
material benefits was exhausted before permission to leave finally came.

Will Israel be really different for me? Will I ever really feel in emotional sympathy with any government? Is it enough to be in a nation
of one's own if that nation and its leaders are not just, or does a man
feel more at home with his own tongue and with friends who share
his convictions? I don't know. Sometimes I think that I would be
better off in the United States or England. There are friends there,
too, and those countries are free. All that I know now is that I feel
dead inside about Russia, and as much as I'll miss my friends, I know
that I'm a Jew and Israel is our only homeland. When Nixon visited
Moscow and many of us were arrested for trying to contact him and
the U.S. government said nothing, I knew that even in free countries,
the leaders were interested in power, not freedom. The U.S. would
rather sell wheat than protect freedom. Where does a man belong?

Where indeed? Grigory Svirsky, a 53-year-old novelist, playwright,
and film writer, was a Communist Party member from the age of 21
until his spirited defense of Aleksandr Solzhenitsyn and his eloquent
exposures of mounting anti-Semitism led to his total official excom-

munication. Several months before he emigrated from the USSR to Israel in April 1972, Svirsky wrote:

> In Stalin's time there was a practice—to deprive the unwanted writer of "fire and water." For a minimum of a year or two. So that he could meditate on an empty stomach.
>
> I was "segregated" from the reader . . . not for a year or two. The blockade is already in its *seventh year*. Its seventh year, but it is no longer a blockade. It is a cynical extrajudicial persecution. In full daylight. To the death! Each anti-Zionist campaign, which was understood by some as anti-Semitic, poured oil onto the fire. . . . if even my name is under the strictest interdict, and this has been going on for seven years, there can be no doubt *I am being killed or pushed out of the country.* . . .
>
> I AM BEING KILLED OR PUSHED OUT OF THE COUNTRY!
>
> I choose the second. But perhaps I exaggerate? Have I the right to call the seven-year blockade of an author murder?
>
> Murder is murder. . . .
>
> The first who could not bear the persecution lasting many years was my wife, lately the bread-winner of the family; exhausted by the intensity of the persecution, by lack of money and of necessities, she fell gravely ill.
>
> There was bitterness in the eyes of our 16-year-old son. His father was being given short shrift under his very eyes. . . . I do not wish to explain or complain any more. I have no more to say to the bureaucratic well-wishers from the Writers' Union: the road to hell is paved with good intentions.
>
> To foist one's love on those who reject one—what can be more insulting! One cannot be loved by force, according to the wisdom of the Russian people.
>
> No, I have not altered my convictions: have not stopped loving the land for which I spilled my blood, my friends, the spontaneous Russian language, which became my life and my fate.
>
> I—a former Russian soldier, who was for four years constantly in battle—wrote in my notebook for '41 . . . the lines of the fallen poet Pavel Kogan, and felt them as my own: "I love the Russian air, the Russian land!"
>
> In those days, my relatives were shot in the back of the head because they were Jews. . . .
>
> I was a Russian writer. I was sure of it. I was accepted into the Union of Writers as a Russian writer. But in 1965, when I started protesting against the anti-Semitism of V. Smirnov, chief editor of the journal *Friendship of the Peoples,* respectable elderly ladies of the official commission flew into a rage, losing the remnants of their respectability: "How is it possible that a Russian writer is a Jew?" . . .
>
> I am a Russian. I believed so for many years. I had grounds for that: I was not alone in defending Russia. My ancestor, grandfather

Girsh, a cantor, a soldier of Nikolai, was wounded nearly 130 years
ago at the first siege of Sebastopol. He served in the Russian army
for twenty-five years and I was named in his honor.

I considered myself a native Russian. But cold, estranged, and
mocking eyes looked at me . . . Enough. Every person has a limit of
endurance. Mine has been reached. Recently, on 29 September 1971,
I reached the age of 50. It is time to stop living feeling like a boy
in a crush in a bus. The boy's nose is on elbow-level. Whoever moves
an elbow, the boy gets a bloody nose. . . .

I do not wish to be the tallest among equals, nor the shortest among
equals.

I want to be equal. . . .

I have had enough of drunk tram hooligans with their saying:
"Hitler did not kill you off" and "Clear off to your Israel!"

Let them be an insignificant part of the people, one could even say
that they are untypical. It does not make it any easier for a man if
somebody untypical spits at him. The spit is typical. . . .

I no longer *believe* in the assimilation of Jews in Russia. At least,
a considerable section of Jews. . . .

Is the assimilation of the branded possible?!

Mimicry is possible. Mimicry is not for me.

I am a Jew.

And having decided this for myself, finally and irrevocably, I want,
I have the right to live . . . among my national majority.

And when the Tsukermans and the Zands, the Rutmans and the
Svirskys get to Israel, what then? The Israeli government has assiduously confirmed that it is not anti-Soviet, but it has discouraged expressions of sympathy by former Soviet Jews for their friends, the
human rights dissenters who remain behind. The purpose is clear.
Israel's leaders do not wish to exacerbate already tenuous relations
with Soviet power, and they believe that more Jews will be released if
no criticism is made of Soviet internal policy. But many Jews who
still retain both ties with and understanding of the Soviet condition
disagree. One such dissenter is Aleksei Tumerman, who said, shortly
after his arrival in Israel:

The regime in the Soviet Union can continue to exist only on one
condition—if absolute lack of freedom continues to rule there. The
granting of some freedom to the inhabitants of the USSR creates a
chain reaction. When people get a little freedom there, then their eyes
are immediately opened and they understand how bad their situation
is. This is the reason for striking such strong blows against intellectual
groups which demanded the freedom of expression, even though they

did not express opposition to the regime itself. In the West, they do not understand that the regime in Russia is not willing to enter into an ideological discussion with opposition groups. This regime simply liquidates anyone who "rebels." The Russians react to criticism, not according to the severity of the criticism, but to the actual damage that it is liable to cause the regime. . . .

Those who think that since the Zionist movement in Russia has no proposals against the Soviet regime itself—in the sense that the democratic movement threatens it—that the Russians will treat the Zionist activists more leniently than the democrats, are mistaken. The Soviets think that the Zionists are likely to bring about a situation in which anyone will be allowed to leave the prison called the Soviet Union, and this is in contradiction to the Russian purpose of preventing the opening of the prison gates. . . . In their opinion, the Zionist movement in the USSR is capable of preventing the signing of the trade agreements between the United States and the USSR . . . so that the Zionist movement constitutes a force liable to harm the most essential interest of the Russian regime if [Senator Henry M.] Jackson succeeds in his struggle. We have already learned that protests alone in these situations do not deter the Russians. The Czechoslovakian invasion is a good example of this. . . . If Jackson fails . . . the Soviet regime will win complete freedom of action and that will be the end of the Zionist movement in the USSR. Only if the Jackson amendment is passed, will the Russians, who are depending on trade with the United States, be forced to increase the rate of emigration from the USSR— not only of Jews, but for everyone who wishes . . .

Even in Israel, Svirsky, Zand, and others have continued to protest the official Soviet persecution of their friends—the mathematician Yury Shikhanovich, for example—just as they signed such petitions and made such protests involving human rights fighters while still in Moscow, but they have done so despite marked official discouragement. On January 25, 1972, at a full plenum of the World Zionist Congress in Jerusalem, a panel of ex-Soviet Jews discussed the dynamics of the Jewish movement. Vladimir Levin, a professor of Russian literature, who described himself as formerly a fully assimilated Russian intellectual but also considered himself a citizen of the world, told of how the 1967 war and the 1968 Czech invasion had drastically altered his views.

Jews in the democratic movement still haven't faced their ultimate reality [Levin said]. Assimilation is a slave psychology. Those Soviet Jews who still wish to be assimilated, who still know nothing of their Jewish heritage, have the psychology of slaves. Two false idols must

be broken—shattered forever. One is the idol of the so-called democratic movement. The other is the illusion that Jewish life is possible
in Russia. I have broken those idols and that is why I am here tonight.

Zand, who was also on the panel, sharply disagreed. Tracing the
origins of the Jewish movement and its relationship to other national
movements in the USSR, he noted that Ukrainians, Lithuanians, Armenians, Georgians—all people with territory on Soviet soil—sought
autonomy within the USSR, but

> the Jewish intention is outward. Jewish culture within the USSR is
> possible only if there is no more Soviet regime. But the Jewish move-
> ment has much in common with other national movements, particu-
> larly if they have no territory, for example, the Crimean Tatars.
> Now they, the Turks, the Germans also want to leave Russia. The
> Jews have influenced these movements.
>   We have had strong contacts and links with the underground move-
> ment, particularly the democrats [Zand continued]. The democratic
> movement is a noble movement. They are a small, heroic group who
> fight a hopeless struggle against a totalitarian society. They are heroes,
> not idols to be broken. These are noble people. Our national move-
> ment could not and would not have existed without the democratic
> movement. They were our mentors. They created the climate that
> made dissent possible. They are men of the law, who helped victims
> in the camps and who always helped Jews. Without their bravery and
> assistance, it would have been difficult to give vent to our views,
> because we had had little experience in such things. We followed the
> path blazed by our teachers—the democrats. This is a matter of basic
> morality. To turn our backs on them would be impossible to us as Jews.

It was Zand who noted that "the democratic movement in the Soviet
Union does not exist as a homogeneous movement." It is composed of
"followers of the law"—legalists like the Soviet Human Rights Committee; practical idealists, best exemplified by the Initiative Group;
liberal Marxists, exemplified by Zhores and Roy Medvedev; and neo-
Christians, of whom Solzhenitsyn is a good example. But the Jewish
movement, *as such*, does not intervene in Soviet internal affairs, despite
the love many Jews bear for the Russian land where they were born,
the Russian language that they know and use so well, the Russian
culture in which they were steeped, and the Russian intelligentsia of
which they were a part. Their only goal is to leave, and their struggle
to do so is, in their view, completely legal and sanctioned by both
Soviet and international law. As Zand has noted,

The fact that we don't intervene in internal Soviet affairs does not mean that we do not sympathize with the democratic movement there, or that the movement does not sympathize with us. Our best friends in the Soviet Union are the Russian intelligentsia, with their democratic and liberal traditions. They understand our feelings, and as far as they can, they help us. Russian intellectuals were present, so to speak, at the trials of Jews in the last years of the Stalin era. They saw the massacre of the Jewish intelligentsia, and as a natural protest against it they became Judeophiles. For Russian intellectuals to be anti-Semites is a shameful thing, and to be a friend of Jews is a matter of honor.

Tragically, simultaneously with "détente" and the expatriation of Jews, the democratic movement is under heavier assault than at any time in its existence. The ultimate logic of the Soviet regime—Stalinism —is reasserting itself. It is a myth that, whatever its intention, the Jewish movement, the democratic movement—or any other form of opposition—is not, in effect, subversive. In a one-party, one-class, one-ideology regime, the ambit of nonconformity is so circumscribed that any ideological variation, any insistence on rule of law, any freedom of the mind, whether it be cultural or scientific, must be subversive to the regime. Political, cultural, national expression, or any freedom of thought or action in a sector the state seeks to occupy, becomes, in the eyes of the state, illegal, anti-Soviet dissent.

And if the Jews are the only ones who have had a measure of success, that is due, not to their moral superiority, but rather to the fact that they have been heard. They exert power because they have millions of lobbyists in the outside world—fellow-Jews and compassionate libertarians who have heard their voice and responded. That is the key difference. That is what must be understood. And to be silent is to be morally bankrupt.

In a letter I have just received, Vladimir Slepak, a heroic Jew who has not been permitted to leave the Soviet Union after more than four years of struggle, wrote:

> I am aware that you are awaiting a detailed letter about the state of our affairs. But, tragically, there is actually nothing to write about. Nothing is happening here now that would be worth mentioning. . . . These are tragic days when newspapers, radio, and TV are silent about us. These are wasted days, days of unfulfilled hopes and despair. For to act is easier than to wait. But it is not always possible and worthwhile to do something that would attract the attention of the

press. On these routine days, it is much more difficult to preserve
one's fortitude than on the days of sit-ins and hunger strikes. Conditions in political camps have become considerably worse now. It was
preceded by a well-organized campaign aimed at limiting the amount
of information coming out of prison camps. . . .

The same thing is happening in what we call the "outer zone," the
rest of the country. Besides the fact that most of our mail is not
delivered, more and more telephones that we used to contact friends
in Israel and in the West are being disconnected. What will be next?
Things seem to be ominously similar, don't they?

So, if one day you find that no more information is coming from
us, that would mean we have been gagged and things are very bad for
us. But be sure that we will stand our ground and be firm, no matter
what happens to us . . .

The freedom of Slepak and the safety of Sakharov depend on those
who care in the West. This book is dedicated to them in the hope that
their voices will be heard.

EPILOGUE

Five years have passed since the first edition of *The Last Exodus* appeared. Given publishing technology, it has been almost six years since the writing of it occurred. This is a miniscule period of time in the life of a people. But, if we date the modern Soviet Jewry Movement from June 1967, when the Six-Day War ignited latent, suppressed Jewish nationalism, half of its contemporary history has been subsequent to the book's preparation. Although it is perhaps presumptuous for me to appraise the continuing validity of what I wrote then, I believe that the passage of time has not created the need to rewrite what was reported.

The Last Exodus sought to chronicle the story of a remarkable, contemporary freedom movement from the perspective of the participants. Time and new knowledge have not altered the factuality of that history, nor the correctness of what was perceived at the time. Time has permitted us to place the meaning of events in a broader perspective—their relationship to modern Jewish and Soviet history. It would be feasible to document the events that have taken place since early 1974. But for a fundamental understanding of the meaning of the Soviet Jewish Movement, the elaboration of facts, however interesting, heroic, controversial, and complex, appears to be unnecessary. I believe that the book can and should remain as written. This epilogue is therefore designed to place it in the broader perspective of historical trends; to comment on the effects of the book itself upon the events it reports; and to note changes, developments, and directions that could not be anticipated or which strongly underline trends that were much murkier more than half a decade ago.

By the end of 1973, a relatively small percentage of the early leading figures in the Movement had been able to leave the Soviet Union. Since then, the overwhelming majority of the people discussed have emigrated. They are free to tell their own story. A number of them have read *The Last Exodus,* and some have discussed it with me. It is a tribute to my original sources that there were virtually no factual errors, and little quarrel with interpretive material, from the participants themselves. Where such errors were verified, changes were made in this edition.

In January 1976, Vitaly Rubin, one of the most sensitive and distinguished scholars, activists, and observers in the Soviet Union, wrote me from Moscow. Rubin, a world-famous Sinologist, the author of *Individual and State in Ancient China* (New York: Columbia University Press, 1976) and many other works, had been seeking permission to leave the Soviet Union since 1972. (Rubin subsequently received his exit visa, and is now a professor at Hebrew University living in Jerusalem.) He wrote:

> Not long ago I read your book for the second time. I prepared a lecture about the 1st Leningrad trial on its 5th anniversary with the help of it. I want to tell you that so far as I know (and I think I am informed), your book is the best history of the first period of the Exodus of Soviet Jewry.
>
> Unfortunately, we are not able to write our own history. The archives are taken by the KGB. Foreign books, magazines and newspapers in libraries are closed for us, and we do have not such first-rate sources as interviews. That's why we ourselves don't know many facts of the struggle of our people in different parts of the Soviet Union, and it is not easy for us to remember the exact sequence of events and to have the whole picture. These reasons make your book invaluable for us. I am happy that several days ago some Americans brought it to me and now I have my own copy. (Before this I borrowed it from Vladimir Slepak.)
>
> The understanding of our movement shown by you is wonderful. . . .

Rubin's letter sought to differentiate the events reported in this volume from what he called the second period of the Movement. He noted:

> . . . I already mentioned that I think you have created a superb book about the first period. As I see it, we are living in the second period, different from the first in many respects. First of all, the second period is a period of *mass* emigration. As a result of the self-sacrifice of the leaders of the first period (*e.g.,* those convicted in the first Leningrad trial), Soviet leadership was forced to open the gate of their giant jail, and through this gate sent to freedom more than 120,000 people. Soviet leadership in August 1972 attempted to close the door again with the "education tax," but without success. Their action aroused vigorous response from the United States Congress, and for the first time in the history of the Soviet regime, they were forced to drop their repressive measure. . . .

We may speak about the differences of the second period from the first period at several levels. On the level of the activity of the Movement, on the level of the response of the regime, and on the international level. When the first generation leaders were no longer active, the scientists, who came to the leadership, created forms of activity peculiar to them, *e.g.*, seminars. The first seminar was initiated by Alexander Voronel in the fall of 1972. In cooperation with him, almost simultaneously there was initiated my seminar concerning Jewish history, religion and philosophy. (I am a rather untypical figure in the leadership, because I am the only scholar, who is not a scientist.) . . .

On the level of the regime's response, one may see their unwillingness to repeat the experiences of 1970-71 with political processes against "anti-Soviet" Zionist activity. It is clear that they did not achieve their goal—to intimidate—and they don't see this experience as positive. When they try people now they do it under different pretexts and tend to avoid mentioning Israel and Zionism. The purpose now is not to create the impression abroad that it is political persecution, yet, on the other hand to intimidate the active Jewish refuseniks, especially in the provinces. In Moscow, they have apparently dropped some forms of harassment and persecution. For instance, the last press conference with foreign journalists that was disrupted by KGB with brutal force, was in October 1973. Since then, we have been able to see foreign newsmen without any difficulty.

And—last but not least—at the international level, contact with foreign representatives of different levels—from U.S. Senators and Congressmen to the people from Jewish organizations and synagogues and also average Jewish tourists—is going without interruption. These contacts have enormous moral meaning for Soviet Jews: they see that they are not alone, they begin to know and to feel what Jewish solidarity is which kept our people alive for millennia. These contacts also educate the Soviet authorities. Although they repeat that there is not a Jewish problem, they don't believe it themselves. They see that the Jewish question is not their internal affair—it is an international question. It is very unpleasant for them, but they cannot change it.

And if you speak in your book about the USSR and Israel, now it makes more sense to speak about the USSR and the USA. All of us will settle in Israel: but we have the feeling that without the support of the West—mainly American Jewry and the American people—we would be in prison camps long ago. Instead of this we are witnessing a strange phenomenon: the group of politically active people (who did not want to be politically active or even to live here) for years have openly expressed their dissident views and yet they are still living in their apartments with their families. I have an impression that the Soviets don't know what to do with us. Finally, they will be forced to make their choice: to put us in prison or to give us permission to emigrate.

Rubin's effort to classify this on-going, unique historical experience into periods was valid. It was an appropriate and characteristic exercise for a historian who was on the scene. His letter is a superior example of the numerous efforts that have been made to explicate with historic logic the dynamic and changing Soviet Jewry Movement. Yet, I believe that no effort

THE LAST EXODUS

at classification—no corseting of the Movement by historic logic; no doctrinal encapsulation of it into a specific, time-limited, historically unique phenomenon—can be wholly successful. Neither Jewish nor Russian-Soviet history begins in 1967. Thus, the contemporary (now twelve-year-old) history of the Soviet Jewish Movement, in my view, can best be comprehended within the context of contemporary (nineteenth and twentieth century) Jewish history. It is not a historic isolate. Contemporary Jewish history, in turn, is inevitably intertwined in the life and events of the primary places where Jews live.

As this is written (May 1979) virtually all of the Leningrad trial defendants have been freed, including Dymshits and Kuznetsov, who had received death sentences, reduced to fifteen years. Silva Zalmanson's sentence was commuted years ago. Most of the prisoners of conscience and Movement leaders discussed in the book now live in Israel, their heroic period behind them, pursuing more or less normal lives except for the permanent emotional scars left by long years in the Gulag. The most intractable refusenik cases have proven not to be "impossible" at all. Polina Epelman, the wife of a defector, and thus by conventional wisdom a permanent prisoner of the regime, received an exit visa; joined her professor husband in Israel; bore a new child; emigrated to Canada and then the United States; has returned to her profession as a pharmacist; and is well on the way to American citizenship. Refusenik scientists, who by virtue of their international status and their indisputably seminal minds were Soviet national assets, and whose emigration was a meaningful technologic increment to the receiving country, have now departed. When Academician Venyamin Levich is permitted to leave as he has been, it would appear that there is no logical, comprehensible constraint that exists to prevent any individual Jewish exodus. By now, refuseniks such as the most distinguished artistic celebrities (Valery Panov); famous scholars (Vitaly Rubin); great scientists (Levich); "dangerous" prisoners serving long terms (Dymshits and Kuznetsov)—all have been freed. No reason exists to believe that there is any category of person who will be permanently held by the regime. But many believe that the *policy* of the regime is purposely unpredictable. There are some hardcore refusenik cases, such as Academician Aleksandr Lerner, whose applications for exit visas, made almost a decade ago, have still not been granted despite constant reapplication, political agitation, and support from abroad. Activist Movement leaders, notably Vladimir Slepak, Grigory Goldstein, Ida Nudel, and Yosef Begin, after years of struggle, have been prosecuted, receiving sentences in labor camps and exile. For some, rights deprivation, harassment, repression, and hopelessness have become chronic. The brutal bureaucracy of the regime has eclipsed hope—despite the activists' knowledge that no hope is too extreme, that nothing is impossible, and that even for them the great Soviet prison doors may open. Conscious random irrationality and example setting remain a potent weapon to discourage the right to leave. The lack of predictable logic as to why some are victimized tends to inhibit all.

Emigration statistics for the total period reveal somewhat more than they obscure and may usefully assist in our quest for historical perspective. An epilogue does not permit the extensive evaluation, refinement, and explication of statistics. We merely note that the numbers vary, depending on the terms used, the political interest of the statistic providers, and other nonstatistical considerations, including propaganda, public relations, and plain inefficiency. The table that follows comes from Israeli sources and is in some minor respects questionable and even confused. Nonetheless, it permits a graphic summary of events.

As of this writing it would appear that 50,000 to 60,000 Jews may be released from the USSR during 1979—by far the largest annual emigration in the history of the USSR. Most of these (perhaps 65-70 percent) are expected to choose the United States as their ultimate haven. Over 200,000 Jews have been permitted to leave the USSR since the contemporary Jewish movement began. A small, but increasing number have left the USSR on visas issued to other countries, such as the United States. This group is

SOVIET JEWISH EMIGRATION SINCE THE SIX-DAY WAR

Year	Israel Visas Issued by USSR	Emigrants Leaving the USSR	Emigrants Arriving in Israel	Emigrants to Countries Other than Israel	New Invitations Sent from Israel
1968	379	229	231	—	6,786
1969	2,902	2,979	3,033	—	27,301
1970	1,046	1,027	999	—	4,830
1971	14,310	13,022	12,819	58	40,794
1972	31,478	31,681	31,652	251	67,895
1973	34.922	34,733	33,477	1,456	58,216
1974	20,181	20,628	16,816	3,879	42,843
1975	13,139	13,221	8,531	4,928	34,145
1976	14,138	14,261	7,279	7,004	36,104
1977	17,159	16,736	8,348	8,483	43,062
1978	30,594	28,865	12,231	16,867	105,711
Total	180,248	177,382	135,416	42,926	467,687

not included in the tabular summary. A continually mounting number of Soviet Jews, including some prominent leaders of the Movement, have lived in Israel for a period of time and then re-emigrated to Western countries, primarily the United States. These facts remain undocumented by reliable statistics. Reasons for the disillusionment of some Soviet Jews with Israel have been frequently documented. One documentation is Ephraim Sevela's book, *Farewell Israel* (South Bend, Indiana: Gateway Editions, 1977). Sevela was a Moscow activist and a well-known Soviet screenwriter and film maker before his emigration to Israel in 1971. More unusual, though far more publicized in Western media, and particularly in the Soviet press, are those Soviet Jews who have left Israel with the intent of returning to the USSR. Many of them still remain, as miserable displaced pariahs, in European cities like Vienna and Brussels. Given a total emigration in excess of 200,000, the few thousand people in such categories are statistically insignificant, although dramatic in their quotient of human misery.

It should be noted that although the number of invitations (*vizovs*) sent from Israel to Soviet Jews approached half a million in the twelve years involved, some of the *vizovs* were to the same family, others were duplicative in varied ways, and more importantly many did not reach their destination because of KGB mail interference. There is no establishable correlation between the number of persons receiving invitations (*vizovs*) from Israel and the number applying for visas to leave from the Soviet authorities (OVIR).

Lastly, it seems important to note that these statistics, interesting as they are, tell us only a small part of the meaningful story. Certainly, historical perspective makes it relevant that the Soviet Jews who came to Israel, became Israeli citizens, and then left—i.e., those who became *yordim* (Jewish emigrants from Israel)—are still much less than 10 percent of those who become *olim* (Jewish immigrants to Israel). This is in marked contrast to *olim* from Western countries who leave Israel at a ratio five to ten times higher than that of Soviet *olim*. Further, the number of *yordim* among Israeli-born Jews has increased. There are now approximately as many *yordim* as *olim* each year, and many times more Israeli *yordim* in America than there are American *olim* in Israel. Viewed in this context, the Zionist steadfastness of the Soviet Jewish Movement remains remarkably high in contrast to overall Jewish constancy toward Israel.

These fundamental patterns lead to other basic observations, distillable from the perspective of a dozen years.

In all likelihood the issue of Soviet Jewry will remain a chronic one, with exacerbations and remissions in its fever level and its effect on the world outside the USSR. Absent some even more extraordinary events than have occurred, or some unspeakable, genocidal tragedy—both essentially not predictable but not excludable—Jews will still be seeking to leave and will be continuing their exodus from the USSR at the beginning of the twenty-first century.

Few Soviet Jews have remained unaffected by the events of the past decade. Even those who are Communist Party members are dramatically affected by the emigration movement. Some documentation indicates that almost 300,000 Jews, constituting approximately 13 percent of the Jewish population, are party members. It seems clear that the Soviet perception of the Jew as the "outsider"—the "rootless cosmopolitan"—has become a self-fulfilling prophecy. Jewish alienation from Soviet society, always present, has become substantially institutionalized on a two-way basis. Although assimilation has been officially encouraged and frequently practiced, it is now increasingly being viewed as unachievable. All Jews, whether assimilated party members or not, are being seen in regime terms as unreliable. Thus, the ability of Soviet Jews to successfully penetrate the upper reaches of the Soviet power structure has been drastically reduced, with its inevitable concomitant—the near universality of Jewish alienation from the society.

The chronicity of the issue arises from the awareness of the future long-term presence of the "Jewish problem"; the substantial size of the Jewish population; the awakening and revival of interest in Jewish religion, culture, and history—all the accoutrements of Judaism as a religious civilization; combined with the almost total absence of access to Jewish experience. Consequently, there will be increasing concern by Soviet Jews and the world Jewish community over the right to have Jewish identity and expression within the Soviet Union.

Endemic Russian anti-Semitism, now buttressed by the official anti-Semitism of the regime (often in the guise of anti-Zionism or anti-Israel politics), has substantially increased, and is seemingly institutionalized in its more overt, rabid form. Anti-Semitism is accompanied by increased discrimination, evidenced by an almost total absence of upward mobility; severe and increasing entry limitations into the heretofore heavily Jewish scientific and art sectors; and widespread understanding that economic opportunity is being curtailed, and that children will have far less chance for advanced educational opportunities than their parents had. Anti-Semitism and discrimination have their profound long-term effect, fueling the already developed emigration pressures.

Any simplistic generalities concerning Soviet Jews should by now have been dispelled. We know that they are far more heterogenous than Jewish populations in any European countries. The major differences in culture, language, and historical experience between the three broad groups (all of which have multiple subdivisions)—(1) Asian Jews (e.g., Georgian, Bukharan, and Mountain Jews), (2) Soviet heartland Ashkenazis (RSFSR, Ukraine, Byelorussia), and (3) Jews from the Western borderlands (the Baltic states and pre-World War II Polish, Rumanian, Hungarian, and Czechoslovakian territories)—lead to ideologic, political, and emigration goal differences. These differences have dramatic manifestations, including the definition of the character of the Movement itself. Unquestionably, in its inception and early years, the Movement not only had the rhetoric of political Zionism, but its behavior was the most dramatic affirmation of Zionism in Zionism's eighty-year history. Until 1973, not more than 2 percent of all Jews who left the USSR chose to go anywhere other than Israel—thus fully supporting the thesis that the Soviet Jewry Movement was indeed a "repatriation movement." To Israeli ideologues this phenomenon was a euphorically staggering vindication. It was not at first noticed or understood that in these early years fully two-thirds of the immigrants to Israel came from the border states and Georgia, although less than 10 percent of all Soviet Jews reside in those areas. On the other hand, the 80 percent of the Jewish population residing in the largely urban heartland republics produced less than 15 percent of the Israel emigration. Soviet Jews from the large population centers (Moscow, Leningrad, Kiev, Odessa, Kharkov, Sverdlovsk, Minsk, etc.) are often third or fourth generation Soviet citizens, far removed in time and understanding from the religio-culture of their people. They are heavy consumers and producers of Russian culture. In the large they are educated, impressed with Western technological and cultural values, urban, and alienated. It is little wonder then that once the reservoir of Zionist-committed Jews (e.g., in Latvia and Georgia) was substantially drained, the relative percentage of Jews emigrating from the far more populous heartland republics increased drastically as did the percentages of Jews going to Western countries rather than Israel. By 1978, almost two-thirds of all Soviet Jews were emigrating to the United States, most of these people from large heartland cities, where the heavy Jewish populations reside. This would clearly appear to be an irreversible trend. Similarly the high level of Zionist commitment of the early years would now seem to have been specific to the time, and of short-term duration. Although Zionist rhetoric remains a fundamental feature of Movement literature, emigration conduct is much more significant.

As the 1967 Six-Day War is a convenient bench mark for the beginning of the Soviet Jewry Movement, the 1973 Yom Kippur War can be similarly useful as the turning point from its predominantly Zionist character to its more historically traditional Jewish conduct. That war demonstrated that the belief in Israel's military invincibility was an illusion. The internal scandals in Israel following the war reminded Jews everywhere that Israel was not a utopian Zionist paradise, but a hard pressed, small nation with all the usual warts and blemishes of states, plus an extraordinary vulnerability to the likelihood of future war. The post-1967 euphoria was replaced by a post-1973 sober reality. The percentage of Soviet Jews going to countries other than Israel rose roughly from 5 percent in 1973 to 20 percent in 1974; 35 percent in 1975; 50 percent in 1976; and continuously upward since then.

All present indications are that the overwhelming majority of Soviet Jews do not leave the USSR because they are Zionists, but because of their perception that their society is anti-Semitic, discriminatory, and that they and their children will be denied upward social mobility. Thus they move *from* a country where they are disadvantaged because of restrictions on Jews, lack of economic opportunity, and bureaucratic repression, which results in their political and intellectual alienation. They move *to* countries where they see the opportunity for upward mobility—particularly in terms of the advanced education of their children, economic opportunity, full utilization of their profession skill, freedom for creative growth and from bureaucratic repression, and where extended family exists. The United States is the principal land of such opportunity, freedom, and family connection. It is therefore no surprise that close to 50,000 Soviet Jews have recently come to the United States and tens of thousands of others wish to do so, if the human right to leave becomes an institutionalized reality. Emigration motivation thus has little to do with Zionist ideology. It has a great deal to do with the characteristic patterns of modern Jewish history and the oppressiveness of Soviet life.

Between 1880 and 1925 (when open emigration to the United States was halted), over 2.5 million Jews, about one-third of the Jewish population of Eastern Europe, came to America. During the same period, despite the ideological and political activity of Zionist parties in all Eastern European Jewish communities, less than a tenth of that number emigrated to Palestine, and a large percentage of those emigrants left the rigors of that life, often moving on to America. Today, after more than thirty years of Jewish statehood, more than five times as many Israelis are living in the United States and Canada than there are American Jews living in Israel. Frustrating and disappointing as these facts are to many Zionists, they constitute a central reality of modern Jewish history. Denigrating epithets such as *"noshrim"* (dropouts), employed with alacrity in recent years to those Soviet Jews who, receiving Israel exit visas, choose Western countries rather than Israel, not only fail to reverse the trend, they show an incomprehension of Jewish history and the basic human right of free choice.

Within the past century, during which freedom of movement has become increasingly technically feasible, Jews have moved *from* lands of oppression *to* lands of opportunity, when the country of oppression permitted migration and the country of opportunity accepted immigrants. In such migrations the opportunity for full religious expression has been much less important than the opportunity for a college degree. Political Zionism—a land of one's own—has been much less important than a house or business of one's own. Much of the Jewish migration of the past century has been by East European Jews, from lands now within the present territorial boundaries of the USSR.

The behavior of contemporary Soviet Jewry can be appropriately contrasted to that of the parents, grandparents, and great-grandparents of most Western Jews who are descendants of this stock. Many commentators have observed that Russian Jewry has been the most prolific, vigorous, and creative people in modern Jewish history. It has supplied much of the leadership and creative vigor of Israel, a substantial part of the leadership of the Jewish communities of America, and has made enormous contributions to science, aesthetics, and scholarship both in the United States and in the USSR. The people composing the current Soviet Jewish Movement, in perspective, are often strikingly reminiscent of those portrayed in *World of Our Fathers: The Journey of the East European Jews to America and the Life They Found and Made,* by Irving Howe (New York: Harcourt Brace Jovanovich, 1976).

Contrary to the early hopes and illusions, the majority of Soviet Jews, like the majority of their ancestors and like the majority of other Jews from other lands, are *not* Zionists, despite the Holocaust and the foundation and continued existence of the state of Israel. (Since it is commonly said that most Jews have become Zionists, it should be noted that I mean by Zionism, a commitment to live in Israel, not simply financial, political, and moral support of that country.)

Although in the early years almost 100 percent of Soviet Jews came as *olim,* casting their lot with the Jewish state and rejecting life in the USSR or any part of the diaspora, after 1973 in increasing numbers those who emigrated voted with their feet to go West. This development led to hysterical, insensitive, extreme reactions from Israeli and Jewish Agency officials. The first manifestation of this was the effort mounted to compel organized Jewish communities to deny any economic assistance to impoverished Soviet Jews who having come to Israel decided to live elsewhere. This was followed by a brutish insistence that funds be totally denied *noshrim*. This astonishing abdication of century-old Jewish community commitment to aid the poor and oppressed was justified to obsequious sycophants in diaspora countries by asserting that Soviet Jews had perpetrated a fraud by accepting visas to Israel and then going to the West. This sophistry ultimately failed, since it was well known that for the Soviet Union the ideology of "repatriation" to Israel and the concept of family reunification were merely convenient rationalizations for the current emigration policy. The regime even used the repatriation pretext when it issued exit visas to Israel for non-Jews who had publicly indicated their intent to go West. It has been obvious that the Israel visa is a comforting fiction to Soviet authorities, and is a pragmatic mechanism for Jewish rescue from the USSR. The continued rejection of Israeli and Jewish Agency pressures to deny funds to Soviet Jews who do not go to Israel can only be counted as a triumph for traditional Jewish values.

These events help verify the perspective that the Soviet Jewry Movement conforms to the main creative forces of Jewish history, rather than being an idealistic Zionist aberration.

In the perspective of a dozen years, some earlier directions have now been confirmed. Most observers agree that once the Soviet Jewry Movement surfaced, was identified in the West, and had developed a sense of its own character and existence as a movement, its continued vitality and successes became largely reliant upon American Jewish supporters and the active and potential intervention of the United States government.

The publication and use of this book constitutes a confirmation of that fact. As Vitaly Rubin noted in his letter to me, Soviet Jews have best learned about themselves from their friends abroad, who by recording their history permit them to see a reflection of their own identity. A people or movement must be nourished by knowledge of their own history. Without a press, journals, research centers, and universities, how can a people know themselves? This book is the first, and still the only, book that tells the story of the contemporary Soviet Jewry Movement through its own eyes. It is particularly valuable for them, since it permits them to be recorded and thus reflected. Soviet Jewry activists in the West have understood this lesson well. Their primary task has been to report, publish, document, spread, and return information to the activists within the Soviet

Union. Telephone links, hot lines, newsletters, press conferences, all have had these purposes: securing popular and governmental support in the West; acting as the voice and reflection of the captive Movement; and being a communication system, keeping Soviet Jews informed about themselves, aware of and in contact with their Western supporters.

Shortly after the first publication of this book, activists in the United States began to smuggle copies of it into the USSR. Later travelers learned that the book had been seen in a number of cities and that typed *samizdat* copies of fifty to sixty pages of the book were being circulated in cities like Kharkov and Kiev. Later there were reports that translations of some of the chapters into Russian had occurred. It became an important source book for Soviet activists preparing their own *samizdat* journals.

This kind of support was vital to the Movement. Crucial factors in the success it has achieved in recent years were extensions and reconfirmations of tactics and directions that had already emerged by 1972. The original assumption of Movement leaders was that the link to Israel and its government was the critical one for implementing their struggle. For many reasons, this became obviously erroneous. All contacts were to be with the Israeli government office with self-delegated authority to coordinate the Soviet Jewry struggle throughout the world. The activists soon learned to call this apparatus, headed since 1970 by Nechemia Levanon, the "office without a name." Nechemia's office proved consistently inept; at times half-hearted and ambiguous; primarily concerned with *aliyah*, not rescue; and the prisoner of a largely inapplicable post-World War II experience and mentality. Most importantly, it lost the confidence of activists, both within the USSR and in Western countries.

The obsession of Soviet leaders with the perceived menace of Chinese power, led to a major Soviet detente gambit in February 1971, which has continued to this date. Detente for the Soviets meant at least the neutralization of the United States in the Sino-Soviet struggle. This, in turn, required the Soviet regime to be finely tuned to congressional sentiments and not to be too insensitive to American public opinion. Furthermore, the increasing dominance of oil in foreign policy changed the Middle East from a secondary focus of international power politics to the primary one, making evident what had long been true—that Israel was a client state of the United States, without power to control events, let alone free Soviet Jews.

Under these circumstances the Soviet Jewry issue became significant in the world politics of the 1970s. Next to the support of Israel it occupied the highest political priority for most Jews in Western countries. Realization of this led to the kinds of tactics Rubin describes in his letter to me. Characteristic of the Movement's focus was their instigation of what became the Jackson-Vanik Bill, and their continued support of that legislation.

In August 1972, when the Soviet regime imposed the notorious education tax that required, as a precondition of emigration, repayment to the state of the claimed massive costs of secondary education, the response of Movement and Soviet democratic leaders was that the United States should condition any economic benefits to the USSR upon Soviet adherence to the fundamental human right to leave one's country. This proposed tactic found expression in Senator Jackson's insistence upon linkage between economic aid and free emigration. The Soviet government ceased requiring payment of the education tax, and the Movement marshaled its forces in support of the Jackson legislation. Years after the passage of the Jackson-Vanik Bill, efforts to eliminate linkage or neutralize its legislative effects still result in vigorous Movement opposition.

Activist Movement leadership knows that if changes are to occur in Soviet policy toward them, these changes will take place because of pressures, in fact or anticipated, from the United States government. Movement leaders appreciate that apart from their own capacity to make direct appeals, they have available to them a potent pressure group—the Jewish communities of the western world. Movement leaders know the names and political attitudes of members of Congress far better than they know details about Soviet elective officials. They have invoked the provisions of the Helsinki Agreement, prepared documentation for the Belgrade Conference, and endlessly cited international human rights covenants, because they know that the Soviet regime, under American prodding, has great sensitivity and vulnerability in these areas. Their first-line allies are the Soviet Jewry activists in the West. Their targets are American public opinion, Congress, and the President. This is where the action is. This is where their *samizdat* literature, letters, petitions, telephone calls, and pleas are directed.

The classic illustrative case of the maturing directions of the Soviet Jewry movement and Soviet and Western responses to it is that of Anatoly Shcharansky. Shcharansky, a talented computer scientist, was arrested in early 1977 to the accompaniment of extensive and exceptional Soviet news charges that he was a CIA-sponsored espionage agent. Shcharansky had, as a very young man, become a part of the Jewish movement in Moscow, applied for an exit visa, and been refused. His young wife, Natalya, received permission to leave Moscow the day after their marriage and has been in Israel (where she adopted the Hebrew first name of Avital) ever since. Meanwhile Shcharansky, who speaks fluent English, was the primary direct contact person for the Movement with the Western press. He was involved in multiple activist ways, his name, face, and voice becoming well known in the West. A British television film company produced two documentaries featuring Shcharansky and his commentaries—audaciously filmed in Moscow. Shcharansky acted as a tour guide of Soviet dissidents, covering the wide spectrum of human rights protest activities. He also became a founder and one of the spokesmen of the Helsinki Watch Committee, a monitoring group committed to seeing that Soviet regime failures to adhere to its Helsinki Agreement human rights commitments would become known to the world. Shcharansky, with his courageous confrontation politics, had committed too many cardinal sins for the regime. He, and virtually all members of the Helsinki Watch committees, were prosecuted, usually on catch-all bases such as "anti-Soviet" activity. Shcharansky was particularly targeted for regime revenge and example-setting by being charged with espionage on behalf of the CIA. The President of the United States took the unprecedented step of publicly denying that Shcharansky had ever been any kind of a CIA agent. Worldwide protest over his arrest was ignored. He remained incommunicado in detention for well over a year, without an attorney or any semblance of what could be described as due process. Shcharansky then endured a predictably rigged trial, distinguished only by the paucity of evidence of anything other than that he was a dissident human rights and Jewish activist. The trial resulted in a thirteen-year sentence; cover pictures on news magazines all over the world; the strong protests of government leaders in the United States and other countries; and the continuing global crisscrossing in his behalf by his beautiful wife, Avital, and her articulate and indefatigable brother, Michael Stiglitz. Shcharansky is indeed a fitting modern hero, and his supporters are admirable and skillful proponents of his cause.

What then distinguishes Shcharansky from earlier Soviet Jewish prisoners of conscience? First, more than any other such case, it has become an international incident of substantial proportions, involving the integrity of the President of the United States, and the stubborn vengeance of the example-setting Soviet authorities. Secondly, Shcharansky is not merely a Zionist hero—he is much more complex, embodying Zionist attachment, human rights commitments, intimate and interlocking connections with the democratic movement and other Soviet dissident groups, and a sophisticated political awareness that permitted him to recognize that political leverage could be applied most effectively by means of Western media and politicians (particularly American). The campaign for his release thus symbolically becomes the most important confrontation in the rapidly expanding Soviet Jewry struggle.

The Israel "office without a name" has, not so strangely, been ambivalent, lukewarm, and sometimes standoffish about the Shcharansky case. The documentation of these attitudes and how they expressed themselves is highly instructive, illustrating some central theses that have become clearer with the passage of time. The Israeli authorities responsible for Soviet Jewry do not tolerate the heresy of diluting Zionism by solidarity with democrats and other dissidents. They fear Soviet Jewry political activity that is not under their control. Thus independent activists within the Soviet Union, in Israel, or in the countries of the West, are suspect to them and subjected to intense criticism. The activists feel that Nechemia's office has been consistently manipulative and obstructionist. The Israelis have felt that Shcharansky was never "their man." The movement in his support has been wholly out of their control. They accurately perceive that it is Shcharansky and his supporters who characterize the future direction of the Movement and its tactics. This spells the end of their power and control.

Like King Canute commanding the waves to retreat, those who would attempt to roll back the Movement to its pristine Zionist days are fated to damp frustration. Soviet Jews are the legitimate descendants of the Jewish generations that preceded them. They are creating exciting new chapters in the long and rich history of the Jewish people—and in the process they are affecting detente and the delicate world power balance.

BIBLIOGRAPHICAL
NOTES

My sources of information include tape-recorded and other conversations and interviews in Israel, Western Europe, the USSR, and the United States with persons discussed in this book. Much of the background material and quoted information comes from *samizdat* documents which I secured in various ways. Some were smuggled or brought to me and were translated into English by persons I knew to be reliable. I have edited or shortened some passages to make them more readable, to eliminate repetition, or to simplify and clarify ideas. Other documents were secured and/or translated by the Israeli office responsible for Soviet Jewish affairs. Still others were received by individuals, and I have generally relied on their translations. Where I have utilized lengthy quotations from *samizdat* materials, I refer to the source of the original English publication or translation.

The news media I consulted are too numerous to cite in detail, but they include *The New York Times,* the *Washington Post,* the *Los Angeles Times,* and American news magazines; *The Times, The Daily Telegraph,* and the *Jewish Chronicle* of London, and other British newspapers and journals; the English-language *Jerusalem Post,* the Hebrew-language *Haaretz* and *Maariv;* and the *International Herald Tribune.*

My most important secondary source was the *News Bulletin on Soviet Jewry,* a collection of news letters and bulletins assembled, translated, and issued by a group in Israel called the Action Committee of Newcomers from the Soviet Union. Ann Shenkar, the American-born wife of a prominent Israeli manufacturer whose family emigrated from the USSR, was the principal English-language editor of the *News Bulletin,* and she, more than any other person, made available in English the continuing documentation of the Jewish movement. The first *News Bulletin,* dated December 31, 1970, was a report of a telephone conversation between Aron Bogdanovsky at the Shenkar home in Givataim, Israel, and Leonid Rigerman, then in Moscow. For the next nine months, the *News Bulletin* frequently but irregularly reported important news as it occurred, and by the fall of 1971, it began to appear regularly. Well edited, detailed, and invaluable, it was, during the period of its existence, the single most important reference. Most of its information was derived from regular telephone conversations between

417

activists in the USSR and activists in Israel, which were recorded. Letters, petitions, and other *samizdat* documents were read over the telephone. *The News Bulletin* also published *samizdat* documents smuggled out of the Soviet Union and information brought out by Soviet Jews who were permitted to go to Israel. Its style and method were copied by others who were far better financed and supported. Thus, having accomplished its purposes, the *News Bulletin* ceased publication in the fall of 1973. Its success led to its death.

Jews in the USSR, a weekly information bulletin published in London since January 14, 1972, is edited by Colin Shindler, a young Englishman, and produced under the auspices of the Board of Deputies of British Jews, the official coordinating and governing body for the Jewish community of the United Kingdom. At first, it depended for its primary sources on material that went to the Israeli government office or to the *News Bulletin*. Later, it developed its own direct telephone contacts with the USSR.

No study of Soviet Jewry could fail to acknowledge *Jews in Eastern Europe,* a periodical survey edited in London by Emanuel Litvinoff since March 1958. Its material has come largely from the Israeli office concerned with Soviet Jewry. From 1958 to 1969, when no similar publications existed, it kept interest alive in Soviet Jewish affairs. Another London-based organization, the Institute of Jewish Affairs (IJA), a research arm of the World Jewish Congress, issues an excellent academic journal, *Soviet Jewish Affairs,* which is a successor to *Bulletin on Soviet Jewish Affairs,* first published in January 1968.

In the United States since the late 1950s, Moshe Decter, director of Jewish Minorities Research and later the Conference on the Status of Soviet Jews, has gathered and edited important research material, as well as occasional pamphlets and newsletters. The official Jewish-establishment coordinating body, the American Conference on Soviet Jewry, founded in 1964, and later the National Conference on Soviet Jewry, has published pamphlets, studies, and, more recently, newsletters containing valuable information. Since October 1970, the Union of Councils on Soviet Jewry, an independent American activist group, has sponsored *Exodus,* the first regularly published newspaper in the United States on Soviet Jewish matters. Some of the separate councils in seventeen U.S. and Canadian cities distribute their own newsletters.

The *samizdat* sources are discussed in the text. *Khronika,* the most important, was issued in English in the West as *A Chronicle of Current Events* by Amnesty International Publications in London. The editor of its twenty-seven issues was Peter Reddaway, senior lecturer in political science at the London School of Economics who made material available to me and provided guidance and advice.

Radio Liberty's Research Department in Munich compiles *Arkhiv Samizdata,* the most comprehensive *samizdat* collection in the world, and its facilities are of inestimable value to any serious student of Soviet affairs and particularly of the Soviet Human Rights Movement.

My interpretations and analyses are based on information from many sources, but except for the foregoing, which I have mentioned specifically because I have constantly used them as reference sources, I have not attempted to list them in detail. My extensive personal research files, however, are available to historians and other scholars.

CHAPTER 1

1. Useful studies of Jews in the Soviet census and mixed marriages among Soviet Jews have been made by the Institute of Jewish Affairs. See particularly

Ivor I. Millman, "Major Centres of Jewish Population in the USSR and a Note on the 1970 Census," *Soviet Jewish Affairs*, Vol 1 No. 1 (June 1971).

2. *The Jews in the Soviet Union*, by Solomon M. Schwarz (Syracuse, N.Y.: Syracuse University Press, 1951), remains the most comprehensive analysis of the position of Jews in Soviet society during the earlier years of the regime. *The Black Years of Soviet Jewry*, by Yehoshua Gilboa (Boston: Little Brown, 1971), is the most complete account of the difficult years between 1939 and 1953.

CHAPTER 2

1. The incident involving U.S. Embassy officials was described to me in personal conversations with embassy staff people in Moscow in August 1972. On January 10, 1974, a U.S. vice consul in Leningrad was beaten on the street by "unidentified Russians" and returned to the United States. Ten days later, a Russian official was accosted in New York by a Jewish Defense League member. U.S. Department of State officials acknowledged "a pattern of retaliation in the past."

2. The secret instruction manual for Soviet censors is reported in *Radio Liberty Research*, November 20, 1972. It has been confirmed in private conversations with a former high-ranking Soviet journalist now in Israel.

CHAPTER 3

1. The Chornobilsky case is reported in *Jews in Eastern Europe*, Vol. III, #6 (May 1967).

2. Information about Boris Kochubiyevsky was obtained from Kochubiyevsky himself as well as from other sources. See *A Hero for Our Time: The Trial and Fate of Boris Kochubiyevsky*, edited by Moshe Decter, with a foreword by Abraham J. Heschel (New York, April 1970). The pamphlet reprinted Kochubiyevsky's own *samizdat* essay and his trial comments, which had previously been available from *Khronika*, Radio Liberty, and other sources.

CHAPTER 4

1. The account of the Leningrad intellectual, now a Tel Aviv doctor, is from a manuscript, portions of which were published under the title "The Road Home: A Russian Jew Discovers his Identity," *Bulletin of Soviet and East European Jewish Affairs* #4 (London: IJA, December 1969). Supplementary information was secured from the author, who prefers to remain anonymous because his aged parents are unable to secure permission to leave Leningrad.

2. The Pechersky and Tsirulnikov cases have been sparsely referred to in the occasional London newspaper *Focus on Soviet Jewry* (November-December 1970) and in several other reports.

3. Information describing the formation and growth of the Leningrad center (group or organization) is derived from conversations with some of the participants; from *samizdat* transcripts of the first and second Leningrad trials and the Riga trial; and from an analysis of conflicting news reports.

4. The experience of Joel Sprayregen comes from conversations with him and a private, unpublished account of his trip.

5. Information from Polina Yudborovskaya was secured in detailed taped interviews with her on May 15, 1972 and from accounts she prepared and gave to me.

CHAPTER 5

1. Leah Pliner Slovin's story and that of the growth of the Jewish movement
in Riga were told to me on several occasions by her and by other friends from
Riga. The quotations are from a taped interview with Leah on July 11, 1972.
2. The accounts of the *samizdat* origins of Leon Uris's *Exodus* were told to
me by Leah Slovin; by Ezra Rusinek in a taped interview on May 3, 1972
(Rusinek's story is also related in a book written by his daughter-in-law, *Like a
Song, Like a Dream*, by Alla Rusinek (New York: Scribner, 1973); by Viktor
Fedoseyev in personal conversations, among others, on December 28, 1972, and
in a taped interview on September 20, 1971; by Anatoly Rubin in some personal
notes to me; and by D. V., a former inmate of Potma Labor Camp Number 7
in an article in *Nasha Strana*, a Russian-language Israeli newspaper in late 1971.
A translation of the *Nasha Strana* account was given me by Si Frumkin, a Los
Angeles businessman who is the chairman of the Southern California Council
for Soviet Jews.
3. A detailed account of the murder of Latvian Jews during World War II
appears in *The Final Solution: The Attempt to Exterminate the Jews of Europe,
1939-1945*, by Gerald Reitlinger (New York: Barnes, 1961). *The Final Solution*
is a basic source for the fate of various Jewish communities in the USSR and is
relied upon in other chapters in this book. In addition, there is a useful chapter
on "Jews in the Baltic Countries under German Occupation," by Joseph Gar, in
the book *Russian Jewry, 1917-1967*, edited by Gregor Aronson *et al.* (New York:
Yoseloff, 1969).
4. The information concerning Mendel Gordin comes from lengthy conversations with him. In addition, I have taped interviews of Gordin, Ruta Aleksandrovich, Sanya Averbukh, Ezra Rusinek, and others taken on April 21-22, 1972.
5. The quotation from Viktor Fedoseyev comes from notes of a personal
conversation in December 1972.
6. The detailed explanation of Ezra Rusinek was given me in a lengthy personal memorandum in May 1972, and was supplemented by a taped interview
on May 3, 1972.
7. The Dora Zak, Mendel Gordin, and U Thant *samizdat* letters first appeared
in *Ishkod*, which collected and published in *samizdat* many of the most significant
early *samizdat* letters, appeals, and petitions. Many were reproduced for the first
time in the United States in *Redemption: Jewish Freedom Letters from Russia*,
edited by Moshe Decter, with a foreword by Bayard Rustin (New York, May
1970). Some were also published by the IJA and in *Jews in Eastern Europe*.
8. Additional background information concerning the Jewish movement in
Riga was secured from many persons not referred to in the discussion in this
chapter. Rivka Aleksandrovich (Leah Slovin's sister and Ruta Aleksandrovich's
mother) was an important source. I discussed these matters in Riga in late August
1972, with, among others, Margarita Shpilberg (Aron's wife), Zhenya Imerman,
Pavel Yorsh, Vladimir Gelfandbein, and Lazar Keet, who then constituted important Jewish activist leadership in that city.

CHAPTER 6

1. Brief, nondetailed references to Moscow prosecutions of Jews in the late
1950s and early 1960s appeared in issues of *Jews in Eastern Europe*.
2. The Dolnik case is reported in *Jews in Eastern Europe*, Vol. III, #6 (May

1967). Prusakov discusses his connection with the case in a *samizdat* document, "To the World Zionist Congress," published in *Survey*, Summer 1972. *Survey*, a quarterly journal of Soviet and East European studies, edited by Leopold Labedz in London, is widely respected by students of Soviet affairs. The quotation is from that document. Other information about the Dolnik case comes from private conversations with recent emigrants from Moscow.

3. For the origin of the *samizdat* documents quoted, see Chapter 5, reference note 7, above.

4. The Moscow activist leaders discussed here have lived in Israel for a number of years. They have been interviewed with some frequency and have discussed many of their experiences publicly. I maintain a file of information on each one. Some are close friends and I have interviewed them extensively. Taped interviews with Viktor and Rakhel Fedoseyev are referred to above. There are also taped interviews with Mikhail Zand on July 14, 1972.

5. Some of the material on *Iskhod* and the production of Jewish *samizdat* appeared in an article by me in the *Jerusalem Post*, March 24, 1972.

6. *Iton Aleph* and *Iton Bet* were translated into English by the Israeli office concerned with Soviet Jewish affairs. Their full text has never been publicly released. The quotations are taken from this translation.

7. Some of the information concerning Luba Bershadskaya is found in greater detail in "Twenty-four Years in the Life of Lyuba Bershadskaya," by Trudie Vocse, *The New York Times Magazine*, March 4, 1971. (Trudie Vocse was a pseudonym of Cynthia Ozick.)

8. I owe many people a special debt of gratitude for detailed information about the Jewish movement in Moscow. In addition to those discussed in this chapter, appreciation must be expressed among others, to my friends Boris and Shura Zuckerman (referred to as Tsukerman in the text), Alla Rusinek, Leonid Rigerman, and Julia Weiner. Among those with whom I discussed this subject at length in Moscow in August 1972 were Roman Rutman and Boris Orlov, now in Israel. Viktor Polsky, Vladimir Slepak, and Valery Krizhak have still not been permitted to leave.

CHAPTER 7

1. The Georgian *samizdat* letters quoted were reproduced in the same fashion as those referred to above.

2. Mrs. Meir's speech was reported in the *Jerusalem Post*.

3. Albert Mikhailashvili's letter was published in *Redemption* (see Chapter 5, reference note 7).

4. Joel Sprayregen's comments are from his unpublished account of his trip to the USSR.

CHAPTER 8

1. The Vilna *samizdat* documents quoted come from the same sources referred to above.

2. Reports of the Ryazan trial were first published in *Khronika*. Later details, including the account of Romiel Orliok, appeared in *Maariv*, July 9, 1971, and additional information was provided in the *News Bulletin on Soviet Jewry*, June 9, 1971.

3. The *Iton* material is taken from the translations already noted.

CHAPTER 9

1. The information concerning the Leningrad hijacking arrests comes from a variety of sources, beginning with the first detailed report appearing in *Khronika*. The entire fourth issue of *Iskhod* was devoted to the arrest and trial; it was translated and published by the IJA. Much additional information about the individual defendants and the events preceding their arrest is found in several other *samizdat* transcripts.

2. Meri Khnokh recounted the events leading to the arrests at a press conference at Beit Agron in Jerusalem on December 13, 1971, and in later conversations with me.

3. *Background Paper No. 19,* "The Leningrad 'Hijack Plot'" published by the IJA in November 1970, contains a brief introduction and seven appendices. The appendixes—English translations of *samizdat* commenting on the arrests and upcoming trials—include relevant portions of *Khronika;* protest letters from *Ishkod* No. 2; the first communiqué from Riga describing the searches and arrests and giving biographical information about the arrestees; and a similar extensive document from Leningrad.

4. Eduard Kuznetsov's diary was smuggled out of the USSR in early fall 1972. Portions of it were first printed in the West in the Italian weekly *L'Espresso,* October 12, 1972, and excerpts have been reprinted elsewhere. Additional background information about Kuznetsov was provided to me by Elena (Mrs. Andrei) Sakharov in conversations in Moscow in August 1972.

5. The Vertlib and Shur letter, as well as the Boguslavsky letter, appeared first in *Iskhod* No. 2, and were reprinted in IJA's *Background Paper No. 19*. The IJA also published the letters of the Moscow Jews.

CHAPTER 10

1. Of the various informal transcripts of the first Leningrad trial, that published in *Iskhod* No. 4, which was translated and published by the IJA, is the most useful. It contains, in addition to direct testimony, a summary of witness testimony and descriptive material about the courtroom and events that occurred there and outside. The footnotes prepared by Viktor Fedoseyev for *Iskhod* are particularly useful. In addition, I have a typed manuscript of the taped testimony and a final statement of Leib (Arie) Khnokh which is more detailed than any of the other transcripts. It was secured through his brother, Dr. Pinkus Khnokh.

2. For background on Soviet law, an invaluable book is *Soviet Criminal Law and Procedure,* by Harold J. Berman, 2d ed. (Cambridge, Mass.: Harvard University Press, 1972), which contains translations of the Criminal Code of the RSFSR and the Code of Criminal Procedure.

3. The *samizdat* pamphlet "Your Mother Tongue" was made available to me personally.

4. The operation of the "red line" was related to me in private conversations by Vladimir Telnikov, Galya Ladyzhenskaya, and Pavel Gilman, who participated in the procedure.

5. The post-trial protest letters and telegrams appeared in *Iskhod* No. 4.

6. The text of the appeal decision in the first Leningrad trial reached London through *samizdat* channels in May 1972 and was published by IJA in a research report on June 1, 1972.

CHAPTER 11

1. Dr. Pinkus Khnokh made his comments at a Jerusalem press conference on December 13, 1971. He had related information to me, both prior to and subsequent to that time.

2. I interviewed Boris Maftser several times. On April 20, 1972, I conducted a lengthy taped interview of him with Alla Rusinek as my translator.

3. The story of the Testament was related to me by Ezra Rusinek, Ilya Volk, and Mendel Gordin in April 1972. The microfilm copy was sent to me in May 1973 after being smuggled out of the USSR. Additional information was secured from friends in Riga in late August 1972.

4. On a number of occasions, Sanya Averbukh and his wife Ruta Aleksandrovich discussed with me the matters referred to in this chapter. The quotation from Averbukh is part of a tape recording I made on April 21, 1972.

5. Sprayregen's account of the meeting with Mogilever in Leningrad appears in his unpublished account of his trip to the USSR.

6. Some of the information concerning Mogilever's contacts with Scandinavian visitors, and Butman's comments on these matters and their alleged meaning are found in the incomplete *samizdat* transcript of the second Leningrad trial.

7. Quotations from Kuznetsov come from his diary. Those of Silva Zalmanson were made during the course of her testimony at the trial.

8. Ezra Rusinek's comments were made to me in a private memorandum in May 1972, and were supplemented by a taped conversation.

9. The petition of the eighty-two Soviet Jews to President Podgorny of January 6, 1973 appears in the *News Bulletin on Soviet Jewry*, February 4, 1973.

CHAPTER 12

1. The details of the trial of Igor Borisov were communicated on December 31, 1970 by telephone by Leonid Rigerman, then in Moscow, to Aron Bogdanovsky, formerly of Kharkov, and now a resident of Haifa. The telephone conversation was tape recorded at the home of Israel and Ann Shenkar in Givataim, Israel.

2. The Israeli government office responsible for Soviet Jewry matters compiles internal reports on Soviet press and radio comments. Its issues of May 27, May 31, and July 16, 1971 deal with Soviet media comments on the second Leningrad trial. References to Soviet press comments are taken from these detailed reports. Edited *samizdat* transcripts have appeared. The most complete one is reproduced in *Jews in Eastern Europe*, Vol. IV, #7 (November 1971). Quotations utilized are taken from the manuscript.

3. Butman's final statement and other details were brought to Israel several months after the trial by Vladimir Knopov, a former Leningrad attorney and Jewish activist who had been in the courtroom for much of the trial.

4. Gelfand's analysis, published in *Nasha Strana*, May 20, 1971, was translated by Si Frumkin.

5. Mrs. Meir's address was reported in the *Jerusalem Post*, May 21, 1971.

6. Polina Yudborovskaya's comments were made to me in an extensive taped interview, May 15, 1972.

7. The details about Boris Azernikov were provided by Vladimir Knopov.

8. The material about Nikolai Yavor was communicated by telephone to the West, and most of it was first published in the London newsletter *Jews in the USSR*.

Chapter 13

1. Reports of the Bendery trial of Suslensky and Mishener are found in *Khronika.* Margarita Shpilberg provided additional details in conversations in Riga in late August 1972.

2. The Khantsis case is reported most fully in *News Bulletins on Soviet Jewry.* Many details were learned as the result of tape-recorded telephone conversations between Soviet Jewish activists in Toronto, Ontario, and Kishinev Jews. The official court record dated August 30, 1972 containing the indictment was smuggled to the West and published in *Khronika's* English-language successor, *A Chronicle of Human Rights in the USSR,* Issue No. 1, published by Khronika Press in New York City, whose founders were Peter Reddaway and Edward Kline. It is now edited by Valery Chalidze.

3. In personal conversations, Galya Ladyzhenskaya provided me with information about her interrogation by the KGB.

4. Some details of the Kishinev trial can be found in *Jews in Eastern Europe,* Vol. IV, #7 (November 1971). The Soviet version of the events is set forth in the unpublished Israeli government report #468(S), "The Kishinev Trial as Presented in the Soviet Press and Radio," July 13, 1971.

5. As noted, the Chernoglaz search is officially set forth in the KGB document printed in *Iskhod* No. 3. The search of Voloshin's apartment is described in a statement he prepared after he arrived in Israel in late fall 1972. Hillel Shur's lengthy letter of October 25, 1971 from prison to the Presidium of the Supreme Soviet, in which he describes, among many other things, the search of his apartment, was brought out of prison and taken to the West. I have a translated copy of the *samizdat* document. Subsequently, after Shur arrived in Israel, he "repeated and reaffirmed" this declaration in Tel Aviv on December 12, 1972. The document is reproduced in *USSR Labor Camps,* Part 2, Hearings Before the Subcommittee to Investigate the Administration of the Internal Security Act of the Committee on the Judiciary, U.S. Senate, 93 Congress, February 1-2, 1973. An appendix to this congressional hearing includes statements of former Soviet citizens now in Israel—Shur and Voloshin, among others.

6. Additional information about Hillel Shur was secured in conversations with his sister Kreina, in Israel, and from friends in Leningrad in early September 1972—most notably from Lev Lerner, then an important Jewish activist leader.

Chapter 14

1. Information about the forthcoming Riga trial was provided almost daily during the spring of 1971 in telephone contacts, between Leah Slovin in Tel Aviv and her sister Rivka Aleksandrovich in Riga. Other ex-Rigaites in Israel maintained similar connections. I was privy to these conversations at the time and made notes concerning them. On April 26, 1971, before the trial began, Rivka Aleksandrovich arrived in Israel with additional information.

2. Subsequent to the Riga trial, a detailed transcript was smuggled to Rivka Aleksandrovich in Jerusalem who translated it. The original typed English version of 43 legal-sized, single-spaced pages in my possession was later supplemented by personal interviews with Ruta Aleksandrovich Averbukh, her husband Isai (Sanya) Averbukh, her father Yitzhak Aleksandrovich, Boris Maftser, Ilya Volk, Mendel Gordin, Ezra Rusinek, and other Jews of Riga. On May 24, 1972, a four-hour press conference commemorating the first anniversary of the trial

occurred in Jerusalem. I have a tape recording of those proceedings, as well as of many of the earlier interviews.

3. Ruta's letter, "In the Expectation of Arrest," was widely circulated in the West. My copy was secured from her aunt Leah.

4. Rivka's description of Ruta's arrest was prepared on April 30, 1971 upon her arrival in Israel and was first published in the *News Bulletin on Soviet Jewry,* May 5, 1971.

5. The document, "Appeal to the Jewish People," and the letter to Rabbi Unterman were written by Sanya Averbukh and were sent to Israel to Leah Slovin and Sanya's brother Igor (Yitzhak) Averbukh, who made them available immediately.

6. My broadcast text comparing Angela Davis and Ruta Aleksandrovich is taken from the original copy I prepared for the BBC program.

7. The comments by Maftser, Ruta Aleksandrovich, and Silva Zalmanson concerning *Domoi* are taken from the unofficial trial transcript, as are the other quoted portions of testimony or closing statements by the four defendants and the comments of the various counsel.

8. The Soviet view of the Riga trial can be found in translated excerpts in an unpublished Israeli government report, Document #460(S).

9. Leah's comments at the wedding were made directly to me.

10. Ruta's comments on Maftser are contained in a one-page statement of May 24, 1972, "Why I Can't Take Part in this Press Conference." The original is in my possession.

11. Maftser's comments are taken from taped interviews referred to in reference 2 to this chapter.

CHAPTER 15

1. The major sources of information about Raiza Palatnik were her younger sister Katya, with whom I discussed the case many times in Jerusalem, and Katya's fiancé, Igor (Yitzhak) Averbukh, a friend of mine. On February 4, 1972, I tape recorded an extensive interview with Katya; Yitzhak was also present. Irina Schneer, a friend of Katya's and also a Russian immigrant, translated when that was required. She also translated a lengthy account of the Palatnik case Katya had prepared for me. (The document is in my possession.) Aleksandr Chapla, a friend of Raiza's from Odessa, who emigrated to Israel in the early spring of 1971, carried out the first detailed information about her. He worked extensively in her behalf and provided me with much early information about her case.

2. Raiza's open letter of November 20, 1970 was first published in *News Bulletin on Soviet Jewry,* April 23, 1971.

3. The quotation from Katya is from the document she prepared for me, mentioned in reference note 1 to this chapter.

4. Raiza's closing speech was first reproduced in the *News Bulletin on Soviet Jewry,* September 11, 1971.

CHAPTER 16

1. The Schecter affair in Chernovtsy is reported in *Between Hammer and Sickle,* by Arie L. Eliav, updated edition (New York: Signet Books, 1969). It is also referred to in *Jews in Eastern Europe.*

2. The Ontman trial is reported in *Les Juifs en Union Sovietique*, Paris, August 1970.

3. Dr. Yury (Chaim) Rennert's trial was reported in the *News Bulletin on Soviet Jewry*, June 14, 1971. An earlier version appeared in *Maariv*, June 3, 1971. The Potik case also was first reported in the *News Bulletin*.

4. The translation of Ulrikh Gait's open letter is in my possession. It was subsequently published in the *News Bulletin*, June 9, 1971.

5. Rita Gluzman told me her story in early July 1971, and I assisted her in contacting Mrs. Hauser. Her case was subsequently reported in the *News Bulletin*, July 18, 1971.

6. The quotation is from 41-year-old A.K., who preferred to remain anonymous because his parents remain in Lvov. He provided an account of the exit process in August 1972. (I have the notes in my files.)

7. Details about the Jewish movement in Kharkov were obtained in personal conversations in Israel with Aron Bogdanovsky, Yefim (Chaim) Spivakovsky, Alex Volkov, his former wife Lena Volkov, and others.

8. The Kolchinsky story came from a number of sources. The quotation from Kolchinsky's report to General of the Army Yepishev was transmitted by telephone by Spivakovsky in Kharkov to Bogdanovsky in Tel Aviv at 1 a.m. on February 20, 1971. I have a transcript made at the time. The Volkovs brought out other documents, original copies of which are in my files.

9. The Yuli Brind case was most fully covered in the *News Bulletin on Soviet Jewry*, April 6 and May 3, 1971. Spivakovsky prepared a detailed statement about it on May 18, 1972 which is in my possession.

10. The quotation from the letter to Mrs. Meir is from the *Jerusalem Post*, August 19, 1970. Among its signers was Anatoly Gerenrot who subsequently told me of the incident and the failure to respond to the letter.

11. The synagogue incidents in Kiev have been reported in various places. Many details were provided to me by M. A. Barboy in a lengthy written report he gave me on May 14, 1972. Barboy had recently emigrated from Kiev to Beersheba, Israel.

12. The appeal of April 20, 1973 from Kiev activists appeared in the *News Bulletin on Soviet Jewry* in June 1973.

13. The Shkolnik case, reported in great detail in *Jews in the USSR*, received considerable attention in the British press. Mrs. Shkolnik's first letter to Rudenko appeared in the issue of March 16, 1973; the second letter appeared in the issue of April 13, 1973, and the appeal to Brezhnev in the issue of September 4, 1973.

CHAPTER 17

1. The story of the Jewish movement in Minsk was told to me by Anatoly Rubin, with his wife Karny translating. Rubin has written a book on the subject which has not yet been published. Additional details about the movement in Minsk were provided in numerous conversations with Dr. Yakov Schultz and his wife Larisa. I also spent a very intensive two days in Riga, in late August 1972, talking to Larisa's sister Asya and her activist husband, Ernst Levin, about the Jewish movement in Minsk.

2. The quotations from Rubin are from his brief description of his book in a letter to me.

3. Colonel Ovsishcher's letter to President Podgorny appeared in *Jews in the USSR*, December 24, 1972.

4. Facts concerning Case 97 in Minsk have been reported in various places. The single best collection of information is found in an excellent pamphlet, *Terror in Minsk, KGB Case Number 97: The Jewish Officers' "Plot,"* edited, with an introduction, by Moshe Decter, foreword by Morris B. Abram (New York: National Conference on Soviet Jewry, 1973).

5. Colonel Davidovich's letter to Brezhnev of December 19, 1972, as well as later letters and documents that are quoted, was carried in the *News Bulletin on Soviet Jewry,* December 27, 1972, *Jews in the USSR,* January 12, 1973, and elsewhere. They are all collected in *Terror in Minsk,* from which I have taken the extracts used.

6. A copy of the letter from former Minsk Jews living in Israel to American Jews, in late April 1973, was sent to me.

CHAPTER 18

1. The experiences of Jews in Sverdlovsk were described to me in tape-recorded interviews in Arad, Israel, with Jewish activists from that city on March 15, 1972. Ella Kukuy, Vladimir Aks, and Ilya Voitovetsky were among those interviewed. Larisa Schultz acted as translator. Meyer Levin, the author, also took part in the interviews. On March 22, 1972, the *Jerusalem Post* carried my detailed story describing the events. Some of the material that appears here was first published in that article. The quoted comments were made in these interviews and are found in my notes and the transcripts of tapes in my possession.

2. There is a detailed 27-page informal transcript of the trial of Valery Kukuy. A translated copy is in my files.

3. The appeal of Dr. Andrei Sakharov and Valery Chalidze to the Supreme Court of the RSFSR following the conviction of Kukuy appears in *Khronika* No. 21 (September 11, 1971).

4. A copy of the open letter to *Izvestia* by Sverdlovsk Jews on August 8, 1971 was given to me by the signers after they arrived in Israel. The letter of September 1971 by the Sverdlovsk activists was given to me at the same time.

5. Portions of the official court record in the Markman trial appeared in *Jews in Eastern Europe,* November 1972.

6. I was present during some of the telephone conversation between Markman in Sverdlovsk and Voitovetsky in Beersheba. It seemed clear then that Markman was in danger of arrest.

7. Leonid Zabelyshensky's protest against the methods of interrogation is quoted from the *News Bulletin on Soviet Jewry,* December 2, 1972.

8. Kosharovsky's appeal was being prepared while I was in Moscow. Its text was discussed in my presence and it was signed by most of the leading activists. It was reproduced in *Jews in Eastern Europe,* November 1972.

9. Mrs. Markman's letter to Rae Sharfman of Detroit was reproduced in New York by the Student Struggle for Soviet Jewry.

CHAPTER 19

1. The saga of Lazar Lyubarsky was first reported in the *News Bulletin on Soviet Jewry* in early 1971, and later issues followed his problems throughout their course. *Jews in the USSR* provided detailed coverage in the later stages. An excellent, comprehensive booklet that includes virtually all of the important documentation is *The Lonely Course of Lazar Liubarsky,* edited by Moshe Decter, with a foreword by Paul O'Dwyer (New York: National Conference on

Soviet Jewry, 1973). The quotations utilized here were taken from the documents included in that source.

2. I was in Moscow in August 1972 when the KGB interrogated some of the Moscow activists about Lyubarsky. I discussed their KGB questioning with them after it had occurred.

CHAPTER 20

1. The publication in December 1973 of *The Gulag Archipelego, 1918–1956,* by Aleksandr Solzhenitsyn, again focused world-wide attention on Soviet prison camps and the number of political prisoners being held in them. See "Soviets Said to Hold Millions in Prison, Including 10,000 on Political Charges," *The New York Times,* January 13, 1974, which estimates that between 1 million and 2.5 million people are held in such camps. The article relies heavily on Peter Reddaway's estimates of the number of political prisoners. The most carefully documented recent study is *The Forced Labor Camps in the USSR Today: An Unrecognized Example of Modern Inhumanity,* by Peter Reddaway, a report presented to the International Committee for the Defense of Human Rights in the USSR, Brussels, February 26, 1973. Professor Reddaway will soon publish a book on the subject. The best earlier study remains *My Testimony,* by Anatoly Marchenko (London: Pall Mall Press; New York: Praeger, 1969).

2. Kochubiyevsky's report appeared in the *News Bulletin on Soviet Jewry,* October 25, 1971.

3. The 1969–70 arrests and trials of Kharkov Jews Nedobora, Ponomarov, and Levin were reported by *Khronika* in various issues that discussed the Action Group's Kharkov supporters, led by Genrikh Altunyan, of which they were a part.

4. Kochubiyevsky also related the fate of a Jewish prisoner, Bendarsky, who was caught attempting to escape to Israel without official permission. Bendarsky died in the camps under mysterious circumstances, labeled a suicide. Other Jews serving sentences for attempting to escape from the USSR included a Moscow musician, Natan Pinson, who was confined from 1969 to 1972 for attempting to cross the Romanian border after repeatedly being denied exit permission. Pinson arrived in Israel in the spring of 1973.

5. On October 17, 1973, the Jewish Telegraphic Agency reported two cases announced by the Student Struggle for Soviet Jewry. In Kishinev, in December 1969, Yakov Stromwasser, a Kishinev Jew and former Nazi concentration-camp inmate, was sentenced to three years under Article 190-1 for writing an anonymous letter criticizing Soviet society and policy toward Israel. Anatoly Glod, a 39-year-old dentist, was sentenced to fifteen years for diamond smuggling. He had received his exit visa to Israel and was arrested on the plane.

6. Emilia Trakhtenberg's background and an account of her trial appeared in *Khronika* No. 22 (November 10, 1971). It had been reported earlier but less extensively in the *News Bulletin,* September 13, 1971.

7. *Maariv* first noted the Yakov Kaufman trial on January 18, 1973.

8. Information about Arnold Finger and the situation in Alma Ata came from extensive interviews with Chanan Finger, who first contacted me in April 1971 to assist him in defending his son and securing the release of Arnold and his family from the USSR. I subsequently also interviewed Gita Cherkez, who had studied in Alma Ata and arrived in Israel in December 1971 from Chernovtsy. Subsequently, I met and interviewed Arnold Finger and his family when they arrived in Israel on April 24, 1972.

9. Anatoly Radygin's case was reported in *Khronika* No. 24 (March 5, 1972). After his arrival in Israel in July 1973 he confirmed the facts.

10. Those like Chaim Rennert and Anatoly Glod, who were charged with economic crimes (see note 5 above), received little attention. The recent case of Petya Pinkhasov, a 27-year-old carpenter from Derbent in Dagestan, a region of the Azerbaidzhan SSR on the Caspian Sea, has attracted more notice. Pinkhasov received a five-year sentence on November 13, 1973, allegedly for having received money for private carpentry work. He was not arrested until after he, his wife, and six children had received an exit visa to Israel. His family and friends claim the charge for an economic crime was a pretext to persecute him for Zionist aspirations.

11. I was in Moscow when Ilya Glezer was tried. I learned of the sentence at the U.S. Embassy and had the unpleasant experience of being the first to tell the news to some of the Jewish activists. They told me about the background of the case.

12. The information about Boris Davarashvili came from his family and was reported in the *News Bulletin,* August 24, 1972.

13. Information about the Goldshtein brothers of Tbilisi was reported in *Jews in the USSR,* beginning in January 1973. Isai's letter to *Izvestia* appeared in the issue of March 23, 1973.

14. Dr. Andrei Sakharov told me about Dr. Gluzman in a conversation in Moscow on August 24, 1972.

CHAPTER 21

1. Accounts of the demonstrations appeared in various issues of the *News Bulletin on Soviet Jewry.* The petition of September 16, 1971 containing the demands of the Central Committee of the Communist Party respecting emigration was made available in December 1971, upon his arrival in Israel, by Pavel Goldshtein, one of the five spokesmen of the group.

2. Among the most remarkable *samizdat* documents smuggled out of the USSR is *The White Book of Exodus,* a 91-page collection of documents—letters, complaints, applications, demands, and commentary—edited by a group of Moscow activists, including Roman Rutman, Yury Breitbart, Vladimir Kogan, and Vyacheslav Gaukhman, and completed on April 18, 1972, in time to be published before President Nixon's visit to the USSR. It was reproduced by the National Conference on Soviet Jewry, but not in time or with sufficient circulation to accomplish its political objectives, in the view of the editors. When I was in Moscow in August 1972, I was told that a second *White Book of Exodus* (our code name was WB-2) was in the process of completion covering the events leading up to the visit of President Nixon, what occurred while he was in the USSR, and the immediate aftermath of his visit, which provoked great bitterness among Soviet Jews. The editors of WB-2 included Rutman, Kogan, and Gaukhman, whose departure for Israel that fall slowed completion of the 54-page collection, microfilms of which were not smuggled out until the spring of 1973. *The White Book of Exodus, No. 2,* edited by Dr. Louis Rosenblum of Cleveland, Ohio, was reproduced by the Union of Councils for Soviet Jews. The quotations utilized are taken from it.

3. For a more detailed exploration of the citizenship issues involved, see Leonard Schroeter, "Soviet Jews and Israeli Citizenship: The Nationality Amendment Law of 1971," *Soviet Jewish Affairs,* Vol. 1, No. 2 (November

1971), and Leonard Schroeter, "Indecision Keeps Russian Jews from Getting Israel Nationality," *Jerusalem Post*, February 27, 1972.

4. Copies of Leah Slovin's 1969 letters to Shaul Avigur and the Israeli Foreign Ministry are in my possession.

5. The arrest and sentencing of young Soviet Jews (who seek exit visas) for failing to report for military service has continued since the convictions of Pokh and Berman in Odessa, and Shapiro and Nashpits in Moscow. In January 1974, it was learned that Mark Lutsker, a mathematician, 25, from Kiev, who had been expelled from Voronezh University for seeking a *kharakteristika* for emigration, and who had been working as a porter in Kutaisi, Georgia, had received a two-year sentence in August 1973 for evasion of military duty.

6. The appeal of the seven former prisoners was published in *Jews in the USSR*, January 19, 1973.

7. The complaint of cruelty by the six prisoners of conscience to the UN appeared in the *News Bulletin on Soviet Jewry*, October 31, 1972. It is one of a large number of *samizdat* documents that confirm in detail prison-camp treatment and the militancy of the prisoners.

CHAPTER 22

1. For a more detailed analysis of the emigration experience through the fall of 1972, see Leonard Schroeter, "How They Left: Varieties of Soviet Jewish Exit Experiences," Soviet Jewish Affairs, Vol. 2, No. 2 (1972).

2. The Jewish Agency statistics quoted are contained in a confidential "Fact Sheet on Immigration from the Soviet Union in 1972 and Costs of Absorption in Israel" of February 22, 1972. The "informed sources" referred to are reported in the *Jewish Chronicle*, February 11, 1972, in connection with a speech by Israeli Finance Minister Pinhas Sapir.

3. Other statistical breakdowns appeared in a variety of newspaper reports, statements from Jewish organizations, Soviet overseas press services, etc. The 80,000-*vizov* figure was the one consistently utilized by "Nechemiah's Office" from the spring of 1970 until the winter of 1972–73.

4. In response to my direct query to Jewish activists in Moscow as to the accuracy of official Soviet statements in July 1973 that 1,300 Jews granted exit visas in 1972 had chosen not to emigrate, and that 172 out of a list of 1,000 hardship cases in 1973 had changed their minds about emigrating, I was informed: "We have no way to verify the 1,300 figure officially. Our inquiries indicate, however, that there are very few known cases. We believe there are considerably fewer than 100. We have checked the list of 1,000 names and find only seven persons in Leningrad and none in Moscow who have temporarily withdrawn their exit applications, for reasons peculiar to their personal circumstances. The Soviet statement is nonsense."

5. Feldman's article first apeared in *Zion*, a bimonthly Russian-language magazine published in Israel by the Coordinating Committee of the *Assirei Tsion* (Prisoners of Zion), composed mostly of former Soviet political prisoners. It was translated by Si Frumkin.

6. Viktor Yakhot's article appeared in a remarkable *samizdat* journal, *Jews in the USSR: Collection of Materials on the History, Culture and Problems of Jews in the USSR*, No. 1, October 1972, edited by Yakhot and Dr. Aleksandr Voronel. It was published in the United States as *I Am a Jew: Essays on Jewish Identity in the Soviet Union*, edited by Moshe Decter (New York: Anti-Defamation League of B'nai B'rith, 1973).

7. The letter of April 20, 1973 to Senator Edward M. Kennedy, as chairman of the Subcommittee on Refugees, following inquiries he made to the State Department, was signed by Marshall Wright, acting assistant secretary for congressional relations.

8. Viktor Polsky's statement was made to me in Moscow on August 26, 1972.

9. The Bershadskaya statement was printed in an article, "A Jew's Disillusionment With Life in the West," by Peter Worthington, *Los Angeles Times,* August 5, 1973. Worthington quotes from an article she allegedly wrote that appeared in *Sovietish Heimland,* the Soviet Union's only Yiddish journal. Subsequently queried about the article by a San Francisco friend with whom she maintains regular correspondence, Bershadskaya denied writing it and denied that she had been quoted correctly. A letter she wrote in early December 1973 indicated that she was awaiting approval of an application for an exit visa to the United States and that she would never return to the USSR. She came to America in early 1974.

10. The letter to the U.S. Congress signed by 100 Soviet Jews was released on April 30, 1973 by the National Conference on Soviet Jewry.

11. I reported the Epelman case in greater detail in an article, "Russia's Captive Wives," *Jerusalem Post,* January 17, 1972. Mikhail Epelman is a friend with whom I have frequently discussed this and other matters. I discussed Polina Epelman's case with her in Leningrad on August 31, 1972, and we remain in contact by letter and telephone. My file includes many letters, Mikhail Epelman's formal request to the Israeli government, and his petitions.

12. The Viktor Yoran-Stella Goldberg story was related to me on a number of occasions by Yoran.

13. The Panov case has received extensive attention in the press. The Panovs' November 1973 hunger strike failed, but the official withdrawal in January 1974 of the invitation to the Kivov Ballet to visit the United States appears more likely to result in the freeing of Panov and his wife.

14. The documentation of the Temkin affair and the quotations from the various appeals have appeared in issues of the *News Bulletin on Soviet Jewry* and *Jews in the USSR.* The Union of Councils for Soviet Jews has published most of the information as well as a fact sheet on the Ilona Dreizner case.

15. Press reports in January 1974 quoted Soviet sources as stating that 34,750 Jews had left the USSR in 1973. Other estimates were as high as 36,000. *The New York Times* reported on November 4, 1973 that of 101 Soviet Jews who emigrated to West Berlin during the first nine months of 1973, 15 were resettled as "ethnic Germans." The rest, arriving "on the Soviet Union's Jewish quota, had gone first to Vienna." Under a West German-Soviet agreement, 3,420 ethnic Germans also were permitted to emigrate during the same period.

CHAPTER 23

1. Dzyuba's address was circulated widely in *samizdat,* and has been republished several times, one of the first being in *The Commentator,* February 1968, a Ukrainian-English-language journal published in Toronto, Ontario.

2. For discussion of the Action (Initiative) Group for the Defense of Civil Rights, and other aspects of the Soviet dissent movement, see *Uncensored Russia: The Human Rights Movement,* edited by Peter Reddaway (London: Cape, 1972); *The Voices of the Silent,* by Cornelia Gerstenmaier (New York:

Hart, 1972); *In Quest of Justice: Protest and Dissent in the Soviet Union Today,* edited by Abraham Brumberg (New York: Praeger, 1970).

3. The Initiative Group's statement on the arrest of Piotr Yakir appeared in *Khronika* No. 26 (July 5, 1972).

4. The documents and statements of the Soviet Committee on Human Rights appeared in *Obshchestvennye Problemy* (Social Problems). *Khronika* also regularly reported them.

5. Sakharov's open letter to the U.S. Congress on September 14, 1973 was reported in the press. I have a copy of the full text.

6. The letter of Azbel, Einbinder, Braylovsky, Voronel, Levich, Lunts, Orlov, Raginsky, and Temkin of September 9, 1973 in support of Sakharov and Solzhenitsyn was circulated in *samizdat* and telephoned to the West. I have a copy of the telephone transcription.

7. Mikhail Grobman's criticism of Solzhenitsyn appeared in the *Jerusalem Post,* November 14, 1972. The answer from Moscow Jews was printed in the *Jerusalem Post,* January 26, 1973.

8. I met Larisa Bogoraz in Moscow in August 1972 and have maintained correspondence with her since that time. I have a copy of the essay from which I quote. It subsequently appeared in *I Am a Jew* (see Chapter 22, reference note 6, above). Her final statement on October 11, 1968 at her trial for demonstrating at Red Square against the Czech invasion is reported in several sources; see particularly *Red Square at Noon,* by Natalya Gorbanevskaya (London: Deutsch, 1972).

9. Boris Tsukerman's comments were made to me in a taped interview in July 1972. I had first met Tsukerman in early February 1971, shortly after his arrival from the USSR. We became friends and saw each other frequently during the next eighteen months.

10. Roman Rutman's quotation is from notes I took of conversations with him in Moscow in late August 1972. We continued to correspond thereafter. (He wrote from Moscow and later from Israel.) I also saw him when he visited the United States in 1973.

11. Grigory Svirsky's statement—an open letter to the Secretariat of the Moscow Section of the RSFSR Writers' Union—appeared in *Survey,* Spring 1972.

12. Aleksei Tumerman's remarks appeared in *Haaretz,* May 15, 1973, shortly after he arrived in Israel.

13. A summary of the comments made at the Twenty-eighth Zionist Congress in Jerusalem can be found in Bulletin No. 6, January 25, 1972, issued by the Executive of the World Zionist Organization. I was present and took extensive notes of the proceedings. I subsequently confirmed Zand's remarks in personal conversations with him. Zand's analysis of the relationships between the Jewish movement and the democratic movement was made on October 6, 1971, at a lecture at Columbia University; it was published in *Soviet Jewry Today,* November 1971, published by the Academic Committee on Soviet Jewry.

14. For a discussion of the attitude of Soviet Jewish emigrants in Israel toward the democrats, see Leonard Schroeter, "Bukovsky and the Jews," *Jerusalem Post,* February 11, 1972.

15. I received Vladimir Slepak's letter in November 1973.

INDEX

Nashpits, Mark, 343-45, 368, 418
Nedobora, Vladislav, 308-10, 416
"Nekhama Has Come," 165
Netiva, code-name, 189
New York Times, 31, 115, 201, 242, 405, 416, 419
Newman, Paul, 369
News Bulletin on Soviet Jewry, 405-6, 409, 411, 412, 413, 414, 415, 416, 417, 418, 419
Nikiforov, I.I., 280
Ninth Fort, 41, 132-34
Nixon, Patricia, 337, 339
Nixon, Richard M., 33, 175-76, 284, 336-39, 393-94, 417
Novosti, 189, 197, 200, 201, 362
Nudelman, Yuli, 336
Nureyev, Rudolf, 369n

O'Dwyer, Paul, 415
Okudzhava, Bulat, 243
Olivier, Laurence, 369
Omsk Polytechnical Institute, 392
One Day in the Life of Ivan Denisovich, 27, 41
"On Socialist Realism," 243
Ontman, Lilia, 251, 346, 413
Orliok, Romiel, 137, 409
Orlov, Boris, 336, 338, 388, 409, 420
Ovchinnikov, Colonel, 253
OVIR (Department of Visas and Registration), 46, 46n, 75, 76, 80, 93, 95, 107, 122, 129, 134, 139, 150, 161-63, 165-67, 176-78, 184, 192, 196, 205, 210-11, 216, 221, 246-47, 251-55, 257-58, 261, 263, 265, 276-78, 301, 311, 314, 328-31, 335-36, 350-51, 363, 368-69, 371-72, 375, 387, 391, 394
Ovsishcher, Colonel Lev, 278, 282, 285, 414
Ozick, Cynthia, 409

Palatnik, Katya, 239, 243, 246-47, 413
Palatnik, Raiza, 239-47, 251, 290, 346, 413
"Palmoni, N.," 111
Panov, Valery, 369, 419
Parushov, KGB major, 228
Pasternak, Boris, 41, 243, 289
Pavlovsky, KGB investigator, 181
Pechersky, Dr. Gedalia, 55, 86, 407

Peled, Natan, 358
Penson, Boris, 142, 150, 158-59, 164, 166, 171-73
Peter the Great, 50, 147
Petlyura, Semyon, 40
Petronin, procurator, 149
Pevzner, counsel, 171
Pevzner, Dr. Galina, 304
Pevzner, Iosif, 301
Phoenix, 145
Pinkhasov, Petya, 417
Pinson, Natan, 416
Platonov, writer, 245
Pliner, Leah, 62–64, 68–74, 77, 226–27, 236, 256, 277, 408, 412, 413, 418
Pliner, Rivka, 62, 70, 74, 226, 408, 412, 413
Plisetskaya, Maya, 114
Plotkina, Rosalia, 108
Podgorny, Nikolai, 58, 78, 81, 94, 175, 176, 193, 217, 265, 278, 283, 301-2, 329, 411, 414
Pokh, Yury, 247-48, 418
Poliachek, Solomon, 283
Polsky, Elena, 332
Polsky, Viktor, 118, 294, 305, 319, 332-33, 336, 337-38, 363, 409, 419
Ponomaryov, Vladimir, 308-9, 416
Pravda, 105, 257, 261, 301, 317, 333
Pravda Vostoka, 312
Prayers, Rites, and Religious Laws of the Jewish People, 222
Prestin, Vladimir, 115, 118, 294, 303, 305, 319, 333, 337-38
Princeton University, 391
Progress, Co-existence, and Intellectual Freedom, 384
Protocols of the Elders of Zion, 26, 283
Prussakov, Valentin, 87, 305, 408
Prutkin, 291
Pulkhan, Isak, 68
"Purim and Pesach," 103
Pushkariov, investigator, 296-97
Pushkin, Aleksandr, 133

Rabinovich, Boris, 289-91
Rabinovich, David, 143, 218-20, 223-24
Radek, 18
Radianska Ukraina, 39
Radio Free Europe, 33
Radio Liberty, 29, 33, 267, 288, 339,